GREVEL LINDOP was born in 1948 and educated at Wadham College and Wolfson College, Oxford. He is currently British Academy Reader in English at Manchester University, and is heading a group of scholars who are preparing a new edition of De Quincey's collected writings. His publications include many articles on Romantic and modern literature, three volumes of poems and *A Literary Guide to the Lake District*.

GREVEL LINDOP

The Opium-Eater

A LIFE OF THOMAS DE QUINCEY

WEIDENFELD · LONDON

First published in Weidenfeld paperback in 1993
by Weidenfeld & Nicolson,
a division of the Orion Publishing Group,
Orion House, 5 Upper St Martin's Lane,
London WC2H 9EA

A catalogue record for this book is
available from the British Library.

ISBN 0 297 81404 4

Printed in Great Britain by
Butler & Tanner Ltd,
Frome and London

Contents

Illustrations

For my father
and in memory of my mother

Preface

Sometimes a new book on a literary subject seems to require elaborate justification. Where much has already been written, it may not be obvious that more is needed. This is not the case with a life of De Quincey. The last biographies, Edward Sackville-West's *A Flame in Sunlight: The Life and Works of Thomas De Quincey* and Horace A. Eaton's *Thomas De Quincey: A Biography* both appeared in 1936, and since then no one has attempted another. Yet over the years a great deal of important work has been done on particular aspects of De Quincey's life. We know much more about the details of his career than we did forty years ago, and the appearance of new biographies of his friends and associates, and new editions of their letters and journals, has added to our opportunities of understanding his personality and relationships. Part of the present book's object is to synthesize such material; another part has been to draw on the many manuscript sources which have become available during the past few years in British and American libraries. To give only one example, the National Library of Scotland now houses all the archives of William Blackwood and Sons for the period of De Quincey's association with the firm, so that both sides of an intimate correspondence between author and publisher, continuing sporadically for some twenty-five years, are readily accessible, giving a remarkable opportunity to watch the day-to-day vicissitudes of De Quincey's private and professional life.

Whilst uncovering some things, however, time has obscured others. The great mass of papers formerly held by De Quincey's descendants has been dispersed to the four quarters of the globe, some into private hands and some into public collections. Certainly this material will never again be brought together, and for this reason among others Eaton's monumental biography, written with access to the complete body of papers, will remain indispensable. But it may perhaps be said without harshness that from Eaton's meticulous and fairminded treatment De Quincey, as a living personality, somehow escapes. It is the personality that I have tried to capture in this book, for it is at the root of all that De Quincey's readers most value in his art. His work has the qualities of good conversation: it creates a *rapport,* a sense of closeness to the audience, and however carefully selected may be the confidences it imparts, it seems to invite further intimacy. Biography is an appropriate response to such an appeal, the more so as De Quincey's life was a strange and adventurous one. He was an explorer of society, of ideas and of the human mind, and his readiness at times to disregard the conventions in pursuit of his personal quest led him into regions of trouble, exaltation and insight a good way off the beaten tracks of experience. I have not attempted a 'critical' biography, but I hope that an account of his life may add to the material available for interpreting his works, as well as winning him some new readers and perhaps encouraging those who know *The Confessions of an English Opium-Eater* to go on to some of his less famous but equally characteristic writings.

A central factor in De Quincey's personal and literary life was his opium addiction, and I have tried to give a coherent account of how it developed, reading his own reports in the light of external evidence and modern medical and psychological views of addiction. How and why De Quincey became an opium addict – the stages by which his addiction progressed, and the personal tendencies that predisposed him to it – have not previously been very clear. I have tried to find a way through these perplexities by treating his addiction not as an accident but as a form of behaviour integrally related to his emotional make-up and characteristic ways of responding to life's problems. The reader must judge how far I have succeeded in deducing order from the chaos of conflicting evidence; I hope I have managed at least to clarify a few points.

Throughout the book I have had to draw for important material on De Quincey's autobiographical writings. This raises a problem, for while the nature of his experience was often such that only he could tell us about it, we know that his statements are not always accurate on matters of fact. I have tried to reduce the risks by scutinizing his testimony for internal consistency and checking it, wherever possible, against external evidence. Where I am dependent entirely on his published reminiscences I have indicated the fact. Inevitably I shall have believed too much for some readers and too little for others, but I see no solution to the problem.

One other aspect of this book perhaps calls for comment. Following the thread of De Quincey's complicated working life, I have found myself led to a number of literary works, previously unidentified, which internal and external evidence seem to mark out as his. These include several essays, a short story, and a political letter to *The Times* which is probably his first published piece of prose. There is also an anonymous sentimental novel, *The Stranger's Grave*, which was tentatively indicated in 1870 as possibly by De Quincey, but which seems not to have been closely examined since then with a view to establishing its authorship. I have therefore thought it worth while to reopen the investigation, and I believe that *The Stranger's Grave* is indeed De Quincey's work. Together with a closely related short story, 'The Peasant of Portugal', it adds some interesting facets to our view of De Quincey's personality, though neither item will do much to advance his literary standing, a point which may go some way towards explaining the reluctance of previous researchers to examine *The Stranger's Grave* for signs of his workmanship. In all these cases, fully detailed arguments for attribution would have been out of place in the present book. I have merely indicated briefly the kinds of evidence that seem to support the attributions, leaving the minutiae for examination elsewhere.

It remains for me to express my gratitude to some of the many people and institutions without whose help the book could not have been written. It is a particular pleasure to begin by thanking Mrs Rosemary Blok van Cronesteyn, De Quincey's great great granddaughter. In every generation De Quincey's descendants have been friendly and helpful to biographers, and Mrs Blok and her family have carried on this fine tradition. I am grateful to Mrs Blok for her kindness and hospitality, as well as for permission to examine manuscripts and to reproduce the De Quincey family portraits in her possession. Several scholars have been most generous in allowing me to draw upon their own unpublished research: for such favours I am grateful to Mr Norman Brennan, Mr Richard Downing, Dr Robert Glen, Dr F. Samuel Janzow and Mr Paul Mallinson. Mr Mallinson kindly read part of the book in manuscript. Valuable help was also given by Dr Ian Jack, Professor John E. Jordan, Mr Huw Lawrence, Professor Judson S. Lyon and Mr Jonathan Whittington. The present custodians of various landmarks in De Quincey's erratic career were most co-operative, and I am grateful to Mr D. Maland, High Master and Mr

M. Ricketts, Surmaster of Manchester Grammar School for access to the school's archives; to Mr William B. Gardner, editor of the *Westmorland Gazette,* for permission to examine the *Gazette*'s files and to quote from the proprietors' Minute Book; to Mr J. Campbell, Librarian and Miss Lesley Montgomery, Assistant Librarian of Worcester College, Oxford, for access to the College's archives and manuscripts; and to Dr J.G. Campbell, present owner of De Quincey's cottage at Lasswade, for hospitality and much valuable information. The Trustees of Dove Cottage kindly gave me access to the cottage and the Wordsworth Library, and their staff did much to make my visits pleasant and productive. I am particularly grateful to Mr Charles Shaw; and to Dr Peter Laver, who read part of the book in manuscript and helped in countless other ways.

Medical, psychiatric and pharmacological matters have necessarily loomed large at many points and I have been fortunate in receiving expert guidance from a number of specialists at Manchester University and its associated teaching hospitals. For such guidance I am grateful to Dr John H. Clark, Dr R.F. Hobson, Dr J.M.H. Rees, Professor L.A. Turnberg and Professor Peter O. Yates. Whatever is sound in my treatment of opium addiction and the illnesses of De Quincey and his family is owed directly to their patient and willing explanation of technical matters through which I could never have found my way unaided. Any errors, on the other hand, are certainly my own. Special thanks are due to Dr Hobson and Dr Rees, both of whom read substantial portions of the manuscript and gave warm encouragement, as well as advice without which my blunders would have been far more numerous. For help in other areas I must thank Professor D.S.L. Cardwell of the Department of History of Science and Technology, UMIST; Mr J.V. Earle of the Victoria and Albert Museum; Mrs M.A. Pattenden of the Post Office Records Department; Dr D. Vaughan of the Science Museum; and Dr John Vassie of the Institute of Oceanographic Sciences.

Manuscript material is reproduced by kind permission of the Provost and Fellows of Worcester College, Oxford; the Bodleian Library; the Houghton Library; the Henry W. and Albert A. Berg Collection, the New York Public Library (Astor, Lenox and Tilden Foundations); the Cornell University Library; the Trustees of Dove Cottage; the Trustees of the National Library of Scotland; the British Library; the Liverpool City Libraries; and the Manchester Central Library. Extracts from Dr Robert Glen's article 'The Manchester

Grammar School in the Early Nineteenth Century: A New Account'
are quoted by permission of Dr Glen and the Bancroft Library. Quotations from De Quincey's letter of 5 March 1840 to Thomas Noon
Talfourd are given with the permission of The Carl and Lily Pforzheimer Foundation, Inc. Letters from William, Robert and John
Blackwood are quoted by permission of William Blackwood and Sons,
Ltd.

For permission to quote from published material I am grateful to
the authors and publishers of the following works: J.M. Dent and Sons
Ltd: *Henry Crabb Robinson on Books and Their Writers*, ed. Edith J.
Morley; Duke University Press: *Collected Letters of Thomas and Jane
Welsh Carlyle*, ed. C.R. Sanders (Copyright 1970 by Duke University
Press); Macmillan and Co. Ltd: *Journals of Dorothy Wordsworth*, ed.
E. De Selincourt; Manchester University Press: *The Manchester
Grammar School, 1515-1965*, ed. J.A. Graham and B.A. Phythian;
Oxford University Press: *The Letters of William and Dorothy Words-
worth*, ed. E. de Selincourt, revised by C.L. Shaver, Mary Moorman
and A.G. Hill; *Collected Letters of Samuel Taylor Coleridge*, ed. E.L.
Griggs; and *Thomas De Quincey: A Biography* by Horace A. Eaton;
Routledge and Kegan Paul Ltd: *The Letters of Sara Hutchinson,
1800-1835*, ed. Kathleen Coburn; University of California Press: *De
Quincey to Wordsworth: A Biography of a Relationship*, by John E.
Jordan.

Dr Elizabeth Lomax kindly authorized quotation from her article
'The Uses and Abuses of Opiates in Nineteenth-Century England'.
The illustration of 'Greenhay' is reproduced by permission of Messrs.
A. and C. Black from *The Collected Writings of Thomas De Quincey*,
ed. D. Masson; the portraits of De Quincey's father, Richard De
Quincey and De Quincey aged sixteen are reproduced by permission
of The Bodley Head from *A Flame in Sunlight: The Life and Works of
Thomas De Quincey* by E. Sackville-West, ed. John E. Jordan. Other
illustrations are reproduced by permission of Mrs R. Blok van Cronesteyn; Dr J.G. Campbell; the Liverpool City Libraries; William Blackwood and Sons Ltd.; the Trustees of Dove Cottage; the Manchester
Public Libraries; the Trustees of the National Galleries of Scotland;
and the Trustees of the National Portrait Gallery.

Particular thanks are due to the staff of the John Rylands University Library of Manchester, at whose Deansgate building much of the
book was written; to my editors, Jocelyn Burton and Peter Shellard,
who managed to combine eager interest in the project with an admir-

able tolerance of missed deadlines; to Joan Blackburn, Gill Williams and Louise Banda who typed with speed and accuracy successive stages of a very difficult manuscript; and to Amanda Cox, for meticulous proof-reading as well as constant reassurance and encouragement over four De Quincey-dominated years.

Manchester 1981   Grevel Lindop

Postscript

The Opium-Eater appeared twelve years ago. At that time interest in De Quincey was rare: he was a marginal figure, and many well-read people did not know who he was. From the years when I was writing the book, I cherish the memory of two conversations in particular, one with the person who asked, 'Didn't he write *The Imitation of Christ*?' (No, that was Thomas à Kempis), and the other with someone who, in a worried tone, enquired, 'Do you mean to say he really existed? I thought he was invented by Flann O'Brien. Didn't he have theories about bicycles?' (No, that was the mad scientist De Selby in *The Third Policeman*).

Since then De Quincey's reputation has grown immensely. He is now read and studied everywhere, and no account of Romantic or Victorian literature is complete without some discussion of him. I do not think *The Opium-Eater* has dated too much; but as more people have thought and written about De Quincey, we have come to understand his stature better: I see now that he is a greater writer than, working in isolation more than a decade ago, I could dare to assert.

Readers who want to follow recent critical debate should know R. L. Snyder's *Thomas De Quincey: Bicentenary Studies* (1985), Edmund Baxter's *De Quincey's Art of Autobiography* (1990) and John Barrell's *The Infection of Thomas De Quincey* (1992). Those who want the latest news about *The Stranger's Grave* should see Barry Symonds's article in *The Charles Lamb Bulletin* (summer 1993). A new critical edition of De Quincey's works is now in progress, and will appear (all being well) before the end of the century.

Grevel Lindop
April 1993

Part I
'My Labyrinthine Childhood'

1
Brothers and Sisters

Among his earliest memories were dreams. One was 'a remarkable dream of terrific grandeur about a favourite nurse' which, he later calculated, he dreamed before he was two years old. A little later came a dream about meeting a lion. It was a recurring dream: each time he would be terrified but 'spellbound from even trying to escape' and, to his shame and horror, would find himself submitting to the lion, lying down in front of it. This dream persisted throughout his childhood and made such an impression that in later life he wondered if all children did not dream it. Might not the lion-dream, and the failure of will it symbolized, point to a kind of original sin, a self-betrayal first suffered in infancy?[1] De Quincey saw the intensity of his childhood dreams as proof that his lifelong gift for dream and reverie was 'constitutional', and not dependent upon opium. He may have been right, but perhaps he was exceptional, rather, in that he did not forget such experiences or lose touch with the intense, vulnerable world of childhood. Another memory from his first two years was one he could scarcely put into words: it concerned 'having connected a profound sense of pathos with the reappearance, very early in spring, of some crocuses'[2] – a memory, no doubt, of the farm near Manchester where he spent most of his first six years.

His father, Thomas Quincey, was a linen merchant who came, probably, from Boston in Lincolnshire. We know almost nothing about his origins, but he seems to have known Boston well and had friends and relations there,[3] though it has been claimed, on doubtful authority, that he was born near Ashby-de-la-Zouche, one of the twenty-two children of a country gentleman.[4] However that may be, the family name was at first just Quincey, a name which (with its variants Quinsey and Quince) occurs in Lincolnshire parish registers as far back as the sixteenth century. Quincey had a natural flair for business, and starting with a patrimony of £6,000[5] he entered the textile trade in London before moving to Manchester in the late 1770s with John Quincey, his brother and business partner.[6] The Quinceys

2

imported linen and cotton goods from Ireland and the West Indies and sold them wholesale and retail. Manchester was the obvious place for such a business, for it was already the centre of cotton manufacture and distribution in England. It was well served by canal and road transport and only thirty-five miles from Liverpool, where trading vessels from the West Indies and Ireland landed their cargoes, including the muslins and Drogheda linens which the Quinceys handled.

The brothers built up a flourishing business in Cromford Court, Market-street Lane,[7] and in 1780, when he was about twenty-five, Thomas Quincey felt his prospects secure enough to marry Elizabeth Penson, a girl whose family held a rather higher social position than his own. The Pensons lived in London and the couple were married there, at St George's, Queen Square.[8] Thomas and Elizabeth at first lived over the shop in Market-street Lane, John Quincey moving to a house in nearby Deansgate. But soon the partnership was dissolved and Thomas forged ahead on his own. In 1783 he announced his intention to 'decline all *Retail* Trade'[9] and concentrate on the import and wholesale business. This signified a rise in the social scale: he was now a 'merchant' rather than a mere shopkeeper. The Penson in-laws must have been pleased.

The Quincey's first child, William, had been born in 1781 or early 1782. He was followed by Elizabeth (born in 1783) and Mary (1784),[10] and then by Thomas, who was born on 15 August 1785, probably in the house at Market-street Lane.[11] He was baptized at St Anne's Church, Manchester by the Rev. Samuel Hall, curate of the church and a family friend, and named Thomas Penson, after his mother's brother. The next year another daughter, Jane, was born, and then in 1789 another boy, Richard. Jane, as we shall see, did not live long, and when, some time after her death in 1790, another daughter was born, the Quinceys christened her Jane too.

The family lived for only a short time in central Manchester. Soon after Thomas's birth the Quinceys felt that a larger house in a more pleasant situation was called for, and in 1785 or 1786 they moved to The Farm, Moss Side, in the open country beyond the city boundaries. This was to be only an interim residence. The Farm was not just an oddly named country house, as De Quincey's recollections imply, but a real farm (in 1796 the local press carried advertisements for a sale of crops and agricultural implements to be held there)[12] and if the Quinceys rented the whole house someone else must have continued to farm the adjoining land. For the time being, however, it was home, and

3

from it Thomas dated his earliest memories. He was not a strong child. From his second to his fourth year he was continuously ill with some ailment called, in the vague terminology of the day, 'an ague'. When he was three he also had whooping-cough so badly that he was 'carried for change of air to different places on the Lancashire coast'.[13] During this period of illness he grew accustomed to being the pet of the family. He was quiet, well behaved and very small for his age so that adults tended to fuss over him, and even after his health had improved he seems to have tried to prolong as far as possible the physical and emotional security of babyhood. It may be symptomatic of this reluctance to lose the special status of a 'youngest child' that in later life he wrote of his younger sister Jane as his 'older sister', adding three years to her age to put her ahead of him.[14] Moreover, like many children who experience prolonged illness early in life, he may have learned the dangerous lesson that illness can be used to win sympathy and attention.

Thomas's parents, meanwhile, were planning to build themselves a new house fit for the prosperity the future seemed bound to bring. Business was flourishing, not least because of Quincey's gift for inspiring confidence in those with whom he dealt: his son recalled that for years after his father's death he would occasionally meet people who would say, in almost the same words, 'Sir, I knew your father: he was the most upright man I ever met.'[15] And a business contact in the West Indies, hearing that Quincey was about to build a house, sent him as a gift a consignment of mahogany for the doors and window frames.[16] In November 1790 Quincey bought three acres of land not far from Moss Side, space enough for a substantial house and gardens. The house was designed by Mrs Quincey, who had definite ideas of her own about what was required. She also gave it a name: 'Greenhay'.[17] It was built during 1791.

Greenhay was a splendid place for a child. It was in the midst of open country near a hamlet called Greenhill. The outskirts of Manchester were over a mile away by road, the house was surrounded by fields, and a stream, the Cornbrook, ran by the front gate. It was so much the most prominent building in the area that it gave its name to the district, which is still known as Greenheys. A contemporary painting showed it as a large, square, two-storeyed building with a lawn and gravel path before it, clumps of trees and a shrubbery at one side, stables at the other. There was also a conservatory – the largest room in the house, as Thomas recalled. Besides fresh air and open space, the

4

Quincey children enjoyed at Greenhay surroundings which reflected the best aspects of their father's cultural milieu. Throughout the principal rooms 'were scattered a small collection of paintings by old Italian masters', and De Quincey stresses that this was typical of the homes of the Manchester merchant class, who frequently 'applied a very considerable portion of [their] expenditure to intellectual pleasures – to pictures, . . . and, in a large measure, to books'.[18]

At Greenhay there were books in plenty. The children had a generous stock in the nursery, including the usual favourites of the age: Mrs Barbauld's *Hymns in Prose for Children*, Bewick's *Quadrupeds*, the *Adventures of Baron Munchausen* and the *Arabian Nights*. The latter was a particular favourite and in adult life Thomas, like so many writers of that period, was to find in his childhood memories of these tales a rich store of romantic imagery. There was also a large illustrated Bible, and the children enjoyed sitting by the nursery fire whilst a nursemaid read stories from it, holding up the pictures for inspection: Thomas's first imaginative glimpse of the oriental landscapes which were to return, garishly intensified, as a setting for his adult nightmares.[19] As for his father's library, to Thomas the range of books seemed vast. 'It was impossible', he tells us, 'to name a book in the classes of history, biography, voyages and travels, *belles-lettres* or popular divinity, which was wanting.' There was a comprehensive collection of the 'Tours' and topographical works so popular with eighteenth-century readers, and the children must often have pored over the large engraved plates which folded out from these volumes to show route-maps and panoramic views: forty years later Thomas still remembered them vividly.[20] Mr Quincey had himself made a modest contribution to topographical literature, publishing a *Short Tour in the Midland Counties of England* in the *Gentleman's Magazine* in 1774 and then as a separate volume in 1775. On the evidence of his *Tour* Quincey's taste in landscape was not adventurous (the famous crooked spire at Chesterfield is dismissed as 'disgusting . . . being so much warped that I discerned its crookedness at three miles distance'),[21] but he observed details of agriculture and industry with a sharp eye and took a great interest in the new 'navigations' or canals and in the draining and enclosure of fenlands. The *Tour* was his only literary venture, and it confirms Thomas's account of him as 'a plain and unpretending man' – but also a thoughtful and intelligent one.

The Quinceys, indeed, seem to have been rather well placed in the intellectual society of Manchester. Mr Quincey was a founder member of the Manchester Literary and Philosophical Society; regular visitors to their house included Samuel Clowes, the first translator into English of Swedenborg, and Thomas Percival, physician, author and pioneer of public health reform. Quincey seems to have shared the Whig sympathies of most Manchester intellectuals. Certainly he opposed the slave trade, and at one time went so far as to forbid the use of sugar in his house in support of a campaign to put pressure on the plantation owners.[22]

After the move to Greenhay, however, the children saw almost nothing of their father. His health had begun to suffer, for he was tubercular and the damp Manchester climate led to a rapid deterioration in the condition of his lungs. In 1788 he had entered into a new partnership, the firm becoming Quincey and Duck.[23] The partnership set him free to travel, and he sought the warm, sunny places which were supposed to have some effect in countering pulmonary consumption. The West Indies, in particular, gave him the opportunity to take care of the firm's business interests and his own health at once; but he also visited Portugal and Madeira. He returned to England for brief visits 'and met my mother', De Quincey wrote later, 'at watering-places on the south coast of Devonshire, etc.'[24] Thomas, as a very young child, did not go with her on these occasions, so that his father remained essentially a stranger to him.

The children spent their earliest years mainly in the care of the nurse-maids always employed in families of their rank. Thomas found himself in a completely female world until his younger brother Richard began to grow up. The eldest child, William, had from a very early age been found 'wholly unmanageable' and whilst Thomas was still very young had made himself such a nuisance that he was sent away to boarding school to restore peace to the household. It seems surprising that the Quinceys should have been content to banish him, as they must have done, at the age of five or six. One suspects that the decision came not from the mild Mr Quincey, who can never have been much of a disciplinarian, but from his wife, who could be very tough-minded and seems to have found boys troublesome. Whatever the reason, William was at Louth Grammar School and until Thomas was eight years old the two brothers hardly ever met.

The dominant figure at Greenhay was, undoubtedly, Mrs Quincey. She carried on the day-to-day running of her large household with considerable efficiency, and she had decided ideas about how her children should be brought up. Unfortunately she seems to have held her emotions strictly in check and the children had to turn to one another, or to the female servants, for the spontaneous affection they needed. Even Thomas failed to draw much apparent warmth from her: he mentions that when at the age of seven he made his first journey alone away from home – to visit relatives at Boston about Christmas time – the maidservants gave him a far fonder farewell than did his mother.[25] She already had traces of that moral earnestness which led her later to Evangelicalism, and Mr Quincey's absence had left her with a heavy responsibility. Handling her large family alone, she seems often to have tackled childish crises and complexities with impatient strictness. 'If I could presume to descry a fault in my mother', De Quincey wrote later, 'it was that she turned the chilling aspects of her . . . character too exclusively upon those whom, in any degree, she knew or supposed to be promoters of evil. Sometimes her austerity might even seem to be unjust.'[26] Nor had she much patience when explanations were offered: she 'was predisposed to think ill of all causes that required many words', and Thomas, who even in childhood found it hard to be brief, often felt himself misunderstood. Indeed, he found that he did not naturally feel much love for his mother, and in adult life was well aware that there had been an emotional gap in his childhood experience. 'It may seem odd, according to most people's ideas of mothers,' he wrote, 'that some part of my redundant love did not overflow upon mine. And the more so, if the reader happened to know that she was one whom her grown-up friends made the object of idolizing reverence. But she delighted not in infancy, nor infancy in her.' She was 'freezing in excess' and 'austere . . . in a degree which fitted her for the lady president of rebellious nunneries. Rigid in her exactions of duty from those around her, but also from herself; upright, sternly conscientious, munificent in her charities, pure-minded in so absolute a degree that you would have been tempted to call her "holy", – she could yet not win hearts by the graciousness of her manner.' The relationship between her and her children was based on 'filial duty (a quality much valued at that date) . . . rather than love'. Over-anxious that her children be perfectly disciplined, she would listen too readily to any complaint about their behaviour, but would reject any praise they might receive lest it make them conceited.[27]

Daily routine was carried on in almost military fashion (Elizabeth

Quincey's two brothers and her father were all soldiers): every morning the children were marched, or in the case of the younger ones carried, to morning parade in her dressing-room to be inspected from head to toe for neatness and cleanliness. When she was satisfied, 'we were dismissed, but with two ceremonies that to us were mysterious and allegorical – first, that our hair and faces were sprinkled with lavender-water and milk of roses; secondly, that we received a kiss on the forehead'.[28] The whole business was uncomfortably formal.

In domestic matters Mrs Quincey used the housekeeper as *aide-de-camp* and never communicated directly with her servants, wanting to make sure that distinctions of rank did not become blurred. The servants regarded her aloofness with a mixture of awe and amusement. Even when a dispute arose no one was eager to consult Mrs Quincey for a judgment: De Quincey remembers that one housemaid, 'being asked why in a case of supposed wrong she had not spoken to her mistress, replied – "Speak to mistress! Would I speak to a ghost?" '[29] In these circumstances Thomas, not surprisingly, developed a hunger for affection and approval. In his earliest years these were supplied mainly by his sisters, especially Elizabeth, who was two years older than he. Elizabeth was a pretty, affectionate and highly intelligent girl and she seems to have mothered Thomas a good deal. She was his favourite companion in nursery games, shared his love of fantasy and enjoyed the same books. More than anyone else she understood him and was able to enter his imaginative world. This relationship was especially important to Thomas because the rather awesome distance kept by his mother laid him open to deep feelings of insecurity. The earliest onset of such feelings seems to have been associated with the death of his younger sister Jane in 1790, when he was four and a half. In itself, her death did not affect him deeply. His reaction, he tells us, was not so much sorrow as 'a sad perplexity', death being then 'scarcely intelligible to me'. He was miserable at her absence, but thought she might come back. But he learned, probably from conversations overheard and half-understood, that 'a female servant, who by accident was drawn off from her proper duties to attend . . . Jane for a day or two, had on one occasion treated her harshly, if not brutally' a few days before her death.[30] Just what had happened, he does not say: perhaps the servant lost her temper with Jane and hit her. He was shocked and frightened by what he heard, and felt a fearful revulsion from the woman concerned. In a household where Mother was somewhat aloof and the children were at the mercy of servants and nurses for most of each day his terror was natural enough.

A far worse blow was to follow, however, for two years later, when he was seven years old and his emotional dependence on Elizabeth was stronger than ever, she too fell ill. It was thought that she had taken a fever whilst walking home one evening through the dewy fields around Greenhay. She soon grew seriously ill and after a couple of days the other children were no longer allowed to see her. Her condition was diagnosed as 'hydrocephalus'; it was probably what we should call cerebro-spinal meningitis. At first Thomas was only dimly aware of what was happening. Certainly he expected his sister to recover and when, at length, one of the nurses told him that Elizabeth's death was inevitable, it came as a shocking blow. How far he was conscious of her sufferings we do not know, not least because De Quincey himself could not face the memory of her last days. Upon hearing that she must die, he says, he was plunged into utter misery of the kind that 'cannot be remembered': 'Blank anarchy and confusion of mind fell upon me . . . I wish not to recall the circumstances of that time.'[31] Shortly afterwards, Elizabeth died. Thomas was stunned. She had been the main prop of his world, and separation from her was still unthinkable for him.

In the early afternoon of the day after her death, he chose a moment when nobody was about and crept up the back stairs to the room where his sister's body lay. There would, no doubt, be the usual decorous family viewing of the body, but he wanted to see her alone. The door was locked but the key was still in the lock. Turning it, he opened the door and tiptoed in, closing it as quietly as possible behind him. 'Then,' he recalls, 'turning round, I sought my sister's face. But the bed had been moved, and the back was now turned towards myself. Nothing met my eyes but one large window, wide open, through which the sun of midsummer at mid-day was showering down torrents of splendour.'[32] After pausing a moment he walked round to the side of the bed. His sister lay there, beautiful and calm, with no sign of her recent illness and pain, but unmistakably different, with a statue-like, frozen look, the lips like marble, 'the stiffening hands laid palm to palm' – an awesome being, and not quite his sister any more. His attention was caught by a low surge of wind outside the open window, and listening to it for a moment he was carried on the sound of the breeze into a kind of trance: his bodily senses were suspended and, 'A vault seemed to open in the zenith of the far blue sky, a shaft which ran up forever; and the billows seemed to pursue the throne of God; but that also ran before us and fled away continually . . . some mighty relation between God and death struggled to evolve itself' until, after what seemed 'a *very* long interval', he regained normal consciousness and found himself standing, as before, by his sister's bed.[33] We have only the adult writer's account of the episode, but in essentials it may well be true to what the child experienced. Such trance-like suspensions of consciousness, following upon the profound shock of first seeing the corpse of someone dearly loved, are not unusual. As he came to himself, he heard (or thought he heard) a footstep on one of the lower flights of stairs. Quickly he kissed his sister's lips and 'slunk, like a guilty thing, with stealthy steps from the room'. He sensed that he was breaking some taboo. Children were not expected to pay their last respect like adults, alone and in secret. And perhaps his motives were confused: simple curiosity, even the sense of a 'dare', may have mingled with the longing to see his sister once more. Perhaps, moreover, Thomas wanted to assert at the last a particular bond with his sister, to prove to himself and her that his love was special and greater than the rest of the family's.

The next day a group of doctors came to perform a *post-mortem* examination of the dead girl's brain. When they were gone, Thomas again crept to the room. Again the door was locked, but this time, fortunately, the key was gone.

Then came the funeral. Thomas was dressed up in black and taken to the churchyard in a carriage with two gentlemen who chatted together about this and that on the journey. 'At the church', he tells us, 'I was told to hold a white handkerchief to my eyes' – the ceremonious outward show of grief was expected. 'During that part of the service which passed within the church, I made an effort to attend; but I sank back continually into my own solitary darkness, and I heard little consciously except some fugitive strains from the sublime chapter of St Paul, which in England is always read at burials.'[34] De Quincey, a fervent believer in the power of childhood experience to shape the mind of the grown man, believed that Elizabeth's death gave his mind a permanent tinge of melancholy; and that she was the original, the archetype, around whom crystallized, from many sources, the images of suffering female innocence which haunted his nightmares and reveries throughout his adult life. The girl or woman of these visions consistently awoke mingled feelings of exaltation and anguish, sensations which may have been distant reverberations of the visionary experience he underwent in Elizabeth's death-chamber. What De Quincey seems never to have realized, though, is the importance of his inability to face memories of her illness and death. The 'blank anarchy and confusion of mind' and his wish 'not to recall the circumstances of that time, when *my* agony was at its height, and hers, in another sense, was approaching', provided the motive force which drove Elizabeth's image into his dreams. Experience we cannot bear to live through with the mind fully awake will find its way back into consciousness by unexpected paths.

He tells us that Elizabeth's death intensified his natural tendency to solitude. Perhaps we can be more specific, and suggest that Thomas – still only seven years old – was withdrawing from the other children so that he could create a private mental world where he could not be harmed, where such suffering as Elizabeth's need not be reckoned with. The evasion could not, of course, be complete, and some of the terrors it tried to conceal began to return almost at once. At church with the family on Sunday mornings after her death, Thomas would daydream, and pass the time by dazzling his eyes, gazing at the stained-glass windows until, during the prayer for 'all sick persons and young children', he would find the inevitable associations called forth and see amidst the stained-glass panels, in the clear glass at the centre of the window, 'white, fleecy clouds sailing over the azure depths of the sky', which would shape themselves to 'visions of beds with white lawny curtains; and in the beds lay sick children, that were tossing in anguish, and weeping clamorously for death. God, for some mysterious reason, could not suddenly release them from their pain; but he suffered the beds, as it seemed, to rise slowly through the clouds.'[35] However the experience may have been reshaped by the adult writer's art, we surely have here a simple displacement of memories of Elizabeth's dreadful sickness, decorated and generalized to avoid their coming too close to the unbearable fact. In such ways Thomas began to learn how to apply the ointment of dreams to the wounds inflicted by experience: an ointment that soothed the hurt but would never quite let it heal. Solitude and daydream were in any case natural refuges for a child who had lost his closest companion and who seems to have been discouraged from expressing his grief. He speaks of being 'taunted insultingly with "my girlish tears" '[36] – perhaps by his elder brother William, who may have come home briefly – and his mother was intolerant of displays of violent grief. Even the fact that he had loved Elizabeth far more than he loved his mother must have given rise

11

to painful feelings of guilt. It was not so much the shock of Elizabeth's death as Thomas's inability to complete his mourning and resolve his grief that conferred on the event a lasting significance.

The third in this series of family deaths was that of Thomas's father. The West Indian climate had failed to preserve his health, and in 1793, at the age of forty, he came home at last, knowing that death from tuberculosis was imminent. During the few weeks between Quincey's return home and his death, father and son had their sole opportunity to get to know one another. Perhaps Thomas's main feeling at his father's arrival was one of curiosity: he certainly felt no deep excitement about the event. To the last, in fact, he was able to know his father in only the vaguest way. Once Quincey was back at Greenhay, Thomas spent a good part of the time with him. He was a quiet, biddable child, and no doubt entertained his father without tiring or disturbing him. The father rested on a sofa, sometimes amusing his son with books and pictures brought from the West Indies, and growing steadily weaker. Thomas did not understand what was happening but was aware of a general atmosphere of depression about the house. One morning he found everyone speaking in whispers and 'all the women of the family' weeping.

> Soon after, all of us, being then four, able to understand such a scene, were carried into the bedroom in which my father was at that moment dying. Whether he had asked for us, I know not: if so, his senses had left him before we came. He was delirious, and talked at intervals — always on the same subject. He was ascending a mountain, and he had met with some great obstacle, which to him was insurmountable without help. This he called for from various people, naming them, and complaining of their desertion.[37]

Most poignantly, as Thomas confided to Dorothy Wordsworth many years later, Quincey cried out to his wife, 'Oh Betty Betty! why will you never come and help me to raise this weight?'[38] The root of the delusion was, no doubt, the dreadful effort of breathing; but perhaps Quincey's words testified to a long-endured sense of loneliness. Someone took up Quincey's hand and placed it for a moment on Thomas's head. Then the children left the room, and in a minute or two their father was dead.

Thomas was nearly eight when his father died on 18 July 1793. The death did not immediately have any drastic effect on the family's way of life, for Thomas Quincey had faced death as he had lived his short span: with prudence, consideration and practical intelligence.

He left his wife Greenhay and its contents, his pew in St Peter's Church, and half the income from the capital raised by selling his various business ventures: the linen business, a share in the New Linen Hall at Chester, and an eighth part in a trading vessel, the 'Isabella Brigantine, of Drogheda'. The other half of the income was to be spent on the upbringing and education of the children. The total income would be about £1,600 a year — not a large amount, but enough. When the children reached the age of twenty-one their half of the income was to be divided amongst them so that the boys had one-third more than the girls; and on Mrs Quincey's death her income was to be shared in the same way.[39] For the children he appointed five guardians: Mrs Quincey herself, with Samuel Hall, James Entwhistle, Thomas Belcher and Henry Gee. These were trusted friends of Quincey's but they turned out to have little business sense and handled the Quincey affairs rather poorly.

Poor Quincey had tried to make everything foolproof, adding to the will a long letter explaining that he would like the family to stay at Greenhay, and that if they should leave, on no account should the house be sold whilst property values were so low. He hoped, he said, that his wife would be able to carry on 'the Jamaica trade' with the aid of his 'principal clerk' Thomas Kelsall, but he gave instructions for the sale of the warehouse and wholesale business: to realize a good price, it should be advertised only in the best London papers; and if it would not make the sale unduly difficult, he added, a sum should be asked for the goodwill he had built up. In London, he noted wistfully, 'a very large sum would be demanded for the enterance of *such* a trade'.[40] In the event, the guardians (who were also the executors) disregarded most of this sound advice, and seriously mismanaged the estate.

For Thomas, the first important consequence of his father's death was the recall of the miscreant William (now aged twelve) from Louth Grammar School, where he had been since Thomas's infancy. School had done nothing to calm William's exuberant talent for mischief, and he at once set about shattering the sheltered calm of the nursery at Greenhay. Fresh from the pugnacious, competitive atmosphere of public school, he treated Thomas, four years his junior and small for his age, with lordly contempt. He thought him physically puny and intellectually backward, and said so; adding (with some justice) that Thomas had 'always been tied to the apron-strings of women or girls'.

13

He conceded Thomas a good moral character, but in terms of hearty schoolboy contempt: 'You're honest,' he said; 'you're willing, though lazy; you *would* pull, if you had the strength of a flea; and, though a monstrous coward, you don't run away.'[41] Not for the first time, Thomas tried to protect himself by retreat: he submitted to these strictures, and even succeeded in getting a sort of enjoyment from his inferior status. 'I had a perfect craze for being despised,' he writes; 'I doted on it; and considered contempt a sort of luxury that I was in continual fear of losing.' Perhaps he had traded on his delicate physique and role as the baby until he needed a sense of inferiority to feel safe. He convinced himself, part of the time at least, that he was stupid, and took care to appear so. This was the easier as Mrs Quincey's superstitious fear of anything that might tempt her children to pride saw to it that none of them ever received explicit praise for intellectual accomplishments. But at times self-respect would break in and Thomas would allow himself to show some sparks of intelligence. One such occasions William's sense of superiority was threatened and he would respond with verbal bullying or hazardous 'dares' which Thomas had not the moral courage to refuse.

William soon established unquestioned dominance over the other children. He had a powerful and riotous imagination. He despised books but would write his own and insist on reading them aloud to the others: fireworks, conjuring and the occult were among his favourite subjects. Or he would scare them with gruesome fantasies; warning them, for example, that there might be a conspiracy amongst the dead to band together, outnumber the living and take over the earth. In the nursery he tested techniques for flying and walking on the ceiling. These were a failure, but he was more successful in building toy hot-air balloons and dropping cats by parachute. 'For some time,' De Quincey recalls, 'he turned his thoughts to philosophy, and read lectures to us every night upon some branch or other of physics', until his audience rebelled. Then he turned to drama, composing bloody tragedies in which the others were expected to act.

However mixed his feelings at the time, Thomas benefited a good deal from William's impact on the quiet routine of Greenhay. Self-pity became less of a temptation, life became unpredictable and exciting. And when, in the autumn of 1793, Thomas and William began to go together to a tutor in Salford, Thomas's protective screen of assumed stupidity was soon broken down.

William was kept away from school, perhaps to save expense. He and Thomas were now to go for their lessons to the Rev. Samuel Hall in Salford, the town which merges with Manchester at the latter's north side. Hall was one of the guardians named in Quincey's will, an old and trusted family friend. In 1793 he was still curate at St Anne's Church, where eight years before he had christened Thomas. Mr Quincey seems to have suggested him as a tutor, and Mrs Quincey probably thought him a suitable teacher for her sons because he was a fairly 'low' churchman, on good terms with the local dissenting ministers, yet with no hint of social inferiority about him: St Anne's was extremely fashionable, its services attended by the smartest of the Manchester middle class, and Hall had a high reputation as a preacher.

For the next three years Hall was to have a strong influence on Thomas's life. On weekdays the boys went to his home to learn Latin and Greek; on Sundays they went to St Anne's to hear him preach. Thomas's feelings towards Hall were rather cool. He could not help seeing the dullness of Hall's mind, for his teaching and preaching were equally uninspired. De Quincey remembered him later as one of 'that class . . . who sympathize with no spiritual sense or spiritual capacities in man; who understand by religion simply a respectable code of ethics, leaning for support on some great mysteries dimly traced in the background'. Hall's preaching ran on an efficient but mechanical system:

> He had composed a body of about 330 sermons, which thus, at the rate of two every Sunday, revolved through a cycle of three years; that period being modestly assumed as sufficient for ensuring to their eloquence total oblivion. Possibly to a cynic some shorter cycle might have seemed equal to that effect, since their topics rose but rarely above the level of prudential ethics, and the style, though scholarly, was not impressive.[42]

These sermons were turned into an instrument of educational torment for Thomas. Every week he was set the task of memorizing the Sunday morning sermon as it was preached, and on Monday he was expected to give a precise summary of its argument, couched as far as possible in the original words, with the sequence of ideas preserved intact. Since he often found the order of thoughts in Hall's sermons quite arbitrary, the latter part of the task was especially hard. Every weekend was overshadowed by this awful exercise. Instead of daydreaming in church, he would sit in fearful anxiety making supreme mental efforts to retain 'the somewhat torpid sermon of [his] somewhat torpid

15

guardian'. Fear of the Monday morning test disturbed his sleep on Sunday nights. This mental pressure gave rise to a hatred for Hall which seems to have frightened Thomas so that he found it hard to admit his feelings even to himself. Recalling them thirty years later, he claims not to have resented Hall's exactions in any way; yet he calls the task 'odious . . . in the most abominable excess'. 'My guardian and I', he tells us, 'went on cordially'. But then again,

> I believe my guardian, like many of the grim Pagan divinities, inhaled a flavour of fragrant incense from the fretting and stinging of anxiety which, as it were by some holy vestal fire, he kept alive by this periodic exaction. It gave him pleasure that he could reach me in the very recesses of my dreams, where even a pariah may look for rest.[43]

Eighteenth-century education placed a heavy emphasis on rote-learning: long before he began to visit Hall, Thomas had been set to learn spelling by *memorizing* a dictionary, starting at the letter A – a task which he had flatly refused![44] Hall, however, would not be disobeyed, and it seems likely that besides developing in De Quincey remarkably accurate powers of recall, Hall's memory-task, and its invasion of his sleep and dreams, gave rise to his recurrent horrified fascination with feats of memory and rooted dislike of rote-learning as a means of teaching children.

More invigorating than the mental gymnastics imposed by Hall were the new exploits in which William involved him. To reach Hall's house the boys had to follow the single main road from the open country near Greenhay into the centre of Manchester. As it approached the town, the road crossed the River Medlock, and beside the bridge stood a large cotton mill – at this time the only factory in the area. On one of their first visits to Hall the brothers, crossing the bridge, were spied by one of the factory lads, who, moved to disgust by their elegant and expensive clothes, sang out derisively, 'Holloa, Bucks!' Then, noticing that the boys wore Hessian boots (knee-high boots with tasselled tops which were the latest fashion, but decidedly outlandish for Lancashire), he began to jeer 'Boots! Boots!' Thomas would have preferred to ignore these provocations and hurry on to Hall's. Not so the belligerent William, who 'made a dead stop' and challenged the boy to fight. The boy declined his invitation with 'a most contemptuous and plebian gesture', upon which William 'drove him in with a shower of stones'.[45]

From that time onwards a miniature class war raged daily between

16

the Quincey brothers and the boy operatives at the mill. The brothers passed the mill twice a day, and at their approach a crowd of boys would come out to join battle. In the mornings conflict was sometimes avoided, but in the afternoons the Quinceys went by just as the factory bell signalled the end of the shift. The usual weapons were stones and, says De Quincey, 'by continual practice both parties became expert in throwing them'. The factory lads 'were slovenly and forlorn in their dress, often unwashed, their hair totally neglected, and always covered with flakes of cotton . . . But . . . they were perfectly independent, getting very high wages, and these wages in a mode of industry which was then taking vast strides ahead.' William and Thomas made inviting targets with their cultured voices and smart clothes.

William, for his part, felt that the dignity of his family and class had to be maintained. There was no escape for Thomas. William announced that from now on, military discipline should prevail: *he* was commander-in-chief, and Thomas his subordinate. Twice daily Thomas was ordered into battle beside William, who would work out elaborate strategems for driving the enemy from the bridge with pieces of brick and stone. Any appearance of cowardice or disobedience on Thomas's part was punishable by court-martial and the burden of William's withering contempt.

Generally the battles of the Oxford Road Bridge would end with the Quinceys running away – a fact which William ignored, preferring to invent each week a suitable quota of victories. Sometimes things went worse still and Thomas was taken prisoner. Once he was sent back with kicks and an insulting message for his brother; on another occasion he was picked up and kissed by a group of factory girls (after the initial surprise, he enjoyed it: he was used to being cossetted by the nurses and servant girls at Greenhay). William, of course, was furious, considering that his army had sustained a humiliating defeat, and Thomas's weak submission to the insults of the enemy was published in the twice-weekly gazette which William produced for the entertainment of Mrs Evans, the housekeeper at Greenhay. It seems odd that neither Mrs Quincey nor Hall put a stop to the warfare. It may be an illustration of how little real 'bringing-up' the Quincey boys had: no one reported the battles directly to Hall or Mrs Quincey, and neither of them took enough personal interest in the children to find out.

Perhaps William was especially keen to show his dominance over Thomas because Hall's tuition in the classics was beginning to reveal

Thomas's superior intelligence. In fairness to William, we should remember what a pampered pet Thomas must have seemed to him. Returning from boarding school, he probably felt a secret envy of the younger boy, who had been allowed to enjoy the ease and security of Greenhay whilst he had been exiled. Thomas was making rapid progress at his studies, and the love of reading was becoming a ruling passion. When he began to study under Hall, his mother started to give him 'a large weekly allowance of pocket-money, too large for my age,' according to De Quincey, 'but safely entrusted to myself, who never spent or desired to spend one fraction of it upon anything but books'. But the eight-year-old Thomas, already apparently a book-buyer on the grand scale, soon outran these generous means and found himself three guineas in debt to the bookseller. Typically, he shrank from telling anyone and for three years worried over the debt, dreading the day when the bookseller would lose patience and demand his money. The day never came, for the bookseller, knowing that Thomas frequently ordered and collected books for his tutor, had long since charged the sum to Hall, who had paid it unknowingly.[46]

Yet he also discovered that learning could bring material rewards. The same bookseller one day handed him a Latin Testament and asked him if he could translate a chapter. He pointed to Chapter 1 of the First Epistle to the Corinthians – the chapter which had been read at Elizabeth's funeral, and one that Thomas had often read to himself in the English version. He knew it by heart; and the Latin was comparitively easy. He was able to give an impressive translation at sight, and the bookseller was so pleased that he made him a present of the volume. It was during this moment of reading and translation, too, that Thomas's gift for languages seems to have crystallized. 'The deep memory of the English words had forced me into seeing the precise correspondence of the two concurrent streams – English and Latin',[47] and this intuitive grasp of the underlying relationship between languages stayed with him. His Latin at once improved strikingly, and he never afterwards found any difficulty in learning languages.

William, however, made him pay a high price. Like many boys, the Quincey brothers created imaginary countries, of which they were kings. William's was named, ferociously enough, Tigrosylvania; Thomas's had the odd name of Gombroon. William lost no time in turning this fantasy world into another arena of fraternal warfare. Thomas, hearing that Tigrosylvania was in the far north, prudently placed Gombroon in the tropics, keeping a respectful distance to reduce the risk of conflict. But William announced that his land extended a full eighty or ninety degrees south so that in fact the kingdoms were near neighbours. From that point the logic of the game was set, and its course predictable. Thomas (always one to defend himself by a prudent retreat) made Gombroon so poor as to be not worth invading. William announced that he knew of an unworked diamond mine in Gombroon, which made it imperative that Tigrosylvania invade and exploit its untapped wealth. And so on. For a time Thomas felt more anxiety over Gombroon than over the daily battles at the bridge. The conflict was, in a way, more intimate. Just as Hall invaded his dreams with the memory-test, so William was invading his fantasies. But at length William went too far and killed off the Gombroon fantasy. Hall had been illustrating some points of Greek idiom by reading the boys a passage from Lord Monboddo, the eccentric eighteenth-century anthropologist and theorist of language. He left Monboddo's works lying in the study and one day William picked up a volume and came upon a passage where the author, putting forward a crudely evolutionary theory of human development, quoted an account of the men of Nicobar, who were said to be so primitive that they had 'tails like cats'.[48] William seized on this hint and soon announced his discovery that the people of Gombroon also had tails. Now that Gombroonians had been degraded below the level of human existence Thomas abandoned the game, though not without a sense of defeat.

The period with Hall provided other experiences more puzzling than that of brotherly conflict. Hall's household was not a tranquil place, and Thomas 'being, on account of my age,' as he tells us, 'nobody at all, or very near it, I sometimes witnessed things that perhaps it had not been meant for anybody to witness'.[49] He discovered that amongst the Hall children there were 'two young girls, of what exact age I really do not know, but apparently from twelve to fourteen, twins, remarkably plain in person and features, unhealthy, and obscurely reported to be idiots'. Their names were Mary and Sarah. They were not in fact twins, but were less than a year apart in age. Both were partially deaf, and they may not actually have suffered from any mental handicap.[50] But Mrs Hall hated them, and made no effort to conceal her feelings. She used them as menial servants about the house, dressing them shabbily, keeping them apart from their brothers and sisters and continually scolding them. From time to time Thomas saw these miserable scarecrow daughters hurrying about their household tasks or snatching a few minutes' rest before Mrs Hall's piercing voice rang through the house to call them back to work. Their plight made Thomas miserable, but more frightening was his guardian-tutor's calculated blindness to what was happening in his own house. Sometimes he would remonstrate feebly with his wife, but more often he simply avoided noticing her cruelty. His normal response to family tension was to shut himself into his study and read. The girls died of scarlet fever in 1797 but they left a powerful image in Thomas's mind, and he was grimly fascinated by it, as he had been by the story of the servant who had ill-treated Jane before her death. In imagination he completed the macabre tale by picturing Mrs Hall tormented by agonies of remorse.

Although Hall was the most important of the guardians, the Quincey children did occasionally see the others. Thomas Belcher, who lived close to Greenhay, did his duty by inviting them to stay for a few days now and then. The Belcher children were musically talented (music seems to have been rather neglected at Greenhay) and at their house Thomas's love of music was first awakened. In particular the music of Cherubini made an immediate and lasting impression on him. It was the first music (apart from Handel's) that he had ever heard adequately performed, and although he had imagined the possibility of music as fine as this it now, he says, for the first time 'interpreted itself, as a physical possibility, to my ear'.[51] This memory seems to date from about his tenth year.

The Belchers' house was in other respects like Greenhay – a large, pleasant country house with extensive gardens and stables, potentially a paradise for children but marred for Thomas by the incorrigible William, who took delight in daring him to go as high as possible on a terrifying swing in the garden. 'Horror was at my heart regularly as the swing reached its most aerial altitude; for the oily, swallow-like fluency of the swoop downwards threatened always to make me sick, in which case it is probable that I must have relaxed my hold of the ropes . . . But in defiance of all this miserable panic, I continued to swing whenever he tauntingly invited me.'[52] Fear was easier to bear than his brother's contempt. But he did refuse one challenge: William, who from sheer bravado enjoyed riding a particularly vicious horse, dared him to get up and ride behind on the crupper – the most insecure position. Thomas refused. He reflected later that, 'It was well that my brother's path in life soon ceased to coincide with my own; else I should infallibly have broken my neck in confronting perils which brought me neither honour nor profit.'[53]

The time of these perils soon drew to an end. During their last year with Hall, the Quinceys were joined by a new pupil who in summer rode to Salford on a half-wild mountain pony. The new ally soon joined in with their battles, and one morning helped them to victory by charging his pony straight at the boys on the bridge. The pony was a ferocious-looking beast, and the sight was enough to send the factory lads flying in confusion. But even as the boys celebrated their victory they discovered that Thomas Belcher had been passing and had seen everything. A family inquiry was held, the story of the daily brawls was extracted from Thomas and William, and an end to the feud was ordered. It was soon found necessary for the peace of the household to send William away again; and since he had shown a talent for drawing he was sent to London to study under P.J. de Loutherbourg, RA, a fashionable painter of landscapes and historical subjects. Thus abruptly ended Thomas's relationship with his feared and idolized brother. They never met again, for William contracted typhus and died at de Loutherbourg's house in Hammersmith Terrace. He was buried at St Paul's Church, Hammersmith, on 1 December 1797.[54]

In 1796 Mrs Quincey decided, against her late husband's advice, to leave Greenhay. It had become too expensive to maintain, perhaps because the guardians were making a poor job of managing the Quincey estate. So it was put up for sale. The affair was organized as badly as possible. War with revolutionary France was raging and the papers were full of the threat of invasion, so that house prices were very depressed. The sale was poorly advertised. Nature took a hand, and on the evening chosen for the auction there was torrential rain. The sale went ahead, and the house, which had cost £6,000, went for £2,500 – the sole bid, so far as De Quincey could recall.

Mrs Quincey left at once for Bath, taking with her the servants and three of the children: Jane, Mary and the youngest, Henry, who had been born shortly after his father's death. Thomas stayed on with his younger brother Richard (always known in the family as 'Pink' because of his beautiful complexion) to study a little longer with Samuel Hall. They boarded with Thomas Kelsall, their father's former 'principal clerk', now a merchant in his own right, and for a few months became part of the Kelsall family. Thomas was at first rather startled and then delighted by the friendly atmosphere of the household. The Kelsalls had one daughter, two years old, and the Quincey boys were made to feel like older brothers. Kelsall and his wife were idyllically happy; the children were treated lovingly; even the servants were addressed with courtesy and friendliness.[55] The contrast with the régime at Greenhay was complete. For a few months – from August to November 1796 – Thomas and 'Pink' rejoiced in the parental affection they needed so much and which the Kelsalls were able to supply, and then they left Manchester, to join their mother at her elegant lodgings in North Parade, Bath.

2

A Sentence of Exile

Mrs Quincey had taken rooms at a good address. North Parade was only five minutes from the Pump Room, centre of Bath's health-spa society, and less than half a mile from the fashionable pleasure grounds known as Sydney Gardens. The street was a quiet cul-de-sac, whose main drawback was its low-lying situation near the river. It was rather damp and in summer could be airless and smelly. But the rent was reasonable and on balance it suited Mrs Quincey well enough. 'Bath', according to De Quincey, 'seemed, on all accounts, the natural station for a person in my mother's situation.' It was still smart, but no longer too smart. Many retired people – clergy, army officers, colonial administrators – lived there, besides younger and livelier people of fashion. From Mrs Quincey's point of view this was ideal. She could associate easily with people of her own class and even find scope for a little judicious social climbing, yet the city was eminently respectable and she would be kept in countenance by multitudes of well-to-do widows and evangelically inclined churchgoers.

For the children, however, North Parade must have been a purgatory. The lack of space, enervating air and urban surroundings were terribly oppressive after Greenhay. Boredom was no doubt a perennial problem. Poor 'Pink', a strikingly pretty child, was tormented by the attentions of enthusiastic ladies every time he ventured out into the streets: for an eight-year-old boy the cries of delight, the strokes and pats of the women were a perpetual embarrassment, and Mrs Quincey no doubt continued to dress him in the stylish, even dandified, clothes which invited such treatment – one recalls the showy boots which started the cotton-factory skirmishes. As for Thomas, he amused himself by reading and going to play in Sydney Gardens, whose attractions included a fascinating maze.[1] He was especially fond of this maze: it appealed to his love of the mysterious, and we may presume that he often played there alone.

The previous tenant of the North Parade rooms had been Edmund Burke. The great statesman had left, in the throes of his final illness, about a month before Mrs Quincey arrived. When Thomas and 'Pink' came from Manchester later in the year visitors were still turning up, hoping to see Burke or hear news of his health. Mrs Quincey, it seems, did not fail to pick up these useful social windfalls, and she must have made some good contacts. Poor 'Pink' had of course to undergo the ritual petting when there were ladies in the party.[2]

School, when it began, must have been a great relief. Thomas was enrolled on 6 November at Bath Grammar School – an excellent school, and perhaps a contributory reason for the move to Bath. The school conferred a new sort of freedom: the claustrophobia of too-close family life and private tutoring was exchanged for the company of boys of his own age and an atmosphere of real intellectual challenge. Thomas needed to stretch himself mentally, and at Bath he had just the stimulus he needed, since he found himself comparatively backward in Greek, then an important part of the school curriculum, and had an exhilarating struggle to catch up. Samuel Hall had been, in his pupil's words, 'a feeble Grecian'.[3] Thomas, who wanted to go straight into the top class at the Grammar School to be taught by the headmaster, Mr Morgan, found himself relegated instead to the second class under a lesser scholar, Mr Wilkins. He was already fiercely competitive where learning was concerned. His cleverness had enabled him to hold on to his self-respect through all William's browbeating, and now he struggled to assert himself in the same way at school, striving to raise the standard of his Greek and also making a special effort at Latin verse, for which he had shown a talent under Hall's tuition. These efforts brought quick returns: within a month his verses were being sent up to the headmaster, who praised them in front of the whole school. To Thomas, starved of praise at home and hungry for reassurance, such approval brought intense pleasure, but it provoked the inevitable reaction. Mr Morgan was unwise enough to use his work as a goad to older and duller pupils and, says De Quincey, 'was continually throwing in their teeth the brilliance of my verses at eleven or twelve, by comparison with theirs at seventeen, eighteen, or even nineteen'.[4] Resentment smouldered until one day a senior boy 'strode up to me in the public playground; and, delivering a blow on my shoulder, . . . asked me, "What the devil I meant by bolting out of the course, and annoying other people in that manner? Were other people to have no rest from me and my verses, which, after all, were horribly bad?" . . . I was briefly admonished to see that I wrote worse for the future, or else –.'[5]

Alarming as this might be, the situation was familiar: it was the conflict with William over again. And, after all, it proved that he was making his mark in the school. So Thomas held his ground and tried to write better than ever. When the results of the next exercise were read out there were murmurs amongst the senior boys, and the chief antagonist was seen to shake his fist. The conflict continued by fits and starts for about a year, but fortunately it never spilled over into serious physical bullying and it ended in victory for Thomas. He had shown that he was not to be intimidated, and his friendliness and charm tended to disarm hostility, especially as he was not unwilling to help others: his verses did deteriorate eventually, but only because by the end of his first year he was doing Latin homework for several of his classmates and sacrificing quality to quantity.

The labour he invested in Greek also brought its rewards. By the end of his second year at Bath he was composing good Greek verse, and when he wanted to show off could even talk quite fluently in Greek: a product of his instinctive feeling for languages, developed by the self-imposed daily exercise of translating newspaper articles aloud into the best Greek he could muster on the spur of the moment. Mr Morgan remained fond of pointing him out as a star pupil. 'That boy', he told one visitor to the school, 'could harangue an Athenian mob, better than you or I could address an English one.'[6]

He was very happy at the Grammar School, and one might have expected his mother to be delighted with his progress. There were, however, odd contradictions in Mrs Quincey's character. Despite the austerity of her moral views she was well aware that Bath offered invaluable social contacts for her sons as well as herself. It is easy to see her hand, for example, in the choice of Thomas and 'Pink' as two of the three boys chosen to visit Captain Sir Sidney Smith in 1798 to present congratulations on behalf of his old school when he returned home to Bath after a daring escape from a French prison.[7] On the other hand she had little regard for her son's educational opportunities at Bath and quite unexpectedly she intervened to remove him from the Grammar School, much against his will, when he had been there just over two years.

The occasion was a rather strange illness, caused by a trivial accident at school in late January 1799. Thomas was now in the top class. One morning Mr Morgan was called out of the room and in his absence some horseplay started among the boys. The usher (an ex-pupil retained at the school as a sort of apprentice teacher) tried to restore order in the usual manner of the day by striking out with the cane. He missed the boy he was aiming for and the cane came down on Thomas's head. The sequel is told in a letter Thomas wrote later to his sister Mary, who was away at school in Bristol:

> As soon as I came home my mother sent for Mr Grant; about three o'clock he came. I was then shaved on the place, and bled with six leaches; and two of the old jockies were so fond of my head that they staid on for three hours, and would not have departed then, had not Mr Grant (who came again at nine o'clock) flogged them off with some salt . . . . . . For three weeks I neither read, nor wrote, nor talked, nor eat meat, nor went out of the back drawing-room, except when I went to bed . . . I am not to go to school till Easter.[8]

But what was supposed to be wrong with him? Mild concussion seems the worst possibility, and since he completed his lesson before going home after the accident, even that is unlikely. The clue probably lies in a retrospective comment De Quincey made in 1834: 'I doubt whether in reality anything very serious had happened. In fact, I was always under a nervous panic for my head; and certainly exaggerated my internal feelings without meaning to do so, and this misled the medical attendants.'[9] Thomas's anxiety about his head was connected with memories of Elizabeth's death from 'hydrocephalus'. He may well have scared himself with the notion that the same disease might be lying in wait for him – especially as it was commonly thought to afflict highly intelligent children and to be caused by premature intellectual growth. Once he had convinced himself, the panic infected his mother and the doctors.

The immediate results were pleasant enough. He was kept at home, but with the compensating pleasure of being the centre of attention. He was not allowed to read; but his mother read aloud to him by the hour. Her exertions were truly heroic, for she entertained him with, among other things, the whole of *Orlando Furioso* in English verse translation, and *Paradise Lost* – his first encounter with the poem, and a rather strange one, since it was in Bentley's eccentric edition, full of ill-judged emendations.

In his letter to Mary, Thomas also mentions among books newly delivered to North Parade, apparently for him, ' "Asiatic Researches" (Sir William Jones' work), Goldsmith's Histories of Greece and England, Milner's "Ecclesiastical History", "Rambler", . . . Hoole's

"Tasso", Venn's "Duty of Man", Ogden's "Sermon", &c.'[10] The influence of Mrs Quincey's piety is visible here, but also Thomas's own lifelong interest in history ancient and modern, already developed to a degree rather startling in a thirteen-year-old. But perhaps he reeled off the titles of these weighty volumes to impress his sister, who was a year or so older than he. The general tone of the letter is humorously patronizing, and Thomas clearly wants to display his mastery of an adult epistolary style, even to the point of parody:

> My mother wishes to know whether onny of the *little innocents* are coming to Bath; because she would wish you to come with them. I should suppose old madam Richardson or Ingleby, or some of those old jockies, will come, and then you might take a Saturday-afternoon coach and come to tea; so write as early as you can. I believe you will be in time for Mademoiselle's ball, which was put off (as I suppose) on my account.
>
> I was introduced last Thursday night to young Lord Westport (Lord Altamont's only child), and on Sunday I dined with him at his house at Lansdown. He is a very nice boy, about my size. My mother will call upon Mr and Mrs Grace (N.B. Mr Grace is his tutor), and invite them and Lord W. to our house, where I shall have the opportunity of introducing him to you . . . My mother desires her love to you. Mrs Pratt continues to grow better; she has no complaint, but is still unable to walk even upstairs without help. She goes out every day in a chair . . .
>
> Believe me, your affectionate sister,
> Tabitha Quincey.[11]

This unexpected signature shows Thomas consciously sending-up the gossipy, old-maidish tone he has fallen into ('Mrs Pratt continues to grow better . . .'). Perhaps 'Tabitha Quincey' was a private joke among the children, a personification of the archetypal maiden aunt. At any rate it would be a mistake to take too seriously the touches of pomposity and fussiness in the letter: they probably belong to Tabitha, not Thomas. Yet the letter affords some revealing glimpses: we see Mrs Quincey hard at work cultivating social opportunities for her son, and Thomas letting slip a word or two implying self-consciousness over his small stature, which in adult life was to remain a cause of embarrassment to him: Lord Westport (a couple of years younger than he) is 'a very nice boy, about my size'.

But Thomas, reckoning on a return to school after his convalescence, was in for a shock. His mother decided, in her impetuous way, to remove him from the Grammar School. We can only guess at her reasons. Perhaps the fundamental reason for this as for some of her other misjudgments was simply that it was not in her nature to leave well alone. She never even told Thomas why he was not to go back. Her word, as a parent's word, was law; and that was all he could learn. But he made two guesses. One was that she was trying, as usual, to shield him from praise. Mr Morgan, the headmaster, was anxious to see him back at school, and, unaware that with a perverse lady like Mrs Quincey he was doing the worst possible thing, he paid a call, De Quincey tells us,

> in company with his son-in-law, Mr. Wilkins, as did a certain Irish Colonel Bowes, who had sons at the school, requesting earnestly, in terms most flattering to myself, that I might be suffered to remain there. But it illustrates my mother's moral austerity that she was shocked at my hearing compliments to my own merits, and was altogether disturbed at what doubtless these gentlemen expected to see received with maternal pride.[12]

This, however, can be only part of the story. Clearly Morgan and the others called because they already had an idea of Mrs Quincey's plans. The other reason, Thomas guessed, was that one of his friends, Bowes (son of the Colonel mentioned above), had somehow offended a certain Mrs Pratt, one of Mrs Quincey's closest Bath friends. Exactly what Bowes had done remains a mystery; but Thomas had been with him at the time and so had been implicated in the crime. His mother concluded that he was getting into bad company. Once the decision was made it was final. Thomas protested vehemently but without effect. A year later he was still arguing and pleading, and trying to excuse the mysterious incident of Mrs Pratt, but his mother would not relent.[13]

In consequence of this perverse decision Thomas's schooling was broken off and he passed into the hands of tutors until a new school could be found. One tutor was a Frenchman: there were many French émigrés in Bath, fugitives from the Revolution. Thomas found him a bore, and expressed his resentment by spending his lesson-time making faces at an old lady who lived on the opposite side of the street.[14]

It was at about this time that the Quinceys became the De Quinceys. There was a family tradition, perhaps no more than a piece of wishful thinking, that the Quinceys were descendants of the De Quincis who came over with the Conqueror. In the heady atmosphere of Bath, and apparently with the encouragement of the troublesome Mrs

Pratt, this notion had ripened into a determination on the part of Thomas's mother to refurbish the family name – a measure her late husband would no doubt have resisted. The new surname appears first in a letter from 'Pink', who wrote home to Thomas in 1799 from his new school at Winkfield, Wiltshire, signing himself 'your ever affectionate brother, R. de Quincey'.[15] (The question of whether 'de' had a large or small 'D' was never settled.)

At the end of the summer Thomas was packed off to join 'Pink' at Winkfield (today called Wingfield), Wiltshire. The school was near Bath, and Mrs De Quincey, as we must now call her, no doubt meant to keep Thomas under her eye more closely than had been possible at the Bath school, a large, independent establishment with little scope for parental meddling. Unlike Mr Morgan, the Rev. Spencer, headmaster of Winkfield, was a mere amateur and no match for Mrs De Quincey. If she did not already know Spencer she knew friends of his who had recommended his school, and by the time Thomas had been there a few months Spencer's daughters were visiting her at Bath and she was coming to stay at Winkfield for a fortnight at a time. This must have been most oppressive for the boys, but the truth was that Mrs De Quincey could not rest unless she felt herself in personal control of everything her family did. Better an inferior school with herself at the teacher's side, she reasoned, than the best school away from her supervision.

If the move to a new school was intended to humble Thomas's pride, it failed utterly, for Winkfield School was tiny – with only about thirty boys – and Thomas found himself by far the cleverest and most mature among them. There was not much for Mr Spencer to teach him (Thomas recalled him later as 'a blockhead, who was in a perpetual panic, lest I should expose his ignorance')[16] so that his only interesting activities at the school were really extras, taken up to pass the time and use some of the surplus energy which the school could not engage. He looked after 'Pink'; he wrote for the boys' weekly paper, *The Observer*; he helped the younger ones with their lessons; he organized his fellow pupils into rival bands of 'Greeks and Trojans' for mock battles, taking the part of cunning Odysseus for himself, with 'Pink', inevitably, cast as the handsome Paris; he entered competitions in the *Monthly Preceptor or Juvenile Library* and won prizes for translation (seventh prize for a passage of Cicero; third for one of Horace's odes);[17] and he became a favourite with Spencer's young daughters, showing his usual knack for finding friendly female company. In short, he marked time and sought out every possible means of keeping boredom at bay.

Periodically his mother turned up, inspiring awe in the other boys, who were further impressed when they heard that she was now a friend of the famous Evangelical writer, Hannah More. Also from Bath came Dr Mapleton, who was to look after Thomas's health, since he still complained of pains in the head – now, no doubt, just a physical manifestation of frustration and unhappiness. But his spirits were not altogether damped, and a letter written to his sister Mary in June 1800 shows him still playing Tabitha Quincey and indulging in elaborate absurdity. It also shows how fully school and family life had become interwoven:

> My Dear Sister,
>   The tip of my nose is covered with confusion, my young toe blusheth and my old one is ashamed, when I consider my profound impudence in disobeying your commands. But, my dear, I have had very little time to write to you, considering that I have almost twenty-five boys' business to do every day . . .
>   Next Tuesday being the 18th, I hope to see the tip of the turkey carpet in our dining-room . . . We shall be in Bath by eleven o'clock. I believe Miss Spencer is coming with us to Bath; and Miss Cristiana, Miss Betsy, and Amey are at Oxford. What beautiful paper! What charming writing!
>   My mother (I meant to write it with a great M) has been here about a fortnight. Remember, when you write to me, child (which you mustn't do before the holidays), never to write the day of the month in figures, but at full length in what-d'ye-call-ums, for it's very disrespectful to use contractions to your superiors.[18]

Even this nonsense is full of talent. His mother, meanwhile, continued to enjoy a bustling social life, seasoned with a dash of moral self-righteousness: 'Poor L[or]d Carbery continues very ill,' she writes to Thomas, '. . . her Ladyship was here on Wednesday evening, and is as handsome and amiable as ever; but I fear terribly surrounded with Irish people of rank who wish to make her racket about like themselves.' The argument about Bowes's misconduct is still going on, it seems: 'My dear boy, I will never after this mention the affair of Bowes, and perhaps shall never think of it again, but just to remark that you are wrong to blame Mr Pratt about it.' There is also news of Samuel Hall, or rather of his son: 'Poor miserable Edward Hall has been running away from his father, meaning, had he had so much sense, as to have found the way to Liverpool, to have been a sailor, instead of which he went to Bolton and Rochdale, and found himself at night entering Manchester, which he imagined himself forty miles away from.'[19]

It was at about this time that Thomas first discovered the poetry of Wordsworth, which was to have such a powerful effect on the course of his life. 'In 1799,' he tells us, 'I had become acquainted with "We are Seven" at Bath. In the winter of 1801–2 I read the whole of "Ruth".'[20] 'We are Seven' had been 'handed about in manuscript' at Bath, where he was shown it during a school holiday.[21] Who showed it to him we do not know, but Cottle, original publisher of the *Lyrical Ballads*, had given copies of the book to several West Country friends, including Hannah More. By some such channel the poem found its way to the De Quincey household, where Thomas was impressed by its depth of feeling and powerful simplicity. As one who had lost a father, an admired brother and two dearly loved sisters, he must have felt an intimate response to the certainty of the little girl in the poem that though 'Two of us in the churchyard lie,/My sister and my brother –' yet death has not divided the family. 'Ruth' he found reprinted in a London newspaper two and a half years later.[22]

This discovery of Wordsworth may have been linked with the first stirrings of poetic aspirations within himself, for in the spring or early summer of 1800 he began to dream of writing poems in the romantic manner. Previously he had harboured vague ambitions of performing some great service for his country – military or political, perhaps[23] – but he seems not to have thought of a poetic vocation. He had, of course, written verse: not just the Latin exercises of the classroom, but his prize translation of the Horation ode, and at least one humorous song for the entertainment of his schoolmates at Winkfield. But these productions were not meant seriously. No doubt he liked to show himself a skilful versifier in English as well as Latin, but the impulse behind these schoolboy pieces is no more profound than that. His translation from Horace began

> Fuscus! the man whose heart is pure,
>   Whose life unsullied by offence,
> Needs not the jav'lins of the Moor
>   In his defence.

And so it continued: neat, economical, cool. More energy is shown in the school rhyme (it was an answer to a challenge from another local school) of which the following survives:

> Since Ames's skinny school has dared
>   To challenge Spencer's boys,
> We thus to them bold answer give
>   To prove ourselves 'no toys'.
>
> Full thirty hardy boys we are,
>   As brave as e'er was known;
> We will nor threats nor dangers mind
>   To make you change your tone![24]

None of this shows any sign of a desire to use verse for personal expression. Now, however, he was planning 'A *poetic and pathetic ballad* reciting the wanderings of two young children (brother and sister) and their falling asleep on a frosty moonlight night among the lanes . . . and so perishing', and 'A *pathetic poem* describing the emotions (strange and wild) of a man dying on a rock in the sea . . . which he had swum to from shipwreck . . . within sight of his native cottage and his paternal hills'[25] – subjects akin to those of the *Lyrical Ballads* and fitted (to quote the 'Preface' Wordsworth was soon to add) to display 'the real language of men in a state of vivid sensation'.

The summer holiday of 1800 must have been doubly welcome: not only did it mean a break from the stultifying life of Winkfield, but it brought a magnificent holiday in Ireland. Mrs De Quincey's labours in the drawing-rooms of Bath had borne fruit. The young Lord Westport (the 'very nice boy, about my size' whom Thomas had met the summer before) was the son of an Irish peer, Lord Altamont, who had an estate in County Mayo. Altamont had had some dealings with Thomas Quincey senior, probably over flax or linen, for Altamont was a hard-headed business man with an interest in scientific methods of agriculture. Mrs De Quincey had cultivated his acquaintance after meeting him in Bath. She had seen to it that Altamont met Thomas and was duly impressed with the boy's cleverness and social graces, and her reward was an invitation for Thomas to spend six weeks with Westport in the summer, travelling to the estate in Mayo and back, stopping en route at the country houses of various members of the Irish gentry and peerage.

This was not the first time Mrs De Quincey had managed to pair up Thomas with a travelling companion of some standing. When he was nine he had gone to spend Christmas with his father's relatives in Lincolnshire, and as there was no stage coach service his mother had arranged for him to share the expense of a hired post-chaise with 'a young gentleman, the son of a wealthy banker'[26] who was making the same journey. On that occasion the acquaintance had not prospered: the 'young gentleman', twice Thomas's age, treated him with some haughtiness and alarmed him by priming a pair of duelling pistols in the carriage, talking with obvious relish about the likelihood of their meeting highwaymen on the road. Peter Howe Browne, Viscount Westport seemed a better prospect. He was two or three years younger than Thomas, who was now fifteen, and his father and Mr Grace, his tutor, hoped that Thomas would be a 'good influence' on him. The two boys got on well together and there was no awkwardness in their relationship. Their holiday, however, had unexpected consequences. Instead of forging a lasting link between Thomas and Westport it merely completed the process of unfitting Thomas for further schooling, preparing the way for an adolescent crisis whose consequences were to affect his whole future life.

The journey began calmly enough. Thomas left Bath some time before 14 July,[27] taking a coach to Eton, where Westport was at school. On arrival he found that Westport, with his tutor in tow, had already gone to Frogmore to attend a fête given by Queen Charlotte. Thomas followed, and with Westport watched the dancing for a while, explored the gardens and then, finding nothing else of interest, returned to Eton. When he wrote to tell his mother about the visit – he dutifully kept his 'Dear and honoured Mother' informed about his doings from the beginning to the end of the holiday – her reaction was quite typical: she was simply appalled to hear that he had gone to a royal ball in his travelling clothes! Thomas did his best to soothe her, his tone suggesting a blend of anxious child and nonchalant adult: 'My travelling dress was a very good one, (much better than what Lord Westport had on), and my boots were cleaned . . . Besides, I hardly saw five persons in the garden; for the ball had begun then, and the ball-room was so crowded, that it was impossible for any person to see what I was dressed in.'[28]

Also at Frogmore, a few days later, he met King George III. The two boys were playing in the gardens, Thomas giving Westport a lecture, with practical demonstrations, on the art of stonethrowing – on which he was, as we know, something of an expert. Suddenly they saw the King and his attendants approaching, and had no choice but to go and present themselves. The King chatted amiably and, commenting on Thomas's unusual surname, asked whether the De Quinceys

33

had come to England in the seventeenth century as Huguenot refugees. This was a sore point: Thomas had already acquired an intense dislike of the French, perhaps from his mother, to whom as an Evangelical Tory France represented a hellish brew of Popery and revolution. He hastened to set the King right by telling him that the family had been in England since the Conquest. 'How do you know?' asked the King. This was tricky, but after a moment's hesitation Thomas rose to the occasion and mentioned that the name appeared in 'Robert of Gloucester's *Metrical Chronicle*, which I understood, from internal evidence, to have been written about 1280'.[29] That was quite enough for the King who refrained from pressing the matter any further and, murmuring affably 'I know, I know,' went on his way, leaving the fifteen-year-old genealogist in secure possession of his family dignity.

More important was Thomas's first sight of London, a day or two earlier. What impressed him most was its size, and the 'Babylonian confusion' of noise, people and carriages, the latter brought to a halt at frequent intervals by a traffic jam or 'lock': 'a line of carriages of every description inextricably massed and obstructing each other, far as the eye could stretch'.[30] It took two hours to get from the suburbs to the centre of London, partly because the tutor, Mr Grace, drove the carriage himself and was not sure of the way. At last the boys were deposited at an inn somewhere in the city and left for three-and-a-half hours to 'see London' while the tutor attended to some business. They decided to choose one sight to see, and settled on St Paul's. When they entered the cathedral Thomas was again struck by an overwhelming consciousness of size, the dim emptiness of the dome and the vast aisles presenting a hollow immensity as striking in its way as the noisy, crowded immensity of the city outside. But it was the famous Whispering Gallery which particularly caught his imagination. The boys climbed the narrow stone staircase up to the gallery, which runs around the base of the great dome, and tested the acoustic magic of the place, Westport walking round to the far side and whispering close to the wall, so that 'after running along the walls of the gallery', Thomas tells us, the whisper 'reached me as a deafening menace in tempestuous uproars'.[31] The experience moved him with a delightful kind of fear and, as he later recalled, this weird amplification struck him as a vivid symbol of the fact that words and actions are irrevocable: the lightest utterance may come to have consequences of thunderous magnitude.

This sounds like an impressive glimpse of the adolescent De Quincey's sensitivity and poetic imagination, and as such most readers of the 1856 *Confessions*, where the incident is related, have taken it. But as every visitor to St Paul's will know, De Quincey's account of the Whispering Gallery is wrong. The Gallery does not magnify sounds. It carries them round, with uncanny crispness and clarity, at their original volume. Moreover, De Quincey speaks of his friend as standing at 'the earlier end of the gallery', and of the whisper as 'running along the walls of the gallery' to 'the further end' – as if he is thinking of a rectangular gallery, not a circular one. Apparently memory is confusing the acoustic effects of St Paul's with others encountered in the course of his wide and curious reading later in life. The alteration must have been unconscious, for he could hardly have counted on public forgetfulness of such a well-known tourist attraction. It is merely that, as so often in cases of experience embodying what De Quincey liked to call 'the dark sublime', imagination blended insensibly into memory, transmuting a fact into a poetic symbol.

In the late afternoon of that day in 1801 the two boys went on with Mr Grace to visit Westport's grandmother, at whose house they met a Scottish nobleman, Lord Morton, who had somehow heard of the success of Thomas's translation from Horace – and 'protested loudly', after the poem had been read to the company, that it deserved first prize, not third. It was thus, Thomas recalled, that 'for the first time in my life, I found myself somewhat in the situation of a *"lion"* ',[32] which naturally he thoroughly enjoyed. Next day the boys returned to Eton, where their social life continued at the same fevered pitch. There were more royal fêtes, though Thomas soon grew bored with them and but for his delight in the music, he says, would have 'had some difficulty in avoiding so monstrous an indecorum as yawning'.[33]

It was nearly time to leave for Ireland, but before they left Westport initiated Thomas into a new and forbidden pleasure: the theatre. Thomas wrote home a few days later, confessing the incident and apologizing as for a serious offence:

> On Friday evening, Lord Westport came to me and desired me to go with him to the play. I tried to escape by saying that I had letters to write (which in fact I had); however, as he seemed much disappointed at not going on the last evening of his being near a playhouse, and as he declared he would not go without me, I consented at length to accompany him to the Windsor Theatre. But be assured, my dear mother, I would not have done this for the world if I could have helped it, had I no other reason for avoiding public amusements than the earnest desire of obliging and obeying you.[34]

The mother who liked nothing better than for her son (properly dressed, of course) to rub shoulders with the aristocracy at royal fêtes had a pious horror of the theatre. Thomas later became passionately devoted to theatre-going, and even at fifteen he was so hungry for new experience that we need not take very seriously this picture of the sedate youth, dragged protesting from his writing desk, manfully enduring a visit to the theatre to keep his weak-minded friend company. But writing home to mother, what else could he say?

The next day, Thomas, Westport and Mr Grace set off for Ireland. Thomas described the stage-coach journey to Holyhead in a vivid letter to his mother:

> The road through Wales was much finer than anything I have ever seen, or ever expected to see. From Oswestry to Llangollen was the first remarkably beautiful stage. If you went that road any time when you were in Wales, you will probably remember that we travel on the side of a mountain looking down into an immensely deep valley surrounded by
>
> > 'Mountains and rocks which rise
> > In rugged grandeur to the skies.'
>
> The sun was then setting, and the effect of his glowing light on the roads, the winding river, and the cattle below, and on the distant mountains, and gigantic rocks above, was far more beautiful in the former, and sublime in the latter, than I am able to describe. The road from Llangollen to Corwen, I am told, is still more delightful; but as we travelled that stage between nine and twelve o'clock, I saw very little of it. At first, indeed, the dusky hills, seen 'through the horizontal misty air,' were mournful, but in a short time the increasing twilight prevented me from having any but a very indistinct view of the fine scenes we were passing through . . .[35]

His letter shows a striking facility for landscape description, and a strong response to natural beauty. Nor is his taste uneducated: he classifies the elements of the scene (perhaps a trifle self-consciously) in the terms of late eighteenth-century aesthetics: the gentler, softer aspects are 'beautiful', in contrast with the more awe-inspiring 'sublime' of the distant mountains.

Just before they reached Holyhead something odd happened. Mr Grace, who was to see them as far as the boat, suddenly took offence at something the boys had 'done, or said, or omitted' and stopped speaking to them. They could remember no misdemeanours committed on the journey and Mr Grace would neither explain nor allow them to ask him. 'To the last moment, however,' says De Quincey, 'he manifested a punctilious regard to the duties of his charge. He accompanied us in our boat, on a dark and gusty night, to the packet, which lay a little out at sea. He saw us on board; and then, standing up for one moment, he said, "Is all right on deck?" – "All right, sir," sang out the ship's steward. – "Have you, Lord Westport, got your boat-cloak with you?" – "Yes, sir." – "Then pull away, boatmen." ' And he was gone into the dark. Later on, Westport showed Thomas a piece of paper: part of a torn-up letter which, he believed, had been left purposely by the tutor where the boys could see it. If so, the fragment must have been the wrong one. It was from a letter in Mr Grace's handwriting to Westport's mother, and it read, 'With respect to your ladyship's anxiety to know how far the acquaintance with Mr. De Q. is likely to be of service to your son, I think I may now venture to say that –'. And there the mystery rested.[36]

The boys soon forgot Mr Grace, for on the boat they were taken up by a certain Lady Conyngham, who was also travelling to Dublin. De Quincey recalled her as 'a woman . . . celebrated for her beauty; and not undeservedly; for a lovely creature she was. The body of her travelling coach had been . . . unslung from the "carriage" (by which is technically meant the wheels and perch), and placed upon deck. This she used as a place of retreat from the sun during the day, and as a resting place at night.'[37] This pretty and amusing lady (later to win fame as the Prince Regent's mistress) took a particular fancy to Thomas and (to quote from his letter home) 'seeing me sitting on deck reading, called me to the carriage window, where she talked with me for about five minutes, and then made me come into the coach, and stay the remainder of the day with her. She conversed with me for above eight hours, and seemed a very sensible woman.'[38] The sequel, however, Thomas did not mention to his mother. That night, the weather being 'very sultry', the boys decided to sleep on deck in their cloaks. As they lay under the stars they were awakened by a stealthy tread close by their heads. A man was making his way across the deck to the Countess's coach. 'Our first thought', says De Quincey, 'was to raise an alarm, scarcely doubting that the purpose of the man was to rob the unprotected Lady of her watch or purse. But, to our astonishment, we saw the coach-door silently swing open under a touch from *within*. All was silent as a dream; the figure entered, the door closed, and we were left to interpret the case as we might.' To complete the interest of the episode, the lovely Countess remained unaware that the

boys had witnessed her lover's clandestine visit. The ship reached
Kingstown next morning and she went with them in a small boat to
the shore, friendly and charming as ever, 'and looking as beautiful,
and hardly less innocent than an angel'. Later they met her again in
Dublin, where she introduced them to her husband, who invited
them to stay at his home, Slane Castle. But the boys declined the
invitation.

Arrived at 9, Sackville Street, Dublin, the town house of his host's
family, Thomas was introduced to Lord Altamont, Westport's father,
whom he describes in a letter as

> a very fat man, and so lame that he is obliged to have two servants to
> support him whenever he stirs. He is a very sensible man, I think, and
> one of the most loyal persons I know. He abhors the very idea of
> gaming, and does not like to see a pack of cards. He will on no account
> permit Westport to play for money, and would be very angry if he saw
> him playing at all, though it were for nothing. He never swears,
> because he thinks it both a blackguard and a foolish practice. He
> always goes to church once on a Sunday, makes all the responses,
> seems very attentive, and loves to talk with me about the sermon as we
> are coming home from church. He does not conceive there is any harm
> in a clergyman's going to the play, and was quite astonished to hear
> that Mr Grace had never seen 'Bluebeard'.[39]

Thomas is painfully anxious to convince his mother that he is in safe
hands: Altamont is loyal, devout, opposed to gambling and swearing.
But there is an ironic edge to the last sentence, with its dig at Altamont's naivety about the theatre, and his taste in pantomime.

Much of the two-and-a-half weeks in Dublin was taken up with
official gatherings, for the Irish Parliament was being dissolved in
preparation for direct government from Westminster, a measure provoked by the rebellion of 1798. In reward for voting their own House
of Lords out of existence, under the Act of Union, twenty-eight peers,
Altamont among them, were elected to the English Parliament, and
had various decorations conferred upon them. Thomas was present
for much of this showy business. He sat in the House of Lords when
the Act of Union received the royal assent on 1 August, saw Altamont
invested as a Knight of the Order of the Blue Ribbon at Dublin Castle
on 6 August, and went to the ceremony of installation at St Patrick's
Cathedral on the 11th. He grew impatient with these ritual occasions,
however, secretly regretting what seemed to him a humiliation of
Irish national pride and was now eager to leave for the West. They

were able to go at last on 13 August, and spent three days travelling the 150 miles to Westport, County Mayo. The first stage of the journey was by canal boat to Tullamore, a leisurely ride during which Thomas had another romantic adventure which impressed him even more strongly than the episode of Lady Conyngham.

Among the company in the boat was a fashionable Dublin lady, well known as a wit and 'bluestocking'; learning that Westport was a lord she rushed to get into conversation with him, taking care to flatter him by snubbing Thomas as an inferior. Thomas was annoyed and frustrated: he was used to being the centre of interest, but could see no way of reclaiming his rightful position. He was being eclipsed by the snobbery of a vulgar woman. He was saved by the arrival of a certain Miss Blake, who came on deck with her sister, the young widow of an earl. Miss Blake at once befriended him. She was beautiful, amusing and the sister of a countess (so that Thomas now had a title on *his* side too!) and, best of all, she was willing to discuss literature. This was the opening he needed, and with Miss Blake's encouragement he was soon leading the conversation, deposing the discomfitted bluestocking, who retired below deck. Before long he was paying less attention to the company around than to Miss Blake herself. She was extremely pretty, and he awoke to the full power of his feelings for her when, 'Gazing, perhaps, with too earnest an admiration at this generous and spirited young daughter of Ireland, and in that way making her acknowledgments for her goodness which I could not properly clothe in words, I was roused to a sense of my indecorum by seeing her suddenly blush.' With the surprise and confusion of that moment came a revelation: 'Now first,' he says, 'it struck me that life might owe half its attractions and all its graces to female companionship'.[39] He and Westport spent the rest of the day with the delightful Miss Blake, who was only twenty years old. Thomas, however, did not pursue the flirtation, trying decorously to convince her that his admiration 'had, in reality, been addressed to her moral qualities, her enthusiasm, her spirit, and her generosity'. The realization that one might feel both love and respect for a woman perplexed him. Previously he had felt fully at ease only with women of a lower social class than his own; his mother and her friends had always seemed too stern and distant to evoke affection. The encounter with Miss Blake made a deep impression on him. 'From this day,' he says, 'I was an altered creature, never again relapsing into the careless, irreflective mind of childhood.'[40]

The estate at Westport was reached on 16 August. Thomas was

pleased with the place, as he told his mother in his next dispatch.

> The house is very large and handsome . . . The only thing in which I am disappointed is the very one in which I was most certain I should be gratified – I mean the *library*. Even as to *quantity* it is inferior to ours in Bath; . . . However, I hear that the *French* and the *rebels*, who have twice been in possession of this house, have made off with the best books. There is a fine deer-park here, containing nearly 300 acres. Croagh Patrick, the highest mountain I believe in Ireland, is about six miles from us in a direct line . . . We generally ride sixteen or seventeen miles a day, by which means we get to see almost everything worth seeing in this most romantic country.[41]

Thomas was curious about the unsuccessful Irish risings of 1798, which had been supported by a French invasion. Local memories were still fresh; signs of occupation (such as the looted library) were visible everywhere at Westport, and he listened with fascination, but also with scepticism, to what he heard:

> As to the rebellion in Ireland, the English, I think, use the *amplifying*, and the Irish the *diminishing hyperbole; the* former view it with a *magnifying glass,* the latter with a *microscope.* In England, I remember, we heard such horrid accounts of murders, and battles, and robberies, and here everybody tells me the country *is* in as quiet a state as England, and *has* been so for some time past.[42]

He was already a great reader of history, and it intrigued him to try and piece together the truth from conflicting reports.

Daily routine at Westport was quite strict, and the boys were not allowed to neglect their studies:

> I and Westport rise at various times between half-past four and six. I read the Bible before breakfast and Lord Westport writes copies and ciphers. We breakfast with Lord Altamont, then read again, then ride and bathe till about two or three o'clock, when we dine (for neither I nor Wesport are able to wait till six). In the afternoon I read and write and Westport plays with his cousins. At about seven o'clock we sup on bread and milk and fruit (which is also our breakfast), and at nine go to bed.[43]

Thomas was also keeping up his Greek and teaching Westport, who was none too keen on schoolwork, to write Latin verses.

But new worries were on their way. Even from the other side of the Irish Sea Mrs De Quincey was exerting her usual moral pressure.

'Much as I wish to hear from you, my dear mother,' Thomas writes, 'I am sorry you should spend that time in writing to me which, I am sure, your health much requires to be spent in rest.'[44] But she was impervious to hints. Severe and fussy letters continued to arrive (amongst other things, his mother was angry about his visit to the theatre) and Thomas began to grow anxious about her plans for his schooling. Having snatched him away from Bath Grammar School, she would not let him return. But the little school at Winkfield was utterly inadequate. Mr Grace (and probably Lord Altamont) had suggested that Thomas be sent to Eton with Westport, but the idea terrified him. From Westport's conversation he had gained a lurid picture of Eton as an inferno of vice and cruelty. 'From all I can hear,' he tells his mother, 'the discipline of the school is certainly not what one would expect, and surely not what it should be. Westport and Dominic Brown, his cousin, have told me enough to make me sure of that; and the morals of the place are evidently at a low ebb.'[45] Westport, says Thomas, has been corrupted by the school: his nature 'is in ruins, he curses and swears and blasphemes in the most shocking manner,' but is 'reckoned quite virtuous at Eton'.[46] Moreover,

> Anyone who should *attempt* to differ from the rest of the boys . . . would be literally tormented to death. The first thing they do in such a case as this (for a specimen or earnest of what is to follow) is to fling the boy into the Thames with ropes tied to him, by which they pull him out, not, however, before he is so nearly dead as to require medical assistance to recover him. You may judge of the discipline of the school when I tell you that a week ago they beat an old porter (in defiance of the masters, some of whom were standing by, and hardly trying to prevent them) with such brutality that his life, I hear, is despaired of. My situation, as a boy on the foundation, would be still more miserable.[47]

Perhaps Westport and his cousin were amusing themselves by terrifying Thomas; but his fears were probably justified. Boarding school life could be very unpleasant, and what he heard from the Etonians gained credibility from stories told to him at Bath by Dr Mapleton, who had attended him after his head injury. Mapleton had removed his three sons from Winchester when he learned of their ill-treatment by senior boys. Mapleton's account, taken together with Westport's tales of Eton, formed a strong argument for the comparative peace of a provincial grammar school.

He wanted, ideally, to return to the Bath school. But in his letters home he urged his pleas by the very arguments most likely to antagonize his mother:

The thing which makes me most unhappy at a private school is there being no emulation, no ambition, nothing to contend for – no honours to excite one. This was exactly the case at Mr. Spencer's. I was at the head of the school the whole time I was there. No one but myself could make verses, and all those kind of things; but then I had no one to contend with, nor anything higher to aspire to. The consequence was that my powers entirely flagged . . . Nobody (except the boys) knew I was at the top of the school. With them it was considered no merit to be the head boy; and *had* it, I should have derived but little pleasure from the applause of those who, with few exceptions, were nearly approaching to idiots.[48]

One imagines that Mrs De Quincey was not much pleased with this display of competitiveness and intellectual arrogance. It is striking how effectively her attempts to shield Thomas from praise had led him to develop a craving for it. His letter is written from a sense of intense frustration, and overstates the case in a desperate attempt to convey some sense of his needs to a mother who must have seemed to him terribly obtuse. And surely, he pleads, the affair of the offence to Mrs Pratt – 'the only reason (as far as I know) for my not being now at the Grammar School' – can be forgotten? The school, after all, was not to blame.

The matter rested there while the holiday drew to a close. Thomas left the estate on 8 September,[49] travelling with young Westport to Dublin and then by boat to Parkgate. They went on to Birmingham by coach and there parted company. Thomas was to ask at the post office for a letter from his mother: sealed orders telling him where to go next. Wesport waited whilst the coach horses were changed and then rode off for Eton. Thus he passes out of Thomas's life, though not entirely out of literary history, for after taking the title of Lord Altamont he became the boon-companion of Byron, who in February 1808 notes, 'Altamont is a good deal with me, last night at the Opera Masquerade, we supped with seven whores, a *Bawd* and a Ballet-master.'[50]

After Westport's coach had left, Thomas made his way to the post office, where he found his mother's letter 'from which I learned that my sister [Mary] was visiting at Laxton, in Northamptonshire, the seat of an old friend, to which I also had an invitation'.[51] The old friend was Lady Carbery, whose family had long known the Pensons, Mrs De Quincey's parents. She was now closer than ever to the De Quinceys since, like Mrs De Quincey, she had taken up the fervent Evangelical views of Hannah More and the 'Clapham Sect'. Lady Carbery, however, was a warm-hearted and affectionate lady, only ten or a dozen years older than Thomas. In childhood she had often been to visit the family at The Farm and Greenhay, and they had met again at Bath, where Lady Carbery had been with her guardian, Mrs Schreiber. She was inordinately fond of Thomas, and the idea of a visit to Laxton delighted him. There was no coach to Northamptonshire until the next day, so he had to spend the night in 'gloomy, noisy and, at that time, dirty Birmingham'. He stayed at the Hen and Chickens, a large coaching inn in the middle of the city, and spent much of the time lying awake listening to the arrival and departure of stage coaches and the noise of servants knocking up sleeping passengers for the early morning departures.

The next day he set off to Laxton. On the journey, despite his happiness at the prospect of seeing Lady Carbery again, depression began to set in. He knew from his mother's letters that a decision about his education was to be made as soon as he was back in England. Once his mother and the guardians heard that he had reached Laxton, family conferences would be held, pressure would be applied, and he would be sentenced to three years at some dismal school. The idea of going back to school – *any* school – now repelled him. Not having been allowed to stay at one school long enough to settle down, he had not acquired the habit of school-going. He was aware, moreover, that schoolmasters now had little to teach him in the way of book-learning. He was afraid of boredom and bullying. He had just spent six weeks in the company of cultured ladies and gentlemen, who had sought his conversation and treated him as their equal. He had discovered the power of landscape, the pleasures of travel and the attractions of female company. Yet he would soon be back with a mother who treated him as a child, and who would force him, against his true interests, into the ugliness and frustrations of a school environment. At the same time, Laxton held a glimmer of hope. Lady Carbery adored him and admired his intellectual gifts. She also had influence with Mrs De Quincey. Perhaps she would intercede for him. To achieve this would require a difficult balancing act on Thomas's part, because, of course, his mother also had influence on Lady Carbery, who regarded her as a religious mentor and might well give way in the face of stern arguments about the child's duty of absolute obedience to the parent. But with tact and patience something might be done. Otherwise, prospects were grim, and his own desire – leave to travel or study in his own way for a year or two, followed perhaps by entrance to a university – unattainable.

Reaching Laxton, he was greeted by his sister Mary. The first bell was just ringing for dinner, but Mary had a message for him: he was to go at once to Lady Carbery's dressing-room, where her ladyship wanted a private word with him. It turned out – as if to confirm Thomas's self-esteem – that Lady Carbery had been eagerly awaiting his arrival, as she needed someone to entertain an Irish peer, Lord Massey, who was visiting Laxton with his wife – an extended visit, apparently, as his Lordship was having trouble with creditors and found it prudent to stay away from Ireland. Lord Carbery was away, and the guest was feeling the lack of male companionship. Thomas's arrival just before dinner prevented an embarrassing, though trivial, crisis, for custom dictated that after dinner the ladies must withdraw, leaving the gentlemen to drink and talk not just for a few minutes but for something like two hours. If there happened to be only one gentleman, then he must get bored, or read a book: so complete was the tyranny of convention. Thomas was happy to save Lord Massey from this fate; perhaps it also occurred to him that by making himself useful to Lady Carbery he increased his chances of gaining her support when the time came for a battle with his guardians.

Needless to say, Thomas got on well with Lord Massey. He had met some of Massey's friends in Ireland, and was full of anecdotes from his recent visit. Massey shared his interest in books, and on the succeeding days they spent many hours exploring the neglected library at Laxton. October passed pleasantly enough, when Thomas could forget his anxiety over the question of schooling. At some point Mrs De Quincey herself arrived to stay with her friend Mrs Schreiber, who lived some four miles away, but she does not seem to have spent much time at Laxton and for the most part Thomas was alone with Lady Carbery and her guests. Circumstances continued to seem as if in a benevolent conspiracy to force Thomas into his favourite role of scholar-gentleman. Not only was he Lord Massey's confidant at the dinner table and in the library, but Lady Carbery, who was growing increasingly concerned with theological matters, enlisted him as her tutor in biblical studies.

The situation at Laxton was a strange one. Lady Carbery, a bright and lively girl when Thomas had last seen her, had become increasingly depressed since her marriage. Her husband was away and in any case the marriage, after eight years, was not working well. In her loneliness she had turned to a sombre, Calvinistic brand of religion. She had conceived a 'premature disgust with the world', and, Thomas recalls, 'had any mode of monastic life existed for Protestants, I believe she would before this have entered it, supposing Lord Carbery to have consented'.[52] Thomas and Mary De Quincey must have contributed to Laxton such life as it had to show – Lord Massey, and his wife, the only other visitors, seem to have been uninspiring company. Thomas knew little about theology, but he soon convinced Lady Carbery that to study the New Testament in depth she would need to learn some Greek. Mary De Quincey and Lady Massey decided to join in and 'on the very next morning we all rode in to Stamford, our nearest town for such a purpose, and astounded the book-seller's apprentice' by ordering four Greek testaments, three lexicons and three Greek grammars to be sent at once by the mail coach.[53]

Once again, Thomas's learning had helped him to reorganize a social situation and place himself at the centre. Mary and Lady Massey soon gave up, but Lady Carbery took the enterprise seriously and did indeed learn Greek. No doubt Thomas was happy to have his class reduced to one, for he thought Lady Carbery very beautiful and enjoyed the way she indulged him and deferred to him. She was still only twenty-six, and he began to feel himself attracted to her, despite the embarrassing awareness that she had known him from infancy.[54] Lady Carbery, for her part, did her best to make him a more complete gentleman by entrusting him to her groom, who taught him riding for two hours a day, and to a keeper, who tried, without much success, to teach him to shoot. There was also social life outside Laxton: Lady Carbery took Lady Massey and Mary to dine with the local county families, and Thomas went too to make up the party, for Lord Massey, a shy man and sensitive about his social position as a penniless Irish peer, preferred to stay behind. As at Laxton, Thomas sat with the gentlemen after dinner, and regularly heard Lady Massey praised as a notable beauty. He thought it a pity that Massey should miss these tributes to his wife, and innocently enough 'reported to Lord Massey, in terms of unexceptionable decorum, those flattering expressions of homage which sometimes, from the lips of young men partially under the influence of wine, had taken a form somewhat too enthusiastic for literal repetition to a chivalrous and adoring husband'.[55] What Lord Massey made of all this is not recorded.

Thomas and Lady Carbery were just preparing to tackle Herodotus in Greek when Lord Carbery returned home: not, one gathers, to anyone's great enthusiasm. He smiled patronizingly at his wife's studies, and made it clear that he did not share her religious enthusiasm. The plan to read Herodotus was quietly dropped. Meanwhile, Mrs De Quincey had been conferring with the guardians, and by the end of October it was decided that Thomas should be sent to Manchester Grammar School. He argued passionately against the plan, but his mother would not listen. He appealed to Lady Carbery, but she advised submission. It was all just as he had feared, and at the end of the month he passed out through the park gates of Laxton with gloom and anger in his heart to take the coach northwards to Manchester.

The reason repeatedly given to Thomas for the choice of school was that several awards of forty pounds a year at Brasenose College, Oxford, were available to pupils who had studied at the school for three years. The income from the Quincey estate gave Thomas only £150 a year, so that such an award would greatly improve his lot as a student. Still, three more years at school seemed to him a high price to pay. In reality, Mrs De Quincey probably insisted on sending him back to school because of his age. She was not the sort of parent to notice the signs of exceptional gifts in her own child; had she done so, she would only have seen them as temptations to pride. No doubt she chose Manchester Grammar School mainly because Samuel Hall, always the most formidable of the guardians, had three sons there already and was about to send a fourth. In addition, Mr Kelsall, now a merchant and still managing part of the Quincey business interests, was in Manchester. At the Grammar School, therefore, Thomas could be kept under close supervision. The more he resisted the decision, the more Mrs De Quincey was convinced that the discipline of school was exactly what he needed.

On 9 November 1800 Samuel Hall took him to the school and he was enrolled as 'Thomas, son of the late Thomas de Quincey, merchant, Bath'.[56] First impressions were not encouraging. The schoolroom showed 'a dreary expanse of whitewashed walls, . . . bare as the walls of a poorhouse'.[57] The 'High Master', Charles Lawson, who taught the upper school, was equally unprepossessing: he was seventy-two years old, and in poor health. Thomas guessed his age as seventy-five, and suspected 'that his understanding was of a narrow order'.[58] Lawson gave Thomas a brief examination by handing him a volume of the *Spectator* and telling him to translate a page or two into Latin. This, of course, was easily done, and Thomas went into the highest class.

A couple of days later he moved into Lawson's house, at 3, Long Millgate, where he was to board with several other senior boys. Again, first impressions were grim: he arrived on a rainy winter evening to find a cramped, comfortless house full of 'gloomy and unfurnished little rooms'. When he met the other boarders in their common-room things looked brighter: the boys welcomed him with a glass of brandy and as conversation developed he found them friendly and intelligent. Clearly there would be no bullying here. Another fear was laid to rest when he heard that there was no flogging in the upper forms. Earlier in life Lawson had earned himself the nickname of 'the flogging Turk' but he had mellowed with age and nowadays there was no beating; discipline, Thomas learned, was maintained in an easy-going way by the older boys themselves. This seemed reassuring, but once Thomas was enmeshed in the daily routine of school his spirits began to sink once more, and his tendency to solitude began to reassert itself. He had been given a single attic room of his own, bedroom and study combined, on the second floor of Lawson's house, and increasingly he shut himself away there. He and two other boys made up the top class in Greek, and all of them lived in the High Master's house, but still he preferred to keep to himself. His mother paid for him to have a piano and music lessons, but he decided that 'to the deep voluptuous enjoyment of music absolute *passiveness* in the hearer is indispensable',[59] and so he gave it up. Perhaps the real obstacle was impatience with the necessary hours of practice: it sounds rather as if he expected the 'deep voluptuous enjoyment' to come at once.

It has to be admitted that he was determined to dislike the school, but in reality it had defects enough. Most trying of all were the eccentricities of the High Master himself. Lawson had been teaching at the school for fifty years, and had been High Master for thirty-six of them.[60] He was now seriously ill and his inability to cope with his duties had led to a general decline in school's morale. Discipline was ineffectual: the boys had the upper hand, and treated Lawson as a figure of fun as he lunged harmlessly with an old split cane at gangs of unruly scholars. 'Rudeness and vulgarity were the order of the day,' recalled one of Thomas's near-contemporaries. 'Any thing like gentlemanly behaviour was laughed at.'[61] Lawson had retreated into a world of his own where he found it difficult to tell one boy from another. 'His habit', wrote another former pupil, 'was to address everyone as a third person, and with the prefix of "Psha, blockead" . . . To his boys or servants, or to persons in humble life, he would say, "What does he want, pray?" or, "What has he got to say?" '[62] This nervous, contemptuous mode of address infuriated Thomas. In addition, it turned out that his misgivings about Lawson's abilities were justified.

> When I first entered, I remember that we read Sophocles; and it was a constant matter of triumph to us . . . to see our 'Archididascalus' (as he loved to be called) conning our lesson before he went up, and laying a regular train, with lexicon and grammar, for blowing up and blasting (as it were) any difficulties he found in the choruses; whilst *we* never condescended to open our books until the moment of going up, and were generally occupied in writing epigrams upon his wig, or some such important matter.[63]

Lawson's appearance was certainly striking. 'He wore a complete suit of black velvet – I have him before me now –' wrote one of his pupils, 'lace ruffles at his wrists, black silk stockings, and diamond buckles on his shoes, with a well-powdered perruque projecting like a cauliflower, from behind. He used to enter the school with feeble tottering steps as if about to fall.'[64] As Thomas wrote later, 'It is a bad thing for a boy to be, and to know himself to be, far beyond his tutors, whether in knowledge or in power of mind.'[65] He had experienced it before, and the prospect of three more years of the same tedium was almost insupportable.

The school timetable had come to reflect Lawson's infirmities. Determined to fulfil his duties down to the last detail, the old man plodded with agonizing slowness through his daily routine. School began at seven a.m. and was supposed to break for an hour at nine while the boys had breakfast. But Lawson often kept them until half past nine or later, so that they scarcely had time to swallow their meal before school began again. In the same way, the two hours' break over lunch was 'pared down to forty minutes, or less'.[66] Ending at five p.m., school for the top form was thus almost continuous for ten hours a day. The feeling of claustrophobia was intensified by the lack of a playground: during a financial crisis the school had sold its playground for building land and the boys now had to spend their free time inside the buildings or in Long Millgate, one of the narrowest and dirtiest thoroughfares in central Manchester. An account of the school five years later gives a picture which must be close in essentials to what Thomas saw there:

> Most of the scholars who come from a distance lodge with the High Master or second master. Both their houses are in Millgate, closely surrounded by Old Buildings chiefly occupied by poor people, in situations neither healthy nor comfortable. The street is narrow and also serves as the Apple Market so that on two or three days a week it is crowded with horses and carts, making it difficult and dangerous to pass from the masters' houses to the school. There is no playground so boys have no other outlet but the streets where they are prematurely exposed to temptations to the great danger of health and morals. The resorting to taverns and intercourse with women of the town becomes a fashion amongst the Boys in the higher classes of the school, which no vigilance of the masters can suppress. All this makes a serious impression upon the minds of those parents who live at a distance, with the result that for several years the number of scholars has declined.[67]

How far Thomas succumbed to the same temptations as other senior boys, we do not know, though we know that he was visiting prostitutes two years later. At all events we can easily understand why he found life at the school increasingly oppressive.

During his first winter there he endured his lot with the aid of two main consolations. One was literary discovery, for when a new edition of the *Lyrical Ballads* of Wordsworth and Coleridge appeared in January 1801 he bought a copy and was able at last to read the collection as a whole. The passionate honesty of the poems, the urgency of their attempt to communicate human experience with a directness that cut through obstructive conventions of style, found an immediate response in Thomas, whose emotional life since leaving Laxton had been so limited by constricting circumstances. Into the gloomy school the *Lyrical Ballads* brought a fresh breeze redolent of freedom and human sympathy. The volume was anonymous, but inquiries through his mother at Bath yielded the poets' names and Wordsworth was soon established as chief god of Thomas's pantheon, with Coleridge a close second. It was probably now that he resolved, boldly and – one might think – unrealistically, to obtain, some day, the friendship of Wordsworth himself.

At about the same time, he seems to have been reading the poems of Chatterton, the boy-poet who had become almost a legendary figure after his suicide in a London garret in 1770 at the age of seventeen. No doubt Thomas responded less to Chatterton's poetry than to his appeal as a symbol of ill-treated youthful genius. Chatterton had run away from home to seek his fortune at sixteen. In 1801 Thomas too would be sixteen. Chatterton's example – and the warning it implied – must have crossed his mind more than once.

A more social consolation was the hospitality of the Rev. John Clowes, Rector of St John's Church. Like Kelsall and Hall, Clowes was an old friend of Thomas's parents. Unlike them he was neither oppressed with business nor stiffened by the responsibilities of guardianship. In fact he had no delegated responsibility for Thomas's welfare, so it was all the easier for him to be a friend. Clowes was a clergyman of the Church of England, but of a type far removed from his fellow-cleric Hall, for he was a mystic. A follower of the Swedish visionary Emmanuel Swedenborg, he had his own intimate awareness of an ever-present spiritual world, and his character was marked by a warm-hearted serenity that testified to the power of his eccentric faith. He had been a visitor at Greenhay during Thomas's childhood and now, finding him a pleasant and stimulating companion, Thomas took up the acquaintance again. When he could find the time he took the short walk from Long Millgate to Clowes's quiet parsonage at St John's Parade, Deansgate, where he could discuss literature and ideas in a peaceful, civilized atmosphere and forget school for a while.

Clowes was fifty-eight when Thomas began to visit him but he must have seemed older, since his guest later recalled him as 'aged'. He kindly gave Thomas as presents several books from his own library, including a copy of the *Odyssey* which Clowes had read during his first term at Cambridge in 1761. Apart from his generosity, Clowes's main attractions seem to have been his delightful house and his ability to treat Thomas as an equal. He was quiet without pretension, listened to his young visitor with friendly respect, and without forcing his opinions on him opened up for him the tradition of Christian mysticism. Clowes had devoted much of his time to translating Swedenborg, and he seems to have lent copies of his works to Thomas. No doubt other mystics such as William Law and Jacob Boehme were also discussed. De Quincey found Swedenborg's revelations of the spiritual world tedious and earthbound, but his published writings make frequent reference to Swedenborg, and clearly some impression was made, even if not a very favourable one. He also retained an enthusiasm for Boehme and, years later, went so far as to make Coleridge a present of a fine edition of his works. Some part of Clowes's mysticism must have coloured his thinking and helped, perhaps, to strengthen his interest in visionary states of mind and his sense of mysterious realities underlying the apparent surface of experience – themes which are central to the best prose work of his maturity.

Sometimes Thomas and Clowes would exchange memories of life at Greenhay. One vivid episode which they recalled was the visit of Mrs Harriet Lee. Mrs Lee, illegitimate daughter of Sir Francis Dashwood (notorious for his association with the Hell Fire Club), had been passing through Manchester in 1794 and Mrs De Quincey had asked her to dinner – led on as much by the information that 'Mrs Lee was a bold thinker; and . . . for a woman, she had an astonishing command of theological learnings',[68] as by her status as heiress and society lady. Naturally, therefore, she invited also two clergymen – Hall and Clowes – and looked forward to an evening of pious conversation. When Mrs Lee arrived she revealed herself at once as a militant atheist, her knowledge of theology gathered as ammunition against Christianity. She was also (Thomas informs us) young and very beautiful. The two clergymen were no match for her: Clowes, with his intuitive and visionary faith, could not come to grips with her theoretical arguments. Truth to him was clear as day, so why defend it? Hall tried to fight back, but his mind was so slow and his knowledge so stale and narrow that Mrs Lee tied him in logical knots and Thomas, to his secret delight, had the satisfaction of seeing his tutor made to look a fool. Mrs Quincey had brought the evening to a suitable close by throwing a hysterical fit. Thomas now looked back on life at Greenhay with a certain nostalgia. The dingy world of the Grammar School made it all seem very remote. Thus he particularly liked Clowes's house: the parsonage was exotic in its quiet way, having an organ and stained-glass windows (De Quincey tells us) in the library. These details sound improbable, but other sources confirm that Clowes did indeed have a stained-glass window – a present from a French priest whom he had sheltered in his house during the Revolution – and Thomas no doubt saw it in the library, where it was awaiting installation in the church. So perhaps there really was an organ too.

With such comforts Thomas endured the winter, and as far as we know it was not until the spring of 1801 that he began to complain seriously. The first signs come in a letter from Lord Altamont, replying to one, now lost, in which Thomas seems to have been confiding various troubles, including an inability to concentrate on his work. 'The disorder of which you complain is certainly of very recent acquirement, and therefore may the more easily be got the better of, as I sincerely hope it will, and speedily,' writes Altamont. 'I . . . have just sent my boy back to school . . . If he had as little of the disease of idleness as you have, I should do more with him than I expect to do.'[69]

This was in May 1801. Trouble was averted for the time being by the summer holidays, which were spent at Everton near Liverpool, where Mrs De Quincey had rented a cottage. A letter from her survives, giving Thomas minutely detailed instructions for the journey and obviously not crediting him with much common sense. Thomas is to escort his younger brothers, who will be coming from Horwich Moor in Lancashire where they board with a parson, their tutor. 'Whichever way you come,' Mrs De Quincey fusses, 'I beg your principal care may be given to Henry, who is so blind he cannot see a horse until it is close to his elbow, and so frightened when he does see it, that he loses the power of moving . . . I must repeat, do not let Henry go from you a moment, and let Pink mind the luggage. Keep Henry from leaning against the coach-door or over the edge of the boat . . .'[70] – for they will come by canal from Manchester. Everton was then a delightful country village, built on the slopes of a hill overlooking Liverpool Bay, famous for good sea air and a popular site for the holiday villas of the well-to-do. Mrs De Quincey had taken a cottage in Middle Lane (now Everton Terrace). It was a small place: 'You must expect to see us in an Irish cabin, or very little better; when you approach the cottage, you may reach the chimneys with your hat,' she writes. The cottage, belonging to a Mrs Best, was opposite the far grander mansion of William Clarke, a banker who had been a friend and business contact of Thomas Quincey. The De Quinceys were apparently on intimate terms with him, and his society may have been one of the attractions of Everton.

Clarke was impressed by Thomas's charm and intelligence, and gave him free access to his house, which included a library and a gallery of paintings. Clarke's house was the centre of a circle of minor writers and local intellectuals, most of them involved in Whig politics. In due course Thomas met these Liverpool worthies and over the summer months observed them at leisure with the merciless eye of intelligent adolescence. They were similar in outlook and social standing to the members of the Literary and Philosophical Society in Manchester. Some had known Thomas Quincey, who had made trips on business to Liverpool. The most conspicuous figures were William Roscoe, historian, Whig politician and a popular though mediocre poet; the Rev. William Shepherd, Presbyterian minister of Gateacre and the author of much rollicking satirical verse on political themes; and Dr James Currie, biographer of Burns and a pioneer of medical research. They were often the best company to be had at Everton, but they irritated Thomas by their inflated literary pretensions and their Whig politics, which they discussed continually. They were all, to some extent, 'Radicals', and Thomas, an uninformed but instinctive Tory, must have felt isolated and vulnerable when such topics came up. Shepherd, a hearty and bluntly spoken man, embarrassed the sensitive boy by his coarse humour and by making fun of Mrs De Quincey's famous friend, the pious Hannah More. At the same time Thomas felt an invigorating scorn for the poetry Roscoe and his friends wrote and read aloud to the company. Roscoe's own efforts were full of 'the most timid and blind servility to the narrowest of conventional usages, conventional ways of viewing things, conventional forms of expression'.[71] His pastoral verse represented the last feeble stirrings of eighteenth-century neoclassicism, reducing nature to a pallid backdrop of 'crystal fountains', 'cool retreats' and 'vernal bowers', and it gave Thomas a delightful sense of secret power to sit amongst people who regarded Roscoe as a significant poet and reflect that not one of them had heard of Wordsworth. As he put it many years later,

> to me, who in that year, 1801, already knew of a grand renovation of poetic power – of a new birth in poetry, interesting not so much to England as to the human mind – it was secretly amusing to contrast the little artificial usages of their petty traditional knack with the natural forms of a divine art – the difference being pretty much as between an American lake, Ontario, or Superior, and a carp pond or a tench preserve.[72]

Another consolation was that Mr Clarke wanted to improve his Greek. This gave Thomas a chance to play his favourite role of tutor to his elders, and for much of the summer he visited Clarke early each morning to read Aeschylus with him.

In August Mrs De Quincey set off on an expedition to find a new home, taking her daughters but leaving Thomas, 'Pink' and Henry at Everton. She visited London, High Wycombe and Oxford but failed to find anywhere to her taste.[73] Her intention, Thomas recalled with some exaggeration,

> was to see all England with her own eyes, and to judge upon the
> qualifications of each county, each town . . . and each village . . . for
> contributing the main elements for a home that might justify her in
> building a house. The qualifications insisted upon were these five: –
> good medical advice somewhere in the neighbourhood; first-rate
> means of education; elegant (or what most people might think aristoc-
> ratic) society; agreeable scenery . . . and a Church of England clergy-
> man, who was to be strictly orthodox, faithful to the articles of our
> English Church, yet to these articles as interpreted by evangelical
> divinity.[74]

Of course, these features never turned up together in any one place and
she returned to the North Country thwarted.

In the autumn Thomas went back to serve his second year at
Manchester Grammar School. The place was as dreary as ever, and his
sense of exile from any society outside the school was increased by
friction with the Halls (he was insulted in some way by the sharp-
tongued Mrs Hall)[75] and disillusionment with the Kelsalls, whose
household had once seemed a haven of domestic bliss but who now
seemed to the critical adolescent a couple of typically materialistic
Manchester bourgeois. The gloomy surroundings, 'mud below, smoke
above', contributed to his oppression. And to make matters worse Mrs
De Quincey, though a frequent letter writer, never seemed to take any
notice of what Thomas told her about his doings. Full of her own
news, she treated his communications with offhand impatience. A
typical letter begins: 'My dear Thomas, I have two letters of yours in
my desk, but not easy to find, and I cannot answer, but I will write to
tell you that I purpose being in Manchester on Thursday evening . . .'
Later on, we find, 'I remember you mentioned something about
cravats, which I never answered, nor can I now . . .'[76] She was now
preoccupied with the purchase of a new house, St John's Priory,
Chester, a fine building, medieval in part but with many modern
additions, which was offered for a ridiculous sum of less than £500.
But still, had she taken the trouble to search her desk and pay closer
attention to Thomas's letters, she might have alleviated his feeling of
isolation.

Once again, however, just as crisis point was approaching, there
was a brief respite. To his delight and surprise, the party from Laxton
– Lady Carbery and her friends Lord and Lady Massey, Mrs De
Quincey and Mrs Schreiber, all came to stay in Manchester some time

towards the end of the year. The reason for the journey was the illness of Mrs Schreiber, who was suffering from cancer and needed to be near her trusted physician, the same Mr White who had attended the Quinceys at Greenhay. Thomas, however, was in raptures at seeing Lady Carbery again, and his mood of wintry gloom lifted temporarily, as the High Master gave him 'leave to adjourn for four or five hours' to her drawing-room each evening.[77] He enjoyed showing the visitors the sights of Manchester, and went with them to see Mr White's private museum, a collection of curiosities which included the skeleton of a highwayman, whose body had been bought from the authorities for dissection by Cruikshank, White's anatomy teacher. White told the visitors (how seriously we do not know) that after the hanging the victim had been cut down and taken in a carriage to the lecture-room, where he showed signs of revival. 'I think the subject is not quite dead,' the anatomist had remarked imperturbably. 'Pray' – turning to one of the students – 'put your knife in, Mr.——, at this point.'[78] White had inherited the skeleton from his teacher years later. He was reputed also to own a mummy, the embalmed body of a patient who feared premature burial and had left him a legacy conditional on his embalming and keeping her body. The mummy was said to inhabit a grandfather clock-case, a curtain of white velvet inside the glass hiding the features. The physician, however, declined the visitor's pleas for a sight of the mummy or its case.[79]

Much as he enjoyed seeing Lady Carbery, Thomas somehow found her less entertaining than she had seemed at Laxton. Her appetite for learning whetted by her Greek studies, she was now learning Hebrew, and in Manchester she had tuition from Dr Bailey, a local clergyman chosen for his extremely 'low-church' views which according to De Quincey, 'he pushed into practical extravagances that looked like fanaticism, or even like insanity'. Mrs De Quincey and her friends, of course, were happy to tolerate any extreme of piety, and Lady Carbery persuaded Thomas to join in the Hebrew lessons. These proved tedious, and Thomas soon gave up. On one occasion, however, he went against his better judgment – he knew Lady Carbery to be insensitive to poetry – and 'read to her with a beating heart "The Ancient Mariner" '.[80] He was eager to share his enthusiasm for the new poetry, and hoped that the 'wildness' of the poem, and 'the triple majesties of Solitude, of Mist, and of the Ancient Unknown Sea' might make some impression on her. He was disappointed, of course. Lady Carbery 'laughed at the finest parts', called the Ancient Mariner himself 'an old quiz' and said he would have made a good curate to help Dr Bailey in his overcrowded church. The good lady's orderly sensibility was impervious to the Romantic sublime. But as if to confirm the whole philosophy upon which the *Lyrical Ballads* had been based, the naive Dr Bailey, his mind untrammelled by literary taste of any sort, was deeply impressed, and Thomas 'had a triumph':

> To my great surprise, one day, Lady Carbery suddenly repeated by heart, to Dr Bailey, the beautiful passage:-
>
> 'It ceased, yet still the sails made on,' &c.,
>
> asking what he thought of *that*? As it happened, the simple child-like doctor had more sensibility than herself; for, though he had never in his whole homely life read more of poetry than he had drunk of Tokay or Constantia – in fact, had scarcely heard tell of any poetry but Watts's Hymns – he seemed petrified: and at last, with a deep sigh, as if recovering from the spasms of a new birth, said, 'I never heard anything so beautiful in my whole life.'[81]

Christmas came, and the end of term brought with it the school speech-day, when selected boys declaimed Latin verse or prose to the assembled pupils, parents and friends. Thomas, of course, was included, his task being to recite Latin verses 'on the recent conquest of Malta'. The whole Laxton party attended, with the best of motives, to hear and applaud him when he recited this 'worshipful nonsense', and 'Lady Carbery made a point of bringing in her party every creature whom she could influence'.[82] Thomas writhed with embarrassment at being paraded thus as the complete schoolboy under the eyes of adult friends, to whom he so much wanted to appear an equal. When he had said his piece, 'furious . . . was the applause which greeted me: furious was my own disgust. Frantic were the clamours as I concluded my nonsense: frantic was my inner sense of shame at the childish exhibition to which, unavoidably, I was making myself a party.' The disgust was intensified by a sense of guilt: he guessed that in the audience were many old friends of his dead father's, 'loving his memory, and thinking to honour it by kindness to his son'. His scowling discomfort was visible to all, and, as the applause died down, he made a small but significant gesture. Instead of going back to his seat with the other boys he came over to Lady Carbery and finding a vacant seat next to her he sat down there. He was asserting that he would not be part of the school. His world was the adult world, the world outside, and he was forming a fierce determination to joint it as soon as possible.

Early in 1802 his mother paid another visit to the school, and although she avoided noticing anything amiss, as she was about to leave Thomas could no longer restrain himself and made a passionate outburst to the effect that he must and would leave school forthwith; and that he must either go straight to university or else stay at home until he was deemed old enough to go. This demand was coupled with some attempt to explain that he had already outgrown school and was eager to begin working towards ambitious goals of some kind. Our evidence for this is an angry and startled letter from his mother dated 18 February 1802:

> My dear Thomas,
>   I expected to have received a letter from you by the servants, or by this day's post, to explain your motives for the surprising purpose you disclosed to me on Tuesday morning. As you have not written, I feel myself really constrained to inquire a little further into an affair which certainly, at the time, filled me with amazement and anguish . . .
>   I mean here to expostulate with you, and should be glad that you would not reject and despise my opinions merely because they do not accord with yours. I must repeat again what I believe is true, that you cannot be admitted to the University till you are eighteen . . .
>   Supposing this to be the case, is it possible that you can wish to loiter away two years at home? Surely Mr Lawson's school may afford you better opportunities for study than you could have in any other family! I would urge you to consider that the language you use when you say 'I must' or 'I will' is absolute disobedience to your father's last and most solemn act, which appoints you to submit to the direction of your guardians, to Mr Hall and myself in particular, in what regards your education. I cannot think that a total revolt from our rule will make you in any sense great if you have not the constituents of greatness in you, or that waiting the common course of time and expediency will at all hinder the maturity of your powers, if you have them.
>   What to say to you on the subject of pecuniary advantages I scarcely know, since you are so unhappy as to think £100 a year added to your own fortune despicable, and that the honourable competition of your equals for the reward of literary superiority is a degradation.[83]

There is no way of discovering exactly what arguments there had been over the idea of his trying for an Oxford scholarship. Perhaps Thomas had heard that undergraduates on scholarships were despised by their more affluent fellows.[84] His mother countered by arguing that competing for an award was 'the most independent mode' of financing an education. After urging these and other arguments − supreme among them, of course, being filial duty, a weapon she tended to reach for at the slightest provocation – she awaited a response. None came, and after nearly three weeks she wrote again, deploying the thunders of religion in defence of her position:

> I have an awful account to give as a parent; my charge is one of the talents I must render up with improvement, or meet the just punishment of its neglect or abuse ... Now that I see you threatened with uncommon danger I must endeavour to help you, though I may err in the means, or you may defeat them; my tenderness shall follow you through every change and period of life; if the world forsakes you (a probable thing, though not in the catalogue of your present expectations) I cannot; ... At some period of your life you must be convinced, either to your dismay or advantage, that every human being is brought upon this stage of existence for the great purposes of glorifying God above all, and of doing good, and preparing for his own permanent happiness. Whatever is not planned as a means to these ends, or in subordination to them, is unhallowed; what opposes them must finally be unsuccessful ... the greatest and best men, from this consciousness, are kept humble ... and if any one temper of mind may singly be put to denote the whole anti-Christian character, it is self-glory; and its monstrous adjuncts are independence and pride, which cast angels from heaven, where such tempers are no more admissible now than then.[85]

Thomas seems to have revealed to her something of his literary aspirations, and she identified with remarkable precision the crucial element in his new outlook:

> I know what your ideas are, at least in a considerable measure, and ... I plainly perceive that you have exalted one, and that the most dangerous faculty of the mind, the imagination, over all the rest; but it will desolate your life and hopes, if it be not restrained and brought under religious government; ... you are now carried away, wholly blinded by the bewildering light of your fancy, and that you may never see clearer, your reading is all of a sort to weaken your mental optics![86]

She hastened to prescribe a simple remedy, in terms which show how closely the new movements in literature were linked, in her mind, with subversive doctrines. Perhaps she remembered West Country gossip about the 'Jacobin' Coleridge:

> As your parent, my very dear child, I solemnly request, I command you, in the name of that God whom you must serve or lose, that you do conscientiously read every day at least a chapter in the Gospels or Epistles ... Let your daily reading be the works of men who are

neither infidels nor Jacobins; read history; it will show you the corruption of human nature and the overruling power and providence of God.

Thomas was not satisfied, of course, by this pious advice. He was now feeling resentful and defiant towards his mother, and his misery manifested itself in physical illness, the product of lack of fresh air and exercise, coupled with desperate feelings of frustration and boredom. He tells in the *Confessions* that he began to suffer from some malady affecting the liver, but since in adult life he was fond of explaining every illness by reference to the liver we need not take this too seriously. Probably it was some form of stomach disorder brought on by a combination of poorly cooked, hastily eaten meals and general nervous tension. Samuel Hall, penny-pinching perhaps on behalf of the Quincey estate, would not let him see a physician, who would have charged a fee, but sent him to an aged and incompetent local apothecary. This was a mistake, for apothecaries, prohibited from charging a fee for diagnosis, were under a strong temptation to over-prescribe, to extract the maximum profit from the sale of their drugs. Accordingly, the 'comatose old gentleman' produced a large quantity of some repulsive mixture which, says De Quincey, 'must have suggested itself to him when prescribing for a tiger'.[87]

The medicine aggravated both the complaint and Thomas's sense of grievance. He felt neglected and abused, his illness treated not as an occasion for sympathy but as a trivial matter fit only for the ministrations of an ignorant quack. He had ignored his mother's first letter of remonstrance, but now he made an effort and answered the second, emphasizing that he was utterly miserable at school and wanted to go home. The letter is lost, but part of its contents we can deduce from his mother's reply, dated 12 April. She addresses her letter unexpectedly to 'Mr T. Quincey' and signs it 'E. Quincey': the 'De' has been dropped, and she never again uses it. Perhaps Thomas's supposed pride had led her to renounce the worldly vanity involved in her own refurbished surname. Still she refused to yield any ground. She brushed aside Thomas's feelings with severe reasonableness: 'I see no use in repeating the same things . . . if you only say the old one, that you are miserable. I think it behoves you to show, not only *why* you should leave Mr Lawson's, but *where* you can go, and *how* you can employ your time to *better* advantage . . .'[88] His time would be wasted if he were to spend a year at home; indeed 'a year spent at home in desultory reading, without an object, is an evil of such incalculable extent, that I shall never consent to it'. The fundamental question remains the same: 'Must you govern me or must I govern you? If there are sixteen or eighteen months about which we differ, I must assure you it is *not much* to sacrifice . . . so much time in return for the nights and days and years of solicitude, and the thousand sacrifices I have made for you.'

In answer Thomas set himself to give an exhaustive account of his objections to life at the Grammar School. He planned his letter with extraordinary care, applying to the task that powerful logical intellect which was to be displayed everywhere in his adult writings, and which had already developed to the full by his seventeenth year. He was convinced (because seeing no alternative he had to be convinced) that if he could demolish each of his mother's arguments and establish an opposite set of his own then she must yield. He failed to grasp the plain truth that opposition only strengthened her resolve, and that she would never be brought round except by soothing words and a show of compliance. His letter argued, first, that there would be enough books at home for him to study; that the business of competing for scholarships was unnecessary and degrading; and that school, far from keeping him usefully occupied, 'has no tendency to make me even *not idle*. The truth is that no situation could give me more opportunity of being idle, nor more desire of using that opportunity':

> At Mr. Lawson's, it is true, there is a form of restraint kept up, and only a *form*; for the restraint itself is what any person may elude! I could prove this to you from many instances of the most unbridled licentiousness which have fallen under my observation. But I will observe in general that here I have no motive for resisting the temptation to enjoy that unrestrained liberty which is continually offered to me; – at *home*, while I retained my shame, I should at least have one motive for curbing my passion.[89]

This may be a hint at some kind of sexual temptation, but with characteristic shyness Thomas failed to make a more explicit statement. Indeed, it seems that his mother had at some stage been anxious about his moral character, for he went on to mention, amongst her arguments for keeping him at school, ' "The preserving me from profligacy," which is the conclusion I have made you draw from the three negative advantages of my staying at Mr. Lawson's.' But Mrs Quincey did not take the matter up again and the details of this 'unrestrained liberty' and 'profligacy' remain mysterious. More straightforward are the passages describing general conditions at the school.

> I ask [Thomas writes] whether a person can be happy, or even simply *easy*, who is in a situation which deprives him of *health*, of *society*, of *amusement*, of *liberty*, of *congeniality of pursuits*, and which to complete the precious picture, admits of no *variety*. I think you will hardly say he can; and yet this description was taken from my own case.
>
> As to health, I may say very fairly that I have not passed one quarter of the time I have been at this school in health . . . for there are three things at Mr Lawson's which murder health. The first is want of exercise, which the whole purpose of the school seems purposely directed to deny one; in winter there is, for a considerable length of time, not *one* hour of the day for walking out. The second is the badness of the air, which every day grows worse and worse from the increasing numbers of these diabolical factories. The third is the short time one has to eat one's dinner in; I have rarely time to push it down, and as to chewing it, that is out of the question. This last circumstance is, on me at least, less gradual in its effects than the two former, though they are all three (I should think) enough to ruin any person's health.

Unwisely, perhaps, he went on to complain of the Mancunian *ethos* itself:

> I must beg you to consider that I am living in a town where the sole and universal object of pursuit is precisely that which I hold most in abhorrence. In this place trade is the religion, and money is the god. Every object I see runs counter to the bent of my nature, every sentiment I hear sounds a discord to my own. I cannot stir out of doors but I am nosed by a factory, a cotton-bag, a cotton-dealer, or something else allied to that most detestable commerce. Such an object dissipates the whole train of romantic visions I had conjured up, and frequently gives the colouring to all my associations of ideas during the remainder of the day.
>
> These . . . evils are, in themselves, sufficiently great; but . . . that they admit of no variety – serves to aggravate them all. Every day, and every day, with scarcely a moment's variation, returns the same routine of stupid employments . . . In short, so habitually miserable do I feel, as sometimes hardly to care about myself, and often to think
>
> > 'That I would set my life on any chance
> > To mend it or be rid on't.'[90]

Of course Mrs Quincey's heart was not to be conquered by this cumbersome battery of arguments. She was 'pre-disposed to think ill

61

of all causes that required many words', and this latest letter was a massive document even by Thomas's standards. The force of the simplest, most practical arguments, about his health and the running of the school, must have been neutralized by the pretentious tone of his attacks on Manchester materialism. Mrs Quincey must have been shocked by his sneers at the cotton trade – his late father, after all, had been a worthy linen-and-cotton merchant – and there is something absurdly priggish about his sad picture of a 'whole train of romantic visions' sent flying in confusion by the rude interruption of 'a cotton-bag [or] a cotton-dealer'. In reality, these passages (like that about the school dinner, which he has time to 'push down' but none to chew) are almost certainly intrusions of conscious humour. His letters from first to last show a vein of sly comedy, often at his own expense, and in this letter he seems unable to resist touches of self-parody at the very moments when it is most ill advised. It is not surprising if Mrs Quincey could not take the letter seriously. It was too fluent, too eloquent for a sincere outburst of childish feeling (and she still thought of him as a child). If he were so miserable, how could he find the leisure to discuss romantic visions and the associations of ideas, and to garnish his pleas with apt quotation from Shakespeare? She could not enter his imaginative world enough to understand that in him such things were no more an affectation than were the solemn religious phrases that flowed so easily from her own pen.

What was Mrs Quincey's response to this long letter we do not know. At this point matters become complex, but her two surviving letters to Thomas[91] suggest that she was persuaded to yield in certain minor ways. For when we next hear of Thomas he is staying at Mrs Best's cottage in Everton and his mother sends him, in a letter of 6 June, what looks like the money for six weeks' board and lodging.[92] If this is so, he must have left Manchester in late April, well before the end of the spring term. The probability is that Mrs Quincey was sufficiently alarmed about his health to let him leave school before the end of term and go to Everton to benefit from the fresh sea air and relax away from home, for she foresaw endless quarrels and would not allow him home until the dispute was settled. Indeed, there seems to have been a deliberate break in communication during May.

Mrs Quincey had repeatedly urged that he should confide in some third party, feeling, perhaps that he was inhibited in his letters to her and hoping that discussion with someone else on the spot might allow the problem to be resolved. She had already suggested Samuel Hall:

hardly Thomas's ideal confidant, one feels, but at least easy of access and with the power to make decisions on behalf of the guardians. It seems that some time after receiving Thomas's long document of complaint she decided to put the idea into practice, and decreed that henceforth he must sort out his problems with Hall, and that there must be no direct communication until late May, at which time he should write and tell her the outcome of the negotiations. Thomas, accordingly, discussed and argued with Hall, first in Manchester and then perhaps by letter from Everton. Mrs Quincey seems, through Hall, to have offered – quite unexpectedly – a very substantial concession. If Thomas would stay on at school until the end of the next half-year (that is, until December) she would put his name down at once for entrance to an Oxford college the following year: in late 1803, when he would be eighteen, the required age. She was also prepared to pay him, from the time he left school, an allowance of £100 per year. This was part of the income from the Quincey estate set aside for his schooling. He might live on it during the year between school and university (if he wished, he could go to Oxford and board there whilst reading and studying in preparation for his university course) and the allowance would continue, perhaps with some increase, whilst he studied at the university. This would leave him poor, since he would have to forgo the scholarships he might have won by staying longer at school, but he might still make ends meet. Alternatively, he could have the allowance to live on whilst studying for a profession. All she asked was that he agree to stay at school for another half-year; and that he opt definitely either for university or a profession.

Hall no doubt communicated these terms of treaty with a bad grace, since he was tight-fisted by nature and capable even of standing out against Mrs Quincey where money was concerned.[93] Indeed it is possible that Mrs Quincey was intending to find the £100 allowance out of her own pocket if the other guardians refused to pay it from the fund. Thomas considered his answer, sulked, procrastinated and at last wrote to his mother at the end of May, nearly a week after the deadline she had set. Apparently he accepted the idea of an allowance, and intimated that his mother might as well put down his name for university, though whether or not he would go there was uncertain. As for his plans in the meantime, he would not discuss them, nor would he commit himself to a profession. He expressed resentment towards his mother and perhaps permitted himself some scathing remarks about her attitudes and values. When she replied, it was to repeat old arguments. She told him roundly that his present views were foolish fads, 'swelled into importance by the advocates for early emancipation and other preposterous theories'. As for his arguments, 'I cannot see the force of . . . them; I might as well engage Don Quichotte's wind-mills.' His illness, she told him, was 'produced by your sick mind, which no earthly physician can cure'. She was determined to prevent the malady from spreading, and informed him that though he might come to see her at the Priory, she would not allow Richard or Henry home at all while he was there unless he changed his views. 'I will, to the best of my power,' she resolved, 'keep them from the mischief and misery of hearing your present sentiments; . . . it is sufficiently terrible to those affected by such opinions – that is, you and me – without two more poor children being tormented themselves or tormenting me with demanding unnatural liberty.'

A stalemate had been reached. Mrs Quincey continued, plain-tively, to hold out the inducement of an allowance of £100 a year, but apparently insisted that he complete the year at school. The surviving letters are not very clear on this point, but some such condition must have been made. In June she was expecting him to have only a short time to spend at home, as if assuming that he would return for a new term, and in July he did indeed go back – which he would surely not have done, had any scheme been proposed which offered him instant liberty from school. Moreover, in the *Confessions* De Quincey tells us that, although he negotiated for two months with 'one of my guar-dians' – clearly Hall – he found no compromise possible: 'the *whole* must be conceded, or nothing: since no *mezzo termine* was conceiv-able'.[94] If the object of the argument was, as the adult De Quincey writes, 'to obtain some considerable abbreviation of my school resi-dence', then of course a 'middle term' was possible, and probably such a compromise – a reduction of one year in his schooling – was offered. But if the crux of the argument was whether or not he might leave school *at once*; then indeed only a straight 'yes' or 'no' was conceiv-able. To this, both mother and guardian apparently said no, in the hope of preserving some shreds of their authority; but it was Thomas, in his extreme unhappiness and frustration, who was uncompromis-ing.

Whether or not he spent any part of his holiday at Chester with his mother and brothers is uncertain. But early in July he went back to school. Another 'half-year' or six-month term stretched ahead of him like a desert, the Christmas holidays – his next interval of freedom – dimly visible at the far side. Meanwhile, summer was advancing. Manchester was dirty and smoky and smelly, and the schoolroom a hell of boredom. Outside was adult life, freedom, fresh air and independence. No further overtures could be expected from Mrs Quincey or the guardians. He was on his own. He decided to run away from school, and to strengthen his resolve vowed to be free before his seventeenth birthday. The idea seems to have been in his mind, if only vaguely, for some months; perhaps Edward Hall's escapade had suggested it to him. Thomas's first long letter of complaint, written probably in April, had contained an ominous sentence: 'The objection to my leaving school, if you really do entertain it, I cannot tell how to answer; indeed it admits of none but a practical answer.'[95] The practical answer would now be given, and the long argument would end with his escape.

When he first settled on the idea of running away it seemed natural to think of the Lake District as his destination. It was not far away to the north; its countryside had been made famous in recent years by writers and landscape painters; and in Westmorland lived Wordsworth, whose presence drew Thomas like a magnet. The Lake District would be the perfect antidote for all he hated about Manchester. He planned the details carefully. To escape, and then to survive, he would need money. So he wrote to Lady Carbery, asking her to lend him five guineas. He trusted that she would help him without asking questions, but did not tell her why he needed the money. He had learnt at Laxton that she would not help him in any plan that went against his mother's wishes. It must have hurt him to know that she would feel deceived when the truth came out, but he was desperate. He waited in feverish impatience for a reply, and when none came his greatest fear was that he might accidentally have given some hint of his plan. After more than a week, however, an answer came. Lady Carbery had been at the seaside, so the letter had been delayed. She enclosed not five but ten guineas, and, De Quincey recalls, 'hinted, that if I should *never* repay her, it would not absolutely ruin her'.[96] He now had twelve guineas – enough, he reckoned, to survive at the cheapest inns for a month or so. Perhaps he assumed that by then a truce would have been made with Hall and his mother. At any rate there was now no turning back.

He chose the day for his flight, and reconsidered his destination. His longing to meet Wordsworth face-to-face was tempered, when he began to consider it realistically, by misgivings about how the great poet would see *him*. If he turned up unannounced, tired and short of money, a runaway from home and school, Wordsworth would not be pleased. It would be sheer impertinence to seek the poet's friendship in such conditions, and if he made a false start now he would also lose any prospect of future acquaintance with him. Better to forget about the Lakes and go instead to North Wales. On the way to Ireland he had gazed from the coach in delight at the magnificent scenery on the road to Holyhead. The best part of the summer lay before him, so why not go and explore that countryside? The road to Wales lay through Chester, and it occurred to him that he might be able to call secretly at the Priory on his way and speak to his sister Mary. She could then tell his mother that he was safe and her anxiety, though not her anger, might be calmed.

The problem of getting out of the school buildings now had to be solved. Some assistance was needed for this. He wanted to leave like a gentleman, not a vagabond, so he took into his confidence Ashhurst Gilbert, the senior boy who came closest to being his friend, and gave him three guineas, to be distributed in tips to the servants: even at this crisis, the perfect manners instilled by his mother did not fail him. He also bribed one of the servants – a groom – to help him. He wanted his departure to be final, which meant that his belongings must go as well as himself. Everything could be packed into one trunk, but it would make a massive load, especially as most of it consisted of books. The groom was to come at dawn on the appointed day, help him lower the trunk down the steep stairs from his attic room, and then take it to a carrier and send it to Chester. As a final precaution, he hinted to one or two fellow pupils that he thought of running away, and mentioned the Lakes as his probable destination. That would take care of pursuers. He decided to leave shortly after dawn on Tuesday, 20 July.

He had planned the escape with his usual care for detail, but of course there was an unexpected upset. On the Monday morning a letter arrived addressed, strangely, *A Monsieur Monsieur de Quincy, Chester*. It had been forwarded from Chester, but the postmark said 'Hamburg'. He tore it open and out fell a bank draft for 'somewhere about forty guineas'.[97] There was also a letter, dated from Normandy, in an almost illegible hand. For a moment his hopes soared: it seemed magically appropriate that a windfall of forty guineas should land at his feet just as he was about to set out on his 'perilous adventure' with nine guineas in his pocket. But the letter dispelled his euphoria. He could make out enough to see that it was meant for a poor French émigré living at Chester who now wanted to go home, taking advantage of the recent Peace of Amiens. The letter had been mistakenly forwarded by the post office to Thomas, 'as the oldest male member of a family at that time necessarily well known in Chester,' – an explanation which incidentally gives some idea of the social position Mrs Quincey had built up for herself there. There was no time to take the letter to the Post Office that day: Lawson's relentless routine saw to that. Lessons finished at five o'clock with prayers, the whole school assembled as the High Master read the evening service. It was a hot evening, the sun still brilliant (or so Thomas remembered it later) as the time drew on towards eight o'clock, when he would see Lawson and his fellow boarders for the last time. He was nervous, and now that he stood on the brink of freedom he had some doubts about the wisdom of what he was about to do. But the commitment had already been made. At length roll call was held for the boarders in the courtyard of the house and Thomas, savouring all the irony of the moment, waited for his name – first on the list – to be called. Then, 'stepping forward, I passed Mr Lawson, [and] bowed to him, looking earnestly in his face, and saying to myself, "He is old and infirm, and in this world I shall not see him again" . . . He looked at me complacently; smiled placidly; returned my salutation (not knowing it to be my valediction); and we parted for ever.'

Thomas slept little that night. He says that he got up at half past three just as the dawn of 'a cloudless July morning' was beginning to show. He was conscious of the absolute silence around him, and all the more aware of his own nervousness.

> I dressed myself [he recalls], took my hat and gloves, and lingered a little in the room. For nearly a year and a-half this room had been my 'pensive citadel'; here I had read and studied through all the hours of the night . . . I shed tears as I looked around on the chair, hearth, writing-table, and other familiar objects, knowing too certainly that I looked upon them for the last time.[98]

Whether the youth's feelings had quite the degree of sentiment attributed to them by the adult author may be doubted. But his last act before leaving the room, as he describes it, sounds credible and characteristic. Over the mantelpiece hung 'the picture of a lovely lady' – the seventeenth-century Duchess of Somerset, benefactress of the school and, incidentally, provider of those scholarships to Brasenose College which Thomas found so distasteful. 'The eyes and mouth,' he says,

'. . . were so beautiful, and the whole countenance so radiant with divine tranquillity, that I had a thousand times laid down my pen, or my book, to gather consolation from it, as a devotee from his patron saint.'[99] He was looking at this painting when he heard the nearby cathedral clock strike four. He went up to the picture and kissed it before leaving the room. The friendly groom arrived on time to help with the trunk. He insisted on taking it single-handed, and carried it most of the way down the attic stairs until, near the bottom, his foot slipped and he dropped the trunk, which thundered down the stairs, shot across the narrow passage and slammed into the door of Lawson's bedroom. The groom burst out laughing and Thomas was sure the game was up but, amazingly, no sound came from Lawson's room. Thomas could only suppose that the illness which normally prevented the old man from sleeping must make his slumbers, when they did come, exceptionally heavy. Outside the house, the groom put the trunk on a wheelbarrow and went off with it for the carrier's. And Thomas, carrying some clothes made up into a small parcel under his arm, with 'an odd volume, containing about one-half of Cantor's "Euripedes" ' in one pocket, and a volume of Wordsworth in the other, set off on foot for Chester and the Welsh border.

3

The Compassion of Strangers

A couple of hours' walk brought him to Altrincham, a small town some eight miles from Manchester. Here he bought breakfast, and surveying the colourful, bustling market-place at eight o'clock he rejoiced in his freedom. The 'gloom and despondency' of school fell away.[1] The weather continued fine and he covered the remaining thirty miles to Chester easily by the end of the next day, spending the intervening night at a roadside inn. On reaching Chester he again put up at an inn, as he hoped to make contact with Mary at the Priory. The problem of approaching the house without alerting his mother was a formidable one. Lawson would undoubtedly have sent word there as soon as his escape was discovered, and in addition there was the wretched business of the forty-guinea letter, still in his pocket and perhaps drawing criminal suspicions after him as he travelled. He worried obsessively about the letter. As long as he kept it, he was a thief; but he was afraid that if he went to a post office to hand it back, he might be arrested. Fraudently cashing a bank draft constituted forgery and was punishable by death; but surely no one would suspect him of intent to commit a crime of such magnitude. Perhaps no one knew that the letter contained a bank draft. But if 'Monsieur Monsieur de Quincy' of Chester had been expecting it he might already have lodged a complaint with the post office that would send constables or post office servants in pursuit. (In fact, these fears were justified: a man on horseback had been sent from the school to the Priory, and had actually passed Thomas on the road without recognizing him. Meanwhile, someone from the Chester post office had also been to the Priory, and it is clear from De Quincey's account that the household suspected him of stealing the letter. Indeed, only Mary had been loyal enough to believe in him and 'from the very first she had testified the most incredulous disdain of all who fancied *her* brother capable of any thought so base as that of meditating a wrong to a needy exile.'[2]

Meanwhile he still had the letter, and somehow he had to get rid of it. Still unsure of what to do, he walked round the edge of the town,

69

following the medieval city walls to avoid the risk of meeting servants from the Priory, and began to approach the house along the bank of the River Dee. The Priory stood just above the river near the old Dee Bridge. As he walked by the river he was alarmed to see a kind of tidal wave rapidly approaching upstream along the course of the river. He ran to the top of a small hill for safety, and there met a middle-aged countrywoman, with whom he watched the wave pass. She told him it was 'The Bore', a phenomenon well known locally and dependent on tides in the nearby Dee estuary. De Quincey says that he told the woman of his anxiety over the letter and ended by offering her half-a-crown to deliver it to the Chester post office. She returned after two hours to tell him that she had 'given his love' to the post office and that everything had been sorted out.[3] Some readers have found this part of De Quincey's narrative unconvincing, and it has been suggested[4] that in truth he may have held on to the letter until he feared to return it at all and may then have guiltily destroyed it. The evidence, however, is against this theory: the archives of the Chester post office for 1802 do not record any investigation following the loss of a bank draft, and the very fact that Thomas went on to visit the Priory suggests that he was not afraid of arrest. Even the story of the bore on the River Dee seems to be true: it has been calculated that tidal conditions were probably right on the day in question[5] though it must have occurred soon after dawn, and not after breakfast as he recalled many years later.

Having got rid of the letter, Thomas seems to have loitered about for most of the day and approached the Priory at evening through the trees and shrubs that grew in the grounds. He 'reconnoitred the windows . . . in the dusk, hoping in some way to attract [Mary's] attention' but had an unpleasant surprise. Not only were there no lights in Mary's room, but a number of strange servants were moving about the yard and stables. They noticed him, and he could see them conferring suspiciously. He took refuge in the shrubbery again. These servants, whoever they were, had no doubt been warned to look out for him so there was no chance of going away unnoticed. He left the Priory grounds, he says, and 'returned, after an hour's interval, armed with a note to my sister, requesting her to watch for an opportunity of coming out for a few minutes under the shadows of the little ruins in the Priory garden, where I meantime would be waiting'.[6] He gave the note to a servant with instructions to deliver it to Mary.

He waited in the garden as the man receded and a minute later was astonished to find his summons answered not by Mary but by his

Uncle Thomas Penson, who had been in India for ten years and was the last person Thomas expected to see at Chester. This meant an end to secrecy. Everything had to be explained to Penson (Mrs Quincey's brother) and to Mrs Quincey herself. No doubt there was a fearful row to begin with. 'My dear excellent Mother', De Quincey says, looked upon his present 'violent' and 'irregular' proceeding 'much as she would have done upon the opening of the seventh seal in the Revelations',[7] which was not surprising, for not only had he disobeyed her solemn and religious commands in absconding from Manchester, but his disappearance had set off two days of panic at the Priory. Messengers from the school and the Post Office had arrived within an hour of each other on the afternoon of his escape and Mrs Quincey had jumped to the conclusion that he had stolen the bank draft and fled. Within two hours, therefore, 'all the requisite steps having been concerted with one of the Chester banks for getting letters of credit, etc., a carriage-and-four was at the Priory gate', and Mary, a female servant, and 'an elderly gentleman' who was a friend of the family had gone rattling off in pursuit towards Ambleside, where they hoped to catch Thomas and put him on the nearest boat for Holland or France. His plan of misdirecting pursuers towards the Lake District had worked all too well, as it turned out, for Mary and her companions were away for a week chasing him, as they thought, all the way from Ambleside to York, where they gave up and returned to Chester. They covered about six hundred miles all told, and Mrs Quincey saw to it that when Thomas came into his patrimony in 1806 he paid their travelling expenses in full, so that the escapade cost him about £150.[8]

Now he sat in the drawing-room at the Priory facing 'the whole artillery' of his mother's formidable displeasure. We can imagine the kind of things that were said. Thomas, always vulnerable in his craving for the respect and approval of adults, was an easy target for parental reproach. 'Any mother who is a widow has especial claims on the co-operation of her eldest son,' he reflected, 'and, if *any* mother, then by a title how special could my own mother invoke such co-operation, who had on *her* part satisfied all the claims made upon her maternal character by self-sacrifices as varied as privately I knew them to be exemplary.'[9] What sort of co-operation was Thomas offering? What sort of example was he setting the younger children? His mother, still young, had 'sternly refused all countenance, on at least two separate occasions, to distinguished proposals of marriage, out of pure regard to the memory of [her husband], and to the interests of his children'. Was this how he repaid her self-sacrifice? He could find no acceptable defence of his action and sat in hopeless silence. 'If in this world there is one misery having no relief, it is the pressure on the heart from the *Incommunicable*. At this moment,' he recalls, 'sitting in the same room of the Priory with my mother, knowing how reasonable she was – how patient of explanations – how candid – how open to pity – not the less I sank away in a hopelessness that was immeasurable from all effort at explanation.'[10] Even in this recollection of fifty years later we can see touches of the needless guilt and self-pity in which De Quincey often indulged when faced with his mother. We know quite well that she was not at all 'patient of explanations'. Nor was she especially 'open to pity', or 'candid' in the old sense of 'willing to take lenient views'. She was a hard woman to argue with, and he was not quite willing to stand up to her face to face. This was the real trouble. But the feeling of being misunderstood and having no proper explanation to give must nonetheless have been very unpleasant.

Thomas was saved by his uncle, Thomas Penson. This 'bronzed Bengal uncle' was home on extended leave and his visit, from Thomas's point of view, was extremely opportune, for his sympathies were all on his nephew's side. 'Between my mother and my uncle,' De Quincey recalled, 'there existed the very deepest affection . . . But in many features of character no human beings could stand off from each other in more lively repulsion.'[11] The uncle was 'thoroughly a man of the world', and 'it was so exquisitely natural in his eyes that any rational person should prefer moving about amongst the breezy mountains of Wales to a slavish routine of study amongst books grim with dust . . . that he seemed disposed to regard my conduct as an extraordinary act of virtue'. He persuaded Mrs Quincey that Thomas should be left to follow his plan of walking among the Welsh hills and suggested that he be given a regular allowance on which to live. Uncle Penson was all for generosity but at this point Mrs Quincey returned to the attack and refused to hear of any sum being allowed over a guinea a week. Her objection, says De Quincey, was that anything more would 'make proclamation to my two younger brothers that rebellion bore a premium, and that mutiny was the ready road to ease and comfort' – a highly characteristic sentiment. Apparently there was real cause for this anxiety. 'Pink', now thirteen years old, had recently been removed from Horwich, where he and Henry had boarded with a clergyman-tutor, and predictably Mrs Quincey had made a serious mistake in choosing a school, sending him to 'a school governed by a brutal and savage master'.[12] Thomas seems to have known that he was very unhappy there. How much Mrs Quincey knew is uncertain, for 'Pink' was far less articulate than his elder brother and complained less, but it looks as if she was afraid he might follow Thomas's lead.

Thomas was given the option of staying at the Priory for the rest of the summer, as he had demanded several months earlier, to study alone until the autumn, when he could go to Oxford. But he declined the offer, feeling that the atmosphere of the Priory would be unbearably heavy with silent reproach. He evaded as dextrously as ever any commitment to long-term plans, and carelessly assuming that he could live on a guinea a week in Wales for as long as he wanted, he was eager to go. So without even waiting for Mary to return from her wild goose chase around the Lake District he set off for North Wales.

Perhaps at his mother's insistence, he began by sampling the hospitality of various respectable ladies. In nearby Flintshire, a Mrs Warrington and a Mrs Parry, old friends of Mrs Quincey's, put him up for a short time, but they forced him into social engagements which he found dull, and Gresford, the valley where they lived, struck him as too tame – 'a dressed and ornamented pleasure-ground'. So he moved on, still keeping within the compass of his mother's social set, to visit another pair of ladies, the once-famous 'Ladies of Llangollen', Miss Ponsonby and Lady Eleanor Butler. The Ladies, who had eloped from their homes in Ireland twenty-three years before to live together, in a 'romantic retirement' which amounted to marriage, at *Plas Newydd*, a Gothicized cottage near the village of Llangollen, were the objects of much curiosity and fashionable visiting in their day, chiefly because they seemed to be living out a poetic ideal of pastoral retirement. As aristocratic women who had voluntarily chosen the simplicity of life in a Welsh cottage, they were vaguely felt to be worthy of admiration, if not of emulation. How the good ladies received Thomas we do not know, but there can have been little enthusiasm on either side. They were reputed to be interested in poetry, so Thomas did his best to convert them to Wordsworth, but without success. After a short stay he pressed on from Llangollen into the wilder parts of Wales, in quest of a pastoral myth more rugged and dangerous than that which had inspired the genteel Ladies.

From this point on it becomes impossible to trace his movements with certainty. He wandered erratically through Merionethshire and

Caernarvonshire, visiting, among other places, Llanrwst, Conwy, Bangor, Caernarvon, Tan-y-Bwlch, Harlech, Dolgellau, Tal-y-Llyn and Barmouth. He went as far as the borders of South Wales, exploring parts of Cardiganshire and Montgomeryshire. In what order he visited these places, or how often he retraced his steps, we do not know. Probably in later years De Quincey himself would have found it difficult to disentangle the thread of his ramblings. But it was an adventure of just the kind he needed. His health improved immediately and he was soon walking ten or fifteen miles daily and enjoying it. Moreover, the Wales he was discovering was a very different country from any part of England he had known. The countryside, especially the mountainous region around Snowdon, was rich in the 'immense rocks' and 'romantic precipices' that adorned the scenery of his favourite poems and tales. Welsh was spoken everywhere, often to the exclusion of English, and in many households in the smaller villages the Welsh harp was still played as an accompaniment to traditional songs. There was plenty of sightseeing to be done. At Llanrwst he was shown the famous three-arched bridge supposedly built by Inigo Jones in the seventeenth century, its structure so finely balanced, it was said, that the whole bridge could be made to vibrate if one stood at the middle of the central arch and pushed against a large stone in the parapet. Two local girls told him that a small child running across the bridge could set it shaking perceptibly; but there was no child handy to try the experiment.[13] At Bangor he inspected the cathedral, which turned out a disappointment: he had been hoping for choral services, his interest in religion at this period being mainly aesthetic, but there was no choir; and the cemetery, 'at that time famous as the most beautiful in the whole kingdom',[14] turned out to be 'beautiful' in the old-fashioned eighteenth-century sense, with 'the beauty of a well-kept shrubbery' but none of the Romantic charm required by his more advanced taste.

At Bangor also there was a misunderstanding which displays his extreme sensitiveness at this period. He must have meant to stay there some weeks, for he took 'a very miniature suite of rooms – viz. one room and a closet'.[15] He had a garrulous landlady who was inordinately proud of having been a servant in the Bishop of Bangor's household, and who talked about the Bishop at every opportunity. One day she was tactless enough to tell Thomas that she had seen her former employer and told him that she had a lodger. The Bishop, she said, had warned her to take care in choosing her lodgers, for Bangor lay on the main road to the Holyhead ferry so that 'multitudes' of swindlers and debtors, English and Irish, were constantly passing through in flight from the law or their creditors. 'O my lord,' was the landlady's answer, 'I really don't think that this young gentleman is a swindler; because –' – 'You don't *think* me a swindler?' Thomas burst out: 'For the future I shall spare you the trouble of thinking about it.'[16] And in a rage he packed up his belongings and walked out. Clearly the wounds of the bank draft affair were still smarting, so that he took mere careless familiarity for an intolerable insult. He relieved his temper by marching the ten miles to Caernarvon, but for some time afterwards he entertained daydreams of revenging himself on the Bishop by the typically De Quinceyan device of sending him an angry message in Greek, on the assumption that His Grace would not be clever enough to answer with equal fluency in the same language, and would thus be humiliated. Fortunately the adventures of the road soon drove the idea out of his head.

The rooms at Bangor had been cheap enough to allow him to save some of his allowance, and finding no suitable lodgings at Caernarvon he went to stay at an inn. For a time this became his regular means of accommodation. In most parts of North Wales small inns were plentiful, and though conditions were not always comfortable, this merely added to the sense of adventure. In the more remote districts it was often impossible to get a meal consisting of more than bread and butter or bread-and-milk and cheese. The traveller might find himself sharing the dining-room with pigs or poultry, and even in large village inns flaking plaster and holes in the bedroom walls, and myriads of fleas in the beds, were commonplace.[17] But at some places a good dinner could be had for sixpence, and a night in a public house bedroom might cost no more than a couple of shillings.[18] In such conditions, a guinea a week would go a long way. But prices were rising. English travellers in search of the picturesque were on the roads in increasing numbers, the word 'tourist' was already becoming known and several guide books to North Wales had appeared. De Quincey's own impulse to visit Wales was itself a part of this more general movement. Even in the four months of his wanderings (from July to November 1802) abrupt price increases could be noted. Dinner at Tal-y-Llyn in Merionethshire, he recalls, went up from sixpence to three shillings in the course of two months.

Moreover, once the initial excitement of freedom and fresh mountain air had begun to diminish, Thomas found himself in need of congenial company. He wanted someone to talk to, which meant staying from time to time at an expensive hotel, where 'society' could be found. This swallowed up half a guinea a day and was therefore a luxury that could be indulged once or twice a week only if extreme economy were practised on other days. To make matters worse, the smaller Welsh inns were notorious for overcharging English travellers and in some areas haggling over prices – long extinct in England – was still the custom, and must have been difficult at times for a touchy, emotional youth like Thomas.[19] He must also have met with some hostility on account of his appearance and the fact that he went on foot. 'Pedestrians' were often regarded with the deepest suspicion; only seven years before, Coleridge and Southey had been locked into their room at the village inn at Cheddar as suspected footpads. Respectable people, it was thought, did not wander about on foot without luggage or a clear destination.

As summer drew on and his reserve of guineas shrank, he slept in the open several times a week. He made himself a canvas tent, using a walking-stick for a tent-pole as he was shy of attracting notice by carrying anything larger. This tent, 'miserably small' even for Thomas, he pitched at night on sheltered hillsides. On windy nights this was troublesome, and always he was worried, he says, by the thought that 'whilst my sleeping face was upturned to the stars', a stray cow 'might poach her foot into the centre of my face'.[20] But the cows left him alone and in this way he spent four or five nights a week up to the end of October, when the cold grew too severe. On nights when he was not staying at hotels or sleeping under the stars, he found simple accommodation at cottages. Plenty of people would give a stranger a meal and a bed for sixpence or less, and the food sometimes included excellent trout caught in nearby streams.[21] In this way money could be saved for his 'periodical transmigrations back into the character of gentleman-tourist'. Sometimes, De Quincey says, he could not force any money upon his hosts, but paid for his stay by writing letters for them. One such visit he records in detail in the *Confessions*. It was at Glanllynau, a farmhouse at Llanystumdwy near Criccieth, Caernarvonshire.[22] Here, he recalls happily,

> I was entertained for upwards of three days by a family of young people, with an affectionate and fraternal kindness that left an impression upon my heart not yet impaired. The family consisted at that time, of four sisters and three brothers, all grown up, and remarkable for elegance and delicacy of manners ... They spoke English; an

accomplishment not often met with in so many members of one Welsh family, especially in villages remote from the high road. Here I wrote, on my first introduction, a letter about prize-money for one of the three brothers, who had served on board an English man-of-war; and, more privately, two letters to sweethearts for two of the sisters.[23]

The latter, he characteristically notes, were 'both interesting in appearance; and one of uncommon loveliness'. This charming family pressed him to stay, and for about four days he did so, sharing a bedroom (and perhaps a bed) with the brothers. He might have stayed longer, but

On the last morning . . . I perceived upon their countenances, as they sat at breakfast, the approach of some unpleasant communication; and soon after one of the brothers explained to me that, on the day before my arrival, their parents had gone to an annual meeting of Methodists, held at Caernarvon, and in the course of that day were expected to return; 'and, if they should not be so civil as they ought to be,' he begged, on the part of all the young people, that I would not take it amiss. The parents returned with churlish faces, and 'Dym Sassenach' (no English) in answer to all my addresses. I saw how matters stood; and so, taking an affectionate leave of my kind and interesting young hosts, I went my way.[24]

He found other company on the road. At one point he struck up an acquaintance with 'Mr De Haren, an accomplished young German' who had been a lieutenant in the British Navy and was now, since the recent peace, exploring Britain for pleasure. De Haren taught him a little German (which did not stick) and showed him the small clutch of German books he carried in his trunk – for Thomas was beginning to feel starved of books. They included Hippel and Hamann, two obscure humourists, but also Jean Paul Richter. If De Haren translated a page or two of Richter for Thomas's benefit it may have caught his interest in a way that lasted, for when he took up German again a few years later Richter at once became a favourite author, and was to be an important literary influence. He also made friends with a Welsh clergyman, and with two lawyers who travelled a circuit of several small towns so that their scattered clients could consult them on market days. His powers as a conversationalist stood him in good stead when he could afford to visit a respectable inn parlour. One encounter was positively bizarre, for out of curiosity he allowed a cottager to introduce him to an astrologer, a grubby man who lived in a grubby cottage in a valley somewhere near Ruabon. The man asked the date and time of Thomas's birth, prepared some sort of diagram on a dirty piece of paper and then read out his predictions from a large folio volume printed in gothic type. He foretold, among other things, that Thomas would have red hair, and that he would have twenty-seven children and desert them!

But life on the open road could not remain permanently idyllic. As autumn advanced the disadvantages became more apparent. He was growing bored, and during October the nights grew too cold for him to sleep out of doors. He was determined not to go back to Chester: having found freedom he wanted to hold on to it whatever the cost, and in any case his pride would not brook a return home. Yet his allowance of a guinea a week would suffice only if he took rooms for an extended period in some very secluded (and therefore potentially tedious) place. It is not altogether clear how his allowance was reaching him, but it seems likely that he was using the post office of one or more Welsh towns as a *poste-restante* and collecting the money when he passed through. This supposition is based on the fact that a letter survives from the Marquis of Sligo (who had now resigned the title of Earl of Altamont to his son) addressed to Thomas at 'Post-Office, Bangor'.[25] The letter is dated 'Westport House, November 8, 1802' and refers to 'the note you so kindly addressed to me from Bangor, which came to my hands yesterday' – which proves that Thomas was in the vicinity of Bangor at the end of October or the beginning of November. One would like to know why Thomas had written and what he had said. Sligo's letter is short, bland and chatty, and obviously written in ignorance of Thomas's current problems. He hopes that he will revisit Westport, and adds general remarks on politics and the condition of the estate. So far as we know, however, Thomas never corresponded with the Marquis again.

At some time in November he decided to leave Wales. 'Suddenly,' he says, 'I took a fierce resolution to sacrifice my weekly allowance, to slip my anchor, and to throw myself in desperation upon London.'[26] Why he chose London remains obscure. Perhaps his brief visit to the city with young Westport a year and a half before had left him with a curiosity to see more of the place. Another motive was the belief that in London he would be able to find money-lenders who would advance him money against his 'expectations' so that he could live in his own way, out of reach of the guardians, until he was twenty-one, when he would be legally his own master. This ingenuous scheme he fancied he could best carry out in London. He therefore wrote to various money-lenders and discussed the plan with his Welsh friends, the clergyman and the lawyers. The latter offered to lend him any cash he might need to visit London. Whether they also had the sense to warn him against such a hazardous undertaking we do not know; but he would in any case have been quite capable of keeping them in the dark about the precise nature of the people he intended to visit in London. The outcome was that they lent him twelve guineas and he made his way back to England, where his first halting place was Oswestry in Shropshire. By coincidence he met there one of the lawyers – 'the very warmest amongst my Welsh friends' – who lived at Oswestry when he was not going the rounds of the market towns on business. Of course he invited Thomas to stay, and his hospitality was worth having, for 'his library was already large, and as select as under the ordinary chances of provincial book-collection could reasonably be expected . . . so that, what between the library and the mercurial conversation of its proprietor, elated by the rare advantage of fraternal sympathy, I was in danger of finding attractions strong enough to lay me asleep over the proprieties of the case'[27] – for Thomas came to suspect that his presence was hindering his host's business affairs, and with his usual politeness insisted on leaving without further ado.

It was now late November, but a warm spell was in progress, so he decided to walk to Shrewsbury and there pick up the mail coach from Holyhead, which would take him to London. His good-natured host promised to book him a place as the coach passed through Oswestry, so he could be sure of a seat when he joined the coach, and they walked together for five miles along the road out of Oswestry before parting. Thomas walked the remaining thirteen miles alone, reaching Shrewsbury 'at least two hours after nightfall', at about seven o'clock. He made for the Lion Inn, where the London coaches stopped on their way from Holyhead. Experience had made him apprehensive as to how he would be received, as a foot-traveller, but his statement that he was booked for a place on the night mail secured him good treatment. Indeed, his hours of waiting at the Lion were passed, unexpectedly, in eerie splendour, for when he asked for a room (coach passengers commonly hired a private room in which to wait) he discovered that the inn was undergoing structural repairs and that he was to have the inn ballroom all to himself, no other room being available. Four servants were summoned to light the way with candles and the procession set off for the ballroom, which was on the first floor at the back of the building and was reached by going out through the inn-yard and up a broad stone staircase. He followed his torch-bearers into the great ballroom, a dim lofty place from whose ceiling twenty feet above hung 'three gorgeous chandeliers' glittering in the candle-light. The flames lit up two galleries for musicians, a domed lantern in the ceiling and fine plaster mouldings in the delicate style of the Adam brothers. Here he was left in a chair on the great oak dancing-floor to doze or look around him at this silent arena of departed eighteenth-century gaiety.

He was apprehensive about his venture into London, now that it was almost on him, and pondered the possibility that he was making a serious mistake. It would be a declaration of total defiance to his mother and guardians, and whether or not it would prove easy to borrow money he did not know. A storm was blowing up outside and about ten o'clock he left the chair where he had been drowsing to watch it from the windows. Rain and wind raged and beat against the panes. Nothing could be seen except that 'at intervals, when the wind, shifting continually, swept in such a direction as to clear away the vast curtain of vapour, the stars shone out, though with a light unusually dim and distant'. At other moments (or so he says) he imagined how the dance floor and its adjoining rooms must have looked, full of youthful dancers 'at seasons when every room rang with music': a reminiscence, perhaps, of those over-long fêtes at Frogmore when only the music had held his attention and the whirling figures in the dance had faded from conscious notice before his eyes. Perhaps the fancy was inspired also by the emblematic figures of Music and Dancing painted on the door-panels of the ballroom.[28] Between midnight and two in the morning, when the coach was due, his mood reached its nadir. He spent the two hours, he says, in 'heart-shaking reflections', in that particularly unpleasant state where one simultaneously knows that one is about to make a serious mistake, and is entirely determined to go ahead and make it. Pride, and the fear of losing freedom, would not let him turn back. At last he heard the sound of wheels and hoofs, and the Holyhead Mail 'was announced as having changed horses'. He went out to take his place in the coach, and was off for London.

Thomas's decision to break off communications with his mother and guardians, to leave his meagre but useful allowance untouched and to throw himself on the mercies of London money-lenders remains, in its fundamental motives, something of a mystery. True, he felt that he could not lead a pleasant or useful life in Wales on his allowance; he was not ready to settle matters by opting for a profession and could not face another year at home. True, also, that he was innocent enough to believe he could borrow £200 on his own security and live on it for four years. Yet none of this makes a great deal of sense. Why should fifty pounds a year make him comfortable in London, when an allowance of fifty-two guineas had failed to do so in Wales? And how did he mean to spend those four years? There was something distinctly irrational about the London venture. De Quincey himself in later years was inclined to view it sombrely as a wilful folly, though since it was to become a formative episode in his life he could hardly disown it or view it without a certain degree of pride. He tended to be especially tolerant of his own errors of judgment when they were extreme enough to set him apart in some way from other men. In retrospect he would examine their consequences with considerable subtlety, but he generally failed to give an adequate account of their causes, preferring to convey the impression that he acted under the force of some mysterious compulsion. This was how he saw the flight from Manchester Grammar School, and how he was to portray his progress into opium addiction.

His reckless venture into London, accordingly, was put into the same category. J.R. Findlay, who knew De Quincey in his old age, records that 'he confessed to occasional accesses of an almost irresistible impulse to flee to the labyrinthine shelter of some great city like London or Paris – there to dwell solitary amid a multitude, buried by day in the cloister-like recesses of mighty libraries, and stealing away by night to some obscure lodging'.[29] This tendency to secretiveness may well have grown from a childhood response to his mother's habit of supervising every aspect of his life and presuming guilt in every doubtful case. Feeling too much observed and judged, he may have experienced freedom only in concealment, so that he now needed to disappear completely from the knowledge of the family to assert his independence. The example of the boy-poet Chatterton, who had flown to London to seek his fortune, may also have encouraged him. On a more practical level, De Quincey tells us that he feared being traced by his guardians and forced to return to school. At first sight this looks absurd, for matters had been sorted out at the Priory, the allowance granted, and he was apparently free. But it may not have been as simple as this. The arrangement had been worked out by Thomas, his mother and his uncle. None of the other guardians had been consulted, and we know that Samuel Hall at least was prepared to defy Mrs Quincey where the treatment of Thomas was concerned. His attitude to Thomas was generally harsher than hers: did he refuse to ratify the arrangement and decree that by the end of the year Thomas must be found and compelled back to school?

Whatever the reasons, Thomas found himself on the London coach and, twenty-eight tedious and bumpy hours later, he stepped down into Lombard Street ready for a new adventure. The essentials of what followed are vividly described in *The Confessions*, and form one of the best-known episodes of De Quincey's life. His first business was with a money-lender, 'a Jew named Dell'[30], and by ten o'clock in the morning he was at Dell's office, ready for an interview. Perhaps he expected Dell to hand him the £200 over the counter. But 'the money-lender, as it turned out, had one fixed rule of action. He never granted a personal interview to any man . . . One and all – myself, therefore, among the crowd – he referred for information, and for the means of prosecuting any kind of negotiation, to an attorney.'[31]

This was an unexpected check, but the next step, clearly, was to see the attorney, whose office was at 38, Greek Street, Soho. The house, when he found it, 'wore an unhappy countenance of gloom and unsocial fretfulness, due in reality to the long neglect of painting, cleansing and in some instances of repairing. There were, however, no fractured panes of glass in the windows – and the deep silence which invested the house . . . sufficiently accounted for the desolation, by suggesting an excuse not strictly true – *viz*. that it might be tenantless.'[32] He knocked, and at length saw someone peering at him through a narrow side-window by the front door. Then the door opened, and he was face to face with the attorney, who escorted him through to the office at the back of the house. His name seemed to be Brunell, though he sometimes called himself Brown and Thomas was never sure which was the real name. He may be the John Brown of Greek Street whose name occurs in Poor Rate books for the parish in 1802–3.[33] He was a large man of cheerful but somewhat furtive countenance, and he made only guarded response to Thomas's polite overtures, as if anxious not to give too much away. They discussed Thomas's position, and the only outcome of the interview was the information that nothing could be done immediately, that there were various investigations to be made and formalities to be completed before the money would be ready, and that he would have to wait.

Assuming that there would be only a brief delay, Thomas found himself lodgings somewhere in the area – poor rooms, which he considered 'barely decent', rented apparently at the rate of half-a-guinea a week, in which he could live 'more parsimoniously' on his meagre reserve of cash until the loan made its appearance. There began a tedious, heart-sickening routine of visits to Brunell *alias* Brown, who continually put him off with new delays, new (imaginary) documents requiring stamps which had to be paid for by Thomas, and promises that the money would be available soon, but only after this and that further business had been settled. Thomas watched with dismay as his money dwindled and the delays continued, but he was still naive enough to believe that the business would be brought to a conclusion shortly. (In adulthood, with much bitter experience of money-lenders behind him, he would reckon that six months was the very shortest time in which a sizable loan could be negotiated.) Apparently Dell had – or was soon to earn – a bad reputation: in 1809, during a parliamentary investigation of corruption, a letter was read out in the House of Commons in which the Duke of York's mistress, Mrs Clarke, told a correspondent, 'I have a letter which says you are a money-lender, in colleague with a notorious man call'd Dell!!'[34]

How Thomas passed his days, other than in visits to the attorney, we do not know. Presumably he sat in his rooms or wandered about the town. If he had grown bored with Wales, London must have been infinitely worse for a youth with no friends and no money. He says that this period lasted for seven or eight weeks, though in fact it was probably less. December at least passed in this way, until he was so short of money that he saw he could no longer afford to keep lodgings. To avoid starvation he gave up his rooms, requested an interview with Brunell 'and, stating exactly the circumstances in which I stood, requested permission . . . to make use of his large house as a nightly asylum from the open air'.[35] Brunell agreed – saving him from the expedient of sleeping in the street in midwinter – and urged him to come the same evening and make himself as comfortable as he could. The house was not well equipped for residence, being dilapidated, dusty and virtually without furniture. It was also very cold. But it turned out not to be quite empty at night, for when Thomas moved in that afternoon towards dusk he found there a small girl,

> a poor, friendless child, apparently ten years old; but she seemed hunger-bitten; and sufferings of that sort often make children look older than they are. From this forlorn child I learned that she had slept and lived there alone for some time before I came; and great joy the poor creature expressed when she found that I was in future to be her

companion through the hours of darkness. The house could hardly be called large – that is, it was not large on each separate storey; but, having four storeys in all, it was large enough to impress vividly the sense of its echoing loneliness; and, from the want of furniture, the noise of the rats made a prodigious uproar on the staircase and hall, so that, amidst the real fleshly ills of cold and hunger, the foresaken child had found leisure to suffer still more from the self-created one of ghosts'.[36]

The two of them slept huddled together for warmth and comfort on the floor, 'with a bundle of law-papers for a pillow, but with no other covering than a large horseman's cloak' – as, apparently, the little girl was accustomed to sleeping every night. A few nights later, however, Thomas braved the ghosts and led an expedition upstairs to the attics, where they found 'an old sofa-cover, a small piece of rug, and some fragments of other articles, which added a little to our comfort'.[37]

It was Brunell's custom to return at unpredictable hours. He 'sometimes came in upon us suddenly, and very early; sometimes not at all'. Since he was 'in constant fear of bailiffs', he slept in a different part of London every night, or so Thomas gathered, and he never opened the front door without first inspecting the caller through the side window. The small girl was used by Brunell as a servant, and as soon as he arrived in the morning she would hurry to brush his coat and clean his shoes, and would then retreat to the basement kitchen where she spent the whole day unless Brunell sent her out on an errand. For some reason, Thomas suspected that she might be an illegitimate daughter of Brunell's. Why he made this guess he does not say, but he adds that 'she did not herself know' whether or not Brunell was her father – a disclosure that conveys some idea of the emotional void in which the poor child must have existed. Brunell usually began the day by having breakfast in his office. To Thomas, who could now barely afford to eat, this was a painful and humiliating business, for despite the wretched poverty of Brunell's meal ('little more than a roll, or a few biscuits, purchased on the road from the place where he had slept') Thomas 'generally contrived a reason for lounging in; and, with an air of as much indifference as I could assume, took up such fragments as might chance to remain; sometimes, indeed, nothing at all remained'.[38]

In this condition of near-starvation he continued for weeks whilst negotiations with Dell dawdled along. It became apparent that one obstacle to the speedy granting of the loan was doubt as to whether

Thomas, the youth living mouse-like in Brunell's house, was actually the Thomas Quincey junior mentioned in the will of the late Thomas Quincey of Greenhay, Manchester. The loss of social identity was now virtually complete: not only had he vanished from his guardians to become a shabby stray in a huge city, but his very name and parentage were questioned. An appeal to his mother was out of the question, and Dell must have seen that he would instantly lose his client if he made inquiries at Chester. The best expedient Thomas could think of was to produce letters which he carried with him from Westport and his father, the Marquis of Sligo. Encouraging words were dispensed as usual and he was left to wait again.

Oddly enough, De Quincey described Brunell in retrospect, when he came to write the *Confessions* in 1821, in rather generous terms. One can only assume that Brunell caught his fancy as a 'character'. He knew quite well that much of Brunell's 'legal' work was in some degree dishonest, but found the man 'obliging, and, to the extent of his power, generous' towards him personally. A major point in his favour, as Thomas saw it, was that he had a great enthusiasm for literature and some literary education, which, he said, had been suddenly broken off by the violent death of his father, which had left him no choice but to take up an opening in the low branches of the legal profession. Like so many other people Brunell was charmed by Thomas's manners and his learned conversation and it may have been precisely for this reason that he gave him the run of the house at night time rather than let him sleep in the streets or under bridges with the countless other outcasts of London. Brunell specialized in negotiating loans for those who could offer no security; by the same token he had to handle debtors, and in this side of the business he was helped by one Pyment or Pyemont, a combination of clerk and strong-arm man who also came to work at the house in Greek Street. Brunell and Pyemont kept up their spirits during working hours by waging a regular war of insults and Thomas, despite the misery of his situation, found some amusement in their antics and in observing 'scenes of London intrigues, and complex chicanery, . . . at which I sometimes smile to this day – and at which I smiled then'.

Through all the troubles of this time he clung tenaciously to his dream of going to the Lake District to meet Wordsworth. Steadiness of purpose is not a quality with which De Quincey has often been credited, yet there is surely something impressive in the fact that he should have succeeded in fulfilling a desire so apparently hopeless.

During this winter in London the thought of Wordsworth and Grasmere became a spiritual life-line to him:

> Oftentimes, on moonlight nights, . . . my consolation was (if such it
> could be thought) to gaze from Oxford Street up every avenue in
> succession which pierces northwards through the heart of
> Marylebone to the fields and the woods; for *that*, said I, travelling
> with my eyes up the long vistas which lay part in light and part in shade
> – '*that* is the road to the north, and, therefore, to Grasmere' (upon
> which, though as yet unknown to me, I had a presentiment that I
> should fix my choice for a residence); 'and, if I had the wings of a dove,
> *that* way would I fly for rest.'[39]

The dream had a particular wistful intensity about it, distilled by the
sufferings of the time, and he was to recall these yearnings with mixed
feelings when, years later, he lived at Grasmere, fulfilling his youthful
plan to the letter but amidst agonies and pleasures inconceivable to the
seventeen-year-old waif who had set the direction his older self must
follow.

Meanwhile, near starvation, cold and anxiety were affecting his body
as well as his mind. He began to suffer from some internal disorder
which produced severe stomach pains and, especially at night, 'a
hideous sensation' which he could only describe as 'a sort of twitching
(I know not where, but apparently about the region of my stomach),
which compelled me violently to throw out my feet for the sake of
relieving it. This sensation coming on as soon as I began to sleep, and
the effort to relieve it constantly awaking me, at length I slept only
from exhaustion; and from increasing weakness . . . I was constantly
falling asleep, and constantly awaking.'[40] When he tried to eat solid
food he would be sick, but strangely enough wine brought temporary
relief. This ailment, which returned to plague him for much of his
adult life, has resisted all attempts at applying a modern diagnosis. In
some respects the symptoms seem to have resembled those of a
duodenal ulcer, but the extreme rarity of cases of duodenal ulcer
before the twentieth century renders this unlikely. A more plausible
suggestion, perhaps, is pancreatitis, which can give rise to severe pain
of the kind De Quincey describes and may be temporarily relieved by
alcohol. A third possibility is, of course, that the symptoms were
largely psychological and not directly attributable to any organic
condition.

Perhaps the most important element in Thomas's London experience, however, arose from the fact that he had to leave Brunell's house and wander the streets during the daytime. 'As soon as the hours of business commenced,' he recalls, 'I saw that my absence would be acceptable; and, in general, therefore, I went off and sat in the parks or elsewhere until the approach of twilight.'[41] It was during these cold, dull days, as he later claimed, that he made friends with a number of 'unfortunate' women, the prostitutes of the Oxford Street area, and in particular with the girl whom he was to make famous as 'Ann', who was to become an important symbolic figure in his lyrical prose works.

At this point we are faced with a riddle, for 'Ann of Oxford-Street' may be a fiction, a personification synthesizing De Quincey's observations of various young street-walkers, drawing perhaps on youthful fantasies of the kind of companion he would have wished for during this lonely, anxious period; on the other hand her story as he outlines it may be factually true, however ordered and intensified by literary artifice. It is hard to imagine what sort of evidence, short of a statement by the girl herself, could settle the question. No such evidence exists, and De Quincey nowhere refers to Ann outside a consciously literary context, so the uncertainty must remain. All we have is De Quincey's own account. 'Being myself,' he says, 'at that time of necessity a peripatetic, or a walker of the streets, I naturally fell in more frequently with those female peripatetics who are technically called street-walkers. Some of these women had occasionally taken my part against watchmen who wished to drive me off the steps of houses where I was sitting; others had protected me against more serious aggressions. But to one amongst them . . . I owe it that I am at this time alive. For many weeks I had walked, at nights, with this poor friendless girl up and down Oxford Street, or had rested with her on steps and under the shelter of porticos.'[42] This was Ann, a girl of less than sixteen who, De Quincey says, had been forced to live by prostitution as a result of wrongs done to her by a 'brutal ruffian who had plundered her little property', a phrase which could equally be a direct reference to theft or fraud, or a covert reference to rape or seduction. Whichever it may have been,

> hers was a case [says De Quincey] of ordinary occurrence (as I have since had reason to think), and one in which, if London beneficence had better adapted its arrangements to meet it, the power of the law might oftener be interposed to protect and to avenge . . . In any case, however, I saw that part of her injuries might have been redressed; and

I urged her often and earnestly to lay her complaint before a magistrate . . . She promised me often that she would; but she delayed taking
the steps I pointed out, from time to time; for she was timid and
dejected to a degree which showed how deeply sorrow had taken hold
of her young heart; and perhaps she thought justly that the most
upright judge and the most righteous tribunals could do nothing to
repair her heaviest wrongs.[43]

But in what sense did he owe his life to her?

One night [he recalls], when we were pacing slowly along Oxford
Street, and after a day when I had felt unusually ill and faint, I
requested her to turn off with me into Soho Square. Thither we went
and we sat down on the steps of a house, which to this hour I never
pass without a pang of grief, and an inner act of homage to the spirit of
that unhappy girl, in memory of the noble act which she there performed. Suddenly, as we sat, I grew much worse. I had been leaning
my head against her bosom, and all at once I sank from her arms, and
fell backwards on the steps. From the sensations I then had, I felt an
inner conviction of the liveliest kind that, without some powerful and
reviving stimulus, I should either have died on the spot, or should, at
least, have sunk to a point of exhaustion from which all re-ascent,
under my friendless circumstances, would soon have become hopeless. Then it was, at this crisis of my fate, that my poor orphan
companion, who had herself met with little but injuries in this world,
stretched out a saving hand to me. Uttering a cry of terror, but without
a moment's delay, she ran off into Oxford Street, and in less time than
could be imagined, returned to me with a glass of port wine and spices,
that acted on my empty stomach (which at that time would have
rejected all solid food) with an instantaneous power of restoration;
and for this glass the generous girl, without a murmur, paid out of her
own humble purse, at a time, be it remembered, when she had scarcely
wherewithal to purchase the bare necessities of life, and when she
could have no reason to expect that I should ever be able to reimburse
her.[44]

This touching story is at least possible, and many of its details accord
well with what we know of De Quincey's nature and condition at this
period. There is an obvious plausibility about his being adopted by a
young woman who, although younger, would certainly have been a
great deal more experienced than he: he was clearly attractive to
women, and his obvious helplessness no doubt increased the appeal.
And nothing is more likely than that, in his wanderings about London's West End, he should have come into contact with prostitutes.
They were numerous in this part of the town and in the evenings much

soliciting took place in Oxford Street. De Quincey, despite his sheltered upbringing, was always ready to mix – on a temporary basis – with any company that came his way, so long as he was treated with due consideration. His boast in the *Confessions* that 'from my very earliest youth, it has been my pride to converse familiarly, *more Socratico*, with all human beings – man, woman, and child – that chance might fling in my way' was strictly true, and in the present crisis his philosophical curiosity about people was supplemented by loneliness, and the real risks of physical violence which threatened a delicate and rather undersized youth in the unpoliced streets – those 'more serious aggressions' against which, he says, the women had protected him. Nor is there anything implausible in Ann's age. Many girls of less than sixteen were on the streets in the 1800s. To this extent, the 'noble-minded Ann', De Quincey's 'youthful benefactress', is a representative figure, accurately reflecting human suffering as he had encountered it, and at the same time a typically Romantic literary creation, demonstrating that natural goodness and unselfconscious nobility may be found in the lowest of social outcasts. Perhaps he named her after the parish in which Soho was situated, the Parish of St Anne's, Westminster, which then possessed an Ann[e] Street, a Little St Ann[e] Street, and a St Ann[e]'s Court.

The nature of Thomas's relationship with her is, of course, imponderable. Apart from wandering the streets together, pausing on occasion to listen to the music of a barrel organ, how they spent their time is not specified in the *Confessions*. One can only speculate about how and when Ann pursued her trade, and what Thomas felt about it. He tells us that their relationship was purely one of affectionate companionship and 'perfect love' – an emotional attachment in which sexual desire took no part, or was entirely transcended. Such an idealized view of emotion is perhaps unconvincing, though it seems plausible that the sensitive De Quincey should have been powerfully attached to this girl without having the confidence to declare his feelings. In such a case, idealization would be natural enough.

It appears that in late December or early January he grew so desperate that he began to think of a reconciliation with the guardians. He seems to have written to Samuel Hall putting forward some conditions for his return home. Hall sent a characteristically icy reply on 7 January:

Sir,

    As you have thought proper to revolt from your Duty in a Point of the utmost Importance to your present Interest and future Welfare – as you have hitherto persisted in rejecting the Wishes of your Guardians, who could be governed by no Motives but those of promoting your real Benefit, you can not be surprised to hear that they have no new proposition to make.

    But notwithstanding all that has passed if you have any Plans in agitation that seem intitled to notice they are willing to pay them every Degree of consideration.

    They trust that by this Time you are convinced that it was (to speak the least of it) a rash step for a young Man of 17 to throw himself out of the protection of his Friends and relations into the wide World, and to have nothing to trust to but the Charity or Compassion of Strangers, and they still cherish the Hope that you will renounce your Errors, and endeavour to remove the Impression of former misconduct by correct and proper Behaviour for the future.

    I am Sir, your very hum: Svt

Saml. Hall.[45]

There the dialogue seems to have ended. But subsequently there was a more propitious incident:

I met in Albemarle Street a gentleman of his late Majesty's household. This gentleman had received hospitalities, on different occasions, from my family; and he challenged me upon the strength of my family likeness. I did not attempt any disguise, but answered his questions ingenuously; and, on his pledging his word of honour that he would not betray me to my guardians, I gave him my real address in Greek Street. The next day I received from him a ten-pound bank note. The letter enclosing it was delivered, with other letters of business, to the attorney; but, though his look and manner informed me that he suspected its contents, he gave it up to me honourably, and without demur.[46]

The first thing Thomas did with the note was to go to a baker and buy himself some bread. Brunell, however, gave chase to the money pretty soon afterwards, and found pretexts for charging him another three guineas in respect of stamp duty on documents being drawn up and sums mysteriously due to Mr Dell. It appears that Dell – or some other money-lender, for De Quincey is vague about how many he was dealing with – had now decided to supply 'two or three hundred pounds', on condition that the young Lord Westport, whose letters

Thomas had used as credentials, could be persuaded to guarantee the payment 'on [their] joint coming of age'. Altamont being two or three years younger than Thomas, this sounds rather ridiculous and of dubious legality, but we should realize that, as De Quincey shrewdly surmised many years later, the man's final object was 'not the trifling profit he could expect to make by me, but the prospect of establishing a connexion with my noble friend, whose expectations were well known to him'[47] and amounted to some £30,000 a year. Predictably, Thomas's ill-judged bid for financial independence had ended by making him a pawn in the money-lender's game.

If Westport were to guarantee the repayment of the loan, it would be necessary for Thomas to go to Eton and talk him round. To set off cap-in-hand to ask Westport to help him get into debt must have humbled his pride painfully, but it seemed the only way, and he prepared for the ordeal. He had some five pounds left from the family friend's ten-pound note. Fifteen shillings of this he spent, he says, in 're-establishing (though in a very humble way) my dress', and 'of the remainder, I gave one-quarter (something more than a guinea) to Ann, meaning, on my return, to have divided with her whatever might remain'.[48] Not much would remain, in any case, for there were coach fares to be paid. He decided to take one of the West Country mails as far as Slough and walk the rest of the way.

'Soon after six o'clock, on a dark winter evening,' he says, 'I set off, accompanied by Ann, towards Piccadilly', where the Bristol mail waited at the Gloucester coffee house before going off at a quarter past eight. There was plenty of time to spare (De Quincey does not say so, but Soho is rather less than half a mile from Piccadilly) and so, 'not wishing to part in the tumult and blaze of Piccadilly', he sat down with Ann in Golden Square 'near the corner of Sherrard Street': or Gerrard Street, as it is now called. The details, however, cannot be precise, for Gerrard Streed ends a quarter of a mile away from Golden Square. Here, it seems, Thomas came as close as possible to a full declaration of his feelings:

> I had told Ann of my plans some time before, and now I assured her again that she should share in my good fortune, if I met with any, and that I would never forsake her, as soon as I had power to protect her. This, I fully intended, as much from inclination as from a sense of duty; for setting aside gratitude (which in any case must have made me her debtor for life), I loved her as affectionately as if she had been my sister; and at this moment with sevenfold tenderness, from pity at

91

witnessing her extreme dejection. I had apparently most reason for dejection, because I was leaving the saviour of my life; yet I, considering the shock my health had received, was cheerful and full of hope. She, on the contrary, who was parting with one who had had little means of serving her, except by kindness and brotherly treatment, was overcome by sorrow, so that, when I kissed her at our final farewell, she put her arms about my neck, and wept, without speaking a word.[49]

Quite what Thomas planned to do when he returned, and what part Ann played in the scheme, we do not know, but he says that she had at last agreed to go with him to a magistrate and seek legal redress for the wrongs she had suffered. She had put up protracted resistance to this idealistic plan, and her capitulation now may be a sign that she did not intend to see him again after his return from Eton. She may well have sensed that once he was restored to respectability her presence would be an embarrassment to him.

However that may have been, they agreed that she should wait for him, beginning on the fifth night following, every night at six o'clock, 'near the bottom of Great Titchfield Street', a meeting place they had regularly used before. Later he was to reproach himself with having failed to ask her surname, as a means of tracing her, in case they should miss each other; 'My final anxieties,' he says, 'being spent in comforting her with hopes, and in pressing upon her the necessity of getting some medicine for a violent cough with which she was troubled, I wholly forgot this precaution until it was too late to recall her.'[50] They said goodbye and Thomas made his way to Piccadilly. The parting was expected to last no more than a week, but, as all readers of the *Confessions* will know, they never saw each other again.

Thomas caught the Bristol Mail and took his place on the roof. Soon after the coach started he fell asleep from sheer exhaustion. Oddly enough, the ailment which had so regularly jerked him back from the brink of sleep with intense abdominal discomfort did not disturb him, and, lulled by the rolling motion of the coach, he enjoyed the first easy and refreshing sleep he had had for weeks. The only disturbance occurred because of the heaviness of his sleep. He could not keep his place – 'if the road had been less smooth and level than it was,' he recalls, 'I should have fallen off from weakness' – and at every jolt in the road he fell against the passenger who sat next to him. The man made no secret of his annoyance and seemed 'a surly and almost brutal fellow' until Thomas apologized and explained the reasons for his weakness, earnestly promising to try not to fall asleep again. When he next awoke he found that the man had put an arm round him to keep him from falling, and for the rest of the journey the man treated him with the greatest kindness. He slept so soundly that he missed his stop next morning and had to trudge back some nine miles to reach Eton. So weak was he that this stretch of road occupied him from eleven in the morning until dusk. He had still not reached Eton when darkness came down, and in his weariness he lay down by the roadside and slept. About dawn he was awakened by the sound of a voice and opened his eyes to find a man – 'an ill-looking fellow' – standing over him. But the man did not hinder him and he went doggedly on to Eton. He crept unnoticed through Windsor, for few people were yet out, and found a public house where he was able to wash himself and tidy his clothes. Then he returned to Eton and asked for Westport, only to be told that he had left school and gone to Jesus College, Cambridge. Matters seemed to be taking a nightmarish turn, with one disaster following another. In desperation he asked for Viscount Castle Cuffe, Altamont's cousin whom he had met in Ireland two years before.

The young Viscount, fortunately, was there, and he greeted Thomas kindly, inviting him at once to breakfast. It was a magnificent meal, and the first proper meal of any kind that Thomas had seen for weeks, but he found that he could eat nothing. His appetite was gone and the food repelled him. Curiously enough, however, he had a craving for wine. This was brought and he drank eagerly. After such hospitality he dreaded having to ask his host if he, in Altamont's stead, would agree to be bound in security for the loan, but so much effort had been spent on the journey that he could not bear to go away without asking, and ask he did. The young nobleman 'faltered' at this request, as well he might. 'He acknowledged that he did not like to have any dealings with money-lenders, and feared lest such a transaction might come to the ears of his connexions.' But at length he agreed – on certain conditions which De Quincey does not reveal. Having to be satisfied with this, Thomas caught a coach from Windsor, arriving back in London after a three days' absence. More disappointment awaited him here. The money-lenders would not accept Viscount Castle Cuffe's conditions.

Thomas was back where he had started weeks before but with an added sense of hopelessness. But there was a worse blow in store for, he says, Ann failed to keep her appointment in Great Titchfield Street. He stood at the appointed place on the night of his return and every night thereafter, but she did not come. He searched the street where she had lodged, but found no trace of her: he did not know the number of her house, and remembered in any case that she had spoken of leaving owing to trouble with her landlord. He asked everyone who might know her, but the members of the floating street-population could tell him nothing: some laughed at him, others thought he might be pursuing the girl on account of something she had stolen from him and were 'naturally and excusably indisposed' to give any clue. She had vanished utterly. Some misfortune, he thought, must have befallen her. It seems never to have occurred to him that she might have disappeared deliberately to avoid future trouble and embarrassment on both sides. On each of his subsequent visits to London, De Quincey claims, he scrutinized thousands of passing faces in the crowded streets in the hope of seeing her again. 'I should know her again,' he wrote, 'amongst thousands, and if seen but for a moment. Handsome she was not; but she had a sweet expression of countenance, and a peculiarly graceful carriage of the head.'[51] He never found her, and at last allowed himself to hope that she was dead rather than suffering the whole course of the miseries to which her way of life seemed to condemn her: 'her cough,' he wrote in 1821, 'which grieved me when I parted with her, is now my consolation'.

Imagining such an end for her, he completed the process of trans-forming Ann into a symbol of suffering female innocence, a powerful goddess in the mythology of Romanticism. Whether she ever existed as an individual outside De Quincey's imagination we cannot be sure. Certainly, he later claimed that his loss of her was the 'heaviest affliction' of his life. For this or some other reason, soon after his return from Eton his powers of resistance seem to have flagged. Somehow — perhaps through the family friend who had previously met him and given him money — 'an opening was made' for reconciliation with the guardians. Whatever terms were proposed, Thomas accepted them. His desperate bid for independence had failed and he agreed to return to the Priory, Chester, and his mother. On the day he left London, he says, he sought out the only person who he was sure knew Ann by sight and gave her, to pass on to Ann, his address at the Priory. If this is true, he must have been desperate indeed: one can well imagine the sort of reception Ann would have received upon applying to Mrs Quincey at Chester as one of Thomas's London friends! As for Thomas, he returned to Chester in March 1803 ill, exhausted and old beyond his years with a burden of unhappy experience whose conse-quences were to affect every subsequent phase of his life. His guardians had gained a temporary victory over him but he was not broken, and from now on he would be his own man. Their chance to mould his character and life was gone.

Part II
The Dark Idol

4

The Secret of Happiness

The intimate connection, which exists between the body and the mind, has never (to my knowledge) been sufficiently enlarged on in theory or insisted on in practice. To shew the ultimate cause of this would be very difficult though not (I think) impossible. But on the present occasion it would be almost superfluous; because, throughout the whole of the following system, I suppose previously that the reader admits the fundamental points on which it is grounded; and, even though he should not, I don't care a damn . . .[1]

The writer is Thomas De Quincey; the date, March 1803; the place Mrs Best's cottage at Everton. Thomas and his mother still finding it difficult to live under the same roof, he had been packed off, soon after his return from London, to his accustomed place of exile to recover his health, consider his future and form some notion of how he meant to employ himself for the next few years. As we shall see, he had distinct ideas on that subject, but they were not of a kind to be revealed to his mother or Samuel Hall, who had been driven near to desperation over the past two years by their failure to extract any hint as to what he meant to do with his life. Alarmed perhaps by the impact of the London ordeal on his mind and body, the delinquent youth sat at his table in Everton with a notebook, sketching the plan of a complete system of physical and mental culture. Whilst Mrs Quincey and Samuel Hall might have approved the robust foundations of the plan, which stressed Gymnastics, Bathing and 'Manual labours', their gloomiest suspicions would have been confirmed by the information that the plan was to attain its main objects 'by producing on the mind these two effects 1. continually calling forth (and thus invigorating) the passions; 2. by relieving – varying – and so rendering more exquisite those fits of visionary and romantic luxuriating or of tender pensive melancholy – the necessary and grand accompaniments of that state of mind to which this system of education professes to lead . . .'[2]

The 'system of education', however, ended with its first chapter and Thomas filled the remainder of the notebook with a diary. Like most diaries, this one was kept most assiduously because there was so little to record. Thomas was bored at Everton, and the general atmosphere of the diary is one of mild depression. He was living in a kind of limbo, dwelling alone in the cottage and dining daily with a Mr Cragg, an old family friend, a merchant and presumably a former associate of Thomas Quincey senior. Frequently he wandered over to see a family called the Wrights, where he sat for hours at a time drinking tea or coffee, talking or reading the latest books (Mr Wright was a bookseller) and, since there were ladies at the Wrights', frequently showing off and flirting. Add to this churchgoing ('Went to St Ann's; – heard an ass preach'),[3] visits to the circulating libraries and dispirited wanderings along the lanes and seashore near Everton, and we have virtually the whole round of his movements. (There is one significant exception, for whatever the case may have been earlier, he now had a sexual life of sorts, though to judge from the single brief reference in the diary any sort of pleasure or satisfaction was hardly to be expected: 'Go to the same fat whore's as I was at last time;' he noted, 'give her 1s. and a cambrick pocket hand-kerchief; – go home miserable.')[4] Depression undermined his self-respect, and the diary shows him amusing himself cynically with petty dishonesty. At the circulating library he hands over his half-guinea deposit and is about to leave with the book when he is called back: the half-guinea is a 'bad' one. Three days later, 'looking in booksellers' shops; – see "Mary Stewart" (Schiller's) in a window; go in; ask price; – "4s. Sir"; – "Change me this half-guinea"; – "it's a bad one, Sir"; "Is it? Well I'll call again". Go to the library in Dale Street where I got it; – I take 3rd volume of Miss Lee's *"Recess"*; – leave my half-guinea, receiving 6s.6d. change out of it.'[5]

Mr Cragg seems to have had responsibility for keeping an eye on Thomas, and he paid occasional visits to Chester, no doubt to report to Mrs Quincey. Cragg was just the sort of kindly, paternal, well-meaning, half-educated person whom Thomas loved to despise, and he noted fragments of their after-dinner conversations, which give some idea of his mood:

> On C[ragg]'s asking me . . . if I liked the *Odyssey* which he himself thought mightily entertaining. I said that I could not bear it; and, as a reason, observed that, independent of the insipidity of the story, there was no character in it: 'What? not Telemachus?' said C. 'No,' said I coolly.[6]

In the evenings he was, in fact, dutifully plodding through Cowper's translation of the *Iliad:* 'the wretched drivellings of that old dotart

Homer,' as he snarled to his notebook.[7] His preferred reading was the Gothic novel, the pulp fiction of the period. He was cultivating his mind with *The Ghost Seer; The Italian, or, the Confessional of the Black Penitents; The Dagger; The Accusing Spirit; The Infidel Father; Tales of Wonder;* and many more. Often he read aloud from such books to the assembled ladies at the Wrights': Mrs Wright, Mrs Edmunds, a Miss Barcroft, a Mrs Cartwright and others. When not chilling their blood deliciously with *Tales of Superstition* and the like he entertained them with poetry: 'Burns's *Ode to Despondence* – ode to Ruin – 6 stanzas of the "lament of Mary, Queen of Scots" . . . and also my own stanzas on May morning – not telling however the name of the author'[8] – for he was now again trying to write poetry. Sadly, the attempts at verse in the diary are feeble. There are fragments of a poem on Senacherib, given a wry autobiographical twist at the end:

> At noon Senacherib look'd at the sun;
> And his hour was come, he knew:
> For the angel of Fate had fixed the hour;
> And the face of a spirit of Ocean blue
> Looked through the hawthorn bow'r.

> 'Now God thee bless' to Senacherib said
> The woman who liv'd at that house;
> But the man of that house
> Was tilling the ground

– Senacherib now looked at the sun; and immediately, going down stairs – and taking leave of his hostess, he set off on the road to Caernarvon.[9]

– a reference to his discomfiture by the tactless episcopal landlady at Bangor. None of the verse in the diary is much better than this.

It seems rather surprising that the young De Quincey should reveal such a complete lack of the poetic gift. He certainly had no inkling of his own deficiency. In May he proclaimed to the diary, 'I have . . . always intended of course that *poems* should form the corner-stones of my fame; – but I do not (at this moment) recollect any subject that I have chosen for my poetic efforts',[10] except for a few which he listed on the same page, including '*Ethelfrid*, a drama; *Yermak the rebel*, a drama; *Paul*, a drama' which were to be 'Poetic and pathetic'; '*A pathetic tale*, of which a black man is the hero;' and another, 'of which an Englishman is the hero'.[11]

Needless to say, none of these projects came to anything, though in the evenings at Everton he worked at *Yermak the Rebel*, noting on 20

May that, 'Last night I advanced a good deal in the plot of my Arabian drama.'

More important were the signs of a developing critical intelligence. Throughout the spring of 1803 he was preoccupied with questions of literary theory. He lists his favourite poets as follows:

Poets

Edmund Spenser;
William Shakespeare;
John Milton;
James Thomson;
William Collins;
Thomas Chatterton;
James Beattie;
Robert Burns;
Robert Southey;
S.T. Coleridge;
William Wordsworth!!!

Q. Gray? A. *No.*[12]

His critical jottings were concerned especially with the problem of the 'pathetic'. Romantic literary taste much enjoyed the portrayal of suffering, and in narrative poetry and Gothic fiction this enjoyment often became mere gloating. The ideal, however, was the representation of suffering combined with dignity – not a stoical dignity which would suppress the passion upon which Romantic effects depended, but an elevated tone of speech and behaviour which would render suffering at once grander and less deserved. Hence the young De Quincey's desire that his own tales, poems and ballads should be '*pathetic*' and his posing of such questions as, 'What is the essence and classification of *Nature* as distinct from *Pathos* – *Imagery*, etc?' He speculated as to whether there might be a fundamental difference between 'the two *species* of English and French pathos' (French pathos, of course, being shallow and 'noisy'!); resolved that '*Dramatized Pathos* is a perfect definition of Tragedy'; and roundly declared 'that there is no good pastoral in the world but Wordsworth's "*Brothers*"; and that enchanting composition has more pathos (ah! *what* pathos!) than poetry in it'.[13] He sought similes by which to communicate his delight in certain authors: 'Bacon's mind appears to me like a great abyss – on the brink of which the imagination startes and shudders to look down.' 'My imagination flies, like Noah's dove, from the ark of my mind . . . and finds no place on which to rest the sole of her foot except Coleridge – Wordsworth and Southey.'[14]

In Everton, as in the cold streets of London, he dreamed of dove-like flight to Wordsworth and the other 'Lake' poets. His resolve to meet Wordsworth was growing now beyond the world of dreams. A cryptic paragraph in the diary may refer to this intention – the one firm landmark in the present misty confusion of his life: 'It is a plan immoveable as the mountains. Whatever it may be, however weak – however poor – however inefficient, it is yet not built of such frail and slight materials, as that . . .'[15] there the note broke off, but the determination did not, for on the night of 11 May, alone in the cottage at midnight, he began to draw up a letter to Wordsworth.

> Sir,
>   – To most men what I am going to say would seem strange; and to most men therefore I would *not* say it; but to you I will, because your feelings do not follow the current of the world.
>   From the time when I first saw the 'Lyrical Ballads' I made a resolution to obtain (if I could) the friendship of their author. In taking this resolution I was influenced (I believe) by my reverence for the astonishing genius displayed in those delightful poems, and, in an inferior degree, for the dignity of moral character which I persuaded myself their author possessed. Since then I have sought every opportunity – and revolved many a scheme of gaining an introduction into your society. But all have failed; and I am compelled either to take this method of soliciting your friendship (which, I am afraid, you will think a liberty), or of giving up almost every chance for obtaining that without which what good can my life do me?'[16]

In this vein a long letter was composed. Over the next fortnight he revised and reconsidered and at last, on 31 May, composed the final version (it took him most of the day, from nine in the morning until four in the afternoon) and posted it.

> May 31, 1803
>
> Sir,
>   I suppose that most men would think what I am going to say – strange at least or rude: but I am bold enough to imagine that, as you are not yourself 'in the roll of common men', you may be willing to excuse anything uncommon in the liberty I am now taking.
>   My object in troubling you, Sir, is that hereafter I may have the satisfaction of recollecting that I made one effort at least for obtaining

your notice – and that I did not, through any want of exertion on my own part, miss that without which what good can my life do me? I have no other motive for soliciting your friendship than what (I should think) every man, who has read and felt the 'Lyrical Ballads', must have in common with me. There is no need that I should express my admiration and love for those delightful poems; nor is it possible that I should do so. Besides, I am persuaded that the Dignity of your moral character sets you as far above the littleness of any vanity which could be soothed by applause feeble and insignificant as mine – as the transcendency of your genius makes all applause fall beneath it. But I may say in general, without the smallest exaggeration, that the whole aggregate of pleasure I have received from some eight or nine other poets that I have been able to find since the world began – falls infinitely short of what those two enchanting volumes have singly afforded me; – that your name is with me forever linked to the lovely scenes of nature; and that not yourself only but that each place and object you have mentioned – and all the souls in that delightful community of your's – to me

'Are dearer than the sun!'

With such opinions, it is not surprising that I should so earnestly and humbly sue for your friendship; it is not surprising that the hope of that friendship should have sustained me through two years of a life passed partially in the world – and therefore not passed in happiness; – that I should have breathed forth my morning and evening orisons for the accomplishment of that hope; – that I should now consider it as the only object worthy of my nature or capable of rewarding my pains. Sometimes indeed, in the sad and dreary vacuity of worldly inter-course, this hope will touch those chords that have power to rouse me from the lethargy of despair; and sometimes, from many painful circumstances – many bitter recollections, it is my only refuge.

But my reasons for seeking your regard – it would be endless to recount and (I am afraid) useless; for I do not forget that the motives to any intimacy must be mutual: and, alas! to me, unknown and unhon-oured as I am, why should anyone – the meanest of God's creatures – extend his friendship? – What claim then can I urge to a fellowship with a society such as your's – beaming (as it does) with genius so wild and so magnificent? I dare not say that I too have some spark of that heavenly fire which blazes there; for, if I have, it has not yet kindled and shone out in any execution which only could entitle me to your notice. But, though I can shew no positive pretensions to a gift so high, I may yet advance some few negative reasons why you may suffer me, if but at a distance, to buoy myself up with the idea that I am not wholly disregarded in your sight – when I say that my life has been passed chiefly in the contemplation and altogether in the worship of

103

nature – that I am but a boy and therefore could have formed no connection which could draw you one step further from the sweet retreats of poetry to the detested haunts of men – that no one should ever dare, in confidence of any acquaintance he might have with me, to intrude on your hallowed solitude – and lastly that you would at any rate have an opportunity of offering to God the pleasant and grateful incense of a good deed – by blessing the existence of a fellow-creature. As to all external points, I believe that there is nothing in them which would disgrace you.

I cannot say anything more than that, though you may find many minds more congenial to your own – and therefore proportionately more worthy of your regard, you will never find any one more zealously attached to you – more full of admiration for your mental excellence and of reverential love for your moral character – more ready (I speak from my heart!) to sacrifice even his life – whenever it could have a chance of promoting your interest and happiness – than he who now bends the knee before you. And I will add that, to no man on earth except yourself and *one* other (a friend of your's), would I thus lowly and suppliantly prostrate myself.

Dear Sir!

Your's for ever,

Thomas de Quincey.[17]

This was a letter of youthful hero-worship at its most intense, and an answer would require all the tact Wordsworth could muster. Such admiration is a dangerous burden for any man to carry. Expectations so high could hardly fail to be disappointed, for De Quincey was making his hero a symbol of all that he felt himself to lack. In time Wordsworth responded with both tact and common sense, but this problem at the root of their relationship would not easily be resolved. Having posted the letter, addressed to Wordsworth in care of Messrs. Longman and Rees, his publishers, Thomas settled down to await a reply. Almost at once there was an encouraging coincidence: the day after the letter was sent the Wrights took him to visit a Mrs Cartwright, where he was introduced to Miss Barcroft and Mr Bree, from Keswick, who knew something of both Wordsworth and Coleridge. After an evening of wine, whist and conversation, he notes:

These particulars I gathered from Miss Barcroft concerning the Poets! *Coleridge* is very absent – frequently walks half a mile (to her *uncle's*, I think she said) without being sensible that he has no hat on; – has married the sister of *Southey's* wife; – lives (I believe she said this of Coleridge) in a house where he has lodgings; – when she first saw him, (in church) she took him for some great boy just come from school; –

104

Wordsworth is rather handsome; – has a beautiful little cottage; (N.B. both he and C. live near Keswick) – has a sister 29 years old about. Mr Bree surprises me by telling me that *Coleridge* intends to astonish the world with a *Metaphysical* work . . . on which he intends to found his fame; Mrs *Coleridge,* he says, speaks in high terms of it; his conversation is even more wonderful, he says, than his works; – he is so intellectual as to be quite oppressive, he says; – Miss Bearcroft [sic] says she has seen either Charles Lloyd or Charles Lamb (or both) at *W's* or *C's*; says she admires *Coleridge* very much; – Mr Bree has seen *Coleridge* . . . but says he does not know him. We . . . go about 1 o'clock; – the night is wonderfully serene; – I walk home thinking of Coleridge; – am in transports of love and admiration for him . . . I begin to think him the greatest man that has ever appeared and go to sleep.[18]

These were the high points of an otherwise dreary spring. All the old problems were unresolved. He exchanged letters with his mother about 'the Oxford scheme', which was once more up for consideration. Should he go to lodge in Oxford and work privately? This seemed pointless. Should he enter as an undergraduate? Hall refused to allow him the necessary cash, becoming so obstinate that both his former allies, Mr Kelsall and Mrs Quincey, were alienated, and Mrs Quincey urged Thomas to write to Hall in tones of supplication. 'I need not tell you that in order to have a chance of success you must treat him with respect,' she sighed. 'I find writing so useless that I have given it up.'[19] He sent Hall a polite and humble letter but one which, characteristically, failed to produce the necessary appearance of commitment just at the crucial points. He gave his 'assurance' that he was willing to enter a profession after going to university, but not 'an absolute promise' – a distinction whose subtlety no doubt escaped Hall; and, he added, 'going to college is *not* a favourite point' with him.[20]
Naturally enough, this lukewarm tone left Hall unmoved. Mrs Quincey meanwhile urged that even on the bare £100 which had formerly kept him at school, he should be able to make ends meet at university. She, in fact, seems to have been the only person who was now eager to see him continuing his education. Thomas remained inscrutable.

Much of his time was spent in introspection. He jotted down 'Notes on my own character':

A few days ago . . . I became fully convinced that one leading trait in my mental character is – *Facility of Impression*. My hopes and fears are alternately raised and quelled by the minutest – the most trivial

105

circumstances – by the slightest words . . . Witness . . . the *moidera-tion* in which I leave Mrs W[right] if anything is said less flattering than on a preceding day: though, all the while, I am fully conscious that she does not regard me more or less on one day than on another. – Above all, witness the strong effects which striking descriptions of the *new sort* have . . . – To me these are always paintings. Thus is my understanding triumphed over by my heart.[21]

This is accurate self-analysis, and we may agree that now and later sensitivity even to touchiness was an important feature of his charac-ter. Equally significant is his observation that 'striking descriptions' in the new Romantic literature are 'always paintings' to him – in other words, that his mind is powerfully visual, translating words directly into pictorial imagery. Already he was moving towards a conscious development of the 'dreaming faculty' which would play a central part in his literary work. He deliberately explored fantasy, observing it like a film show: 'Last night I imaged to myself the heroine of the novel dying on an island of a lake, her chamber-windows (opening on a lawn) set wide open – and the sweet blooming roses breathing their odours on her dying senses. One of my associations was derived from the *farm*. The morning of this event must be still – calm – balmy – beautifully blue etc.' Here, apparently planning a story of his own, he allowed visual imagination to conjure up the scene for him, drawing on associations not only from The Farm, but from the second Quincey residence, Greenhay, where he had seen the body of his sister Elizabeth lying in that room with wide-open windows, the serene summer sky radiant outside.

Another of these pictorial reveries was of 'Chatterton in the exceeding pain of death! in the exhausted slumber of agony I see his arm weak as a child's . . .'[22] There may have been a certain amount of masochistic self-identification here. Towards the beginning of the diary, he had noted, 'Last night my Chattertonian melancholia state of mind returned for the 1st time this about two years' – which would place the previous attack in the spring of 1801, when he was trying to release himself from the Grammar School. It has been suggested that Chatterton's flight to London may have influenced Thomas's behaviour. But what is 'Chattertonian melancholia'? Is it the self-pity of a gifted youth surrounded by dullards? Or is it perhaps a suicidal mood?

Last night too I image myself looking through a glass. 'What do you see?' I see a man in the dim and shadowy perspective and (as it were) in a dream. He passes along in silence, and the hues of sorrow appear on his countenance. Who is he? 'A man darkly wonderful – above the beings of this world; but whether that shadow of him, which you saw, be the shadow of a man long since passed away or of one yet hid in futurity, I may not tell you. There is something gloomily great in him; he wraps himself up in the dark recesses of his own soul; he looks over mankind of all tongues – languages – and nations 'with an angel's ken'; but his fate is misery such as the world knoweth not; and upon his latter days (and truly on his whole life) sit deep clouds of mystery and darkness and silence . . .'[23]

Precognition? Perhaps. Or it may be that we choose the courses of our own lives more than we know. A few weeks later, at the Wrights', Thomas 'look[ed] into Charlotte Smith's metrical works – particularly "An ode to the poppy" '.[24] This poem, although appearing in the works of Charlotte Smith, one of Thomas's favourite Gothic novelists, was written for Mrs Smith by her friend Lady Henrietta O'Neile. Both ladies were opium addicts[25] and the poem is not without a certain poignancy. Singled out thus for a moment in the course of the desultory reading of the future Opium-Eater, it acquires an extra resonance:

> Thou brilliant weed
> That doest so far exceed
> The richest gifts gay Flora can bestow;
> Heedless I pass'd thee, in life's morning hour,
> (Thou comforter of woe,)
> 'Till sorrow taught me to confess thy power.

Apparently Thomas liked the poem; but he made no further mention of it, or of its subject, in his diary.

It is perhaps surprising that there is nowhere any reference to his recent ordeal in London. Perhaps he regarded it as a humiliating defeat, too painful to contemplate. There are, however, one or two indications that its consequences were still with him. On 10 May he suffered from a stomach ache after an evening of wine drinking; on other occasions he complained of headaches, of feeling ill, of being too unwell to write. But these may have been merely trivial upsets, magnified by his rather obsessive anxiety about his illnesses. Already something of a hypochondriac, he carefully noted how much wine he drank a day, and even how many cups of tea or coffee he drank or refused. The practice of keeping a fussy watch over the details of his health was already well established.

The diary comes to an end in late June 1803. On 3 August Thomas returned to Chester. On the evening before his departure, however, the long-awaited reply from Wordsworth had arrived – at a time when he had begun to despair of ever receiving a word from his hero. Thomas's letter had lain unnoticed at Longman's, and Wordsworth had not received it until nearly two months after it was written. He had hastened to answer, and his reply was dated 29 July, from Grasmere. It was all Thomas could have desired.

> It is needless to say [wrote Wordsworth] that it would be out of nature were I not to have kind feelings towards one who expresses sentiments of such profound esteem and admiration of my writings as you have done . . . You will then perceive that the main end which you proposed to yourself in writing to me is answered, viz. that I am already kindly disposed towards you. My friendship it is not in my power to give: this is a gift which no man can make, it is not in our own power: a sound and healthy friendship is the growth of time and circumstance, it will spring up and thrive like a wildflower when these favour, and when they do not, it is in vain to look for it.

This was a necessary caution: Thomas had been rash enough to ask for Wordsworth's 'friendship', and the older man could see the dangers of such a demand. Modesty led him also to speak of

> the very unreasonable value you set upon my writings, compared with those of others. You are young and ingenuous and I wrote with a hope of pleasing the young, the ingenuous and the unworldly above all others, but sorry indeed should I be to stand in the way of the proper influence of other writers . . .
>
> How many things are there in a man's character of which his writings however miscellaneous or voluminous will give no idea . . . You probably would never guess from anything you know of me that I am the most lazy and impatient Letter writer in the world. You will perhaps have observed that the first two or three Lines of this sheet are in a tolerably fair, legible hand, and, now every Letter, from A to Z, is in complete route, one upon the heals of the other. Indeed so difficult Do I find it to master this ill habit of idleness and impatience, that I have long ceased to write any Letters but upon business. In justice to myself and you I have found myself obliged to mention this, lest you should think me unkind if you find me a slovenly or sluggish Correspondent.
>
> I am going with my friend Coleridge and my Sister upon a tour into Scotland for six weeks or two months . . . If however you write immediately I may have the pleasure of receiving your Letter before our departure . . . I need not add that it will give me great pleasure to see you at Grasmere if you should ever come this way.[26]

The postscript repeated this invitation, with a note of charming spontaneity: 'P.S. I have just looked my letter over, and find that towards the conclusion I have been in a most unwarrantable hurry especially in what I have said on seeing you here. I seem to have expressed myself absolutely with coldness. This is not in my feelings for you I assure you. I shall indeed be very happy to see you at Grasmere . . .' He urged, however, that Thomas should not neglect the 'many engagements of great importance to [his] worldly concerns and future happiness in life' which no doubt pressed upon one so young. Thomas went cheerfully home to Chester, his 'worldly concerns' as uncertain as ever but his 'future happiness' seeming now a good deal more assured. He wrote back to Wordsworth, full of gratitude and relieved that his letter, written at a time of depression, had not struck the wrong note. Again he asserted his admiration for Wordsworth's poems, though he was careful now to emphasize that he meant no disparagement to the earlier masters of English verse – Spenser, Shakespeare, Milton, Thomson and Collins – and tentatively accepted the invitation to Grasmere, though he seems almost too overawed to believe in its reality. But it will have to wait, he says, until next summer, for, 'Unfortunately . . . I am not yet my own master; and (in compliance with the wishes of my Mother and my guardians) I am going, in a month or two, to enter myself at Oxford.'[27] Greatly daring, he adds a Postscript: 'You mention Miss Wordsworth (I speak at a venture) and Mr Coleridge; and this emboldens me to use the privilege of a friend and take a liberty which I should not otherwise have done – when I beg you to convey my most sincere and respectful good wishes to them both.' 'The privilege of a friend': somehow the demand for friendship will out, however he tries to suppress it.

Thomas returned to find the Priory in a stir. The fragile peace between Britain and France had broken down in May 1803. Now a local militia was being raised in each town for defence in case of a French invasion, and Uncle Thomas Penson was organizing a volunteer cavalry force for Chester. He and two fellow officers bustled about the Priory, now a military headquarters, whilst Thomas mooned about, feeling in the way, passing the time until he could go to Oxford. Hall was still making difficulties over the question of money so Thomas stayed on until even Uncle Penson, who was generally very fond of him, found him becoming rather a nuisance. They spent much time talking together but Penson was less tolerant than Mr Cragg had been of Thomas's cutting comments and air of intellectual superiority. One day, Penson, his temper sharpened by the fact that he was immobilized with his leg in splints after a riding accident, took offence at his nephew's attempt to debunk one of his favourite books and asked angrily what he was doing idling away his time at home. They discussed the problem of finance, and when Penson suggested that life could be supported at Oxford on £100 a year Thomas readily agreed. Penson spoke to Mrs Quincey, and a week later Thomas went to Oxford.[28]

He arrived 'late on a winter's night, in the latter half of December, 1803, when a snow-storm, and a heavy one, was already gathering in the air'. The coach deposited him at the Golden Cross, 'a shabby coach-inn, situated in the Corn Market'.[29] Here he spent the night, leaving until the next morning the complicated question of how to get himself admitted to the university – for, of course, neither his mother nor anyone else had given a moment's thought to such details as what college he should enter, whether he should be admitted as a commoner or gentleman-commoner, and so on. It was all, bewilderingly, left to him. In the morning he called together the few Oxford undergraduates he knew – former pupils from Winkfield and Manchester Grammar School – and held a conference. He would prefer, he said, to enter a large college, where he could remain inconspicuous, for he would be unable to afford the extravagant social life pursued by many of the students; he would also prefer a college where good music was to be heard during the chapel services, daily attendance being compulsory for all undergraduates. With these conditions in mind, which college would they recommend?

The answer to this conundrum was agreed by the assembly to be Christ Church, the largest college, which was incorporated with the Cathedral of Oxford. No doubt the idea of aiming high appealed to the young De Quincey, so to the surprise of his friends he set off at once for Christ Church to seek an interview with the Dean, Dr Cyril Jackson. A footman introduced him into the spacious library where the great Dr Jackson was sitting. He treated Thomas with politeness and gave him an informal interview on his previous education and present reading, but when he realized that Thomas was seeking immediate admission his answer was firm. He would have liked, he said, to admit Thomas. ' "But sir," he said, in a tone of some sharpness, "your guardians have acted improperly. It was their duty to have given me at least one year's notice of their intention to place you at Christ Church. At present I have not a dog-kennel in my college untenanted." '³⁰ When Thomas explained that his guardians were giving him no support in his application the Dean's interest was aroused and he seemed disposed to relent, but at that moment a visitor 'of high rank' was announced and after an instant of hesitation the Dean put an end to the interview. Thomas found himself in the street again, contemplating the ruins of his plan and no doubt cursing Samuel Hall more fervently than ever.

He spent several days of indecision staying at the Golden Cross, his Oxford friends helping him to get rapidly through the fifty guineas he had brought from Chester, and at last was forced to choose Worcester College, for the simple reason that the amount of 'caution money' demanded from the students as a deposit against unpaid bills was lower at Worcester than elsewhere and it was thus the only college he could now afford to enter. He consoled himself with the thought that Worcester had a reputation for lax discipline, which meant that he would be able to do very much as he pleased. He entered Worcester College as a commoner on 17 December 1803. His subsequent Oxford life remains shadowy, and we know little about how he spent his time. He stayed at Oxford intermittently until May 1808, and during these five years many of the most significant events of his life took place; but they happened mainly during the vacations, and on the whole Oxford features as a series of dim and not very happy interludes between brightly lit scenes of excitement and discovery in London, the Lake District and the West Country.

Worcester College in 1803 was far from being the grandest of Oxford colleges. It was rather small and it had no organ – thus failing to meet either of Thomas's original demands. Nor had it a garden. With the possible exception of Robert Bourne, Professor of Physics, it boasted not one Fellow of any real distinction and its generally low reputation, together with its situation some distance away from the town centre where the older-established colleges had their buildings, made it a regular butt of student wit. A humorist contemporary with De Quincey, for example, claimed to have taken three years to discover 'that there was a very respectable college of the name of Worcester somewhere out in the country, and that some of the members of it had been known to ride the whole distance down into Oxford without changing horses . . .'³¹ Clearly, De Quincey's life there would be as secluded as he could wish. 'The first rooms assigned me,' he says, 'being small and ill-lighted, as part of an old Gothic building, were charged at four guineas a year. These I soon exchanged for others a little better, and for them I paid six guineas. Finally, by privilege of seniority, I obtained a handsome set of well-proportioned rooms, in a modern section of the college, charged at ten guineas a year.'[32] The quality of the accommodation improved, it seems, as the amount of money available for his expenses increased. During the first few months he had to budget very carefully indeed.

Having moved into his small, dim rooms, he kept very much to himself. He began to pursue his own omnivorous course of reading, allowing the college routine to interfere as little as possible. Some participation in the collective life of the college, of course, could not be avoided. The day would begin at half past seven, when a bell would summon the students from their beds to dress hastily and run to chapel for the compulsory morning service. At half past eight breakfast was brought by a college servant to the students' rooms, and at nine-thirty or ten lectures would begin, continuing until one o'clock. Dinner, at which attendance was compulsory, was served in the college Hall at three in the afternoon, after which there was chapel again, this time voluntary and sparsely attended. Tea and supper would be served in the rooms of students willing to pay for them at six and nine in the evening. No one might leave the college after nine o'clock, and the gates were locked at eleven.[33] The more affluent students enlivened their evenings with wine parties and their afternoons with fox-hunting, hare-coursing, cock-fighting and boxing. The last-mentioned sport could be pursued by students as either spectators or participants: John Wilson, a contemporary of De Quincey's at Oxford and later to become his close friend, was well known in student circles not only as a leader of the Oxford 'Fancy' but as an invincible 'bruiser' in his own right, willing to take on any local champion at boxing or wrestling. De Quincey, however had neither the means nor the desire to cultivate the sporting side of student life, and after accepting a few invitations to wine parties he ceased to take much part in the social life of the college, limiting himself to giving an occasional breakfast party, thus fulfilling what he felt to be the minimum obligation of hospitality. The students seemed to him, on the whole, 'a drinking, rattling set, whose conversation was juvenile, commonplace, and quite unintellectual'.[34]

Relations with his tutors were no better. No doubt he attended a certain number of lectures each week, for they were compulsory, but he must have found them unrewarding. They were not lectures in the modern sense, for the students, a dozen or so at a time, sat in the tutor's room and 'lectured' to him: each had a copy of a classical text and in turn translated or construed, the tutor correcting and instructing when necessary. There can have been no creative scope for De Quincey's linguistic talent and the lectures must have been unpleasantly reminiscent of Lawson's schoolroom. Discipline at Worcester being notable by its absence, De Quincey probably 'cut' many of the lectures. Like every undergraduate, he was assigned to an individual tutor who was supposed to keep an eye on his progress and give extra tuition if necessary. In these early years at Oxford he met his tutor only once. He was walking in the quadrangle one fine morning when the tutor stopped, introduced himself, and asked De Quincey what he had been reading lately. As it happened, De Quincey, already growing deeply interested in philosophy, had been reading Parmenides, but with a characteristic blend of shyness and arrogance he declined to tell the truth (he was afraid the tutor might not have heard of Parmenides) and chose to say that he had been reading Paley, whose works on moral philosophy were a standard examination text. 'Ah!' said the tutor affably, 'an excellent author; excellent for his matter; only you must be on your guard as to his style; he is very vicious there.'[35] His pedagogic duty done, the tutor bowed and went on his way, leaving the young philosopher angry and incredulous: for he much admired the old-fashioned colloquial vigour of Paley's style, but thought his philosophy nonsense. The incident confirmed him in the view that he must get his education for himself, and he did not trouble to see his tutor again until almost the end of his student career.

It is obvious, however, that the college cannot take all the blame for De Quincey's morose behaviour at this period.

> There was one reason [he admits] why I sought solitude at that early age, and sought it in a morbid excess ... Past experience of a very peculiar kind, the agitations of many lives crowded into the compass of a year or two, in combination with a peculiar structure of mind, offered one explanation of the very remarkable and unsocial habits which I adopted at college.[36]

A second reason was that, to his dismay, he soon found that his fellow undergraduates showed no enthusiasm for the great works of English literature which had become the vital inspiration for his own life over the past few years. They seemed to know nothing of literature beyond the classical works they had met at school and a few passages from the *Spectator* – familiar because of the standard exercise of putting its essays into Latin. Such ignorance he found intolerable, but he was too shy to go about proselytizing for the beauties of English literature, and the fact that he was in correspondence with Wordsworth earned him no respect in a society where the poet's name was unknown.

Another reason for his melancholy, and one which may explain the neglect with which Mrs Quincey and the guardians treated him at the opening of his Oxford career, was the loss of his favourite brother Richard, who was now fourteen years old. The strange drama of the Quincey sons had entered a new phase. William had been banished in infancy; Thomas had fled from school. Now it was 'Pink's' turn. For over a year 'Pink' had endured the tyranny of a master whose addiction to flogging was exceptional even by the standards of the 1800s. At last he could stand it no longer and some time in late 1803 he had run away from school, determined to go to sea. He reached Liverpool after four days of walking but before he could find a ship was tricked by a seemingly helpful stranger into revealing his name and address. The long-suffering Uncle Penson was fetched from Chester, and 'Pink' was returned to school, though not before the good-humoured uncle had extracted from the master a promise that this time 'Pink' would not be beaten for his offence. As soon as Penson was safely beyond the school precincts, the master broke his promise and at the next opportunity 'Pink' was again on the road for Liverpool. There he went straight to the docks and engaged himself to the captain of a privateer. He sailed for several months, and when he returned in the spring of 1804 he refused to come home, communicating with his mother by letters whose tendency, as described by Mrs Quincey in a letter to her youngest son Henry, sounds very familiar. 'He absolutely rejects everything,' she writes, 'and will return on no condition . . . but that of being his own Master, a condition which neither the Laws of the Land nor the inclinations of his Guardians allow them to accede to.'[37] No agreement was reached, so 'Pink' went as cabin-boy on board a South Sea whaler and, for the time being, no more was heard of him. The affair was a source of great distress to the whole family and Thomas, whilst heartily wishing his brother success in his daring venture, was burdened with guilt, fearing that his example had been an immediate cause of 'Pink's' flight. Mrs Quincey had predicted that Thomas's behaviour would corrupt his brother's, and so it had turned out. If 'Pink' were never to return, would Thomas not be guilty of something like fratricide?

But probably poverty was the greatest obstacle to his forming friends at Oxford. He shrank from allowing others to see how carefully he had to watch his expenditure. His mother offered to help him out with extra money in small sums,[38] but she was not herself well off. When Penson returned to India she moved temporarily to Bath, where she found the cost of living higher than she had expected, and Thomas was unwilling to trouble her with frequent requests. Always he tended to skimp the mere practical needs of life when they came into conflict with more exalted concerns. 'I neglected my dress in one point habitually,' he recalls; 'that is, I wore clothes until they were threadbare – partly in the belief that my gown would conceal their main defects, but much more from carelessness and indisposition to spend upon a tailor what I had destined for a bookseller.' He was warned by a senior member of the college that he must improve his appearance, and meant to do so,

> but always it happened that some book, or set of books, – that passion being absolutely endless, and inexorable as the grave, – stepped between me and my intentions; until one day, upon arranging my toilet hastily before dinner, I suddenly made the discovery that I had no waistcoat . . . which was not torn or otherwise dilapidated; whereupon, buttoning up my coat to the throat, and drawing my gown as close about me as possible, I went into the public 'hall' . . . with no misgiving. However, I was detected; for a grave man, with a superlatively grave countenance, who happened on that day to sit next me, but whom I did not personally know, addressing his friend sitting opposite, begged to know if he had seen the last Gazette, because he understood that it contained an Order in Council laying an interdict upon the future use of waistcoats. His friend replied, with the same perfect gravity, that it was a great satisfaction to his mind that his Majesty's Government should have issued so sensible an order; which he trusted would be soon followed up by an interdict on breeches, they being still more disagreeable to pay for. This said, without the movement on either side of a single muscle, the two gentlemen passed on to other subjects.[39]

Yet there were intellectual consolations. Finding the academic work easy, De Quincey began to follow his own instincts, reading voluminously in literature and philosophy. His knack of discovering new authors did not fail him, and during his first winter in Oxford he bought the first works of Lamb and Landor, then both unknown, on the same morning. Placing Lamb's *John Woodvil* and Landor's *Gebir* on his shelf beside the *Lyrical Ballads*, he smiled wrily, reflecting that he seemed well on the way to collecting a library of books unread by anyone but himself. He also took up the study of German, enlisting the aid of a German Jewish student called Schwartzburg, who gave him private tuition. It may have been from Schwartzburg that he first heard of Kant, whose philosophy was the main subject of intellectual debate in Germany. He longed to read the *Critique of Pure Reason,* and worked hard at his German so that he might tackle the formidable treatise as soon as possible.

His time, however, was not entirely dedicated to secluded study. It happened that in the first week of March 1804 the trial took place, at Oxford, of two students who were charged with the abduction of a certain Mrs Lee — none other, in fact, than the beautiful lady atheist who had routed Samuel Hall and driven Mrs Quincey to a hysterical fit over dinner at Greenhay some years before. De Quincey, of course, determined to be present at the trial, and he was not alone, for Oxford was in a fever of excitement over the case, the charge being a capital one and the defendants, the Gordon brothers, Oxford men. De Quincey was among the crowd which gathered in the streets around the courthouse before dawn, undeterred by heavy rain. The trial was to begin at seven o'clock, and by the time the Judge and Sherriff arrived the street was so crowded that the constables had to force a passage through the mob. Several people were injured and a brawl ensued, but De Quincey managed to get into the courtroom, which was soon full to overflowing with noisy spectators. The case proved to be suitably lurid: the jury had to decide whether Mrs Lee had left her home voluntarily with the two brothers or whether they had dragged her away at gunpoint with the intention of raping her or extorting money from her (she was known to have a fortune of some £50,000). The evidence included the reading of several private letters, and an investigation of Mrs Lee's behaviour and conversation with the Gordons in a post-chaise which, as the local paper put it, 'were too indecent to repeat'.[40] The high point of the day was the appearance of the chief witness, Mrs Lee herself. Much of the confidence she had shown at Greenhay was gone, and at her entry De Quincey thought her 'pitiable'; but some of the old fascination was still there, and once in the witness box she began to make a powerful impact on the hostile crowd: 'first,' De Quincey recalled, 'through her impressive appearance; secondly, through the appalling coolness of her answers'.[41] Her coolness did not save her, for during cross-examination she was trapped into admitting that she did not believe in God. Her evidence, given under oath, was thus rendered invalid, the trial was stopped, and the Gordon brothers were let off with a reprimand. De Quincey's attitude to the wicked lady remained ambivalent: however 'appalled' he may have been at her manner in court, he went round to her lodgings after the trial, hoping to see her on the pretext of their former acquaintance in Manchester. He arrived, however, just in time to see her carriage jeered out of town by an angry mob. The real interest of the episode is that it shows how early De Quincey had developed a taste for courtroom drama, an enjoyment of public scandal as a dramatic spectacle in its own right, which was to be an important element in his work as newspaper editor and essayist.

Worcester was one of the few colleges where a student could keep what was known as 'the short term', attending for a mere thirteen weeks in the year. De Quincey, resolving that 'from the great aversion I have to a college life, I shall pass no more of my time there than is necessary',[42] left the college in March 1804 and took lodgings in the nearby village of Littlemore. From there he wrote to Wordsworth on 14 March, his first letter for six months. Apologizing for this long silence he explained that he had been depressed, and hinted at poverty as one of the causes. More than ever he expressed his admiration for Wordsworth, implying that the moral guidance he found in his poetry was the only stabilizing factor in his confused life. He explained that between twelve and sixteen he had modelled his conduct and aims on characters from legend or the German drama, until 'miserably deluding myself with the thought that I was led on by high aims, & such as were most worthy of my nature I daily intoxicated myself more & more with that delirious and lawless pleasure which I drew from the hope of elevating my name in authority & kingly splendour over every name that is named upon earth. For I felt myself unable to live in the pursuit of common objects, & unfettered by any ties of common restraint.' From these dangerous delusions, he says, he was rescued by the 'mild reproach' which he sensed in nature during his 'long & lonely rambles through many beautiful scenes', and looking for guidance he had realized that it was to be found in Wordsworth's poetry.[43] He saw Wordsworth now as his father-confessor, and clearly he was in a perilous emotional state: lonely, nervous, full of emotion which he could not direct to any object other than his distant hero.

He had no immediate reply, but inquiring at his college nearly a fortnight later he found two letters from Wordsworth awaiting him.

The first had been sent to the Priory, which Mrs Quincey had now left. The second was simply to warn that the first might have gone astray. Both were very friendly. The earlier letter, dated 6 March, gave news of the Wordsworths' tour of the Scottish Highlands, and offered some friendly advice:

> I need not say to you that there is no true dignity but in virtue and temperance, and, let me add, chastity; and that the best safeguard of all these is the cultivation of pure pleasures, namely, those of the intellect and affections ... I do not mean to preach; I speak in simplicity and tender apprehension as one lover of Nature and of Virtue speaking to another. Do not on any account fail to tell me whether you are satisfied with yourself since your migration to Oxford; if not, do your duty to yourself immediately; love Nature and Books; seek these and you will be happy.[44]

This sounds a little distasteful in its inquisitive moralizing, but perhaps it was just what De Quincey wanted. Wordsworth was taking a real interest in him and, although mostly talking down to his young correspondent, putting him for a moment ('as one lover of Nature and of Virtue speaking to another') on his own level. Better still, Wordsworth takes Thomas into his confidence about his new poem:

> I am now writing a Poem on my earlier life; and have just finished that part in which I speak of my residence at the University: it would give me great pleasure to read this work to you at this time. As I am sure, from the interest you have taken in the L.B. that it would please you, and might also be of service to you. This poem will not be published these many years, and never during my lifetime, till I have finished a larger and more important work to which it is tributary.[45]

This may be a clue to the rather surprising degree of interest Wordsworth was showing in his young admirer. Reviving and contemplating the memories of his own student days as he worked on Book III of the poem we know as *The Prelude*, perhaps he saw in De Quincey a counterpart to his own young self, and felt inspired to offer advice which might have helped him, had it been available. He signed himself 'your very affectionate Friend, W. Wordsworth' – as if friendship, 'the growth of time and circumstance' as he had cautiously put it eight months before, were already flourishing.

Thomas sent off a reply without delay. He expressed his concern at the illness which, Wordsworth said, had forced Coleridge to drop out of the Highland tour, but obviously saw in it a possible opening for a meeting with the great man:

If he is advised to try Bath waters (which, I believe, are of great benefit
in rheumatic complaints) and has no friend there whose services he
would prefer on such occasion, I hope that I may be permitted to
procure lodgings and all other accommodations for him. I can never
have any engagements here important enough to detain me from such
an office.[46]

His response to Wordworth's moral exhortation is most revealing:

The interest – so gratifying to me, which you are kind enough to take
in my welfare, would be of itself a sufficient check upon me if I were
unhappily disposed to licentiousness: but I have been through life so
much restrained from dissolute conduct by the ever-waking love of my
mother – and of late years so purified from dissolute propensities by
the new order of pleasures which I have been led to cultivate that I feel
a degree of confidence ... that, even with greater temptations, I
should not by my *conduct* at any rate make you repent the notice you
have taken of me.

There is, he says, some 'intemperance' at college, but he dislikes
college life and it holds few temptations for him. 'I have lived almost
alone since my entrance,' he writes with melancholy pride, 'and until I
see something greater or better, I shall continue to do so.' The letter
was finished on 1 April. A few days later he returned to college, and for
several months we know nothing of his movements except that after
spending the summer term in Oxford he went to his mother's new
home at Hinckley, Leicestershire, for the vacation.

It seems to have been in the early autumn of 1804 that De Quincey
visited London for the first time since he had entered college. His
original purpose in going there can only be guessed at, but the consequences of his visit make it appear, in retrospect, the turning-point of
his life. 'Cardinal events', he wrote later, 'are not to be forgotten; and,
from circumstances connected with it, I remember that [my] inaugura-
tion into the use of opium must be referred to the spring or to the
autumn of 1804; during which seasons I was in London, having come
thither for the first time since my entrance at Oxford.' We can be more
precise: his letters to Wordsworth, together with the archives of
Worcester College, show that he had no prolonged absence from
Oxford in the spring.[47] He returned to Oxford on 18 October for the
Michaelmas term, and it is therefore probable that after visiting his
mother and sisters at Hinckley he went to London for the earlier part

119

of October. And what was he doing in London? Almost certainly he had gone there to borrow money. If, as Charles Lamb says, the human species is composed of two distinct races, the men who borrow and the men who lend, De Quincey belonged, indisputably, to the former. After one term of dreary parsimony his determination to live thriftily had faltered, and being one (as he neatly expressed it) 'who did not delight in the petty details of minute economy'[48] he had taken to spending more than he could afford. In the first three months of 1804 his charges on the college books are average for undergraduates in residence; in April, May and June they rise to put him into the top third.[49] In early summer, undeterred by the terrible experiences of the previous year, he had written again to the money-lender Dell and, 'dating at that time from a respectable college',[50] found Dell ready to change his attitude. He decided to pursue his old plan of borrowing £250 against his patrimony. This he was able to do, at the exorbitant rate of 17½ per cent, and it was probably something connected with this business that now brought him to London.

It was whilst staying in London that he was attacked by the pain which led to his introduction to opium. The story is best told in his own words, as he recalled it seventeen years later:

> From an early age I had been accustomed to wash my head in cold water at least once a day: being suddenly seized with toothache, I attributed it to some relaxation caused by a casual intermission of that practice; jumped out of bed: plunged my head into a basin of cold water; and with hair thus wetted went to sleep. The next morning, as I need hardly say, I awoke with excruciating rheumatic pains of the head and face, from which I had hardly any respite for about twenty days. On the twenty-first day, I think it was, and on a Sunday, that I went out into the streets; rather to run away, if possible from my torments, than with any distinct purpose. By accident I met a college acquaintance who recommended opium. Opium! . . . I had heard of it as I had heard of manna or of ambrosia, but no further: how unmeaning a sound was it at that time! what solemn chords does it now strike upon my heart! what heart-quaking vibrations of sad and happy remembrances! Reverting for a moment to these, I feel a mystic importance attached to the minutest circumstances connected with the place and the time, and the man (if man he was) that first laid open to me the Paradise of Opium-Eaters. It was a Sunday afternoon, wet and cheerless: and a duller spectacle this earth of ours has not to show than a rainy Sunday in London. My road homewards lay through Oxford-street; and near 'the *stately* Pantheon' (as Mr Wordsworth has obligingly called it) I saw a druggist's shop. The druggist, uncon-

scious minister of celestial pleasures! – as if in sympathy with the rainy Sunday, looked dull and stupid, just as any mortal druggist might be expected to look on a Sunday: and, when I asked for the tincture of opium, he gave it to me as any other man might do: and furthermore, out of my shilling, returned to me what seemed to be real copper halfpence, taken out of a real wooden drawer. Nevertheless, in spite of such indications of humanity, he has ever since existed in my mind as the beatific vision of an immortal druggist, sent down to earth on a special mission to myself. And it confirms me in this way of considering him, that, when I next came up to London, I sought him near the stately Pantheon, and found him not . . .

Arrived at my lodgings, it may be supposed that I lost not a moment in taking the quantity prescribed. I was necessarily ignorant of the whole art and mystery of opium-taking: and, what I took, I took under every disadvantage. But I took it:- and in an hour, oh! heavens! what a revulsion!* What an upheaving, from its lowest depths, of the inner spirit! What an apocalypse of the world within me! That my pains had vanished, was now a trifle in my eyes:- this negative effect was swallowed up in the immensity of those positive effects which had suddenly opened before me – in the abyss of divine enjoyment thus revealed. Here was a panacea – a $\phi\acute{\alpha}\rho\mu\alpha\kappa o\nu$ $\nu\eta\pi\epsilon\nu\theta\acute{\epsilon}s$ for all human woes; here was the secret of happiness, about which philosophers had disputed for so many ages, at once discovered: happiness might now be bought for a penny, and carried in the waistcoat pocket: portable ecstasies might be had corked up in a pint bottle: and peace of mind could be sent down in gallons by the mail coach.[51]

* ['Recovery, restoration; . . . A sudden violent change of feeling' (*O.E.D.*)]

5

The Road to Grasmere

Opium is the congealed juice of the seed-heads of *Papaver somniferum,* the opium poppy or 'white poppy' whose flower, contrary to popular belief, is not scarlet but white tinged with purple. Since ancient times it has been cultivated for its medicinal qualities. In De Quincey's day the main centres of opium production were Turkey and the Bengal area of Eastern India. Opium is obtained from the poppy by the painstaking labour of scratching the surface of the bulbous seed-capsules so that the juice 'bleeds' and congeals in a dry brownish deposit which can be scraped off and collected. This is crude opium. Pressed into cakes for distribution and sale, it has much the colour and consistency of treacle toffee. De Quincey had asked his 'immortal druggist' on that wet Sunday afternoon for 'the tincture of opium'. This was laudanum, a solution of crude opium in alcohol containing about one twelfth part by weight of the active ingredients of opium.[1] Laudanum was easily available at any druggist's shop in England, for its medicinal properties, real and imagined, had made it a standard remedy for all kinds of ailments. The most important ingredient of opium is morphine, a painkiller of great power. It has, however, one serious disadvantage, in that repeated doses alter the chemistry of the patient's body to a point where a continued supply of morphine becomes essential to anything like healthy functioning. Once physical dependence has set in, the patient faces two alternatives. With morphine, normal life can continue, though there are certain uncomfortable side-effects. Without morphine, serious illness ensues, accompanied by appalling physical discomfort and an intense craving for the drug. The need to stave off this illness and craving, rather than positive enjoyment of the drug, is what keeps most 'addicts' addicted. With sufficient endurance the dependence can be broken, but in the throes of his sickness the patient is likely to believe that without a renewed dose he will die. Moreover there are psychological factors which make it unlikely that an addict will ever permanently discard his addiction.

These dangers were not clearly recognized in the days of De

Quincey's youth, and the virtues of opium as a painkiller and cough suppressant had led it to be mistaken for a cure in all kinds of cases where it merely suppressed symptoms. Thus, to quote one authority, in nineteenth-century England 'at some time or another the drug was advocated as a specific for diabetes, consumption, syphilis, cholera and rheumatism, as a sedative in delirium tremens, mania and in febrile diseases, as an anti-tussive agent in phthisis and almost every other chest disease and even as a remedy for obstinate constipation'.[2] It might also be prescribed for haemorrhage, diarrhoea, colic, delayed labour and pain from fractures or surgical operations. It had its perilous uses too as a sleeping-draught for adults and a 'soothing syrup' for infants, the notorious Godfrey's Cordial and its many imitators deriving from opium their power to quieten crying babies. De Quincey's college friend was thus making a perfectly normal suggestion when he recommended opium for the raging pain of what was probably a decaying tooth with an abscess. It is characteristic of De Quincey, of course, that his use of opium should have begun with an experiment at self-doctoring. Whether or not it gave rise to the pain which drove him to opium, his rash habit of sousing his head daily in cold water was a typical Quincey fad. Mrs Quincey, the family physician Dr Mapleton and their friend the eminent Dr Currie of Liverpool were all devout believers in the therapeutic value of cold water.[3] It is equally typical of De Quincey that, in agony from a pain which began as toothache, he should have endured it for three weeks and eventually taken a painkiller rather than have the tooth extracted. There were times when he would endure any amount of misery paid out, as it were, by instalments, rather than opt for the intense but short-lived unpleasantness of decisive action.

It will be clear that when De Quincey says 'I had heard of [opium] as I had of manna or of ambrosia, but no further', he does not mean that it was a mere word to him. Laudanum was in every family medicine cupboard: he was probably given it as a child when he had the 'ague'. He means, rather, that he knew nothing of its power to induce psychic and emotional transformation. Yet even that degree of ignorance is unlikely. He must have known something of opium before 1804, for he had a family connection with the most prosperous and highly organized opium industry in the world. His uncle Thomas was a colonel in the military service of the East India Company in Bengal. A major enterprise of the Company in Bengal was the production of opium, which was systematically smuggled into China in huge quantities in defiance of the Chinese government's strict prohibition. The Pensons, Mrs Quincey's family, had been close friends of Colonel Henry Watson, Lady Carbery's father, one of the original entrepreneurs who had urged on the Company the daring policy of smuggling Bengal opium into China. It was a ship owned by Watson which in 1782 had smuggled the first consignment of opium to Macao. On this occasion Watson had smuggled some opium on his own account as well as earning a large shipping fee from the Company, thus adding a respectable sum to the fortune which, at his death, was to come to Thomas's beloved Lady Carbery.[4] During the summer of 1803 De Quincey had spent much time at the Priory debating with his Uncle Thomas the rights and wrongs of British rule in India. Thomas Penson was ready to bow to Mrs Quincey's view that the British had no moral right to be there; De Quincey, on the other hand, defended their presence.[5] That such arguments could have been carried on without reference to the opium trade is not credible. There is, therefore, a possibility that De Quincey was already curious about opium and expected something a little out of the ordinary when he tried it for the first time in his adult life.

Immediate relief of his pain, accompanied by considerable euphoria, was only to be expected. Opium acts differently upon different people but its painkilling properties are not in doubt. When taken to relieve intense pain, its first psychological effect is often a pronounced sense of well-being, an inner glow of warm serenity. There is also a relaxation, when a sizable dose is taken, of any emotional tensions and anxieties with which the mind may have been oppressed. Guilt, fear and inner conflict melt away: external facts may not seem changed, but the weight of worry is lightened so that the subject feels himself raised above mundane problems and able, if it should ever seem important (which it never does), to solve them without effort. Hence that 'abyss of divine enjoyment' which was revealed to De Quincey, and his feeling that he had discovered 'the secret of happiness' and 'a panacea . . . for all human woes'. At the same time, it must be admitted that he showed many of the psychological factors said to predispose an individual to addiction. As he wrote later, 'I confess it, as a besetting infirmity of mine, that I am too much of an Eudaemonist; I hanker too much after a state of happiness, both for myself and others; I cannot face misery, whether my own or not, with an eye of sufficient firmness, and am little capable of encountering present pain for the sake of any reversionary benefit. On some other matters, I can agree . . . in affecting the stoic philosophy; but not in this.'[6] A tendency to shy away from unpleasant experience was combined with a habit of keeping problems to himself and brooding on them until specific issues were lost in a cloudy sense of ill-usage and resentment. Prone to depression, lonely and withdrawn at university, anxious about money and perhaps not without feelings of guilt towards his troubled family, he carried many of the psychological burdens which opium can temporarily lighten. His response to the drug had, therefore, as much to do with his character as with the chemistry of opium. Where many might have observed the experience with curiosity but thought no more of opium once the pain had finally receded, De Quincey had found something that would give him a holiday, when he needed it, from his anxieties and self-doubts. It was thus that a psychological dependence began.

He returned to Oxford in mid-October 1804 and resumed his retired existence, his studies of German and philosophy. He may already have conceived the ambition of doing something original in this line himself, for during the summer his mother had written assuring him, with guarded tolerance, 'Your studies under the name of Moral Philosophy cannot be objected to: and, as you have spoken only in general terms of your object, I conclude as I hope, that there is nothing objectionable either in the plan you are forming or the end you aim at.' She is at pains to warn him, however, that, 'As to any merely speculative scheme which sets aside the Word of God, it can only end where everything of the same root has ended and ought to end, be it more or less finely spun', and commends to him 'the consideration and comprehension of the Gospel morality, which is very little understood – an undertaking which would afford sufficient scope for the finest talents'.[7] Whether this was quite the kind of philosophy Thomas had in mind, we may doubt.

He kept the short term in the autumn of 1804, staying at college from October until 22 November, and it seems to have been during this period that he discovered some of the more surprising psychological by-products of opium. His indulgence in the drug was occasional – he would go for several weeks between doses – and physical dependence had not yet begun. He noticed that 'the day succeeding to that on which I allowed myself this luxury was always a day of unusually good spirits'[8] but he also discovered that the nights after an indulgence in opium were filled with abnormally vivid dreams, often recreating intense childhood experiences which he had not recalled for years. Opium stimulates dreams by a kind of rebound effect: its action inhibits dreaming, but when the drug has worked its way through the system a compensating tendency causes a sudden increase in the quantity and vividness of dreams.[9] In De Quincey's case some inhibition was removed, certain doors of the mind opened, and fearful memories issued forth:

> Once again . . . the nursery of my childhood expanded before me: my sister was moaning in bed; and I was beginning to be restless with fears not intelligible to myself. Once again the elder nurse, but now dilated to colossal proportions, stood as upon some Grecian stage with her uplifted hand, and . . . smote me senseless to the ground. Again I am in the chamber with my sister's corpse, again the pomps of life rise up in silence, the glory of summer, the Syrian sunlights, the frost of death. Dream forms itself mysteriously within dream; within these Oxford dreams remoulds itself continually the trance in my sister's chamber . . .[10]

and so, at this new crisis of his life, there began to return those 'agitations of childhood' with which he had never properly come to terms. He was in what has come to be known as the 'honeymoon phase' of drug experience. He relied upon opium for an occasional lift to his spirits but was not aware of any ill-effects and would go for weeks without a dose. Such use of the drug may be practised for years and may never develop into addiction. For the time being its only effect on De Quincey, if we disregard the periodic disturbance in his dreams, was to confirm him in his habits of solitude and introversion. There may also be a connection with the fact that from now on his Oxford residence was punctuated by frequent visits to London. Here he could find congenial company, when he wanted it; more important, perhaps, he could assume invisibility in the crowd and forget the worries, obligations and forced intimacies of university life. As for his dealings with Mr Dell, his twenty-first birthday was less than two years away and when it arrived he would soon be able to sort out his money troubles.

He visited London at the end of November, returned to spend Christmas in college and went back to London on 10 January 1805. It was on one of these visits that he had his first meeting, face-to-face, with an Author, for he had obtained 'from a Literary friend' a letter of introduction to Charles Lamb. This was part of a devious plan to further a different ambition, for De Quincey was impressed not by Lamb's play *John Woodvil* but by the knowledge that Lamb was a friend of Coleridge. In the event this little piece of duplicity met with the reward it deserved. Armed with a letter representing him as an admirer of Lamb's, he sought him out at the India House in Leadenhall Street where Lamb was a clerk in the Accountant's Office.

> I was shown [De Quincey recalls] into a small room . . . in which was a very lofty writing desk, separated by a still higher railing from that part of the floor on which the profane – the laity, like myself – were allowed to approach the *clerus*, or clerkly rulers of the room. Within the railing sat, to the best of my remembrance, six quill-driving gentlemen . . . all too profoundly immersed in their oriental studies to have any sense of my presence . . . I walked, therefore, into one of the two open doorways of the railing, and stood closely by the high stool of him who occupied the first place within the little aisle. I touched his arm, by way of recalling him from his Leadenhall speculations to this sublunary world; and, presenting my letter, asked if that gentleman (pointing to the address) were really a citizen of the present room; for I had been repeatedly misled, by the directions given me, into wrong rooms. The gentleman smiled; it was a smile not to be forgotten. This was Lamb.[11]

Lamb clambered down from his perch to present himself as nearly as possible on a level with the five-foot-tall De Quincey, shook hands, glanced at the letter and invited him to come to tea at seven.

Charles Lamb, who was twenty-nine, lived in a suite of rooms in the Temple, one of the old Inns of Court, with his sister Mary. Brother and sister shared their lives as much from compulsion as from choice, for Mary was subject to periodic fits of insanity and in 1796, during a particularly violent attack, had snatched up a knife and fatally stabbed her mother. Charles had saved her from the lunatic asylum by becoming her legal guardian and undertaking to give her continual supervision. By hard work and unfailing kindness to his sister Lamb had made a tolerable life for them, but the time of his literary fame had not yet come. His strange and flawlessly written essays, with their sharply controlled undercurrent of melancholy, had not yet been written and he was gloomily aware that his play *John Woodvil* was a failure from every point of view. De Quincey, of course, knew nothing of all this. When the young 'admirer' arrived at seven o'clock he was made welcome, but, unwisely perhaps, 'turned the conversation, upon the first opening which offered, to the subject of Coleridge'. This led to trouble. He questioned the Lambs about Coleridge, and one can imagine the eagerness with which he listened to their answers and the note of veneration that must have crept into his voice as he spoke of the poet. Lamb was provoked by all this. He was an old and faithful friend of Coleridge, but he disliked hero-worship and was not without some traces of natural envy. As usual with Lamb, all this found expression in a disconcerting outburst of absurdity. He simmered quietly whilst Miss Lamb obliged De Quincey, answering his questions 'satisfactorily, because seriously', but when his turn came he 'took a pleasure', De Quincey says, 'in baffling me, or in throwing ridicule upon the subject'. To De Quincey's 'sensitive horror', Lamb began to direct 'a burning ridicule' at Wordsworth and Coleridge and everything connected with them – 'their books, their thoughts, their places, their persons'. Inevitably, the *Ancient Mariner* came in for its share of critical attention and,

> At length, when he had given utterance to some ferocious canon of judgment, which seemed to question the entire value of the poem, I said, perspiring (I dare say) in this debatable crisis – 'But, Mr. Lamb, good heavens! how is it possible you can allow yourself in such opinions? What instance could you bring from the poem that would bear you out in these insinuations?' 'Instances!' said Lamb: 'oh, I'll instance you, if you come to that. Instance, indeed! Pray, what do you say to this –
>
> > 'The many men so beautiful,
> > And they all dead did lie'?
>
> So *beautiful*, indeed! Beautiful! Just think of such a gang of Wapping vagabonds, all covered with pitch, and chewing tobacco; and the old gentleman himself, – what do you call him? – the bright-eyed fellow?' What more might follow I never heard; for, at this point, in a perfect rapture of horror, I raised my hands – both hands – to both ears; and without stopping to think or to apologize, I endeavoured to restore equanimity to my disturbed sensibilities by shutting out all further knowledge of Lamb's impieties. At length he seemed to have finished; so I, on my part, thought I might venture to take off the embargo: and in fact he *had* ceased – but no sooner did he find me restored to my hearing than he said with a most sarcastic smile – which he could assume upon occasion – 'If you please, sir, we'll say grace before we begin.'[12]

Mary Lamb did her best to smooth things over, and 'for the rest of the evening,' De Quincey says, 'she was so pointedly kind and conciliatory in her manner that I felt greatly ashamed of my boyish failure in self-command'.

But Lamb's frivolity had offended De Quincey. 'Knowing nothing of Lamb's propensity to mystify a stranger' he felt puzzled and hurt. He could not know that Lamb was one of the earliest and most perceptive admirers of the *Ancient Mariner*, or that one day he and Lamb would delight in each other's company. 'Lamb,' he says, 'after this one visit . . . I did not trouble with my calls for some years.' And – most irritating of all, perhaps? – he had never had the slightest chance of angling for an introduction to Coleridge.

His movements during the rest of 1805 are obscure. He was playing truant again from college, it appears, from January through March. At some time in the spring he visited Everton, and he certainly spent part of the year in London. He began to co-ordinate his London visits with his opium-taking so as to enjoy urban pleasures the more intensely. He cultivated a new kind of hedonism – subtle, and in a sense intellectual, but hedonism none the less. 'The late Duke of Norfolk', De Quincey explains, 'used to say, "Next Monday, wind and weather permitting, I purpose to be drunk"; and in the same manner I used to fix beforehand how often within a given time, when, and with what accessory circumstances of festal joy, I would commit a debauch of opium.'[13] Generally he chose Tuesday or Saturday nights, when he could indulge his love of music by going to the King's Theatre or the Opera House to hear Josephina Grassini, the celebrated contralto, in grand opera. Between 1804 and 1807 Grassini was the object of rapturous admiration from the London musical public. There was some controversy about the quality of her voice, certain critics contending that she had lost the natural *timbre* of her high notes and that her singing had a harsh, forced quality. Others – including De Quincey – found these same high notes intensely beautiful and never missed an opportunity of hearing her. Normally he took a five-shilling seat in the gallery: he could have found the half-guinea for a place in the pit, but typically he avoided this because it involved 'the troublesome condition' of wearing evening dress. In the *Confessions* he gives a vivid impression of his state as he sat in the gallery, his mood and senses heightened by a dose of opium:

> Thrilling was the pleasure with which almost always I heard this angelic Grassini. Shivering with expectation I sat, when the time drew near for her golden epiphany; shivering I rose from my seat, incapable of rest, when that heavenly and harp-like voice sang its own victorious

welcome in its prelusive *threttanelo-threttanelo*. The choruses were divine to hear; and, when Grassini appeared in some interlude, as she often did, and poured forth her passionate soul as Andromache at the tomb of Hector, &c., I question whether any Turk, of all that entered the paradise of opium-eaters, can have had half the pleasure I had.[14]

He noticed that often the mind's relation to the ear was transformed so that music could be *seen* spatially as an ornate decorative structure:

a chorus, &c., of elaborate harmony displayed before me, as in a piece of arras-work, the whole of my past life – not as if recalled by an act of memory, but as if present and incarnated in the music; no longer painful to dwell upon, but the detail of its incidents removed, or blended in some hazy abstraction, and its passions exalted, spiritualized and sublimed.[15]

It is interesting that for De Quincey the music should have presented the imagery of his past life. There is a remarkably consistent quality of regression in De Quincey's thinking: always the past is more real to him than the present or future. Much of the time he has little or no idea of the future and lives from day to day. But he is always ready to reminisce and analyse his personal history. His individual psychological constitution must also have something to do with the fact that his opium experience so often took the form of dreams or visual fantasies. Opium is not an hallucinogenic drug, nor does it normally enrich mental imagery; De Quincey's experience is exceptional in this respect. If we recall the episodes of daydreaming recorded in the Everton diary we may be able to understand why. He had consciously cultivated his mental imagery, and was inclined to regard 'fits of visionary and romantic luxuriating' as the main pleasure of life. Given such an exceptionally visual mind, it is not surprising that the drug should have produced 'visionary' experience.

The opera was not the only place into which De Quincey deliberately introduced his drug-heightened sensibility at this period. Wrapped in his secret detachment as in a cloak of invisibility, he 'used often, on Saturday nights, after I had taken opium, to wander forth, without much regarding the direction or the distance, to all the markets, and other parts of London, whither the poor resort on a Saturday night for laying out their wages'. He would listen to families debating 'the strength of their exchequer, or the price of household articles'. Occasionally (and no doubt to the astonishment of those concerned) he would join the conversation and proffer his advice. He felt that he shared, vicariously, the pleasures and anxieties of the poor on these

Saturday-night excursions, but it seems clear enough that there could be no real contact between him and them. They were a picturesque spectacle, a live painting (Breughel's *Peasant Wedding,* Hogarth's *Gin Lane*) into which he could step undefiled, clad in the psychological armour of opium. No doubt he remembered his own desperate poverty in London a couple of years before, but if so it gave rise to nothing more than a pleasurable *frisson.* He is honest enough to admit that, if on occasion he witnessed unhappiness, 'I drew from opium some means of consolation. For opium . . . can overrule all feelings into a compliance with the master-key.'[16] During these visits to London, he claims, he habitually scrutinized the crowd for the face of Ann. He did not find her, but this disappointment, too, was soothed by opium.

Meanwhile, his intellectual appetite had not slackened. He had mastered the pronunciation of German, and 'in the spirit of fierce (perhaps foolish) independence, which governed most of my actions at that time of life', he says, he had insisted on learning the grammar unaided. His facility at language-learning had not failed him and during 1805 he was able to begin a serious exploration of German literature. He could now read Schiller, whom he had enjoyed in translation a few years earlier; and, more exciting, such authors as Lessing, Herder and 'Jean Paul' Richter, all practically unknown in England. Once again he was in the advance guard of the literary taste of the day. His primary interest at this time being philosophy, he was aware that 'the very tree of knowledge in the midst of this [literary] Eden' was Immanuel Kant, and accordingly he tackled the bulky *Kritik der reinen Vernunft* and seems to have made his way with a fair degree of comprehension through Kant's knotty prose. He had probably read the dominant British empirical philosophers such as Locke and Hartley without much enthusiasm, and the first impact of Kant's system was favourable. The clarity of Kant's thought, under the superficial tangles of his prose style, the essential simplicity and grandeur of his demonstration that the modes in which the mind comprehends the world are not derived from the contingencies of experience but reveal the anatomy of consciousness itself, gave him initially a sense of 'the profoundest revelation'.

The feeling grew in him that philosophy was to be his vocation, and for a time he flattered himself with daydreams of leaving, after completing his studies, for 'the woods of Lower Canada', where he would live in forest-bound retirement and pursue the further development of the Transcendental Philosophy. He had even chosen the spot – at Stoneham Township, about seventeen miles from Quebec – where he would build 'a cottage and a considerable library': a dream inspired by his reading of Isaac Weld's *Travels Through North America,* where Stoneham, a tiny hamlet built by English settlers amidst 'highly picturesque' lakeland scenery, is given an enticing description. This vision, of course, was too good to last, and further Kantian study induced serious doubts. Kant's argument that we can know nothing of 'things in themselves' apart from our perceptions seemed to abolish the possibility of objective knowledge, and De Quincey felt that the depths of this philosophy had turned out *'culs-de-sac,* passages that lead to nothing; . . . upon every path a barrier faces you insurmountable to human steps'.[17] The idea that space and time, causation, even logic itself might all be merely properties of human consciousness with no basis in external reality was one which he found terrifying to confront: 'Let a man meditate but a little on this or other aspects of this transcendental philosophy, and he will find the steadfast earth itself rocking as it were beneath his feet.'[18]

Disappointment in Kant helped to cast him into another phase of depression, which was aggravated by anxiety over his health. Visiting his mother at Wrington near Bristol in the summer of 1805, he consulted 'the physicians at Clifton and the Bristol Hotwells' about certain symptoms which had alarmed him. They included a flushed face, 'nocturnal perspirations', a 'growing embarrassment of the respiration, and other expressions of gathering feebleness under any attempts at taking exercise'.[19] The physicians looked gloomy, and although they tried to sound encouraging their verdict came as a severe shock to De Quincey, for they diagnosed consumption. Out of 'the common decencies of humanity' they pointed out that constitutions varied infinitely, that a cure might be found or that the 'healing resources of nature herself' might fight off the disease, but there was no concealing the fact that a firm diagnosis of consumption was a death warrant. De Quincey himself 'offered at the first glance', he says, 'to a medical eye, every symptom of *phthisis* broadly and conspicuously developed'.[20] Out of the eight Quincey children, Thomas most resembled his father in physical constitution, and his father, as he was not likely to forget, had died of consumption at the age of thirty-nine.

The diagnosis, however, might have been rather different had Thomas not seen fit to conceal from his doctors one relevant fact: namely, that he was taking opium regularly. He found himself facing an unpleasant dilemma, for he had kept his opium-taking a secret from his mother, and could not now reveal it to doctors who were probably friends of hers. If the truth came out there would be terrible scenes — she disapproved even of theatre-going, so opium-taking would have seemed to her a monstrous form of self-indulgence — and the doctors would have ordered him to stop taking the drug. He would soon have drawn upon himself the vociferous zeal of an army of doctors, evangelical clergymen and strong-willed ladies eager to save him from himself, for Mrs Quincey was now within easy reach of Hannah More and Wrington was becoming a social centre for the 'Clapham Sect'. He could, of course, have stayed away from home to avoid recriminations, or he could have pretended to give up opium and then practised 'habitual and complex dissimulation' to keep on taking it; but either course would have been unpleasant, as would open defiance, which would have thrown him into what he chose to regard as a 'vortex of hotheaded ignorance upon the very name of opium'. It will be seen that the idea of giving up opium did not occur to him. It had already become indispensable, though physical dependence had not set in, and the habit was still only psychological.

So during the medical examinations he kept quiet and hugged his guilty secret to him, whilst the doctors diagnosed consumption from what were probably the symptoms of withdrawal from mild morphine-dependence. The ups and downs of his opium indulgence, perhaps including occasional prolonged sessions of two or three days, must have been disrupting his system sufficiently to produce, from time to time, symptoms of hectic complexion, abnormal sweating and general bodily discomfort which Thomas did not recognize (or at a deeper level, did not want to recognize) as connected with opium. Moreover, the drug can precipitate asthmatic attacks, and there are signs that he was subject to asthma at other periods of his life. Given that doctors at Bath and Clifton made their living by treating sufferers from consumption who sought relief at the West Country spas, this is quite enough to explain the diagnosis. And if the doctors did not know of a remedy, De Quincey did. It was a common fallacy amongst the working people in cold, damp areas that laudanum was a prophylactic against respiratory diseases. Lancashire cotton workers took it against consumption and bronchitis; in the Fen country it was held to be sovereign against 'malaria' and was said to be taken by the majority of the population.[21] Somehow, perhaps in Manchester, De Quincey had picked up this idea, and even as the fear of his illness made indulgence in opium more necessary to him, so his belief in it as a medicine enabled him to justify the indulgence to himself.

> I kept my own counsel; said nothing; awakened no suspicions; perse-
> vered more and more determinedly in the use of opium; and finally
> effected so absolute a conquest over all pulmonary symptoms as could
> not have failed to fix upon me the astonishment of Clifton, had not the
> sense of wonder been broken by the lingering time consumed in the
> several stages of the malady, and still more effectually by my own
> personal withdrawal from Clifton and its neighbourhoods.[22]

It may not have been solely fear of moral disapproval that led him
to keep his opium use a secret. Despite the widespread use of
laudanum in England some evidence was available —mainly in the
form of travellers' tales from the East — to show that opium could have
destructive effects on its users. One who read so copiously as De
Quincey could hardly have missed all this evidence. John Fryer, in the
late seventeenth century, had described the 'Devourers of *Opium*' in
Persia, explaining that 'having once begun, they must continue it, or
else they dye; . . . those that live at this rate are always as lean as
skeletons, and seldom themselves'. Sir John Chardin, around the same
period, had reported that 'the *Persians* find that it entertains their
Fancies with pleasant Visions, and a kind of Rapture', but had warned
of its addictive properties, adding that regular users suffered from
depression and physical pain and never lived long. Tavernier, a French
traveller, had noted that Turkish opium-takers 'dare not give over, for
fear of endangering their lives', and that they rarely reached the age of
forty. Hasselquist, in 1767, explained that opium was going out of use
amongst the Turks because it was 'a custom so evidently destructive'.[23]
It seems likely that De Quincey knew he was playing a dangerous game
but convinced himself that the hazards were exaggerated, putting
down tales of opium addiction as 'lies' and 'hotheaded ignorance'.
And after all, now that he had been diagnosed as consumptive, he had
the perfect justification. Opium might kill him or cure him; it could
hardly make his plight worse.

After leaving Wrington, his 'illness' diagnosed, he made a trip to
the Lake District, intending to call on Wordsworth. He got as far as
Coniston, but lost his nerve and turned back rather than face the great
man. His feelings of inadequacy were now intensified by guilty fears
that Wordsworth would think him rude for staying out of touch for so
long. From Coniston he went to Everton and the cottage where he had
spent so many troubled hours in recent years. Here he could be alone,
as he preferred to be, his only companion the opium whose mysterious

alchemy he observed with ever-growing curiosity. His *Confessions* give us a glimpse of him, now or in a later year, at Mrs Best's cottage, gazing out in rapt fascination at the strangeness and tranquillity of a landscape seen through opium:

> More than once it has happened to me, on a summer night, when I have been at an open window, in a room from which I could overlook the sea at a mile below me, and could command a view of the great town of L[iverpool], at about the same distance, that I have sat, from sun-set to sun-rise, motionless, and without wishing to move.[24]

The following year, 1806, saw him engaged on a second timid advance towards Grasmere, followed again by a retreat in confusion. In April he wrote to Wordsworth, apologizing for his two years' silence with a parade of excuses that included poverty, depression, anxiety over Richard's disappearance and the frightening struggle with 'pulmonary consumption'. His health, he said, was now 'fully restored', and he hoped soon to visit Grasmere. Might he call at Wordsworth's cottage?[25] Wordsworth replied enthusiastically and invited him to stay in late May. 'I cannot bear the thought', he wrote, 'that you should be in the North and I not see you.'[26] But De Quincey heard that Richard's ship, the Cambridge, was to dock at Liverpool, and postponed his holiday plans while he waited at Everton to greet his lost brother. Richard, however, did not arrive, and by the time hope of seeing him had faded, arrangements with Wordsworth had also broken down. Nonetheless, some time in August, De Quincey set out for the Lake District and, as before, made a secret approach to Grasmere from Coniston, coming close enough to see not only Grasmere Vale but the lake, the fields at the far side and, beyond the fields, 'a little white cottage gleaming from the midst of trees, with a vast and seemingly never-ending series of ascents rising above it to the height of more than three thousand feet'.[27] The cottage he knew to be Wordsworth's, but as he stood gazing at it he was overwhelmed once again by a sense of his own unworthiness and he shyly retreated ('like a guilty thing' as he puts it, echoing a favourite passage from Wordsworth's 'Immortality Ode'), returning 'faintheartedly' to Coniston.

He must have been in or near Coniston – perhaps, even, on his way to Grasmere – on 15 August. To this day he had long looked forward, for it was his twenty-first birthday, and henceforth his share of his father's modest fortune was his own to use as he pleased. There was an end to the legal authority of his mother and guardians. How he spent his birthday, or if he celebrated his coming-of-age, we do not know. It

135

must have prompted some self-examination, however, for sitting at 'the little rustic inn . . . at Church Coniston' on 18 August he jotted down a series of notes under the heading 'constituents of Happiness'.[28] He lists twelve 'constituents', the first of which is highly characteristic: 'A capacity of thinking – *i.e.*, of abstraction and reverie.' This is followed – perhaps as a necessary counterbalance – by, 'The cultivation of an interest in all that concerns human life and human nature . . . A fixed, and not merely temporary, residence in some spot of natural beauty . . . Such an interchange of solitude and interesting society as that each may give to each an intenser glow of pleasure' and, of course, '*Books*' – he underlines it – and 'some great intellectual project, to which all intellectual pursuits may be made tributary.' Number 7 is 'Health and vigour'. Then come 'moral elevation and purity' and 'a vast predominance of contemplation, varied with only so much of action as the feelings may prompt by way of relief and invigoration to the faculty of contemplation'.[29] Subsidiary to this is the tenth item, 'a more than ordinary emancipation from worldly cares, anxieties, and connections, and from all that is comprehended under the term business . . . To this end one's fortune should be concentrated in one secure depository, so as that the interest may be most easily collected; and all family arrangements should be definite and simple, and therefore not requiring much superintendence.' Number 11 is unexpected: 'The education of a child.' And the twelfth item introduces a rather touching personal confession:

> 12. One which, not being within the range of any man's control, I should not mention, only that experience has read me a painful lesson on its value – a personal appearance tolerably respectable. I do not mean to say attractive . . . but so far not repulsive, and on a level with the persons of men in general, as that though, apart from the intellectual superiority of its owner, there should be nothing to excite interest – there should . . . be nothing in its general effect to contradict that interest.

Where even 'a mediocrity of personal advantages' is lacking, he speculates, something may be done to mend the defect by 'temperate and unostentatious dignity of manners' and 'by acquiring a high literary name'. Clearly the main problem here was his smallness: it is amusing that he refers in such apt metaphor to his longing to be 'on a level with the persons of men generally', for this, literally, was the source of his anxiety. It would be absurd to take very seriously his notion that 'a high literary name' would compensate for his small stature, but it is a revealing example of the importance De Quincey consistently attached to his dreams of becoming a famous writer at a period long before he had written anything. Taking this goal with that of 'residence in some spot of eminent beauty', one is struck again by the extraordinary tenacity he showed in pursuing his central purposes. Always he moved gradually towards them, however apparently aimless in the short term.

From Coniston he seems to have returned to Oxford. If he had expected to be prosperous once his patrimony was in his hands he was now disappointed, for it came to a mere £2,600,[30] of which £600 was already owed for debts contracted during the past three years. Where the money had gone remains uncertain, but book-buying on a grand scale probably accounts for much of it. Still, for the immediate future borrowing and penny-pinching could stop and a degree of comfort entered his Oxford life. It seems that some belated recognition was also being given to his intellectual abilities. A Latin oration had to be written and delivered on some ceremonial occasion by one of his college, and De Quincey was given the task. He did it so well that instead of the politely bored silence which usually greeted such productions, 'it . . . caused some sensation in the auditors', and he was congratulated by senior members of the university. The head of the college took notice of him and his company began to be sought by the more intelligent of his fellow students, so that his isolation broke down to some extent. The fact that he could now afford to entertain a little no doubt helped.

The oration also brought home to his tutor the fact that here, unregarded, was an exceptionally promising student. The tutor therefore roused himself from the indifference he had so far displayed and began to urge De Quincey to try for honours rather than the more common ordinary degree. Perhaps this took place in 1807, when De Quincey would be in his fourth year at university and approaching the time when he might be expected to enter for the examinations for the degree of Bachelor of Arts. How long a student waited before taking his examinations was up to him, and De Quincey, far from feeling eager to try for honours, was not sure that he wished to take a degree at all. His usual indecisiveness, combined with contempt for his tutors (and, one suspects, a niggling anxiety as to whether, with all his brilliance, he had really done enough of the required work to succeed in the honours examination) led him to shy away from the prospect of finishing his studies and take refuge instead in grander, vaguer plans.

One such notion was that he would leave Oxford without a degree and go to travel and study in Germany, where 'the name of having been of Oxford would [be] of service and an introduction to him abroad as a scholar'.[31]

For the time being, he continued to stay away from college as much as possible. He also continued to take laudanum at irregular intervals for although the scare about consumption was over, he was now emotionally attached to the drug as a means of escape from the guilt and anxiety which so often oppressed him. An opium binge would be followed by bizarre dreams, and it was probably in late 1806 or 1807 that he began to confront the nightmare beings of whom he was to write many years later as 'Levana and Our Ladies of Sorrow'.[32] They appeared first in his daydreams, where fantasy was partly under conscious guidance, but soon, by a process that was to become very familiar to him, they made their way into dreams that came to him in sleep. The precise form of these dreams is not known but they were related in some way to the disturbing memories of early childhood which had begun to flood his dreams in 1804. The essential feature of this new phase was the brooding presence of a group of terrible women who struck profound foreboding into the sleeper's heart. There were four of them. One, their leader, seemed to be a goddess; the status of the other three was less certain. They watched him and they talked about him amongst themselves, the goddess whispering to the three ladies, who would reply silently, as if by mental communication or some language of hidden symbols. As they talked, he *knew*, with the strange certainty of dream-knowledge, that they were deciding his future, devoting him to dreadful experiences which he must suffer blindly since they would give him no hint of what lay in his path.[33]

It is easy enough to see in these ghostly visitants the avenging furies bred of guilt and a severe but heavily repressed anxiety about the future. At some level De Quincey must have sensed that he was failing to fulfil the responsible tasks of life, and that he was becoming dependent upon opium to help him endure the situation. During waking life he could avoid looking steadily at the truth, but in his dreams it was more difficult to hide, and his heart's misgivings returned upon him as three Fates or Weird Sisters and their tutelary goddess. We have seen that De Quincey always responded more intensely to women than to men, and he himself, recalling these dreams many years later, hinted that the mysterious women were composite figures, archetypes drawn from the females who peopled his own past.

The goddess herself, he says, he recognized 'by her Roman symbols' – whatever these were – as Levana. Lemprière's *Classical Dictionary*, the standard reference work of De Quincey's day, explains Levana as 'a goddess at Rome, who presided over the action of the person who took up from the ground a newly born child, after it had been placed there by the midwife. This ceremony was generally performed by the father, and so religiously observed, that the legitimacy of a child could be disputed without it.' She was also, says De Quincey, the goddess who 'controls the education of the nursery'. She must have been brought to his notice by Jean Paul Richter's *Levana, or the Doctrine of Education,* which appeared in 1806. It is obvious that we are dealing here with a symbol which goes back to De Quincey's earliest infancy, and one suspects that this nursery-goddess embodies memories of that 'elder nurse' who, towering over the child with colossal hand uplifted, struck him 'senseless to the ground', and who had broken the news of Elizabeth's imminent death. Perhaps Mrs Quincey contributed her share also. As for the three Ladies of Sorrow, he recognized only one of them, (although he felt that he would come to know the others) and this one seems to have been founded upon Elizabeth herself. She represented in some way the pain of the emotional wound left by Elizabeth's death, the grief he had never been able to accept or forget. He associated her particularly with the loss of loved ones. How much of the interpretation of these dreams, and how much even of their content, was the fanciful work of later years, or the elaboration into which these dream-motifs grew as they recurred, we cannot tell. De Quincey claims that they began during his time at Oxford and there is no obvious reason why this should be untrue.

In December 1806 he was again in London, disappointing his mother by failing to make a promised visit home,[34] and returning to college at the beginning of February, late for the new term. He was still restless and vaguely considered changing his college, though nothing came of it. During April he was in touch with Wordsworth, who was visiting London and hoping to see his elusive young admirer there. But once again De Quincey dithered, despite the news that Coleridge was also in London,[35] and when he at last went there, in May, the two poets had left. From India Uncle Thomas sent a gift of fifty pounds, and his mother knew him well enough to contact him in London when the money arrived, to tell him that he might draw it from Kelsall's bank; 'supposing', as she puts it, 'you may wish for the money while you are among the Booksellers'.[36] One would like to know what he was doing besides buying books. Was he simply reading, going to the opera and trying to forget about Oxford? Was he hunting for Ann? He stayed until 23 June, when he returned to Oxford to put in an appearance before the summer term ended,[37] and a month later he joined his mother at Bristol for the vacation.

It was there that someone brought him a thrilling piece of news: Coleridge was staying less than a day's journey away, at Nether Stowey in the Quantocks. Probably the message came by Joseph Cottle, who had contact with the Evangelical circle in Bristol and knew that Thomas was a worshipper of Coleridge. Certainly Cottle supplied De Quincey with a letter of introduction to Thomas Poole, with whom Coleridge was staying.[38] The news must have been coupled with an invitation: De Quincey found the idea of Coleridge less intimidating than that of Wordsworth, but still he would hardly have wished to travel forty miles without the assurance of some sort of welcome when he arrived. It must have been mentioned that he would be welcome to dinner and a bed for the night if he cared to go over to Nether Stowey and meet the great man.

Coleridge, with his wife and three children, had arrived at Poole's house early in June for a fortnight's stay which had gradually extended itself to some two months.[39] Coleridge was resting and hoping to improve his health before settling down to some work which might bring in the money he so desperately needed. Whether De Quincey knew this, and whether West Country gossip had already told him of Coleridge's opium addiction, the real source of his ill-health, is unknown. Certainly De Quincey knew that Coleridge had returned the previous year from a visit to Malta, where he had been in a vain attempt to recover his health, and had entertained some vague hopes of seeing him on his return. He was now more interested, perhaps, in Coleridge the philosopher than in Coleridge the poet. His delight in the *Ancient Mariner* had not abated, but he had sought out Coleridge's other published poems and been generally disappointed (most of the poems on which Coleridge's fame rests today had not yet appeared in print). But Mr Bree at Everton had told him that Coleridge now 'applied his whole mind to metaphysics and psychology'[40] and the information had excited De Quincey, for was he not now involved in just the same pursuit?

The news that he could so easily meet Coleridge startled the normally irresolute youth into decisive action and 'in that same hour' he left his mother's house and, on horseback, took the road for Nether

Stowey. With him he carried what he hoped would be a suitable gift in token of his admiration for S.T.C.: a copy of a scarce Latin pamphlet, *De Ideis,* by Hartley – the philosopher in whose honour S.T.C. had named his eldest son. He reached Poole's house early in the evening, but was told that Coleridge had taken his family on a round of visits to Somerset friends, and might be absent for days. Still, this was no great misfortune, for Poole and De Quincey took a liking to each other, and before long Poole was inviting the young man to stay and make himself at home until such time as the errant philosopher and his entourage should return. De Quincey (casting a hungry eye over Poole's remarkably well-stocked library) accepted at once.

Poole was a prosperous farmer and tanner, a self-educated man and a radical in politics. His loud voice, with a strong Somerset accent, could sound aggressive to those who did not know him well, and he was a compulsive and messy snuff-taker: not, perhaps, the sort of person with whom one would expect De Quincey to strike up a good relationship. But his cheerful humour, hospitality and genuine interest in intellectual matters appealed to his guest, who came to entertain considerable respect for him. The morning after De Quincey's arrival Poole took him on a pilgrimage to Alfoxden, where Wordsworth had lived ten years before. On their return, they dined at Poole's house, and, as De Quincey afterwards asserted, there took place a curious conversation about the absent Coleridge. Poole, it seems, began to speak of Coleridge's manner of spinning brilliant impromptu theories on philosophical themes in the course of conversation, and came round to confessing that he suspected Coleridge of 'borrowing' some of his theories from little-known authors and passing them off, with a great show of brilliance, as his own. As a case in point, Poole recalled that a few days previously S.T.C. had been holding forth on the subject of the Pythagorean philosophy, and had ventured to offer his own explanation of the well-known enigma as to why Pythagoras had forbidden his disciples to eat beans. To put it plainly, 'Coleridge', said Poole, 'gave us an interpretation which, from his manner, I suspect to have been not original. Think, therefore,' he challenged De Quincey, 'if you have anywhere read a plausible solution.'[41] De Quincey, according to his own testimony, had the answer ready at once. Yes: in a minor German writer ('a poor stick of a man', he hastened to add, 'not to be named on the same day with Coleridge') he had come across such a theory: beans in ancient Greece were used as tokens in voting, and the prohibition had referred not to eating but to meddling in politics. 'By Jove,' was Poole's reply, 'that is the very explanation he gave us!' From the way in which he had raised the subject, it appeared, says De Quincey, that Poole, far from disparaging his eminent friend, was acting kindly in trying to save De Quincey from the rude shock he might have suffered if he had suddenly begun to notice Coleridge, in philosophical conversation, stealing the matter of his arguments from German sources not merely without acknowledgement but with every pretence of originality. Poole had become aware of Coleridge as a kind of intellectual kleptomaniac who, in De Quincey's words, 'with the riches of El Dorado lying about him . . . would condescend to filch a handful of gold from any man whose purse he fancied',[42] and wanted to break the news gently to the young idealist.

If such a conversation did indeed take place, it must have come as an unpleasant surprise to De Quincey, however delicately Poole conveyed the information. But did it take place? We have only De Quincey's word for it, and the story is told in an essay written twenty-seven years later. After De Quincey published the anecdote in 1834, Poole himself commented plainly enough: '*It must be incorrect;* for as I never considered Coleridge as a plagiarist, I never could have said what he has given me.'[43] There are other reasons for regarding the story as a fabrication. Is it likely that Coleridge would have given himself away by the tone of his voice, had he wanted to conceal his obligation to a fellow writer? He was far too accomplished a rhetorician for that. In any case, there is hardly such a thing as plagiarism in conversation. We do not expect a man scrupulously to identify the sources of every bright idea he produces over the dinner table. But seen as a retrospective invention of De Quincey's the story makes much better sense. De Quincey was indeed jealous of the ideas he expressed in conversation, and could feel bitter towards those who used them without acknowledgment.[44] The example he chooses – the explanation of an obscure Pythagorean doctrine – could be of no possible interest to Poole, but concerns just the sort of historical riddle which had an inordinate interest for De Quincey. The obvious explanation is that in 1834, after Coleridge's death, De Quincey decided to break the news of S.T.C.'s casual way with literary obligations – resenting, perhaps, borrowings from his own conversation which could never be proved in print. To strengthen his position, he introduced the topic by means of a supposed statement from Poole, Coleridge's good friend, who, unlike De Quincey himself, could not be accused of literary rivalry. The matter of Coleridge's conversational borrowings having been dealt with, De

Quincey in his own voice could then bring up harder evidence concerning S.T.C.'s plagiarism in print.

We may safely assume, therefore, that Poole said nothing to tarnish the young man's glittering notion of Coleridge's character and intellect. De Quincey learned something of S.T.C.'s genius for procrastination, however, from Lord Egmont, who appeared a day or two later, with a canister of snuff as a present for Coleridge, who like Poole was a great snuff-taker. Egmont and Poole discussed Coleridge at length and Egmont 'spoke of Coleridge in the terms of excessive admiration' but insisted that the great man must somehow be persuaded to apply himself to some work adequate to his learning and talents. A History of Christianity was one suggestion. 'But at any rate,' said his Lordship, 'let him do something, for at present he talks very much like an angel, and does nothing at all.'[45] It seems possible that Egmont was as impressed as Poole had been by De Quincey's intelligence, for twelve years later (in the *Westmorland Gazette* for 2 January 1819) De Quincey claimed that 'at the age of twenty-two' he had declined the political patronage of 'a powerful nobleman', who apparently offered him the chance of a seat in Parliament. If this is true, it must refer to Egmont, whose brother was Chancellor of the Exchequer, and who wielded considerable political influence. Perhaps De Quincey and Egmont kept in touch after leaving Nether Stowey: the offer could hardly have been made during an hour or two's conversation at Poole's house.

De Quincey wanted to know when Coleridge could be expected back at Nether Stowey. Lord Egmont explained that he had lent his carriage to take the Coleridges to Bridgwater, where they were to stay for one night. The 'one night', it appeared, was something of a joke, for Coleridge never kept an engagement and there was no saying when he would be back. De Quincey decided to put an end to his suspense. Obtaining directions to the house of the Chubbs at Bridgwater, where S.T.C. was thought to be staying, he saddled his horse and set off. 'Riding down a main street of Bridgwater,' he says, 'I noticed a gateway corresponding to the description given me. Under this was standing, and gazing about him, a man about five feet eight inches tall,' whose person was 'broad and full, and tended even to corpulence; his complexion was fair, though not what painters technically style fair, because it was associated with black hair; his eyes were large, and soft in their expression; and it was from the peculiar appearance of haze or dreaminess which mixed in their light that I recognized my object. This was Coleridge.'[46]

De Quincey dismounted, entrusted his horse to an ostler at the nearby inn and went to introduce himself to Coleridge, who was startled at the sudden apparition of this shy, polite young stranger but quickly revealed his habitual warmth and friendliness. Inviting De Quincey into the Chubbs' house, he showed him to the drawing-room, rang the bell for refreshments with as little ceremony as if he had been in his own home and, explaining that there was to be 'a very large dinner-party' in the evening, invited him to stay and join the party – provided, he said, De Quincey did not mind a room full of strangers. Such an invitation was not to be declined.[47]

Feeling the moment to be right, De Quincey gave Coleridge the pamphlet he had brought as a gift. This unexpectedly set Coleridge off upon one of his extraordinary philosophical monologues. He began by discussing Hartley, then moved on to another of his youthful enthusiasms, Unitarianism, and explained the reasons for his abandonment of that creed for orthodox Trinitarianism. De Quincey was overawed by the flood of theological learning: the Coleridgean monologue swept along 'like some great river, the Orellana, or the St Lawrence', and he found it 'certainly the most novel, the most finely illustrated, and traversing the most spacious fields of thought by transitions the most just and logical, that it was possible to conceive'.[48] But it was hardly conversation in the normal sense: Coleridge 'did not leave openings for contribution' and De Quincey was far too shy to interrupt. This had been going on for an hour or more when (says De Quincey)

> the door opened, and a lady entered. She was in person full and rather below the common height; whilst her face showed to my eye some prettiness of a commonplace order. Coleridge paused upon her entrance; his features, however, announced no particular complacency, and did not relax into a smile. In a frigid tone he said, whilst turning to me, 'Mrs. Coleridge'; in some slight way he then presented me to her: I bowed; and the lady almost immediately retired.[49]

De Quincey soon realized that relations between Coleridge and his wife were strained, and he had the impression that Coleridge was depressed:

> At dinner, when a very numerous party had assembled, he [Coleridge] knew that he was expected to talk, and exerted himself to meet the expectation. But he was evidently struggling with gloomy thoughts that prompted him to silence, and perhaps to solitude: he talked with effort, and passively resigned himself to the repeated misrepresentations of several amongst his hearers.[50]

According to De Quincey, one further incident of particular significance took place before he left the Chubbs' house that night. De
Quincey claims to have mentioned 'accidentally' that a toothache had
obliged him to take a few drops of laudanum. On hearing this,
Coleridge 'entered into spontaneous explanation of [the] unhappy
overclouding of his life', and 'the peculiar emphasis of horror with
which he warned me against forming a habit of the same kind impressed upon my mind a feeling that he never hoped to liberate himself
from the bondage'.[51] It seems unlikely that Coleridge would have
opened his heart in this way to such a new acquaintance, and such a
young one. The episode looks like a retrospective fabrication on De
Quincey's part, of the same kind as the supposed conversation with
Poole about Coleridge's plagiarism. But it may possibly have happened. Coleridge was at about this period suffering the depression and
physical misery of a temporary withdrawal from opium[52] and within a
few months would be discussing with his friends the need for medical
supervision to help him break the habit. At some time on that late-
summer evening De Quincey and Coleridge took a walk around
Bridgwater together, so perhaps the conversation occurred then. One
cannot help wondering whether De Quincey had heard from Cottle of
Coleridge's addiction, and deliberately let slip an 'accidental' reference to laudanum to test the reaction. There is no way of knowing.

De Quincey left the Chubbs' house at ten, too excited to think of
sleep, and determined to return the forty miles to his mother's house,
rather than go back to Poole's. He rode slowly home under the stars,
through the silent and eerily deserted countryside (even the turnpike
gates, he says, were 'opened by a mechanical contrivance from a
bedroom window'), alone with his thoughts about 'the greatest man
that has ever appeared'.

De Quincey spent August and September at Everton.[53] On his return
he heard that Coleridge's family was staying with Mrs Coleridge's
sisters Eliza and Martha Fricker at College Street, Bristol. He sought
them out and soon became a regular visitor: after S.T.C. had arrived,
in October 1807, he copied De Quincey's Bristol address – 'Dowry
Parade, Hot Wells' – into his notebook.[54] De Quincey had begun to
visit College Street in September, whilst S.T.C. himself was still at
Poole's. The Coleridge children loved him and he sometimes looked
after them alone, giving Mrs Coleridge a few hours of much-needed

rest. On 15 September he wrote to his sister, 'Hartley Coleridge dined with me a few days ago; and I gained his special favour, I believe, by taking him – at the risk of our respective necks – through every dell and tangled path of Leighwood. However, Derwent still continues my favourite.'[55] Subsequently Coleridge joined his family. It was not a happy household. Coleridge was fretting about a course of lectures which he was to give at the Royal Institution and which, he said, required him to go at once to London to begin the preparation of his material. But he showed no sign of going, and Mrs Coleridge waited in uncertainty, not daring to ask about his movements for fear of provoking a tantrum. Coleridge had for some time been talking of separating from his wife on grounds of incompatibility (or, as he expressed it to his brother George, because 'Mrs Coleridge has a temper & general tone of feeling, which after a long – & for six years at least – a patient Trial I have found wholly incompatible with even an endurable Life, & such as to preclude all chance of my ever developing the talents, which my Maker has entrusted to me.')[56] So far Mrs Coleridge was not taking the threat very seriously, but the atmosphere at College Street must have been tense.

De Quincey must by now have become aware that Coleridge's troubles were connected with opium. But he also came to feel that there was a deeper cause, in the form of financial insecurity. He went to see Cottle, who confirmed that Coleridge was very short of money. Having expected this answer, De Quincey now asked Cottle diffidently whether he thought Coleridge would be willing to accept 'a hundred or two pounds'.[57] Cottle agreed to make tactful inquiries, and wrote to Coleridge, informing him that 'an opulent friend, a gentleman of the city, a man of great worth, and who has discernment enough rightly to estimate your genius' had proposed making him a present to ease his financial position.

> He is a man of so much delicacy [wrote Cottle], that (from an apprehension that you would be more likely to accept this sum from me than from a stranger) he wished this sum to come directly from *me*. To this, however, I decidedly objected; he then stipulated that his name should be concealed . . .
>
> I must tell you that there is not a man in the Kingdom of whom you would rather accept a favour, and I can assure you he is a character too respectable and too decided to express what he does not mean.[58]

Cottle met Coleridge to discuss the matter, and Coleridge's decision was stated in a letter on 13 October:

I need not say, that it is and has been the cause of serious meditation with me – yet I can give no other answer than what I gave you orally. Undoubtedly, calamities have so thickened on me for the last 2 years & more, that the pecuniary pressures of the moment are the only serious obstacles at present to any completion of those Works, which if compleated would make me easy . . . Finally therefore, if you know that my unknown Benefactor is in such circumstances, that in doing what he offers to do, he transgresses no duty, of morals or of moral prudence, and does not do that from feeling which after reflection may perhaps discountenance – I shall gratefully accept it as an unconditional Loan – which I trust that I shall be able to restore at the close of two years. This however I shall be able to know at the expiration of one year – and shall then beg to know the name of my benefactor, which I should then only feel delight in knowing when I could present to him some substantial Proof, that I have employed the tranquillity of mind which his Kindness had enabled me to enjoy, in sincere endeavours to benefit my fellow-men, now and hereafter.[59]

Cottle communicated this to De Quincey who at once (according to Cottle) announced the intention of 'lending' Coleridge £500. Cottle, startled, persuaded him to moderate his generous enthusiasm a little and limit the sum to £300.[60] This was lucky, for no doubt De Quincey had given the impression that he had a large fortune at his disposal, whereas in truth £500 would have been roughly a quarter of the capital remaining to him. It says much for De Quincey's real warm-heartedness that he was willing to make such a gift; and there was a kind of humility in this rather desperate bid to do something of value by helping a man whom he believed to be immeasurably his superior.

The money had to be obtained from Mr Kelsall, who still had charge of the Quincey finances. His reaction to the proposed gift is not known: perhaps he called Thomas a fool, but he paid out the money and Cottle handed it over. Coleridge received the £300 gratefully, and Cottle was able to tell De Quincey that he had dropped some pretty broad hints as to the identity of the benefactor:

I am satisfied that Coleridge entertains *no doubt* of the source whence the money was derived. The tenor of my conversation with him respecting you must have been conclusive to a mind much less penetrating than Coleridge's, and in a letter which I afterwards addressed to him, I observed the pleasure it wd give me to learn that he had an opportunity of introducing Mr. de Quincey into one of his select literary Societies. I also further revealed that I also knew you to be 'a noble-minded young man'.[61]

If Cottle's well-intentioned behaviour lacked the fastidious discretion De Quincey might have preferred, at least it did no harm, for by the time the transaction was concluded De Quincey was a firm friend of the whole Coleridge family. Since early September Coleridge had been planning to send Mrs Coleridge and the children home to Keswick and make his own way to London, there to submerge himself in lecturing and literary work which had been too long neglected. This was a troublesome business, however. 'It is my present plan,' he wrote, 'to accompany Mrs. C. northward as far as Liverpool (she is at present at Bristol – & it would be cruel indeed to let her go such a journey with so many children by herself) . . . from Liverpool Mrs. C. can easily go without further protection to Keswick – & I mean to diverge to London.'[62] De Quincey suggested a better plan: he would accompany Sara Coleridge and the three children as far as Grasmere, where they intended to pay Wordsworth a visit. In short, De Quincey had at last found the right moment to visit Wordsworth, when he could arrive not as an idle sightseer but as an accredited friend of the Coleridges, glowing with virtuous responsibility as he kindly took care of the poet's family. He was already a favourite with 'Mrs. C.' and the children, Hartley, Derwent and Sara junior. Mrs Coleridge was delighted. 'This was a pleasant scheme for me,' she told Poole later, 'only I was obliged to give up my visits to Birmingham and Liverpool, which I was rather loth to do ['Mr. de Q. being in a hurry on account of his being obliged to be at Oxford by the 16th Novr.'], but it was a small evil when set against the great convenience of travelling all the way in Chaises, and under the protecting wing of kind Mr. de Q.'[63]

The party set out at the end of October. De Quincey was a favourite with the children, and kept them amused for much of the tedious four-day journey. The four-year-old Sara was especially taken with him: years later she remembered how he 'jested with me on the journey, and declared I was to be his wife, which I partly believed. I thought he behaved faithlessly in not claiming my hand.'[64] Arrived in Liverpool, the Coleridges stayed with a Mr Koster and his family whilst De Quincey visited friends at Everton. The Kosters' home was a centre of cultural life in Liverpool, and one of their visitors during the Coleridges' stay was Madame Catalani, the Italian soprano, who was singing at the Opera. De Quincey met her and heard her sing: he would not willingly have missed the opportunity of meeting the singer who was said to surpass in voice and beauty his favourite Grassini.[65]

From Liverpool they went on to Grasmere. The journey took a day and a half and they arrived on 4 November. They reached Ambleside at three in the afternoon but the chaise covered the last few miles so slowly that De Quincey and the children grew impatient. They climbed down from the chaise when it reached the top of White Moss Common, the hill that overlooks Town End, the southern part of the village, and walked together down into the valley, where a sudden turn of the road brought them 'in sight of a white cottage, with two yew-trees breaking the glare of its white walls'. With a shock, De Quincey recognized it as the cottage he had glimpsed from beyond the lake, the summer before: Wordsworth's cottage. He stopped, the 'old panic' starting to rise within him. But Hartley had run on ahead, and was now turning in at the garden gate, so De Quincey took the plunge and followed him towards the cottage door.

> I heard a step [he recalls], a voice, and, like a flash of lightning, I saw the figure emerge of a tallish man, who held out his hand, and saluted me with most cordial expressions of welcome.[66]

But already the chaise was drawing up outside: Wordsworth went out to the road to greet Mrs Coleridge whilst De Quincey, dazed, 'mechanically went forward into the house'. Stepping into the small, dim 'house-place' or parlour – an oak-panelled room with a low ceiling and one diamond-paned window – he came face to face with Mary Wordsworth, the poet's wife, and Dorothy, his sister. Introductions were made, and De Quincey was ushered upstairs to a little sitting-room, where a fire was burning. Wordsworth soon followed, and De Quincey had leisure now to take in the appearance of the man he had so long worshipped from a distance. He found Wordsworth 'not, upon the whole, a well-made man': there was a 'narrowness and a droop about the shoulders', and although he was powerfully built and quite tall (five feet ten inches, De Quincey estimates), his legs seemed in some way not quite in proportion with his body – a little too short, perhaps? De Quincey noted these details, one feels, not wholly without satisfaction. So sensitive was he about his own personal appearance that he may have been relieved to find Wordsworth's physique less than godlike. The poet's face, however, lived up to expectations: the forehead 'remarkable for its breadth and expansive development', the eyes fine and powerfully intellectual in expression, the mouth firm. (De Quincey was later to be startled by Wordsworth's close resemblance to a portrait of Milton.)[67]

At half-past five tea was served, and to De Quincey's surprise it was 'high tea' in the rustic North Country fashion, the main meal of the day. But he found the family's conversation 'superior by much, in its tone and subject, to any which [he] had heard before – one exception only being made in favour of Coleridge',[68] although he was too timid to take much part in it himself. After the meal there was more talk and De Quincey was honoured with some of Wordsworth's views on poetry, in the course of which the poet took up a translation of Tasso into English verse and read aloud to illustrate some critical point. Perhaps he was telling De Quincey of his recent attempt to translate the *Orlando Furioso* of Tasso's master Ariosto: we know that De Quincey saw part of his translation at about this time.[69]

At eleven o'clock, De Quincey was shown to his room: 'a pretty bedroom, about fourteen feet by twelve' which he guessed from its size to be the best bedroom in the tiny cottage. A humbling sense of his hosts' unaffected generosity mingled with the excitement of finding himself at last in Wordsworth's house and favoured with the great man's conversation. And he fell asleep in the happiness of being relieved at last from the weight of guilt and frustration which had lain on his heart for the past four years. No longer would he need to suffer 'vexation and self-blame, almost self-contempt, at my own want of courage to face the man whom of all since the Flood I most yearned to behold'.[70]

Early next morning, recalls De Quincey,

> I was awoke by a little voice, issuing from a little cottage bed in an opposite corner, soliloquizing in a low tone. I soon recognized the words – 'Suffered under Pontius Pilate; was crucified, dead, and buried'; and the voice I easily conjectured to be that of the eldest among Wordsworth's children.[71]

This was four-year-old John Wordsworth. When the child had finished reciting his creed, De Quincey got up, dressed and emerged from the room. To his surprise, he found Dorothy Wordsworth in the sitting-room making breakfast with her own hands. 'No urn was there; no glittering breakfast service; a kettle boiled over the fire, and everything was in harmony with these unpretending arrangements.'[72] Accustomed to the genteel households of Mrs Quincey and her circle, where servants were taken for granted and domestic labour went on unobtrusively behind the scenes, De Quincey was startled, almost embarrassed, by the spectacle. Indeed, he seems to have spent much of this first stay at Town End in a comical state of perplexity, between awe at the Wordsworth's intellectual grandeur and dismay at the countrified plainness of their life-style. The poet's own words — 'Plain living, and high thinking' — came irresistibly to mind, but the fastidious De Quincey found that it was one thing to admire the theory, quite another to see it put into practice.

After breakfast, despite the rain, he set out with William and Dorothy for a walk, making the circuit of Grasmere Lake and Rydal Water (about six miles in all) and getting his first close look at Lakeland scenery with companions whose knowledge of the district — not to mention their sense of the picturesque — left nothing to be desired. De Quincey rapidly came to like Dorothy. At first he seems to have found her as disconcerting as the ménage which, in a way, she epitomized. She was not pale-skinned, as were the well-bred ladies he was accustomed to meeting socially. 'Rarely,' he recalled, 'in a woman of English birth, had I seen a more determinate gipsy tan.'

> Her eyes were . . . wild and startling, and hurried in their motion. Her manner was warm and even ardent; her sensibility seemed constitutionally deep; and some subtle fire of impassioned intellect apparently burned within her, which, being alternately pushed forward into a conspicuous expression by the irresistible instincts of her temperament, and then immediately checked, in obedience to the decorum of her sex and age [she was now nearly 36], and her maidenly condition, gave to her whole demeanour, and to her conversation, an air of embarrassment, and even of self-conflict, that was almost distressing to witness. Even her very utterance and enunciation often suffered, in point of clearness and steadiness, from the agitation of her excessive organic sensibility.[73]

Obviously her manner confused De Quincey, playing havoc with his assumptions about female behaviour: Dorothy was a lady who cared nothing for decorum, a 'natural spirit', yet full of intellect and refined sensibility. Noticing how the intensity of her feelings sometimes overcame her so that at moments of excitement she could only stammer, he probably felt a grateful sense of kinship, for one of his own most painful social embarrassments was that whenever a topic of conversation arose in which he felt deeply interested, he found it hard to stop his voice from trembling and revealing too much emotion, creating, he feared, 'something too like *scene*'[74] — one reason for his shyness in company. He was also impressed with a sense that Dorothy had contributed a vital element to the sensibility of her brother, so that his poems were in a way a collaboration of brother and sister. Wordsworth's intellect, 'by its original tendency, too stern, too austere, too much enamoured of an ascetic harsh sublimity', had been 'humanized' by his sister, who had 'first *couched* his eye to the sense of beauty' and 'engrafted, with her delicate female touch, those graces upon the ruder growths of his nature which . . . clothed the forest of his genius with a foliage corresponding in loveliness and beauty to the strength of its boughs and the massiveness of its trunks'.[75] The attraction of such a relationship for De Quincey, whose first serious unhappiness had come through the death of his sister, must have been powerful. At the same time Dorothy fell short of his feminine ideal. He observed 'the glancing quickness of her motions, and other circumstances in her deportment (such as her stooping attitude when walking), which gave an ungraceful, and even an unsexual character to her appearance when out-of-doors. She did not', he notes tartly, 'cultivate the graces which preside over the person and its carriage.'[76]

De Quincey certainly made a good impression on Dorothy. 'He is a remarkable and very interesting young man,' she wrote to Lady Beaumont:

> very diminutive in person, which, to strangers, makes him appear insignificant; and so modest, and so very shy that even now I wonder how he ever had the courage to address himself to my Brother by letter. I think of this young man with extraordinary pleasure, as he is a remarkable instance of the power of my Brother's poems, over a lonely and contemplative mind, unwarped by any established laws of taste (As far as it is in my power to judge from his letters, and the little I have seen of him) – a pure and innocent mind![77]

Dorothy's picture of the young man as a walking testimony to the beneficial effects of her Brother's poems is partly a matter of sisterly partiality, but it may well be the view of himself which De Quincey preferred to foster. He was overawed by his surroundings. The role of modest and guileless disciple would give him an acceptable position in the household, whilst relieving him of the responsibility to contribute anything striking to the conversation.

Mrs Coleridge and her children left on 5 November to pursue their journey north to Keswick – but not without inviting De Quincey to pay them a visit at Greta Hall, and to meet Southey, in one half of whose house they lived. The Wordsworths were to make a trip north to Ullswater the next day so De Quincey decided to go with them, leave the party at Ullswater and go on with Wordsworth to Penrith, from where he could easily walk the seventeen miles to see Southey and the Coleridges. He assumed that the journey to Ullswater would be made on foot, since the Wordsworths kept no horses, but another surprise awaited him, for when the family assembled ready to leave on the third morning, up to the cottage door trundled a common farm cart driven by a local girl. In this, he realized, the company was to ride. 'Such a vehicle,' he recalls, 'I had never in my life seen used for such a purpose; but what was good enough for the Wordsworths was good enough for me.'[78]

He climbed in with a good grace and the cart set off for Ambleside, attracting (to De Quincey's evident relief) no surprised looks from the passers-by, most of whom seemed to know Dorothy, who greeted everyone they met. From Ambleside the strange equipage (the girl sitting neatly balanced on the shafts to drive) turned northward and ascended Kirkstone Pass, where the road became so steep that the passengers had to get down from the cart and walk. They rode down in the evening to Patterdale where they left the cart at an inn and mounted horses which stood ready for them. Riding along the shores of Ullswater De Quincey was entranced by the spectacle of the thick woods and the buildings occasionally glimpsed among them by the moonlight which at every bend in the road sent up brilliant gleams from the surface of the lake. They spent the night 'at the foot of the lake in a house called Ewsmere', and in the morning De Quincey and Wordsworth left the others and struck out on foot through the woods for Penrith. It seems to have been at some point on this journey that Wordsworth read De Quincey part of his new poem 'The White Doe of Rylstone'. They dined at Emont Bridge outside Penrith, then went to Brougham Hall, the home of Wordsworth's cousin Captain John Wordsworth, a mile or two from Penrith. Here Wordsworth left De Quincey and departed to attend to some private business. He was to be away all the following day so in the morning De Quincey walked over to Greta Hall to see Southey and Mrs Coleridge.

Southey turned out to be pleasant in manner and a generous host, but De Quincey found him rather reserved, and was chiefly struck by the oddity of his appearance — he had 'a remarkable habit of looking up into the air, as if looking at abstractions', and he wore 'a short jacket and pantaloons' which gave him 'much the air of a Tyrolese mountaineer'.[79] De Quincey stayed at Greta Hall and was joined the next day by Wordsworth. From the manner of the two poets he gathered that they were not on particularly friendly terms. At first, cool politeness prevailed. Sources of tension were certainly not lacking: Southey had been harsh in his private criticism of Wordsworth's recent *Poems in Two Volumes*[80] and there was disagreement over the perennial question of what to do about Coleridge, whose wife and children were left under the care of the overworked Southey whilst Coleridge himself, at Bristol or London, struggled with opium and the materials for his Royal Institution lectures. But Southey and Wordsworth preserved a 'mutual esteem', in De Quincey's words, and passed the day amicably enough. Wordsworth stayed overnight and the next morning at breakfast both men were in high good humour. They discussed politics, and De Quincey received possibly the biggest shock he had yet experienced when he heard the great Wordsworth 'giving utterance to sentiments which seemed absolutely disloyal'. His views – tame enough, no doubt – seemed to De Quincey, who had been 'brought up in a frenzied horror of jacobinism . . . in the abhorrence of French excesses, and to worship the name of Pitt', astonishingly subversive. Too young to have shared in the idealism which accompanied the early days of the French Revolution, he was bewildered and hurt at hearing 'opinions avowed most hostile to the reigning family' and to monarchy in general. Characteristically his response was one of self-doubt. If Wordsworth said such things, could they be wrong? And he could not help laughing when Southey proposed that for the good of England the royal family should be supplied with plenty of money and transported to Botany Bay – a notion which Southey turned, impromptu, into a verse petition culminating in the lines

> Therefore, old George, by George we pray
> Of thee forthwith to extend thy sway
> Over the great Botanic Bay![81]

With this the breakfast party broke up and the two guests began their journey back to Grasmere.

On the last day of De Quincey's stay at Town End William and Dorothy had a long-standing invitation to dine with 'a literary lady about four miles distant'. (Mary Wordsworth, it appears, was not invited.) Dorothy, who had already grown fond of De Quincey's company, suggested that he accompany them: his coach to the south would not be passing until after midnight so there would be no risk of his missing it – which was just as well, for unless he returned to Oxford on the night of 12 November he would miss the compulsory minimum of his university term. The dinner was rather a remarkable experience. The hostess, a local woman of some social standing, was not pleased to find an extra guest at her table, and 'the dinner', recalls De Quincey, 'was the very humblest and simplest I had ever seen' and 'flagrantly insufficient in quantity'. One course consisted of a single pheasant, which was to serve six people. The five guests, out of good manners, declined a share of the pheasant, whereupon the hostess complacently ate up the whole bird herself. The company kept straight faces, but as soon as they were out of the house Dorothy 'laughed with undissembled glee' whilst Wordsworth 'thought it was too grave a matter for laughing – he was thoroughly disgusted, and said repeatedly, "A person cannot be honest, positively not honest, who is capable of such an act." '82

By ten o'clock they were at Ambleside, where De Quincey took leave of his host and hostess and entered the post-chaise which was to take him to meet the mail coach at Kendal. He rode along the banks of Windermere and, as the road turned away from the lake, passing under the walls of an estate called Elleray, the odd thought struck him that the road he was now taking might in years to come be as familiar to him as his own home. The idea was already forming in his mind that, once finished at Oxford, he might return here to live. He tried to sense prophetic echoes from the future that might tell him if it would be so, if he moved at this moment as a stranger through his own future environment. But he could not be sure.

6
Irksome Employments

He was back at college on 14 November, and almost at once fell ill with a mysterious illness, diagnosed as 'a determination of blood to the head',[1] which made it hard for him to read or write. It may have been simply a reaction to the excitement of his visit to the Wordsworths, but it came at a bad time, for he had decided to take his examinations early in the summer and much of the basic work had not even been started. The illness enabled him to procrastinate through the term and he spent Christmas in London, where a doctor advised him to drink no wine and avoid bending his head downwards. This treatment (or the relief of being away from Oxford) seemed to work, and he felt better. He stayed in London through January and February 1808. Dorothy Wordsworth had asked him to attend Coleridge's lectures at the Royal Institution and take notes for her.[2] He missed the first lecture on 15 January, but was soon in touch with Coleridge, who was living at 348 Strand over the offices of the *Courier* newspaper.

Coleridge was in a bad way. His introductory lecture, laying the ground for a critical estimate of Shakespeare, had left him prostrate, adding nervous exhaustion to the physical miseries of half-hearted attempts at giving up opium. De Quincey saw him almost daily and for a time became his nurse, agent and secretary, recommending a doctor, scouring the shops for rare books Coleridge needed, and even supplying quotations for use in the lectures when Coleridge was too ill to find them himself. His intelligence and sympathy made such an impression that Coleridge even solicited his judgment on his poems. 'I do earnestly ask of you as a proof of Friendship,' he wrote, 'that you will so far get over your natural modesty & timidity, as without reserve or witholding to tell me exactly what you think and feel on the perusal of any thing, I may submit to you – for even if it be only your feelings, they will be valuable to me.'[3] He seems to have become dependent on De Quincey: a few days without a visit elicited from him a miserable letter full of self-pity and gruesome details of his ailments. His rooms were noisy and uncomfortable. The building was in a perpetual clatter with people coming and going about the *Courier* offices, the rattle of heavy traffic outside and the creaking of the hand-presses on which the paper was printed adding to the din. Coleridge dwelt at the top of the house, but the servant, Mrs Brainbridge, lived in the basement and there was no bell. De Quincey became accustomed to the apparition of S.T.C., risen from his sick bed, 'picturesquely enveloped in nightcaps, surmounted by handkerchiefs indorsed upon handkerchiefs, shouting from the attics . . . down three or four flights of stairs,' trying to make himself heard with long-drawn cries of 'Mistress Brainbridge! I say, Mistress Brainbridge!'[4]

It may have been now that Coleridge warned De Quincey against taking opium. He later claimed to have 'pleaded with flowing tears, and with an agony of forewarning. [De Quincey] utterly denied it, but I fear that I had even then to *deter* perhaps not to forewarn.'[5] It seems that De Quincey was still keeping his opium-taking a secret, but he might have seen enough to frighten him, for Coleridge was suffering from fits of diarrhoea and vomiting; for hours at a time he would perspire until his clothes were soaked; sometimes he could not work or think coherently for days together.[6] His second lecture, prepared under these conditions and delivered on 5 February, was all that might have been expected. Coleridge was visibly 'struggling with pain and overmastering illness. His lips were baked with feverish heat . . . and, in spite of the water which he continued drinking through the whole course of his lecture, he often seemed to labour under an almost paralytic inability to raise the upper jaw from the lower . . . No heart, no soul, was in anything he said.'[7]

This lecture looked as if it might be the last. The Wordsworths heard 'such alarming accounts of the state of . . . poor Coleridge's health'[8] that William travelled up to London to see him and, if possible, bring him back to the Lake District. (Coleridge himself seems to have told the Wordsworths that he was dying – news which they took with a pinch of salt.) Wordsworth reached London in late February and stayed for about a month. He did not take Coleridge back to the North but his company gave De Quincey great pleasure. He had brought the manuscript of 'The White Doe of Rylstone', intending to have it printed at once, and De Quincey had the excitement of hearing him read the new poem in its final form. Coleridge seemed rather better and Wordsworth, who failed to understand the nature of Coleridge's addiction, briskly decided that there was nothing wrong with

157

him – or nothing that 'could not be cured, or at least prevented, by himself'.[9] He seems to have assumed, naturally enough, that it was opium-taking which made Coleridge ill: the reverse of the truth, for an improvement in health was generally a sign that the dosage had been increased again. On 3 March Coleridge was well enough to give a tea party in his rooms. Wordsworth came, of course, and Lamb and William Godwin were there, as well as Southey, Daniel Stuart (editor of the *Courier*) and others. De Quincey expected fiery argument or startling behaviour from Godwin, the philosophical anarchist, but he turned out to be quiet and reserved. Coleridge was in low spirits, Wordsworth was tired and Southey was not in talkative mood so it fell to Lamb to entertain the company, which he did in a style that went some way to correct the bad impression De Quincey had taken away from their previous meeting.

The party marked the end of De Quincey's visit to London, and on 5 March he was back at Oxford with his examination two months away and a vast amount of reading before him. He began to feel ill again (this time his mother sent him a special reading stand so that he could read without bending his head!) and anxiety affected his work badly. He had done so little lately that he told Dorothy Wordsworth he would have to read thirty-three Greek tragedies in one week. Worry kept him awake at night, and though he forced himself to read, he could take nothing in. The feeling of mental paralysis recalled the nightmares of his childhood: 'finding the whole university on tiptoe for the approaching prize-fighting and myself in a state of palsy as to any power of exertion, I felt very much as in dreams which I recollect where I have been chased by a lion and spellbound from even attempting to escape.'[10] Sometimes he would take refuge in affected nonchalance. 'The motives to all this labour [he told Dorothy] are . . . inadequate; for the difference between success and non-success are the being placarded on all the college walls as the Illustrious Mr. A.B.C. or 2ndly, as the *Praiseworthy* Mr. A.B.C. or 3rdly, the not being placarded at all'[11] – a pose encouraged, perhaps, by the Wordsworths' lack of respect for academic qualification: recalling his own university examinations in *The Prelude*, William had written frankly

> Such glory was but little sought by me,
> And little won.[12]

The examination system was certainly of a kind to produce the greatest anxiety. The range of subjects covered was wide; theology,

Greek and Latin language and literature, classical philosophy, logic, ancient history and mathematics might all be included. There was no standard list of books or topics, the candidate having the responsibility of choosing which books, and how many, he was prepared to 'give up'. This was a nerve-racking decision. If the candidate chose too few he would not gain the respect of his examiners; if he chose too many he risked overtaxing his memory, or being thought arrogant and faced with harder questions. In general, students contending for the highest class offered about fifteen books – the whole work of one poet or historian counting as a single 'book'. De Quincey later claimed that he had decided 'instead of giving in any particular Greek books', to offer 'Greek literature generally'.[13] If so, no wonder he was overworked. There was no way to avoid 'cramming', since the questions often concerned trivial details, and he lamented the necessity of 'learning by heart immense . . . collections of unassorted details'.[14]

The examinations were open to spectators and were conducted orally in part, so that the candidate needed to think and remember on his feet in front of an audience. The oral examination might last up to three hours, and questions might be given in either Latin or English.[15] The average student need only scrape through, the examiners putting a few simple questions and dismissing him. For a student who wanted to distinguish himself the case was very different, and whatever he may have told the Wordsworths, De Quincey did want to distinguish himself. In intellectual matters nothing less than excellence would satisfy his hunger for self-respect. He worked as hard as possible. When Dorothy wrote to tell him of the tragic deaths of George and Sarah Green, who had died in a blizzard on the fells above Easedale leaving six children destitute, he sent five pounds to the subscription the Wordsworths were raising for the children's support but had no time to go collecting amongst his fellow students. 'I am now reading every day for 18 hours out of the 24 – and never go at all to bed but only fall asleep on a sofa when I can keep awake no longer,' he explained. 'I am afraid you will think this very foolish; but, having been treated with great kindness by my college, I cannot endure to disappoint their expectations if the time I have remaining will enable me to do what I have undertaken.'[16] When he wrote this, on 8 May 1808, the examinations had already started, but he had put his name down under Q, which gained him a week or two, as candidates were examined in alphabetical order. From his unhappy childhood days with Hall, De Quincey had carried a particular hatred of that 'learning' which consisted of packing the memory with disconnected fragments. His brilliance of mind could not protect him from mental exhaustion, and a touch of fear was added by his belief that mental strain could bring on 'hydrocephalus'. It seems likely that in these last weeks he relied a good deal on opium.

His two days of examinations began on 14 May. There are conflicting accounts of what happened, but it seems that Latin was examined on the first day, a Saturday, and Greek was to be examined on the Monday, the Sunday between being left clear. The first day's examination went very well, and it is said that in the evening one of the examiners spoke to a friend of De Quincey's at Worcester College and called De Quincey 'the cleverest man I ever met with', adding that if his performance on the second day equalled that of the first he would 'carry everything before him'. Interestingly enough, the friend's reply was that 'he feared De Quincey's *viva voca* examination would be comparatively imperfect, even if he presented himself for examination, which he rather doubted'.[17] This was an astute prediction, for on the Sunday De Quincey lost his nerve. He may not have realized that his work on the first day had been outstanding: after so much tension the examination must have seemed an anticlimax and the boy who had offered the whole of Greek literature as his field had a pride which could not face the risk of an inferior result. Instead of staying for the second examination he fled, and when his name was called on Monday 16 May he was not to be found. His name was kept on the college books until 20 December 1810, and it seems that it would still have been possible for him to return and stand examination for a degree until that time. But he never went back.

He went to London, his usual place of refuge. Coleridge was lecturing again, and on 13 June De Quincey was in the audience. When Coleridge left town De Quincey stayed on, solitary, to attend the wedding of an Oxford friend. Early in June Dorothy wrote, inviting him to stay at the Wordsworths' new house, Allan Bank. She made it an enticing prospect. 'We have plenty of room and quietness for you,' she wrote. 'You may always have a sitting-room below stairs, and a bedroom above, to yourself.'[18] But he stayed in London through the summer and had at least one period of illness.[19] Then he went to Everton, still alone.[20] Perhaps he was avoiding his family because of the Oxford fiasco. At last, late in October, he accepted Dorothy's invitation and set off for Grasmere. Wordsworth, having found that the move to a larger house had led to a corresponding rise in the number of visitors, sent a note that was not wholly enthusiastic – 'We shall be very happy to see you; though unfortunately our house is so full we cannot accommodate you with a bed. Coleridge is with us'[21] – but he was not deterred, and when he arrived room was found for him, by the economy of letting him share a bed with little John Wordsworth.

Allan Bank was psychologically as well as physically crowded. The Wordsworths had a new baby, Catharine, born in September, and besides Coleridge himself, always a troublesome inmate, the Coleridge boys, Hartley and Derwent, were there at weekends. Sara Hutchinson, Mary Wordsworth's sister and the object of Coleridge's hopeless passion, was also staying, as (for one week) was Mrs Coleridge herself, now theoretically 'separated' from her husband. With servants the household numbered around thirteen. To enrich the atmosphere further, autumn was revealing the defects of the new house: the rooms were cold, the cellars were wet and the chimneys smoked badly so that furniture and carpets were sprinkled with soot. Coleridge seems to have spent the daylight hours mainly in bed, emerging to face the household at mid-afternoon and working late into the night.[22] He was struggling against illness, opium, business problems and his own disorganized nature to recover his fortunes by launching a 'periodical essay', to be called *The Friend*. With Sara Hutchinson providing secretarial assistance he laboured over subscription lists, printing and distribution arrangements and the collection of literary and philosophical materials.

Wordsworth, meanwhile, had plunged into politics. The Peninsular War had reached a crucial phase in August 1808 when the British Army had seemed on the point of expelling the French from Portugal. Great public indignation had been aroused when, instead of annihilating the French on the battlefield, the British commanding officers had decided to call a halt and clear Portugal of the French at the minimum military cost by agreeing to evacuate them in British ships and return them unmolested to France. In retrospect, it seems that the measure was justified in military terms, for it opened Portugal as a base for the British campaign to drive Napoleon's armies from Spain; but at the time it was widely regarded as a cowardly capitulation to short-term interests and an insult to the Portuguese. The Convention of Cintra, the agreement setting out the terms of the evacuation, became the subject of angry protests in Britain and the government was forced to institute a public inquiry. The shock-waves reached Grasmere. Wordsworth's feelings had been moved by the brave resistance of the Spanish and Portuguese peoples and he felt them betrayed by the Convention. In October he and Southey were organizing a public meeting and hoping to send the King a protest signed by the local gentry. When these plans failed, Wordsworth decided to throw his indignation into a pamphlet attacking the Convention. He began writing it in November,[23] hoping to publish it as a series of essays in the *Courier* 'for the sake of immediate and wide circulation'[24] before its appearance as a pamphlet.

It was into this buzzing complexity of literary, political and emotional energies that De Quincey entered when he arrived at Allan Bank. There was ample opportunity for him to play his accepted role as humble assistant to Wordsworth and Coleridge. He was excited about the projected *Friend* and whilst the Wordsworths took a merely tolerant view of it as just another of Coleridge's foredoomed, impractical schemes, he set to work collecting subscriptions. His contacts at Oxford, his mother and her friends, his sisters and even the Kelsalls were sent copies of the prospectus and persuaded to sign up. In addition De Quincey put himself down for five copies, the largest private subscription order in *The Friend*'s mailing list.[25] He also pondered the question of how *The Friend* was to be printed. There was no press at Grasmere or Keswick, which would make its production a slow business. He therefore proposed that they should establish 'The Grasmere Press', bringing a printing press, type and a compositor to Grasmere at his expense[26] and printing not only *The Friend* but fine books as well. 'It is his determination', wrote Coleridge, 'to have printed under his own Eye immaculate Editions of such of the eminently great Classics, English and Greek as most need it – and to begin with the poetic Works of Milton.'[27] Coleridge had not yet recognized De Quincey as a fellow-dreamer and procrastinator, and was impressed by his apparent energy.

De Quincey quickly became part of the family at Allan Bank. Wordsworth seemed just a shade reserved, but the women and children accepted him wholeheartedly. In December Dorothy wrote to Mrs Clarkson:

> Mr. De Quincey, whom you would love dearly, as I am sure I do, is beside me, quietly turning over the leaves of a Greek book – and God be praised we are breathing a clear air, for the night is calm, and this room (the Dining-room) only smokes very much in a high wind. Mr.

De Q. will stay with us, we hope, at least till the Spring. We feel often as if he were one of the Family – he is loving, gentle and happy – a very good scholar, and an acute Logician – so much for his mind and manners. His person is *unfortunately* diminutive, but there is a sweetness in his looks, especially about the eyes, which soon overcomes the oddness of your first feeling at the sight of so very little a Man. John sleeps with him and is passionately fond of him.[28]

Sara Hutchinson also liked him, though her account shows that De Quincey's shyness could create a poor impression.

Mr. de Quincey has been here 3 weeks & I daresay will make a long stay [she told a friend] – he is a good tempered amiable creature & uncommonly clever & an excellent scholar – but he is very shy & so reverences Wm & C that he chats very little but is content to listen – he looks only like 18 but is nothing like either helpless or dissipid as Joanna [Sara's sister] said: but then he is in much better health than when she saw him.[29]

Southey, too, had mixed feelings: 'Little Mr. De Quincey is at Grasmere,' he told his brother. 'He was here last week, and is coming again. I wish he was not so little, and I wish he would not leave his greatcoat always behind him on the road. But he is a very able man, with a head brimful of information.'[30]

The 'information' was political as well as literary, for De Quincey had lost no time in studying Wordsworth's current preoccupation, Spanish and Portuguese politics, and seems to have become sufficiently involved to write to *The Times* complaining at the poor support given to a public subscription in aid of the 'Spanish Patriots'. A letter to De Quincey from his sister Jane, written early in 1809, mentions that 'we have not been able to get the *Times*, though I have a great curiosity to study your logic'.[31] It does not indicate the date or nature of his contribution, but can refer only to a letter published on 6 January, which bears clear marks of De Quincey's style. 'I have . . . heard the present Subscription', he writes, 'extolled . . . as a great sum of money; and so I should have thought it, had the object been to raise a Statue to the Convention-makers of Cintra; but when the object is no less than to supply the wants, and relieve the hardships of a brave people, struggling for their liberties and lives, . . . thirty or forty thousand pounds is not such a contribution as might have been expected from the first city in the world.' He goes on to calculate, on the basis of London's wealth and population, how much money should have been raised – perhaps the 'logic' about which Jane was

163

curious – and ends by reminding readers of the maxim that 'he gives double who gives without delay'.

Everyone lent a hand with Wordsworth's pamphlet, and for a time Allen Bank was wracked with its birth-pangs. Wordsworth, who disliked the labour of writing, dictated to Dorothy and Sara, undisturbed by the clouds of smoke which filled his study. Coleridge joined in, and when part of the manuscript was lost in transit to the *Courier* he stayed up with Wordsworth until three in the morning helping to rewrite the lost material.[32] De Quincey was entrusted with writing a note for the pamphlet,[33] and seems to have become Wordsworth's general assistant. In the daily anxiety for news from the Peninsula Wordsworth often stayed up until two o'clock in the morning to walk up to Raise-Gap, four miles north of Grasmere, in the hope of meeting the carrier's cart which brought a copy of the *Courier* over from Keswick. On these excursions De Quincey went with him and must have relished the opportunity for undisturbed conversation with the taciturn poet. Once he witnessed a memorable demonstration of Wordsworth's sensitivity to the subtleties of psychological experience. The carrier was late and they had nearly given up hope for that night. Wordsworth, in typically unselfconscious style, several times lay down and put his ear to the surface of the road in the hope of catching the distant rumbling of wheels.

> Once [De Quincey recalls], when he was slowly rising from this effort, his eye caught a bright star that was glittering between the brow of Seat Sandal and of the mighty Helvellyn. He gazed upon it for a minute or so, and then, upon turning away to descend into Grasmere, he made the following explanation:- 'I have often remarked, from my earliest days, that, if . . . the attention is energetically braced up to an act of steady observation, or of steady expectation, then, if this intense condition of vigilance should suddenly relax, at that moment any beautiful, any impressive visual object . . . falling upon the eye, is carried to the heart with a power not known under other circumstances.'[34]

The star, unexpectedly perceived at the instant when the effort of listening had been relaxed, had brought with it, said Wordsworth, 'a pathos and sense of the infinite, that would not have arrested me under other circumstances.' He referred to his poem, 'There was a Boy' as another illustration of the same psychological principle.

Such intimate glimpses of the poet's creative intelligence seem to have been rare, however. De Quincey was liked and trusted, but one senses that Wordsworth could not see him as an equal or take much interest in him as a person. He was consoled by the affection of the women and children of the household – Johnny loved him, and his bedroom was decorated with the pictures De Quincey drew for him: 'the giant's castle and the Magician's temple'.[35] Another consolation was his meeting with John Wilson, who was to become a lifelong friend: in De Quincey's words, 'the only close male friend I ever had'. They met in the breakfast-room at Allan Bank, where De Quincey, entering to borrow one of the numerous books Coleridge kept there, found Wordsworth talking to a young man in sailor's costume who wore 'upon his countenance a powerful expression of ardour and animated intelligence, mixed with much good nature'. This was 'Mr. Wilson of Elleray'.[36] Wilson and De Quincey liked each other at once, and their relationship became distinctly fraternal: many factors were involved, but it seems a sensible guess that De Quincey, failing to find in Wordsworth the father-figure he had sought, was ready to accept Wilson instead as a protective 'elder brother'. Six feet tall and strongly built, confident and extrovert in manner, a champion athlete, full of good humour and scientific curiosity, impatient of books but a talented minor poet himself, Wilson bore a distinct resemblance to De Quincey's dead brother William, but without the latter's propensity for bullying. A further basis for sympathy lay in the fact that the two had been among the earliest of Wordsworth's admirers. Like De Quincey, the young Wilson had ventured an enthusiastic letter to the poet. Wilson's letter, written just over a year before De Quincey's, was more confident but otherwise remarkably similar in tone. He was the same age as De Quincey but physically and emotionally much more mature, whilst De Quincey was learned and intelligent far beyond Wilson's limits. There was something symbiotic in the relationship, and it flourished. On 29 November De Quincey went with Wordsworth to dine at Elleray, and soon Wilson and De Quincey were planning a trip to Spain.

After two instalments of Wordsworth's pamphlet had appeared in the *Courier*, the poet decided to lose no more time and get the whole pamphlet into print as soon as possible, lest public indignation over the Convention cool down. Arrangements for printing and publishing had already been worked out. The printing was to be done by Baldwin, a printer used by Daniel Stuart, who agreed to advertise it in his paper.

It would be published by Longman's. The only problem was the question of proof-reading and general supervision. Wordsworth was too far from London, in view of the poor postal service, to do this job effectively. What was to be done? A solution was soon found: De Quincey volunteered to go to London himself and see the pamphlet through the press. It must have seemed an eminently sensible plan, for he was devoted to Wordsworth, well versed in recent Peninsular politics, and painstaking in matters of detail. Coleridge, indeed, was tempted to sneer at this aspect of De Quincey.

> I believe [he wrote to Stuart] you have seen Mr De Quincey at the Courier office with me. Ho! – He was the very short & boyish-looking modest man, whom I introduced to you in Cuthell's Shop . . . Besides his erudition, he has a great turn for manual operations, and is even to something of old batchelor preciseness accurate, and regular in all, he does.[37]

A further reason for sending him was that Wordsworth, oddly enough, had doubts about his own ability to punctuate prose correctly, and had come to think that De Quincey knew better. 'As the subject of punctuation in prose was one to which I had never attended, and had of course settled no scheme of it in my mind,' he wrote, 'I departed that office to Mr. De Quincey.'[38] Mr De Quincey, needless to say, had a scheme of punctuation in mind. He believed that punctuation, rather than conforming to a 'blind feeling of propriety', should be 'a representation of the logical divisions – and a gamut of the proportions and symmetry of the different members – of each sentence'.[39] Coleridge had no patience with this sort of thing: 'Never was a stranger whim than the notion that , ; : and . could be made logical symbols expressing all the diversities of logical connection,'[40] he grumbled later. But Wordsworth was convinced, and on 20 February 1809 De Quincey left for London.

He spent much of the journey talking politics with the other passengers and laying down the law about Spain – pride in his mission giving him a sense that Allan Bank was the fountainhead of wisdom on Spanish affairs – and arrived in London on 25 February just in time to see the end of the fire which had destroyed the Drury Lane Theatre. He sent a description of the fire to the Wordsworths, with critical comment ('a very fine spectacle' . . . 'fantastic imagery formed by the wreaths of smoke' . . . 'a very sublime effect'):[41] readers of the essay 'On Murder Considered as one of the Fine Arts' will remember that De Quincey thought himself rather a connoisseur of fires.

166

His troubles began when he visited the printing house, to learn that the copy sent on ahead had not been printed. He urged the printers on and succeeded in getting some pages in proof after a week. But no more copy arrived from Wordsworth and he began to worry. When at last part of the manuscript did arrive he set to work checking it, only to find that an important sentence was incomplete. Not daring to guess at the missing words, he felt compelled to write to Wordsworth and await his answer before having the sheet finally printed – just the kind of delay his presence in London was supposed to prevent.[42] A second visit to the printing house gave further cause for anxiety, for he found the compositor 'celebrating the orgies of St. Monday' – relaxing in the workshop with a bottle. There were also problems stemming from Allan Bank. William, Dorothy wrote cheerfully, 'never likes to trust anything fresh away from the Brain'[43] and he was having second thoughts about the text. Corrections and additions began to arrive almost daily and by 11 March, after a fortnight in London, De Quincey had received seven letters containing instalments of text or corrections. The quantities of paper involved must have been formidable, for the 'pamphlet' eventually consisted of 216 printed pages. The task of punctuating, correcting and adding to this mass of closely written manuscript in three different hands (one of them, Wordsworth's, almost illegible) was an exhausting labour.

After the first ninety-six pages were printed he did not dare to proceed until he had Wordsworth's verdict on the incomplete sentence,[44] so he persuaded the printers to set the new copy and give him proofs but not to print them off. Even this work went slowly and day after day he waited, full of impatience, whilst public interest in the Convention of Cintra steadily waned. The labour seemed to grow more and more arduous. Parts of the pamphlet had to be rewritten to keep it up to date. In the third week of March a new compositor took over and (De Quincey reported) 'the proofs are filled with such monstrous errors . . . that I am now obliged to insist on having a *second* proof'.[45] By March, proof-correcting had become such an obsession that he was demanding *three* proofs – 'and, I believe, the compositor thinks that I shall soon after want a dozen'.[46] Worse, he felt that his lonely labour with eye-destroying manuscript and recalcitrant printers was going almost unnoticed by Wordsworth, for the poet was concerned about his pamphlet to the exclusion of all else, and his concerns were contradictory. The work must appear as fast as possible to have its proper impact; yet it must be as well written as possible and fit to stand as a monument for the admiration of posterity. Even as he longed to see it printed and on sale, he could not resist tampering with the text and holding up the work. He sent no less than four letters on 26 March, all of them full of fuss about the pamphlet, and two days later he was at it again. 'I have been not a little jeered this morning,' he confessed, 'when it was seen that I meant to trouble you with another letter. But I am haunted with notions which I cannot get over in cases of this sort that I leave my meaning undeveloped',[47] so he sent yet more alterations. De Quincey found himself invited to read and comment on a French bulletin, to check historical facts about Charles II, to insert new material 'after some expression like this, which I cannot recollect',[48] to revise a transitional passage which Wordsworth 'cannot find . . . in my MS', and to improve various parts at his own discretion. 'Do mend that stupid part of the Note, which I sent you, in fact my brains were utterly dried up when I wrote it,' wrote Wordsworth breezily.

This mass of vague directions, full of references to things the author himself could not find or remember, upset De Quincey. But the most painful blow was that, having composed a note on the siege of Saragossa to bring the pamphlet up to date, he found his note rejected as unnecessary, without Wordsworth's showing any awareness of the time and trouble it had cost.[49] The cancellation probably hurt him especially because he had ventured to refer to himself in the note as 'the friend of the author': pathetic proof of his longing to be admitted to Wordsworth's friendship. Cancelling the note, Wordsworth silenced the public profession of friendship. (De Quincey was not to be defeated so easily, however, and in the 'Postscript' which he contributed to the pamphlet he again called himself 'the [Author's] friend, who corrects the press errors'.[50] So the magic word 'friend' found its way into print at last.) Resenting the disregard of his time and trouble, and having the impression that Wordsworth had misunderstood the note itself, on 1 April, for the first time, he sent a letter containing explicit protest: 'I meant to have written today to Mr. Wordsworth to complain a little of the very great injustice which he has done me . . . How it is possible that the purport of my note should have been so entirely mistaken, I cannot guess.' He agreed to cancel the note, but made no secret of his regrets: 'I cannot say that I ever did anything with so much reluctance in my life.'[51] His tone jolted Wordsworth out of his complacency, and he wrote to apologize. 'It gives me great concern,' he sympathized, 'to find that after all your fatigue, confinement, and vexation, you should have suffered such mortification as you express from such a quarter.' But it was not a gracious apology, especially as the poet put an end to it by complaining, 'I must quit the subject, my penmanship is very bad, and my head aches miserably; I am also in other respects not well', after which he continued for another half-dozen paragraphs on other subjects, which, apparently, did not induce headache.[52]

The vexatious pamphlet did not take up the whole of De Quincey's time, however tiring the labour it demanded. One consolation was that before leaving Grasmere he had arranged with the Wordsworths that he would take over the cottage at Town End, which they had now vacated. On 7 March Dorothy wrote to say that they had taken a new six-year lease on the cottage, and she began to organize repairs and furnishings so that De Quincey might make his permanent home there as soon as possible. Thus, even as he struggled with the difficulties laid upon him by Wordsworth, he was assured that a place was being made ready for him in the circle of Wordsworth intimates. The flood of letters between Allan Bank and his lodgings at 82, Great Tichfield Street, Soho, carried not only queries about the pamphlet but also discussion of furniture and curtains for the cottage. Dorothy, with the Wordsworthian instinct for economy, had suggested ordering furnishing fabrics from Kelsall's warehouse at Manchester, where she could hope for a discount. De Quincey, of course, disliked the idea: for years he had despised the Kelsalls, and he was annoyed that they should be invited to play a further part in his affairs. 'I should have proposed it myself,' he conceded, 'if I had not hated that any Manchester kind of people should say that they had "corresponded" with Mr. or Miss Wordsworth:- However, if it must be, it must: and among Manchester people the Kelsalls are by no means the worst.'[53]

Dorothy kept him informed of domestic news and the progress of work on the cottage, sensing that he found his labour in London a lonely business. Her letters were full of fun and affection, as well as sympathy for his problems. She 'grieved' for his 'miserable cold ride on the outside of the Coach' when he left for London; she worried about the trouble he might have with her Brother's alterations to the pamphlet. She sent news of the children, vividly conveying their keen attachment to him:

> When your Friend Johnny came from school last night, his mother said to him, 'Here is a letter from –.' 'From,' he replied, 'Mr. De Quincey?' And with his own ingenuous blush and smile he came forward to the fireside at a quicker pace, and asked me to read the

letter; which I did . . . When all was over, he says 'but when will he
come? Maybe he'll tell us in his next letter.'[54]

Johnny wanted De Quincey to be told of a mouse which 'makes its
appearance sometimes under the dining-room grate and disappears
we know not how for we can find no hole for its escape'. Johnny
'thinks it is a fairy in the shape of a mouse', for ' "it comes under the
grate, and it does not come over the fender, and there's no hole under
the grate for it to go through" '.[55] She also did her best to make him feel
that Town End was now his home. '*Your* snow-drops are in full
blossom', she told him in March, and in May, 'I hope [the cottage] will
be a very nice place before you come to it, though the poor Laurels in
the garden have been so cruelly mauled . . . that I fear they will never
look like anything but dismembered creatures.'[56]

De Quincey tried to respond cheerfully and as usual made efforts
to please everyone. He was sending out prospectuses for *The Friend*
and collecting from Stuart of the *Courier* hints on how to edit a paper,
which he passed on for Coleridge's benefit. Always a keen observer of
the London scene, he entertained the Wordsworths with news of his
discoveries: '*everything* is to be had in London', he told them, instan-
cing a poster near his lodgings advertising '*Artificial Ears*'; and he
bought a Patent Smoke-Dispenser which he hoped would improve the
Allan Bank chimneys. He told them of his adventures in book-buying:
he had found the missing eleventh volume for Wordsworth's set of
State Trials and 'a set of Milton's Prose works in his own corrected
editions' which would form the basis for the Grasmere Press edition of
Milton, of which he still dreamed. But the Wordsworths were not
interested in these bookish exploits, and, 'No applause ensued,' as he
later complained; 'not an atom of sympathy did I receive.'[57] He was on
safer ground with the children, and never forgot to send some affectionate message for them. He often sent pictures for Johnny – battles
and storms and brightly coloured prints of all kinds – and he wrote
him a long letter about the fairy mouse and about Baldwin's print-
shop, for Johnny had been drawn into the Grasmere Press fantasy and
was eager to read so that he might become a printer, a notion encouraged by his parents, who thought it a useful stimulus to learning. De
Quincey also described a toy carriage he had seen in Hyde Park, in
which children could give each other rides, and promised to get one for
Johnny and Dora. The promise was kept, and the ledger of the Grasmere carpenter, Edward Wilson, records De Quincey's order for a
'childers carridge'.[58]

His favourite among the children was the baby Catharine. She was a sickly child and, according to her aunt, 'very bonny, but not *beautiful* in spite of her blue eyes', though 'exceedingly mild-tempered'.[59] Wordsworth called her 'his little Chinese Maiden', and she was agreed to be a lovable, if funny-looking child. De Quincey had developed a very possessive love for the little girl, and before he left London had decided, with the Wordsworths' agreement, that he, and he alone, was to teach little Kate. In 1805 he had listed 'The education of a child' as one of his 'Constituents of Happiness'. Now he would fulfil that desire. Sending some reading books for Thomas in May 1809, he emphasized that they were not for Kate: 'besides that she is so far off wanting them yet – sweet little love! –, [she] is to be taught by nobody but *me*: this promise Mr. Wordsworth once made me; and therefore I shall think it an act of the highest perfidy, if anybody should attempt to insinuate any learning into Catharine – or to hint at primers – to the prejudice of my exclusive privilege.'[60] A letter from Dorothy to Mrs Clarkson bears this out:

> Mr. De Quincey has made us promise that he is to be her sole Tutor; so we shall not dare to show her a letter in a book when she is old enough to have the wit to learn; and you may expect that she will be a very learned lady, for Mr. de Q. is an excellent scholar. If, however, he fails in inspiring her with a love of learning, I am sure he cannot fail in one thing. His gentle, sweet manners must lead her to sweetness and gentle thoughts. His conversation has been of very great use to John, who is certainly now the finest boy I ever saw.[61]

Nonetheless, De Quincey was lonely and worried. His London friends were all away, and though he met people when he dined in coffee houses he feared to let them know too much about him lest the word get around that he lived in the Lakes near 'the eccentric Mr. Wordsworth' and his cottage be besieged by London 'acquaintances' intruding on his time and privacy. So he spent most of his time quite alone. Among the few people he could visit in London was John Stewart (also known as 'Walking' Stewart), the eccentric explorer and philosopher. Stewart had wandered on foot over nearly every country of Europe and Asia, including Tibet. He was the author of several curious works with titles like *The Roll of a Tennis Ball through the Moral World*, *The Apocalypse of Human Perfectuability* and *Travels . . . to Discover the Source of Moral Motion*. An atheist, a believer in reincarnation and a political radical, he thought his books so subversive that when he gave one to De Quincey he made him promise to bury it, properly wrapped, seven feet below ground in the orchard at Town End to conceal it from the authorities. The two philosophers, who had met in a coffee house, enjoyed discussing Spanish politics and their hours together were among the few consolations of De Quincey's gloomy months in London. Relations with the printers – 'Mr Baldwin's fiends' as he was now calling them[62] – were bad, and De Quincey's taking it upon himself to lecture the compositor on punctuation had not helped. He had lost confidence since the cancelling of his note and was reluctant to do anything without express instructions. A request from Wordsworth that he would write a Postscript on Sir John Moore's letters, just published, may have mollified him a little, but it meant more hard work, and at the beginning of April Easter arrived, putting a stop to the printing.

De Quincey became ill: a sudden cold spell 'brought on all my old rheumatic pains of my head and face'. His health must have been affected in a number of ways. In a letter of 15 April he confessed, 'I felt rather uneasy, and more so perhaps from having unconsciously swallowed I suppose a pretty large quantity . . .' at which point he had second thoughts and crossed out the sentence. Later in the letter he led up to the same subject via the cold weather and the 'rheumatic pains' which had kept him awake at night, so that 'being obliged to put cotton soaked in laudanum into my mouth at times to allay the pains which run around the whole circuit of my teeth, I have at times unavoidably swallowed a good deal – which has much disturbed my head'. One guesses that depression and illness had driven him again to opium. He seems concerned to blame errors of judgment on the drug: why else mention the 'swallowing' of it? He also tormented himself with guilt for not writing more often and cheerfully: 'I feel as if I had been guilty of a crime in not writing to Miss Wordsworth for so long a time,' he laments, after a mere ten days' silence, 'but I will endeavour to make atonement by a more amusing letter, than my late ones have been, next Tuesday night.'[63] And still the pamphlet went slowly. It was now expected on 19 April.

As if all this were not enough, De Quincey had further cause for agitation in news of his runaway brother 'Pink'. It transpired that 'Pink' was now in the Navy, had been captured by the Danes, and was at Gothenburg awaiting release in an exchange of prisoners. This news came early in March, but there was no further word and De Quincey waited on in suspense.[64] Late in April, as work on the pamphlet continued to go at a snail's pace, he received another blow. Daniel

Stuart mentioned that, inquiring at Baldwin's about the pamphlet, he had been told that it was being delayed by De Quincey's endless corrections! De Quincey was alarmed at the notion that an impatient Wordsworth might hold him responsible for the awful delay in publication, so he wrote to give his view of the problem: 'the case is simply this; last week, out of the six days, the man attended *two*; and must then undoubtedly have been drunk from the absurd blunders and omissions which he made: and they *will* not put any other compositor to the work'.[65] Baldwin's accusation was merely a cover for the incompetence of his workers. He suggested that the job be transferred to another printer. Wordsworth's reaction was swift. He wrote immediately to Stuart, asking him 'to procure the immediate finishing of the work, which has been most shamefully and injuriously delayed by a drunken compositor whom Mr. De Quincey cannot get changed'.[66]

The change was made; but the episode made an opening for Coleridge, a close friend of Stuart's, to get involved.

My dear Stuart [he wrote on May 2],

I both respect and have an affection for Mr De Quincey; but saw too much of his turn of mind, anxious yet dilatory, confused from over-accuracy, & at once systematic and labyrinthine, not fully to understand how great a plague he might easily be to a London Printer, his natural Tediousness made yet greater by his zeal & fear of not discharging his Trust, & superadded to Wordsworth's own Sybill's Leaves blown about by the changeful winds of an anxious Author's Second-thoughts.

Watching from the sidelines, Coleridge obviously found the spectacle amusing, and in his struggles to get *The Friend* under way must have taken comfort from the flounderings of Wordsworth and De Quincey. He has written to Wordsworth, he says, to speak his mind on the business, and is going to write again – the burden of these letters being, apparently, that De Quincey and Wordsworth between them are to blame for the delays. 'That Wordsworth has not been quite pleased with my first letter, & will be still less with my letter of today, I know – but that soon passes off', he states with evident satisfaction. Then he returns to the attack:

After the instances, I saw, of De Q's marvellous slowness in writing a note to the Pamphlet when at Grasmere, the sum and meaning of which I had dictated in better & more orderly sentences in five minutes, and considering the superlative importance of Dispatch –

173

since that time, I can never retract my expressions of vexation & surprize, that W. should have entrusted any thing to him beyond the mere correction of the Proofs – but an unwise anxiety to let nothing escape has been the rock, on which W. has split – whereas had he brought it out, such as it was, he might now be adding all, he wished, to a second Edition. But so it is! We cannot be perfect. I do far worse both for myself and others by indifference about my compositions & what is thought or said of them, than he by over-irritability – His is a more natural fault & linked to better qualities.[67]

Coleridge's letters must have been effective in undermining both Wordsworth's and Stuart's confidence in De Quincey. If we stop to ask why he should have taken this attitude, the answer that naturally occurs is jealousy. He must have sensed the Wordsworths' scepticism over *The Friend*'s prospects, and the adoption of De Quincey as Wordsworth's trusted agent and political confidant no doubt galled him a good deal. Perhaps he also found De Quincey's patronage humiliating. Cottle had made it pretty clear where the £300 had come from: Coleridge had been profoundly grateful, but, constantly in De Quincey's company during the winter at Allan Bank, he must have smarted under the sense of obligation. And need De Quincey have subscribed for *five* copies of *The Friend*? It looked too much like charity. Whatever his motives, Coleridge added to the problems for now neither Stuart nor Wordsworth had complete faith in De Quincey's efficiency.

This might not have mattered much, for in early May publication seemed very close and there was little left for De Quincey to do. It was at this point, however, that a new obstruction was hurled into the pamphlet's path. Wordsworth, looking through 'an old Magazine', noticed an article about a libel case of 1799 in which the author of a political pamphlet had been sent to prison and fined £100 for writing unacceptable home truths about a prominent bishop. It dawned on Wordsworth that the same thing might happen to him. His pamphlet contained bitter criticism of Sir Arthur Wellesley (afterwards Duke of Wellington), who, it said, had earned 'the unremovable contempt and hatred' of his countrymen by signing the Convention. Was not this enough to earn him a place in Newgate – especially now that Wellesley had been made Commander-in-Chief of British forces? He wrote to Stuart in a flurry of anxiety:

I beg that, if my Pamphlet be not published, you would take the trouble of reading it over to see whether it may not be made a handle for exercising upon my Person a[n] . . . act of injustice. If any such passages occur let the leaf be cancelled – as to the expense, that I disregard in a case like this.[68]

This was on 3 May. On 5 May he wrote to De Quincey still more anxiously:

Though I left it to the discretion of Mr. Stuart to soften this passage or not, I am now decidedly of the opinion that it is much safer and more prudent to cancel the leaf . . .

I must apologise for making this application so late and unseasonably after all the trouble you have had; but if 'better late than never' be true in any case it is in a case like this. I am influenced chiefly by the consideration of Wellesley being now in so high a station which makes it imprudent, and even improper, to be said now.[69]

Not all at Allan Bank shared the panic. Sara Hutchinson added a postscript:

We females shall be very sorry to find that the pamphlet is not published for we have not the least fear of Newgate – if there was but a Garden to walk in we think we should do very nicely – and a Gaol in the Country would be quite pleasant – But, seriously, I hope that the passage may not be deemed objectionable, for another delay will be most provoking and put Mr. Baldwin out of all patience with you both.[70]

Dorothy took the same attitude. 'William still continues to haunt himself with fancies about Newgate,' she reports. '*We,* however, have no fears, for, even if the words be actionable . . . in these times they would not dare to inflict such a punishment . . . Though the expense of cancelling the leaf and the consequent delay would be serious evils, what I should most grieve for would be your trouble and vexation.'[71]

In London, De Quincey and Stuart conferred with Baldwin and found that the dangerous passage could easily be cancelled and a new leaf with less violent wording substituted. The pamphlet was promised for 11 May. But Wordsworth, now pathetically anxious, wrote again: 'I request very much that you would procure an interview with Mr. Stuart immediately in order, that by your joint efforts everything may be done which is necessary . . . I request that Mr. Stuart would carefully cancel every leaf that contains matter which he thinks or any person . . . thinks would render me liable to a prosecution. . . . I therefore beg again if there be any doubt concerning any passage, that it may be inexorably removed . . .'[72] De Quincey tried to reassure him,

promising to check the whole pamphlet himself, as well as consulting
Stuart's judgment. But he could not take the matter very seriously, and
when he wrote on 12 May he was more concerned with the dramatic
announcement that, 'At length the pamphlet has climbed to the top of
the hill' and the final pages were in proof. Ironically, now that the
moment of consummation approached, speedy publication was the
last thing Wordsworth wanted. He was prepared to endure any
amount of delay rather than risk a libel action. De Quincey failed to
see this. Jokingly, he told Wordsworth 'there is no hope of Newgate'.
He pushed ahead, reluctant to brook any further delay, and when
Stuart found what he thought might be a libellous passage De Quincey,
who disagreed, persuaded him otherwise and the passage was left
intact. All this was cheerfully retailed by letter to Wordsworth, who
was furious to learn that Stuart's judgment was being overridden. It
was a direct defiance of his instructions, and it must have seemed to
him that De Quincey was perversely determined to leave him defence-
less. But it was too late to intervene again. On 17 May De Quincey
corrected the last proof, and that evening four advance copies of the
pamphlet were printed off. He posted them to Wordsworth with
heartfelt relief. Tomorrow, after a final check of the text by Stuart, the
whole edition would be printed and packed up ready for the booksellers.

Next morning he set out in high spirits, immediately after breakfast, for the printing house. When he arrived he learnt that all the
printing had been done earlier that morning: Stuart had had no
opportunity to make his last check for libel! Bearing up stoically under
this piece of news, De Quincey cheered himself with the thought that
at least the thing was now printed and off to Longman, the publisher,
ready for distribution. It had gone, he asked, had it not? 'Oh, no,' he
was told – 'it would take till Monday to dry.' At this, says De Quincey,
'I fell into despair; and instantly went to Longman's'[73] where he saw
one of the directors, and was told that if he could have fifty copies sent
over at once, the damp sheets could be dried by the fire and 'stitched up
and circulated in 2 hours'. He agreed to this plan and by six o'clock in
the evening the pamphlets were being prepared.

Dazed by the stresses of the past nine hours, he was wandering
homeward through Soho when he bumped into two men. As he made
his apologies and was about to pass, one of them stared at him and
then 'cried out – in a voice that shook all Soho – "Mr. Quincey, I am

very happy to see you!" '[74] Aroused from his reverie, De Quincey recognized John Kelsall, who quickly explained that he had come to London in response to a letter from 'Pink', who had been released by the Danes, was in London and wanted to contact his family again. De Quincey was jubilant, but neither he nor Kelsall was able to see 'Pink' at once. Apparently by using an accommodation address, 'Pink' had opened communication without enabling anyone to find him. De Quincey wrote him a note, and the next day 'Pink' replied, in a strange and touching letter. He had formed, he said, a 'resolution of remaining incog. for some time, whatever inconvenience I may suffer from it. You will undoubtedly be surprised at my perseverance in this point, but I assure you that, however wrong or foolish my motives may be, they are so rooted that nothing can remove them.'[75] Part of his anxiety was to do with his physical condition: years of seafaring and captivity had damaged his health, and he wanted to recover before facing his family. He was also depressed, and worried about his mental condition: 'Every feeling is dulled except a sense of pain and sorrow which retain their first strength'; he felt that his 'mental faculties' had been injured 'proportionably' to his bodily sufferings, and he found himself 'subject to strange whims and caprices'. His self-respect was also vulnerable and he would not confront the family from which he had fled until he could seem something more than an abject failure:

> From the peculiar circumstances under which I have been for some years, I feel my credit very closely connected with the success of my undertaking, and as in the present instance my misfortunes have in some measure damp'd professional hopes, perhaps there may be some degree of pride in my refusing to see anybody until prospects brighten; but I cannot suffer pride to interfere with my affection for you, and shall therefore only beg as a favour that our meeting may be deferr'd until I am in a condition to enjoy it more.[76]

Thomas invited him to Grasmere, but he was determined to go to Liverpool for 'sea-bathing and country air' and asked only for advice about books, as, he said, 'I intend in my Retirement to dedicate a considerable time to study.'

The brothers communicated almost daily, and it became apparent that Thomas was the only person 'Pink' felt he could trust. This placed further stress on him at a time when he was still not free of his responsibilities for the pamphlet. By 24 May all the work of production was done, yet still the pamphlet had not gone out to the shops. Nobody seemed willing to admit responsibility for its distribution, but

177

Wordsworth seemed to expect Stuart to take control, so De Quincey mentioned the fact to Stuart and left him to get on with it. The ghastly labour seemed to be fading out in a blur of apathy and anticlimax. When Wordsworth received his first few copies, his response was barely lukewarm.

> My dear Friend [he wrote on May 24],
>
> Last night we received the pamphlet; I have not read the whole, but Miss Hutchinson will transcribe, on the opposite leaf, the most material errors which I have noticed; three of them are important . . . I am surprized how you have been able to get it done so correctly. I am quite satisfied with your note upon Moore, which is very well done; but had I seen his last letter before I entreated you to be so gentle with him, I should not have been so earnest upon that point . . . It is now time that I should congratulate [you] on your escape from so irksome an employment and give you my sincere thanks for all the trouble you have undergone.[77]

He went on to regret that De Quincey had not trusted to Stuart's judgment in every case on the question of libel. In fact, every scrap of praise was balanced by a point of criticism. He ended the letter by saying he was 'obliged to conclude in a great hurry': in her postscript Sara glossed this by explaining, 'Wm. has been in the house all day, so was in a hurry to get his walk before it was too late.'

De Quincey was rather hurt, but felt a little comforted when a second letter followed, for Mary Wordsworth had told her husband that he should have praised De Quincey's work more positively: to say he was 'quite satisfied' was not nearly strong enough. So a somewhat sheepish Wordsworth wrote again to make amends. Yet somehow he could not do it. His letter began well enough, humorously reporting Mrs Wordsworth's rebuke and making it clear that he thought De Quincey a 'master of the subject'. But then he soon slid off again into negative criticism: 'I am sadly grieved about that error in the Press in the Mottoe . . . I regret I did not request the Pamphlet to be sent down when the Body of it was printed' – implying that he should have done his own proof correction; 'the punctuation pleases me much; though there are here and there trifling errors in it. – I think indeed your plan of punctuation admirable.–'[78] The last sentences vividly show Wordsworth's struggles to stop criticizing and find something favourable to say. The fact is that he was deeply dissatisfied. At about the same time he was writing to Stuart to say he had 'no doubt that Mr. De Quincey was the *occasion* . . . of the delay' though not its direct cause.

'Mr De Quincey', he speculated, 'must have insisted upon his punctuation being attended to and the Printer must have been put out of humour by this and therefore refused to go on with the work.'[79] To Lord Lowther, he grumbled that the pamphlet 'ought to have appeared two months ago' – quite unfairly, since it was just two months ago that he had sent De Quincey the last sheets of manuscript! Hearing on 27 May that his work was still not in the shops, he raged: 'if I were superstitious, I should deem that there was a fatality attending this, my first essay in politics. I have kept my temper till last night, but I must say that Mr. De Quincey's letter of last night ruffled me not a little.' His judgment was severe:

> It avails nothing to find fault, especially with one [who] has taken such pains (according to best of his judgement) to forward this business – that he has failed is too clear, and not without great blame on his own part (being a man of great abilities and the best feelings, but as I have found, not fitted for smooth and speedy progress in business).[80]

Fortunately De Quincey remained unaware of these accusations, and he had little opportunity to worry further about the pamphlet, for at the end of May an anxious letter arrived from his mother. Mrs Quincey had received Kelsall's report on his trip to London, and

> Two things [she wrote] present themselves upon the face of Mr. Kelsall's yesterday's Letter: one, that the Person now in London whom you and Mr. Kelsall have been trying to see is not Richard; and the other, that if Richard, he has fallen under some dreadful Power which has quite changed and alienated his mind.[81]

She was convinced that an impostor was at work. The foundation of her belief was simple and unarguable. If Richard had really returned, how could he refuse to see his mother? About this central idea clustered a complex conspiracy theory: 'Pink' had been killed in a mutiny and his identity assumed by an unscrupulous adventurer in league with a man called Rogers, who had once offered to help the family trace him. The point of the plot was to get 'Pink's' share of the Quincey inheritance. It was Thomas's duty to unmask the imposture without delay.

Thomas, of course, took no part in these fantasies. The letters he had had from Richard left no room for doubt, and and he respected his brother's need for privacy: his own adventures must have made it easy for him to see Richard's point of view. His mother, however, continued to bombard him with anxious letters. Eventually, in June,

'Pink' was able to produce documents which established his identity even to his mother's satisfaction. But he insisted on going to Liverpool before seeing the family, and his behaviour remained an enigma to them.

In early June De Quincey could have left London. His plan was to spend the summer at Westhay, his mother's new house near Wrington in Somerset, before taking over the cottage at Grasmere. Instead he stayed on in a state of stupor. His emotional and nervous exhaustion after the ordeal of the past few months was such that he could not face packing for the move. Daily he stared at the two or three hundred books and other items which needed to be sent off to Grasmere and found himself unable to start. Meanwhile, repercussions of the pamphlet affair continued to rumble round the Wordsworth circle. On 4 June Wordsworth discovered that of ten copies sent him by De Quincey, two still contained the 'cancelled' passage supposed to be libellous! How many more copies, he wondered, had gone out uncorrected? Soon afterwards Stuart was favoured with a letter from Coleridge predicting that the pamphlet would not sell, and heaping much of the blame on 'Mr. De Quincey's strange & most mistaken System of punctuation'. The letter was notable also for its two-edged praise of Wordsworth, whose political writing, Coleridge managed to imply, was too *good* to succeed: 'Readers of Sense & Feeling will have no other dread than that the Work, if it should die, would die of a Plethora of the highest qualities of combined philosophic & poetic Genius.' Wordsworth had pitched his rhetoric too high: the picture is 'all foreground, all in hot tints'. 'The apple pie', he punned, '. . . is made all of Quinces.'[82] To blame the pamphlet's failure on De Quincey's 'System' would be absurd, for the punctuation is in fact perfectly normal. Nonetheless, it sold very badly, as most political pamphlets do. (The publishers had told De Quincey that 'they usually calculated that, out of 20 pamphlets on political subjects, *one* would clear it's expenses'.)[83] One might have foreseen that De Quincey would become the scapegoat. His over-eagerness to make himself useful had led him to a position where he stood to take the blame from every side.

Dorothy, however, seems to have made efforts to prevent his falling from favour with her brother and Coleridge. In May she suggested (with William's agreement) that he might write to the newspapers defending William against unfair attacks in the *Edinburgh Review*: De Quincey agreed and began to make notes for the project, but never carried it out. In August she wrote again, this time on

Coleridge's behalf, asking De Quincey to scan the *Edinburgh* and *Monthly Reviews* for follies and blunders on which S.T.C. could exercise his wit in *The Friend*.[84] On De Quincey's side, there is some slight evidence that may suggest that he was developing a romantic attachment to Dorothy, despite the fourteen years between them. In May, his sister Jane wrote to him, 'I should much like to know Miss Wordsworth, and to see what sort of a woman you admire.' Later in the same letter she refers to 'the fair unknown'.[85] Whether or not this is Dorothy remains obscure. In another letter Jane teases him: 'if you are really going to build or furnish a cottage . . . ought not that beautiful and wild-hearted girl to be consulted? She certainly must have taste, and is the best judge of what will please herself.'[86] This may be just a joke, and there is certainly no evidence that he ever thought Dorothy beautiful. But the emphasis on 'taste' and the epithet 'wild-hearted' might well echo a description of Dorothy by De Quincey. In 1839 De Quincey admitted that both he and John Wilson 'heartily agreed in admiring her'[87] – the word 'admire' in such a context having a sexual shade of meaning.

At the beginning of July De Quincey managed to drag himself away from London and join his family at Westhay, his first visit to them for eighteen months. Mrs Quincey's latest experiment in house-building was a mansion designed to a somewhat fanciful plan by herself and Mary, and built with £12,500 supplied by Thomas Penson, who hoped to live there when he retired from service in India. Jane, Mary and Mrs Quincey had moved in ten days previously but nothing was finished and Thomas arrived to find only one room habitable and 'stonemasons, carpenters, painters, plaisterers, bell-hangers & c.' everywhere.[88] The hall was in use as a workshop, the front staircase had not been built, and, dodging the workmen, the family moved successively 'into a parlour of a neighbouring farmhouse;- into a green-house with no floor;- into a room with a floor but no ceiling;- into a closet 6 feet by 6' and at last into a habitable sitting-room. All this was amusing, and De Quincey was not unhappy. His sisters idolized him (just as they did the vagabond 'Pink', although they were hurt by his refusal to see them) and listened admiringly to his news of Wordsworth, Coleridge and Spanish politics. Even his mother seems to have been in good spirits, and if there were any reproaches over the Oxford disaster they have not been recorded.

Less to his taste was the social life of Wrington. Home after such a long absence, he was duty-bound to visit the houses of his mother's friends to make morning calls, drink tea and attend garden parties. His mother's set was the local Evangelical circle, led by Hannah More, whose residence nearby had been a major factor in Mrs Quincey's decision to settle at Wrington. De Quincey detested 'Holy Hannah', whom he privately regarded as a bore and a hypocrite. He managed to behave politely when they met, but she had a way of making remarks that left him speechless with rage. When, for example, someone at one of her parties mentioned poetry, Mrs More's reply was, 'Poetry! oh! as to poetry, I foreswore *that*, and I think everybody else should fore-swear it, together with pink ribbons.'[89] Wrington society in general was no better. Not only was Hannah More admired as a learned woman, but everyone he met seemed to despise the Spaniards, worship Napoleon's military genius and read the *Edinburgh Review,* whose editor, Francis Jeffrey, had written of the 'vulgarity, affectation and silliness' of the *Lyrical Ballads*.[90] So he spent much of his time arguing and had no scruples about upsetting people. 'I have tormented them to the utmost of my power,' he told Mary Wordsworth, '– and have the satisfaction of thinking that I have given extreme pain to all the *refined* part of the community here.'[91] Even poor Cottle came in for his share, and abandoned political argument saying, 'Really you're so furious, there's no talking with you,' which De Quincey took as a compliment. His association with Wordsworth and the Cintra pamphlet had done wonders for his confidence.

In September 'Pink' arrived, to the delight of his family and the admiration of the neighbours. The full story of his exploits could now be told, and it was a remarkable one. He had served on a number of merchant ships until he was captured by pirates off the coast of Peru. The pirates had no trained navigator and finding that 'Pink' could navigate they forced him to sail with them. After two years he man-aged to escape near the River Plate, joined a vessel of the British Navy as a midshipman and, in 1807, was captured on the Baltic coast by the Danes after the British bombardment of Copenhagen. It was from this captivity that he had recently returned. During the earlier part of this career he had secretly visited England twice, and the brothers, compar-ing notes, found that 'Pink' had passed through Oxford (probably in 1805) at a time when Thomas had been there as a student. He had been hungry and penniless, and a man in a university gown had given him a guinea in the street.[92] Thomas wrote exuberantly to Johnny Wordsworth:

As soon as I come to live at Grasmere, I shall begin to teach you all the things that I know that I think you would like to know: one thing will be swimming; another will be how to fly a kite: and another will be swinging: and another walking on Stilts. But the best thing of all will be how to sail a boat upon the lake . . . But it is not I that am to teach you this — but it is my Brother — who is a sailor.[93]

And he went on to describe some of Richard's daring exploits.

It was now time for him to leave for Grasmere. 'All has been in readiness for you, and every one of us wishing to see you for a long long time,' wrote Mary Wordsworth.[94] John Wilson wrote too: he was planning a visit to Spain in October, and would like De Quincey to go with him. But De Quincey, who always found it hard to nerve himself for a move, stayed at Westhay as the days passed and October arrived. Writing to the Wordsworths he frankly admitted the cause of delay: 'my own intolerable procrastination'.[95] At last he managed to uproot himself, however, and on 18 October he caught the Birmingham Mail for the first stage of his journey north.

7

The Fruits of Philosophy

'A mountainous region, with a slender population, and *that* of a simple pastoral character; behold my chief conditions of a pleasant permanent dwelling-place!'[1] So De Quincey wrote in later years. For as long as he could remember he had 'hungered and thirsted' for mountain scenery, and now his appetite could be satisfied. He moved into the cottage at Town End on 21 October, amidst much local curiosity and gossip. 'Even the old people of the vale', he recalled, 'were a little excited by the accounts (somewhat exaggerated, perhaps) of the never ending books that continued to arrive in packing-cases for several months in succession.'[2] Really, exaggeration was unnecessary. 'You may judge of the number of his books,' Dorothy wrote to a friend, 'when I tell you that he has already received 9 or 10 chests, and that 19 more are on the road.' She had equipped the cottage with 'bookshelves in every corner' but even so 'some of these books must be kept in chests on account of the smallness of the house'.[3]

De Quincey's new home had been built in the early seventeenth century as an inn, The Dove and Olive Branch, whence it came – after De Quincey's time – to be known as 'Dove Cottage', though neither he nor the Wordsworths had any special name for it. It stood at Town End, the southern end of Grasmere, on the road from Ambleside to Keswick, separated from the highway by a narrow strip of garden and a fence of upright slate slabs.[4] It had thick walls of local stone, plastered and whitewashed, slate roof and small latticed windows. There were six rooms, two downstairs and four upstairs, as well as a kitchen. The ground floor rooms were panelled from floor to ceiling with oak, which made them dark at most times of day, but the upstairs rooms were lighter and the cottage, though small, was not cramped. The diamond-paned window of the kitchen-parlour offered an unbroken view of Grasmere Lake and of Silver How, the fell that rises beyond it. The Wordsworths had come to live there in 1799 and had improved the cottage imaginatively. On the front walls they had trained up roses, jasmine and rock plants, and they had let ivy grow on the gable-end. They had made a door halfway up the stairs so that one could step straight out into the garden, which sloped so steeply that the ground came up to first-floor level at the back. This garden was one of the cottage's chief delights. Wordsworth had described it in 'A Farewell', written in 1802, as a

> ... rocky corner of the lowest stair
> Of that magnificent temple which doth bound
> One side of our whole vale with grandeur rare;
> Sweet garden orchard, eminently fair

—lines which De Quincey loved to quote, pleased with the accuracy of the word 'stair', for the irregularly shaped little garden was the first stage of the precipitous ascent of Bracken Fell, which dominates the east side of Grasmere Vale. Here the Wordsworths had cultivated fruit trees, vegetables and flowers; they had cleared a terrace and built a 'moss-hut', a summerhouse lined with moss, at the highest point, where it commanded a view of the whole valley. When De Quincey arrived he found the new whitewash too glaring and the garden damaged by workmen. But spring would repair that, and the interior left nothing to be desired. The furnishings had been chosen with his taste in mind: pink or white dimity for the bedrooms and mahogany for the bookcases.[5] When he arrived everything was ready except domestic service: the housekeeper had not yet come, so thirteen-year-old Sally Green came over from Allan Bank in the mornings to make his breakfast. He managed thus for a few days, and even played host to the Wordsworths in the evenings, but soon grew tired of fending so much for himself and moved over to Allan Bank for a month or so until Mary Dawson, a former servant of the Wordsworths and a very good cook, was ready to take charge.[6]

He was on excellent terms with the Wordsworths, and once he was settled at the cottage they saw each other almost daily. Any ill-feeling over Wordsworth's dissatisfaction with the pamphlet had been forgotten. To Dorothy, his occupying cottage meant that 'we have almost a home still, at the old and dearest spot of all'.[7] His library was open to all and, as Dorothy said, 'will be a solid advantage to my Brother'. It was an equally solid advantage to Coleridge, who was at Allan Bank and still spasmodically producing *The Friend*. He carried off books by the armful, at times accumulating as many as five hundred borrowed volumes. It seems to have been recognized by all concerned that the main reason for De Quincey's living at Grasmere was to be near the Wordsworths,[8] and at first everyone was happy with the arrangement. He loved entertaining in his new home, and as Christmas approached Dorothy wrote ecstatically to Mrs Clarkson, 'On Christmas day we are all to dine there, and to meet Mr. Wilson and a friend of his. . . We shall dine in the parlour below stairs. Oh! that you could actually come in among us.'[9] Christmas was eventually spent instead at Wilson's house, Elleray, but still De Quincey, Coleridge, Sara Hutchinson and the Wordsworths went as one happy crowd. And on 2 January De Quincey celebrated New Year by giving a firework party: all the children of the Vale were invited, and 'Mr. De Quincey's House was like a fair'.[10]

The Wordsworth children still played a large part in his life. In May 1810 he and Wilson stood joint godfathers to the latest arrival, William Wordsworth junior, and whenever De Quincey went away he brought back presents for the children. In August 1810, for example, he brought dolls for Kate and Dora and a toy gun for Johnny. Kate was still his favourite, and he found her 'beautiful',[11] though the Wordsworths thought her rather an ugly duckling. 'Catharine', writes Dorothy, 'has not the least atom of beauty except a healthy complexion. Her face is perfectly comic and her motions are uncommonly quick and lively.'[12] She is 'the only funny child in the family', and though 'a plain child, has something peculiar in the cast of her face which probably adds to the comic effect of her looks and gestures'.[13] De Quincey was often happiest with children, perhaps partly because his smallness and shyness troubled him less in their company, and his affection for Kate was especially intense. Kate, who called him 'Kinsey', returned the feeling: when he was away in 1810 she went through every room in the cottage looking for him, and even pulled off the counterpane to see if he were in bed! One morning in April 1810 Kate was suddenly taken ill. She was seized with a fit of vomiting followed by convulsions which left her right hand and leg partly paralysed. For months this was treated by rubbing the arm and leg for two hours daily. According to Dorothy, 'she is *for a time* kept quiet, while we are rubbing her, when we say that she shall "ride away to London to meet Mr. de Quincey" she will then sing to the motion of our Knees and, till she grows uneasy, be contented'.[14] She recovered partially but continued to walk with a limp. De Quincey and the Wordsworths were inclined to blame Sally Green, who had been minding the children and had allowed Kate to swallow some pieces of raw carrot, which were thought to have caused the vomiting. They were probably wrong in this, for Kate's illness was almost certainly a viral encephalitis of which vomiting was a symptom.

Wordsworth himself was hard at work during 1810 on *The Excursion*, an ambitious poem of ideas 'On Man, on Nature, and on Human Life' in a Lakeland setting which was to crystallize in poetic form his own achieved philosophy of life. The work went briskly and the poem, in nine books, was completed in December 1811. Meanwhile, probably during 1810 or 1811, De Quincey was allowed to read in manuscript the untitled autobiographical poem later known as *The Prelude*, which Wordsworth intended, ultimately, as the first part of a huge three-part poem, of which *The Excursion* would form the second part. De Quincey must have been allowed to borrow a copy of *The Prelude*: in a magazine article of 1839 he quoted some twenty-five lines – apparently from memory – with startling accuracy,[15] and in 1848 he told Emerson that he had once possessed a manuscript copy of the poem in five volumes.[16] Perhaps he sat down at Town End and made his own secret copy, recognizing the work as a masterpiece and seeing no prospect of its early publication.

Other friends besides the Wordsworths were close to Town End. He spent much time with John Wilson at Elleray on the shores of Windermere and they talked of visiting Spain and Portugal together until Napoleon put an end to the idea by letting it be known that English civilians found in Spain would be liable to execution as spies; it says much for the innocence of the age that De Quincey was genuinely shocked by this news.[17] Local excursions on foot, however, became a regular part of their friendship. Both men loved walking and thought nothing of a brisk sixteen-mile hike. Wilson was also interested in cock-fighting. He kept his own birds and bred them with meticulous care, matching them against neighbours' birds at 'mains' which attracted crowds of spectators. Once a main of cocks was actually fought in the drawing-room at Elleray, the unfinished flooring being covered with turf for the occasion.[18] No doubt De Quincey was an occasional spectator. From Wilson too he picked up the slang of the boxing fraternity or 'fancy': a vocabulary he was to use with comic effect in several of his published writings.[19]

This improbable friendship was complemented by one with Charles Lloyd and his wife Sophia. Lloyd was a minor poet who knew Lamb and Coleridge well, though his relationship with the latter had soured, partly because Lloyd had published an unpleasant travesty of Coleridge's early career in his novel *Edmund Oliver*. Coleridge profes-

187

The Fruits of Philosophy

sed an 'unfeigned horror' of Lloyd's character[20] and Wordsworth was inclined to agree, with the reservation that 'the habit of my mind is and always has been to think of him as a Madman', and not as a 'moral and accountable Being',[21] for Lloyd was subject to periods of mental instability when he would become shifty, suspicious and irrational, and since 1796 had been troubled with fits of delirium like waking nightmares accompanied by temporary paralysis.[22] By the summer of 1808 he had told Wordsworth privately that he feared he might be losing his sanity and asked to be watched for his own protection.[23] None of this alarming history was known to De Quincey, and when he first met the Lloyds at their house, Old Brathay, near Ambleside, he found them charming and soon became a regular visitor. The Lloyds were a lively and cultivated couple. They had six children and gave the best dinner parties and dances in the neighbourhood. All sorts of interesting people were to be met there: not only writers but musicians and painters, including on one occasion John Constable. De Quincey's friendship with them was deep enough to touch the bedrock of every-day trivia: they borrowed each other's servants, and when De Quincey needed silver spoons he sent a list of his needs to Lloyd, who would pass it on to a relative in trade at Birmingham.[24] It became De Quincey's custom to walk the five miles to Old Brathay at nine or ten o'clock at night whenever the mood took him and sit talking with Lloyd until one in the morning. Their talk was mainly of literature: Lloyd's own poetry was poor stuff but he had a sharp critical intelligence and a remarkable knowledge of the drama, English and foreign, coupled with a deep interest in the psychology of character which derived partly, perhaps, from the nervous sensitivity of his own nature. They also discussed Coleridge and the Wordsworths, and De Quincey learned that Lloyd felt the circle at Allan Bank despised him. He was careful not to endorse this view, but noticed that Lloyd was very shy, and guessed that he could only relax and show his real gifts 'before confidential friends' with whom he felt perfectly secure.[25]

De Quincey also kept up friendly contact with Mrs Coleridge and the Southeys, although Greta Hall, near Penrith, was too far away for them to see much of each other. The Coleridge children and Southey stayed at Town End sometimes and Southey and De Quincey went walking together.[26] On one occasion Southey opened up enough to declare roundly that he disagreed with Wordsworth's ideas about poetic diction and the choice of fit subjects for poetry,[27] but mostly he remained too reserved for real friendship.

De Quincey thus spent his time in walking, seeing his friends and, above all, reading. His cottage was an acceptable substitute for the Canadian hermitage of which he had dreamed during his student days, and his family assumed that philosophy would occupy him: Jane called him 'Monsieur le philosophe' and Henry jokingly inquired 'how many hundreds you have received for metaphysical works'.[28] Metaphysics certainly occupied much of his time. He was studying Fichte, Schelling, Kant (again) and Spinoza – no doubt discussing all of them with Coleridge, who in the autumn of 1809 jotted down a memorandum suggesting that De Quincey make a survey of scientific publications on psychology and the senses.[29] It may have been during these early years at Town End that he began to dream of becoming not merely a philosopher, but 'the first founder of a true Philosophy' – taking the crown from Kant himself by putting the whole subject on a new basis! He planned vaguely to write a book to be called *De Emendatione Humani Intellectus* ('On the Correction of the Human Intellect') after an unfinished work by Spinoza (*Tractatus de Intellectus Emendatione*). A more ambitious project could scarcely be imagined, but part of its appeal undoubtedly lay in the fact that the scale of the task meant nothing very specific need be done in the short term and he could indefinitely postpone putting pen to paper. Meanwhile, under the banner of 'philosophy', he was free to pursue the miscellaneous reading which had always been his delight. During the first year at Town End he was 'amusing' himself 'by reading, in their chronological order, the great classical circumnavigations of the earth'[30] – which must have meant borrowing some of S.T.C.'s numerous books of voyages – followed by the whole of Milton's prose works[31] and much German literature, in particular Richter, one of whose prose poems he translated in 1811, though not with any intention of publishing it. He began to take an interest in political economy and 'look[ed] into loads of books and pamphlets on many branches' of this science, which fascinated him by its very imperfections, as he saw mathematical and logical errors everywhere in the economists he studied.[32] He considered taking up the challenge himself,[33] but for the time being laid the idea aside and took refuge again in his reading.

Not all his time was spent at Grasmere. He paid long visits to London every year between 1810 and 1815, spending the whole summer and autumn there in 1812, and the spring and summer in 1814. In 1815 he walked through Wales from Cardiff to Bangor, revisiting some of the scenes of his boyhood wanderings.[34] Sometimes he was away for six months at a time. His trips to London were usually broken by a visit to his family at Westhay, though he invariably arrived weeks or months late and among his family and friends became a byword for unpunctuality.[35] This may have been an assertion of freedom: keeping his movements unpredictable made it difficult for people to put pressure on him and freed him from their expectations. It was also, perhaps, symptomatic of the opium habit, which residence in Grasmere and the dire example of Coleridge had failed to check. Surrounded by friends and, for the moment, free of debt, De Quincey at Town End might never have needed opium had it not already become part of his way of life. His use of it was still not heavy. No doubt he took it for his frequent toothaches, and in 1812, he says, he was taking opium 'on Saturday nights'.

> And how do I find my health after all this opium-eating? in short, how do I do? Why, pretty well, I thank you, reader. In fact, if I dared to say the real and simple truth, (though in order to satisfy the theories of some medical men, I ought to be ill), I was never better in my life than in the spring of 1812; and I hope sincerely that the quantity of claret, port or 'London particular Madeira' which, in all probability, you, good reader, have taken, and design to take, for every term of eight years during your natural life, may as little disorder your health as mine was disordered by all the opium I had taken (though in quantity such that I might well have bathed and swum in it) for the eight years between 1804 and 1812.[36]

Unlikely as it seems, this jaunty account may be true, for it appears that opiates may be used occasionally by some people without physical dependence developing. To quote a modern authority, 'Occasional intake of heroin at parties, on weekends, or at times of feeling low, serves a supportive and pleasurable function as a rule, with no negative side effects.'[37] This is a close parallel to De Quincey's situation between 1804 and 1812. This pattern of drug use may last for years, and may never lead to physical dependence. When it does, it tends to be referred to as the 'honeymoon stage' and in De Quincey's case this would be appropriate. In 1812, he recalled, he was still

> ignorant and unsuspicious of the avenging terrors which opium has in store for those who abuse its long-suffering. At the same time, as yet I had been only a *dilettante* eater of opium; even eight years' practice, with the single precaution of allowing sufficient intervals between every indulgence, [had] not been sufficient to make opium necessary to me as an article of daily diet.[38]

Unsuspicious? Not quite. That 'precaution' implies that he knew the dangers of the path he was treading.

Having settled into his new life at Grasmere, De Quincey felt in a strong enough position to invite his mother and sisters to stay. They came in late August 1811, and stayed for two months.[39] The visit was a great success. Friendly relations were established at once with the Wordsworths: Mrs Quincey arrived with donations from Hannah More and the 'Clapham Sect' for the Sunday School Dorothy and Mary were helping to establish in the village, there were numerous tea parties, and Dorothy took Jane and Mary on long outings through the countryside. Wordsworth himself was most gracious, showing the ladies the local beauty spots: 'The Misses De Quincey have just called,' he writes at the end of a letter, 'and I must walk with them to the Waterfall at Ghyll-side.'[40] He sounds as if he could think of other ways to spend the time, and it may have been during this visit of his female relatives that De Quincey observed that 'no consideration would ever have induced Wordsworth to burden himself with a lady's reticule, parasol, shawl, or anything exacting trouble and attention'.[41] But they enjoyed his company and were delighted to find him an expert on the 'philosophy of gardening': he advised them on how to plant the fruit trees at Westhay. They made him a present of two birch saplings and on the day of their departure he gave them roots of the decorative Royal Fern for their garden. The Quincey ladies created a stir at Grasmere, and gave the impression that De Quincey was connected with fashionable society. His cottage was the scene of lavish hospitality: 'This afternoon another *route* at Mr. de Qu's', Sara told a correspondent.[42] She was suitably impressed on learning that the Quinceys knew the famous 'Ladies of Llangollen', and appreciated the new life they lent Grasmere Church on Sundays: 'I wish you saw the number of scarlet cloaks and silk pelisses assembled in the Church yard – the Norths – the Tillmans – de Qus – Crumps – Kings – & Miss W. all as fine as –' she chattered, not staying to complete the simile. Peggy Ashburner, the Wordsworths' old neighbour, was more succinct: 'I never expected to see Grasmere come to sic a pass.'[43] The ladies were charmed by the cottage and garden: as soon as they got back to Westhay they set to work on a moss-hut like the one at Town End, and Mary Dawson's cooking pleased them so much that months later they wanted to know if they could lure her away to cook at Westhay.[44]

When his mother and sisters left on 11 November De Quincey must have seemed firmly established as a member of the Wordsworth circle. But within a month the first small crack appeared in the friend-ship, when he decided to make some alterations to the garden at Town End. The reaction was dramatic.

> What do you say [wrote Sara Hutchinson] to de Qu's having polled the Ash Tree & cut down the hedge all round the orchard – every Holly, Heckberry, Hazel, and every twig that skreened it – & all for the sake of the Apple trees that he may have a few more Apples – Mrs Jones* now stands quite alone, that nice high hedge behind her and all above, & where the Mosshut stood, levelled to the ground. [Dorothy] is so hurt and angry that she can never speak to him more: & truly it was a most unfeeling thing when he knew what store they set by that orchard – the Apple trees also are so pruned that instead of its being a little wood, as it used to be, there is neither shade or shelter.[45]

If De Quincey thought the purpose of an orchard was to produce apples, he was wrong. Dorothy had relied upon its being for 'seven years at least a secure covert for the Birds, and undisturbed by the woodman's ax'.[46] She could not help regarding the cottage as Words-worth property, which De Quincey occupied in trust, as a kind of caretaker. The idea that he might prune the trees and demolish the beloved 'moss-hut' was unacceptable. Sara took a dislike to him from this time onwards. Outwardly she remained friendly when Dorothy would not speak to him, but she wrote of him contemptuously, and was on the watch for signs of selfishness:

> Quincey reads the newspapers standing, or rather stooping with Catherine on his back – he is very fond of her but yet does not like to be plagued with her when he feels any thing like a duty which as he has engaged to teach her to read &c, towards her – but he will contrive some how or other to shake this off for he lives only for himself and his Books. He used to talk of escorting Mary into Wales but I do not believe that she will have his company.[47]

In April 1812 Dorothy could still hardly bear to mention him, though Wordsworth was friendly.[48]

De Quincey's reaction to this fuss is not known. If he had to see less of the Wordsworths for a while it cannot have bothered him much for there were other sources of entertainment. A striking feature of his period at Grasmere is the extent to which he joined in the life of the local people. Despite his shyness he preserved a voracious curiosity about people, and his unpretentious behaviour made it easy for him to associate with whom he pleased. On his walks through the Lake

* [a tree?]

country he was observant of the local speech and customs, which he regarded with the rather detached interest that had characterized his explorations of London. He was a frequent attender at household sales, for example: he noted that such sales were important social events in the country and that 'even a gentleman who should happen to present himself on such a festal occasion, by way of seeing the "humours" of the scene, was certain of meeting the most cordial welcome'.[49] Clearly, he was such a gentleman. 'The "humours" of the scene' also formed a good part of the pleasure he took in his nocturnal walks. One frosty March night he was rejoiced by the spectacle of a man in his shirt-sleeves sitting in a garden in an armchair moon-bathing. More often, his walks offered him the contemplative pleasures of the outsider:

> to trace the course of the evening through its household hieroglyphics from the windows which I passed or saw: to see the blazing fires shining through the windows of houses, lurking in nooks far apart from neighbours; sometimes, in solitudes that seemed abandoned to the owl, to catch the sounds of household mirth; then, some miles further, to perceive the time of going to bed; then the gradual sinking to silence of the house; then the reign of the cricket; at intervals to hear church clocks or a little solitary chapel bell, under the brows of mighty hills, proclaiming the hours of night.[50]

A pensive pastime; but, like those of *L'Allegro* in Milton's poem, De Quincey's walks were 'not unseen', and in time his nocturnal rambles became the subject of gossip and local comment, not all of it friendly.[51]

Observation of his neighbours led him to a philological discovery. Stopping for rest at a farmhouse one hot day, he sat in the kitchen talking to the farmer and noticed a young mother playing with a baby. He heard the girl say to the child in her lap, 'No more patten!' – words which she 'repeated two or three times, and accompanied with a playful gesture as though defending her bosom from the busy little hands of the laughing infant'. His attention caught, he asked the girl what 'patten' meant. She blushed and would not tell him, but the old farmer, greatly amused, interpreted 'patten' as 'breast'. This was just as De Quincey had expected: in 1811 he had studied a little Danish, an interest sparked off by Richard's recent captivity in Denmark, and in Danish the word for breast was *patte*. After this he kept his ears open and soon hatched a theory that the Cumbrian dialect was formed by a survival of Danish elements. He obviously delighted in the dialect for its own sake, and the examples he noted are colourful. 'I'll *skyander*

193

him if he comes here again,' he heard an old woman threaten at Ambleside (*skaende* is Danish for 'scold'); Barbara Lewthwaite, the servant girl who replaced Molly Dawson at Town End in 1813, asked him, 'Master, is I to sweep the *attercops* off them books?' (meaning cobwebs: *edderkop* is Danish for 'spider').[52] He noticed that Lakeland place names bore similar 'Danish' traces. Not all his examples are convincing, but his theory seems to have a core of truth; the Lake District certainly had plenty of Viking settlement in the early Middle Ages. He was proud of his discovery and in 1812 offered to supply an appendix on the local dialect for Wordsworth's *Guide to the Lakes,* a favour which Wordsworth declined – none too graciously, it seems.[53]

For De Quincey the Lakeland landscape derived much of its charm from the presence of people. Unlike the Wordsworths he was not a detailed observer of nature, and his ignorance was such that when his sister mentioned teazles he did not know if they were plants or animals.[54] He was so short-sighted that the finer points of views were often lost on him. Nonetheless the peaks and fells, with the endless diorama of cloud patterns above and between them; the smaller, eccentrically grouped hills, thickly grassed; the hedgerows richly cluttered with hazel, dogrose and enormous foxgloves – all these delighted him. He adopted Wordsworth's views on the picturesque, admiring the steepsided, flat-floored Lakeland valleys and preferring them to the narrower, V-shaped Welsh valleys of his earlier adventures. Like Wordsworth, he regretted the prevalence of dazzling whitewash which made the newer houses stand out distractingly in the landscape; and tended, oddly enough, to regard the drystone walls as an eyesore, because they broke up the sweep of the land. The grandeur of the scenery, if not always the subtlety of its detail, he could appreciate. But landscape was not his real interest. His eyes were sharpest when people came on the scene: conversation, emotion, ideas and personalities were his world.

By March 1812 De Quincey could already foresee a time when his meagre capital would be gone, and he decided (without enthusiasm) that some defence must be prepared. He went to London and on 30 March, he told Wordsworth, had seen Dr Stoddart, a barrister practising in Doctors' Commons:

> He was very friendly and communicative; so that I got all the information that was necessary for me in forming a judgement on the Civil

Law as a profession; indeed quite enough to make me anxious for no more, – I have now determined to enter at Gray's Inn; . . . I shall be up . . . in time to keep the Easter term . . . which point is accomplished, as perhaps you know, by masticating for three days in the Hall of that honourable society.[55]

He later said that his object in taking to the law was simply 'to get money, of which I purposed to get the greatest possible quantity in the least possible time',[56] but his lack of enthusiasm doomed the project from the start. He spent part of his time in London attending the sale of the great Roxburghe library, then entered the Middle Temple (not Gray's Inn) on 12 June. He kept terms there until at least 1815, but there is no evidence that he ever opened a law-book.

On this and subsequent visits to London he kept closely in touch with Coleridge, who had left Allan Bank and was now alienated from the Wordsworths by a complicated quarrel which had its origin in the tactlessness of a friend. In March 1810 *The Friend* had collapsed. Coleridge, ill and exhausted, decided to seek medical supervision to help break his opium habit, and in October arranged to go to London with Basil Montague. The plan was that he should live with the Montague family whilst he attempted his cure. Montague, a well-meaning but unimaginative fellow, seems to have supposed that the cure would be easy and that his own household (which ran with clockwork regularity) could easily assimilate S.T.C. as a long-term guest. Wordsworth, foreseeing difficulties, had felt that a word of warning should be uttered and had privately given Montague an account of Coleridge's state and of the kind of lodger he was likely to be. Montague was worried by what he heard, but still hoped for the best. Coleridge was duly collected and the Montagues' post-chaise set off for London. On arrival Montague, who had been thinking things over, may have broached the idea that Coleridge should take lodgings nearby, rather than moving into his own house. If so, Coleridge probably took offence and demanded to know the reasons for this change of plan. At all events, an exchange took place in the course of which Montague – who was famous for his lack of tact – repeated what Wordsworth had told him, with a few improvements of his own. As Coleridge recalled it, in his anger and humiliation, Montague's explanation was that 'Wordsworth *has commissioned* me to tell you, first, that he has no Hope of You'; adding that 'for years past [Coleridge] had been an ABSOLUTE NUISANCE in the Family'; and that he was 'in the habit of running into debt at little Pot-Houses for

Gin.'[57] Probably neither Montague nor Wordsworth said quite such things, but Coleridge's guilt and self-pity made him vulnerable and there was enough truth in the words to make them sting. Coleridge was shocked. He stopped writing to the Wordsworths and it was not until May 1811 that they were startled to hear, indirectly, that he was offended. He remained resentful for a further year, and though in 1812 the affair was patched up the friendship never fully recovered.

Coleridge had of course left the Montagues as soon as possible and De Quincey found him staying with more trustworthy friends, John Morgan and his wife, in Berners Street.[58] Here he no doubt heard S.T.C.'s views on Wordsworth at some length, and sympathized without taking sides, for he avoided getting drawn into the quarrel. Coleridge was still entertaining company and De Quincey was often invited out with him. At one dinner they met Nelson's mistress, Lady Hamilton. She and Coleridge liked each other enormously: he rose in her company to new heights of eloquence, and she responded by treating the party to an impromptu performance of one of Lady Macbeth's scenes. On another occasion, Coleridge was skulking in his room and would see no one. Mrs Morgan had been honoured with a note explaining that he had an attack of gout and would die if disturbed. De Quincey stayed anyway and talked to the Morgans until late at night. Suddenly someone noticed 'a body of smoke turning the corner from Oxford St. into Berners St. accompanied with a strong smell of burning': a piano-maker's shop was on fire. Coleridge was called. He emerged from his room fully dressed and without further ado made off round the corner to watch the fire. Like De Quincey, he enjoyed a good blaze.[59]

On 11 June 1812, when De Quincey was about to enter the Temple, an envelope sealed with black wax arrived from Grasmere. The writing was Dorothy's. Tearing it open, he read:

> My dear Friend,
>   I am grieved to the heart when I write to you – but you must bear the sad tidings – Our sweet little Catharine was seized with convulsions on Wednesday night . . . The fits continued till $\frac{1}{4}$ after 5 in the morning, when she breathed her last. She had been in perfect health, and looked unusually well – her leg and arm had gained strength – and we were full of hope . . . It is a great addition to our affliction that her Father and Mother were not here to witness her last struggles, and to see her in the last happy weeks of her short life – she never forgot Quincey – dear Innocent, she now lies upon her Mother's Bed, a perfect image of peace . . . It is an unspeakable consolation to us that

we are assured that no foresight could have prevented the disease in this last instance . . . The disease lay in the Brain, and if it had been possible for her to recover, it is much to be feared she would not have retained the Faculties of her Mind. God bless you!
Yours affectionately,
D. Wordsworth.[60]

De Quincey was shattered. Kate had been his particular friend, all the dearer for being the 'odd one out' in her family. She had spent much time at his cottage, and he had lavished affection on her. Her intense attachment to him had gone some way to satisfy his carefully concealed hunger for love. Now it was all over. Wordsworth, who was in Suffolk, heard of his daughter's death and immediately came up to London, where he called on his friend Henry Crabb Robinson for consolation. Together they went to see Coleridge, who was now on speaking terms with Wordsworth, and then, in Robinson's words, 'called on a Mr. De Quincey, a friend who had lately visited the Lakes, and was greatly attached to the little child. Mr. De Quincey burst into tears on seeing Wordsworth and seemed to be more affected than the father.'[61]

Wordsworth's grief was deep but restrained. De Quincey, by nature so much more effusive, gave way to emotion. The observation is confirmed by the letters he sent Dorothy. On 12 June he wrote:

My dearest Friend,
  Yesterday morning I received your letter with its bitter tidings. Oh that I might have seen my darling's face once again! Oh what a heavy increase of affliction to me and to her parents is this! What a bitter pang that we might not see her blessed face again . . . My dear friend, – write to me as circumstantially as you can; it cannot add to your grief to do this; and it will be an inexpressible consolation to me . . . Do not, my dear friend, omit anything that you remember.[62]

The next day he wrote again, without waiting for an answer:

My greatest consolation is that she must have lived a most happy life . . . Oh what a thought of comfort it is also that I was one of those who added to her happiness. What tender what happy hours we passed together! Many a time, when we were alone, she would put her sweet arms about my neck and kiss me with a transport that was even then quite affecting to me. Nobody can judge from her manner to me before others what love she shewed to me when we were playing or talking together alone. On the night when she slept with me in the winter, we lay awake all the middle of the night – and talked oh how tenderly together: When we fell asleep, she was lying in my arms; once or twice

I awoke from the pressure of her dear body; but I could not find in my heart to disturb her. Many times on that night – when she was murmuring out tender sounds of endearment, she would lock her little arms with such passionateness round my neck – as if she had known that it was to be the last night we were to pass together. Ah pretty pretty love, would God I might have seen thy face and kissed thy dear lips again!

Oh dear Friend – what a comfortable what a blessed faith is that of a true Christian, who believes that no more change will pass over us than may take away our frailties and our impurities ... and is assured that he shall meet and know again the child *as* a child, and his beloved *as* his beloved![63]

This is only an extract from a much longer letter, written over three days. De Quincey spent his time calling up memories of the girl, and indulging in torrents of emotion strongly tinged with self-pity. To the very last his possessiveness over Kate was conspicuous: 'One thing hurts me, when I think of this: I fear that the custom of the country would oblige you to let many idle gazers look at our darling's face after she was dead – who never gave her a look of love or interest when she was living. But you would not, I am sure, permit this.'[64]

This letter was finished on 15 June. Two days later, Crabb Robinson, who was a barrister, dined at the Middle Temple and found De Quincey dutifully keeping his term by eating dinner in the hall. His concise pen-portrait is worth quoting.

At four o'clock dined in the hall with De Quincey, who was very civil to me, and invited me cordially to visit his cottage in Cumberland. De Quincey is, like myself, an enthusiast for Wordsworth; his person is small, his complexion fair, and his air and manner those of a sickly enfeebled man. From which circumstances his sensibility, which I have no doubt is genuine is in danger of being mistaken for a puling and womanly weakness. At least, coarser and more robustly healthful persons will think so. His conversation is sensible, and I *suppose* him to be a man of information on general subjects. His views in studying the law will never, I think, be realized. He has a small independent fortune, and the only thing he wants is a magnificent library; this he is willing to purchase by giving for it a few years' close attention to the law. But he is resolved on no account to put himself under a special pleader, nor will he live more than six months during the year in London. I represented to him that I feared *nothing* could be expected from the law *so* studied. A man must be altogether or not at all a lawyer.[65]

A very perceptive account, considering it was only Robinson's second meeting with De Quincey. Apparently the latter was showing signs of strain, and the reference to his 'sensibility' suggests that he talked about Kate. Still, it does not sound as if he were in a paroxysm of grief. One has, on the whole, an impression of a reasonably cheerful conversation. Yet on 21 June he sent another long letter to Dorothy, telling her that 'my heart grows heavier and heavier every day'.[66] He had tried work and visits to Coleridge as antidotes, he said, but to no avail. He tortured himself not only with touching memories of Kate but also with fantasies of miseries that never existed: 'what anguish to us all, if she had called upon our names in delirium – and fancied that we would not come to her relief!' and his devotion reached new heights: 'Oh that I could have died for her or with her! Willingly dear friend I would have done this. I do not say it from any burst of grief, but as a feeling that I have ejaculated in truth and sincerity a thousand times since I heard of her death.' On 24 June he returned to Grasmere.

It is impossible not to feel that there was something inappropriate about the intensity of his reaction. Crabb Robinson sensed it; we feel it when we read the letters. The emotion is excessive or misdirected. Of course he was bound to feel great sorrow, but there are reasons for thinking his reaction complicated in ways he failed to understand himself. To begin with, Kate's death had closed the breach between him and Dorothy. She had been cool and distant, but now all was forgiven and he was 'My dear friend' again. He must already have suspected that the children were his closest bond with the Wordsworths, and joy at finding himself suddenly forgiven by Dorothy no doubt swelled the flood of sentiment. Secondly it seems evident that there was a sexual element in his love for Kate. He writes of her exactly as if she were a mistress, and comes to the edge of making the idea explicit. She embraced him 'as if she had known that it was to be the last night we were to pass together' – which suggests that De Quincey, at least, was thinking of future nights. 'In Heaven,' he says, 'the Christian shall meet and know again the child *as* a child, and his beloved *as* his beloved.' Is this to imply that in the next life two aspects confusingly blended on earth will be separate, so that he will be able to look on each with the appropriate feeling? Probably De Quincey was unaware of what he was hinting here. It is worth recalling that the age was in certain aspects oddly innocent. There was nothing remarkable about an adult and a child sharing a bed if space was short – Kate had slept with him at Town End on several occasions[67] – and the very fact that a child was involved enabled him to describe his night with her in detail which would have been considered indecent had she been a grown woman. The fact that sexual attraction to a child was simply unthinkable supplied a further element in his unhappiness. He was mourning her as something more than a child, and yet could not admit this to himself. Hence an element of hysteria in his sorrow, and an irresistible temptation to sentimentalize over Kate's charms and build up fantasies about his terrible separation from her.

There may have been a third and still more powerful factor. It seems likely, and the records of De Quincey's dream and fantasy life strongly suggest, that he was mourning not only for Kate but also for Elizabeth. His sister's death had been the most serious shock of his early life. It had been his discovery of death itself and his first experience of real loneliness, and the process of mourning had been left incomplete: his mother and brother had encouraged him to hide his grief, to suppress his tears. Sometimes he forgot her death, sometimes he fantasized about it, but he could never come to see it as sober fact. Kate, like Elizabeth, had offered him a love that was neither demanding nor threatening. Her death touched on a feeling he had not experienced since childhood and set loose a flood of misery which had been buried within him for years. Once back at Grasmere, he began to act very strangely. For more than two months after his return, he says, he went out to Grasmere churchyard and

> stretched myself . . . upon [Kate's] grave, in fact, often passed the night upon her grave; not (as may readily be supposed) in any parade of grief, on the contrary . . . I was secure enough from observation until morning light began to return; but in mere intensity of sick, frantic yearning after neighbourhood to the darling of my heart.[68]

At the same time he began to experience illusions or hallucinations of the dead girl. He took to walking in lonely fields high up on the hillsides and there he frequently 'saw' her walking towards him. 'Usually I saw her at the opposite side of the field, which might sometimes be at a distance of a quarter of a mile, generally not so much. Almost always she carried a basket on her head . . . uniformly the same little full-formed figure arose, uniformly dressed in the little blue bed-gown and black skirt of Westmoreland, and uniformly with the air of advancing motion.'[69] On nearer approach the visions generally resolved themselves into clumps of fern or foxglove, which De Quincey's mind, abetted by his poor eyesight, had transformed into Kate's figure. Sometimes the visions were involuntary; at other times there was an element of choice involved. Both the indulgence in solitude and the semi-conscious search for visions of the lost beloved were re-enactments of his response to Elizabeth's death.[70]

The consequence of all this, De Quincey claimed, was that he became ill. He continued his solitary wanderings and his vigils at Kate's grave through July and part of August, and, 'It was reasonably to be expected that nature would avenge such senseless self-surrender to passion; for, in fact, so far from making an effort to resist it, I clung to it as a luxury (which, in the midst of suffering, it really was in part).'[71] Nature's vengeance, he says, struck in late August, when he experienced a 'nervous sensation that, for a moment, caused sickness'. He drank a glass of brandy which removed the sickness but replaced it with 'a sting . . . of some stationary torment . . . a torment absolutely indescribable, but under which I felt assured that life could not be borne'. This indescribable torment, accompanied by a peculiar 'anguish' in breathing, drove him, he says, to doctors in several cities who could do nothing for him. In November he was at Clifton, where the malady vanished in the course of one night after producing a 'peculiar sensation' in his legs. Next day he was recovered but 'so much debilitated as with difficulty to stand or walk'. This was cured by 'hot sea baths' at Ilfracombe, and he found that with his illness his grief for Kate had inexplicably left him. When he came back to Town End in January 1813 the sight of a pair of her red shoes (given him as a memento by Mary Wordsworth), or of her grave covered with snow evoked no unhappiness. He later diagnosed his ailment, fancifully, as 'nympholepsy' – the heart-sickness attributed by the ancients to mortal men who had caught a glimpse of a nymph and fallen hopelessly in love. Somehow the spell of his 'nymph' had been broken.

This account has several interesting features. For example, it fails to mention that on 1 December another Wordsworth child, the six-year-old Thomas, died of pneumonia following measles. De Quincey was in Liverpool at the time, and on his way back to Grasmere received Wordsworth's note, begging him, 'Pray come to us as soon as you can' and ending, 'Most tenderly, and truly, with heavy sorrow for you my dear friend' – as if in appreciation of De Quincey's particular liking for the boy.[72] But Thomas's death did not prostrate De Quincey as Kate's had done. As for the symptoms of 'nympholepsy', they are easily explained if we are ready to accept that he may have been a little inaccurate in dating the start of his heavy opium use. He claimed to have been driven to it in 1813, after a recurrence of the stomach ailment he had known in London. This enabled him to argue that bodily suffering rather than self-indulgence drove him to the drug, a view he was eager to establish in the *Confessions*. But on the whole it seems likely that his use of opium was increased earlier, in 1812, soon after Kate's death. Opium was his normal tonic for times of depression, and in the misery that settled on him then it is hard to imagine him failing to use it generously. Moreover, he was a firm believer in opium as a prophylactic against cold and damp. As he 'often' slept the night in Grasmere churchyard he may have had a further reason for dosing himself. If he did step up his opium use in 1812, the illness is easy to explain. Stomach cramps are a common feature of opium withdrawal: the 'nervous sensation' and 'indescribable torment' may well have been the result of abstinence after a period of regular drug use. Convinced, rightly or wrongly, that his London ailment had been re-activated, he may in his ignorance have proceeded to suppress the discomfort by taking more opium – and so on. The other symptoms were no doubt psychosomatic. Difficulty in breathing was nothing new: stress or laudanum probably produced attacks of asthma.

It therefore seems likely that depression following Kate's death was the factor which turned De Quincey into a true opium addict. The change did not happen overnight (he reckoned that consecutive use for about 120 days was required) but in 1813 at latest it was complete and 'from this date' says De Quincey, 'the reader is to consider me as a regular and confirmed opium eater, of whom to ask whether on any particular day he had or had not taken opium, would be to ask whether his lungs had performed respiration, or the heart fulfilled its functions'.[73] How much opium he was taking in 1813 is not known, but he claims that by 1816 his daily dose was 320 grains. His daily morphine intake would thus have been about 32 grains or 2 grams: a heavy but not exceptional oral dose for an addict. His ways of measuring the drug were very rough and ready. In the *Confessions* he gives the dosage in 'drops', but implies that his normal measure was the teaspoon! A small teaspoon, he reckoned, held about 100 drops, which would contain four grains of opium.[74] But he did not take his laudanum from a spoon; he kept it, sometimes at least, in a decanter, and it seems a sensible guess that he drank it from a glass and had some rule-of-thumb about how many teaspoons went to a glass. As the size of teaspoons and the strength of laudanum were both variable his dosage may have fluctuated wildly, though he probably developed an intuitive sense of how much he should swallow at any given time.

It seems that he did make an attempt at controlling the potency of his laudanum, for some time before 1821 he happened to meet a doctor who was also an addict. They discussed the problem, and the doctor offered De Quincey his own answer, which was 'a particular mode of boiling the opium'[75] to remove impurities and obtain a solution of uniform strength. De Quincey never recorded his recipe, but probably it involved breaking up solid opium, boiling it in water, straining it and reducing the product to a sticky consistency, after which it could be diluted with alcohol (probably brandy). For real precision, the impurities strained off could be weighed to give the weight of opium left in the solution. Some such method he used. He kept solid opium at his cottage,[76] and a small balance of the type once used by Chinese druggists is still to be seen there. How it came from China to Grasmere is a mystery, but perhaps he used it to measure out his drug. (The initials on the balance case are T d'Q – not a form De Quincey himself would have sanctioned.)

His graduation to the status of addict passed unnoticed at the time but slowly people became aware that something was wrong. Recent experience with Coleridge had left the Wordsworths only too familiar with the symptoms of addiction, and in October 1814 Mary Wordsworth told Dorothy that she had 'gone to Grasmere to see Q. who has been confined almost to his bed for a week. Mr. S. says he has a diar[rhoea], such a one no doubt as C's – and from the same cause, so I hinted not very darkly to him.'[77] ('Mr. S.' is Scambler, the local apothecary. 'C' is Coleridge). De Quincey's ailment sounds like a symptom of withdrawal: he must have temporarily cut his dose for some reason. A year later, Sara Hutchinson told her sisters that De Quincey 'doses himself with opium and drinks like a f[ish]'.[78] If she knew, everyone in the Wordsworth circle must have known.

It may well be that rumours of his addiction were partly to blame for a further cooling of the relationship between him and the Wordsworths. His situation had always been precarious, for both Wordsworth and Coleridge had been given to making scathing comments about him to other people, whilst finding him too useful to offend. His library and his unfailing readiness to help in their projects made him valuable, and yet they probably did not feel a great personal liking for him. Sara was always ready for a walk or a gossip with him, yet her references to him in letters are invariably malicious. Even Dorothy, who had shown such fondness for him, had been very quick to take offence at his alterations to the garden at Town End. At every point there was something brittle in these relationships, and now they began to give way. In February 1813, Dorothy reported sardonically that John Wordsworth

> now goes to Mr de Quincey for a *nominal hour* every day to learn Latin upon a plan of Mr de Quincey's own 'by which a Boy of the most moderate abilities may be made a good Latin scholar in six weeks!!!!' This said nominal hour now generally is included in the space of twenty minutes; either the scholar learns with such uncommon rapidity that more time is unnecessary, or the Master tires. Which of these conjectures is the more probable I leave you to guess.[79]

For Dorothy this tone is something new. Later she adds, 'Mary Dawson talks to us in private of leaving Mr. de Quincey . . . She is tired of Mr. de Q's meanness and greediness.' The hostility of this is startling. Obviously Mary Dawson had been indulging in some unpleasant tale-bearing. Neither meanness nor greediness was among De Quincey's failings, though to Mary Dawson and those who chose to listen to her his simple way of life may have looked like miserliness. But perhaps Mary was stirring up trouble for reasons of her own. A number of De Quincey's friends, including the Wordsworths, had his permission to borrow the cottage when he was away. It seems that on some occasion, Mary, against her master's wishes, refused to allow the Wordsworths casual use of the place, alleging that he had given orders that no one was to stay.[80] The Wordsworths naturally took offence. Although not a young woman, Mary Dawson was dismissed from Town End in the autumn of 1813 with an illegitimate child, so it seems possible that setting De Quincey and the Wordsworths at odds was part of a strategy to secure her own privacy at Town End during the master's long absences from home.

There were other, subtler sources of tension. De Quincey had come to Grasmere as the young disciple of Wordsworth. Five years later this was no longer a suitable role and he wanted to be respected in his own right, but Wordsworth's attitude would not change. The two men shared certain interests – poetry, psychology, landscape – but Wordsworth, with justice, regarded himself as supreme in these fields and showed little patience when De Quincey wanted to hold forth on the same topics. No doubt his tendency to philosophical long-windedness bored Wordsworth. There were some friends to whom Wordsworth would listen deferentially; but to others, including De Quincey himself, the poet 'did not even appear to listen; but, as if what they said on such a theme must be childish prattle, turned away with an air of perfect indifference; began talking, perhaps, with another person on another subject'.[81] De Quincey felt such snubs deeply. At times, too, he was hurt by comments implying that he was still an outsider. He mentions an occasion when he, Wordsworth and Southey were walking together and talking of Charles Lloyd, who was then in the grip of one of his periods of mental disturbance. Wordsworth was telling Southey something about Lloyd's condition, which De Quincey failed to hear. When asked to repeat it, Wordsworth replied that 'what he had said was a matter of some delicacy, not quite proper to be communicated except to *near friends of the family*'.[82] De Quincey, who knew the Lloyds intimately and knew also that they were not especially fond of Wordsworth, was annoyed, though he persuaded himself that he was merely amused by Wordsworth's arrogance. Other aspects of the poet's character began to irritate him. For example, it was Wordsworth's habit to display a certain contempt for books. This may or may not have been a conscious pose, but it led to some startling behaviour. On one occasion, De Quincey claims, Wordsworth, having tea at Town End, wanted to refer to a passage in one of De Quincey's books. The book was unread and the pages had not yet been cut, so Wordsworth picked up a buttery knife from the tea-table and used it to cut open the pages he wanted, leaving the book smeared with butter.[83] At the same time it is easy to see why the Wordsworths may have begun to find De Quincey tiresome. He took on obligations towards the children but seemed idle about fulfilling them. He had come to Grasmere an avowed disciple of Wordsworth: was it their fault if he also insisted on being a friend, and pressed himself too eagerly at times into the family circle? After 1813 he seemed to be following Coleridge's downhill path as an opium addict, and they did not want a second relationship of that kind.

But if after 1813 close friendship with Wordsworth seemed unattainable, still there was no question of De Quincey's leaving Grasmere. For, in his own words, 'Other attractions had arisen; different in kind; equally potent in degree. These stepped in to enchain me precisely as my previous chains were unlinking themselves and leaving me in freedom.'[84]

On 13 March 1802, Dorothy had recorded in her journal a walk from Grasmere to Rydal. Hail was falling, and as she and William passed The Nab, an old farmhouse at the edge of the lake, she noticed the six-year-old daughter of the house watching them:

Little Peggy Simpson was standing at the door catching the hail stones in her hand — she grows very like her mother. When she is sixteen years old I dare say that to her Grandmother's eye she will seem as like to what her mother was, as any rose in her garden is like the rose that grew three years before.[85]

In 1813 Peggy (properly Margaret) Simpson was seventeen, and she had caught De Quincey's eye. How she met him is not known, but The Nab was only three miles from Town End and no doubt some neighbourly business brought him into contact with her father, John Simpson, who was a "Statesman' (the local word, from 'Estatesman') — a small farmer who farmed his own land. This land had come to Simpson through his wife, whose family had farmed The Nab since 1332, so Margaret could claim venerable ancestry among Westmorland farming folk, but to a contemporary view she was definitely De Quincey's social inferior, and his relationship with her testified to a remarkable carelessness about local opinion. He had known the Simpsons at least since March 1813,[86] and in 1814 a love affair between him and Peggy was flourishing and he was on good terms with the whole family. Peggy was the eldest of six children, the youngest of whom was five in 1813. No doubt De Quincey's knack with children was useful here, and he seems also to have liked Mr Simpson well enough, although political disagreements must have made the atmosphere rather strained at times, for John Simpson was 'a rank Jacobin' (in De Quincey's words) full of hostility to 'the nobility — gentry — clergy — magistracy and institutions of the land'.[87] De Quincey debated with him but his philosophical High Toryism could make no breach in the farmer's forthright radicalism.

The Nab may be seen today much as it was when De Quincey visited Margaret there. A long, two-storied building, plastered and slate-roofed, it stands a little back from the present main road to Grasmere at the edge of Rydal Water. A lozenge-shaped stone slab over the porch carries, roughly carved, the date 1702, though the pointed, stone-mullioned windows look older. A few yards from the porch, on the other side of the road, is the gently sloping shore of the lake, thick with reeds. The cottage faces due south: opposite its windows, in the midst of the lake, is a small wooded island, and beyond the rise the great shouldering masses of Loughrigg Fell, covered in the lower reaches with clumps of trees and smoothly grassed up to the irregular line where the edge of the fell runs against the sky. Behind the house is a field, and then wooded slopes which ascend steeply to the crags of Nab Scar.

Unfortunately we have no portrait or detailed descriptions of Margaret. But there are occasional passages in De Quincey's writings where the tone of personal experience is heard in contexts that suggest that he may have her in mind. The heroine of his story 'The Household Wreck', written soon after her death in 1837, may well be based on her. If so, the story tells us a good deal about De Quincey's attitude to her.

> When I first saw her [the protagonist tells us], she . . . was merely a child, not much (if anything) above sixteen; but, as in perfect woman-hood she retained a most childlike expression of countenance, so even then in absolute childhood she put forward the blossoms and dignity of a woman. Never yet did my eye light upon creature that was born of woman, nor could it enter my heart to conceive her, possessing a figure more matchless in its proportions, more statuesque, and more deliber-ately and advisedly to be characterized by no adequate word but the word *magnificent* . . . Though in the first order of tall women, yet, being full in person and with a symmetry that was absolutely faultless, she seemed to the random sight as little above the ordinary height . . .
>
> To this superb young woman . . . I surrendered my heart forever almost from my first opportunity of seeing her; for so natural and without disguise was her character and so winning the simplicity of her manners, due in part to the deep solitude in which she had been reared, that little penetration was required to put me in possession of all her thoughts and to win her love.[88]

This tallies so exactly with the known facts that, given De Quincey's habit of introducing large slices of autobiographical material into his fiction, there need be little doubt that he is describing Margaret. A comment of Dorothy's[89] confirms that she was rather a large girl, and we know that De Quincey was on other occasions captivated by well-built women – he was enthusiastic, for example, about the 'mag-nificent' Lady Hamilton.[90] It is also noteworthy that he emphasizes the attraction of child-like looks combined with womanhood. If the fic-tional passage shows us how he saw Margaret, it almost implies that he found in her the same blend of qualities that drew him to Kate Wordsworth, but in a reversed relationship. Kate was both 'a child' and 'his beloved'; Margaret was 'merely a child' yet also a 'superb young woman'. She was nearly ten years his junior, and her lack of education, far from discouraging him, was a source of additional delight: it helped him see her as an embodiment of untutored pastoral innocence, and made it easier for him to treat her as a child. (Early in their courtship he gave her a copy of *The Vicar of Wakefield*: she read it, believed every word, and was most upset when he explained to her that it was all made up.)[91] He was frank enough to admit that this sort of thing was no deterrent. 'I could not, perhaps, have loved, with a perfect love, any woman whom I had felt to be my own equal intellectually', he explained, 'but then I never thought of her in that light.'[92] On the other hand, we may suspect that Margaret mothered him at times: taller and bigger than he, she was probably able to supply the protective affection he had missed in childhood.

A more calculating mind than De Quincey's might have been troubled about the social consequences of a love affair between a gentleman and a mere 'statesman's daughter, but he seems to have had no misgivings. He was at his most spontaneous and relaxed with women who were his social inferiors, and if he thought about the matter at all he no doubt saw it as a poetic idyll in real life. Margaret's class position only enhanced her romantic appeal. As he wrote later,

> a beautiful young woman in the very poorest family, unless she enters on a life of domestic servitude, . . . so long in fact as she stays under her father's roof, is as perfectly her own mistress and *sui juris* as the daughter of an earl. This personal dignity, brought into stronger relief by the mercenary employments of her male connexions, and the feminine gentleness of her voice and manners, exhibited under the same advantages of contrast, oftentimes combine to make a young cottage beauty as fascinating an object as any woman of any station.[93]

He did his best, in a rather naive way, to draw the Simpsons and his other friends together. At Christmas 1814 he held a party, and anxiously pressed Wilson to come:

> My dear Friend,
>
> I have promised for you that you will meet a party (viz. young Mrs Jackson, Miss Huddlestone, – the family from the Nab etc.) on Christmas eve; . . . I conjure you, do not bring me your sponsor into discredit, nor disappoint the company (who are all anxious to see you) by not appearing . . . Come to dinner, if you can; but, at any rate, *come.*[94]

However he may have idealized Margaret in thought, De Quincey was no self-tormenting Angel Clare. He fell in love with her, she returned his feelings and he took to visiting the Nab by night as well as by day. When the nocturnal trysts began is not known, but in January

1816 Wilson, who had moved to Edinburgh, paid a return visit to the snowbound Lake District and, he told his wife, 'walked to De Quincey's, which I reached at half-past one o'clock in the morning; he was at the *Nab,* and when he returned about three o'clock, found me asleep in his bed'. [95] John Simpson, for all his radicalism, seems to have been canny enough to turn a blind eye to these goings-on. Perhaps he thought of De Quincey as a rich man and felt that the connexion promised well for the future.

De Quincey's relationship with Margaret must have been one of his few consolatons in the years following 1813, for increasingly things at Grasmere went wrong. His health was dependent on laudanum, and any reduction of his intake produced serious stomach pains — either a withdrawal symptom or, as he thought, the result of some abdominal ailment. He found it increasingly difficult to get up in the mornings[96] and tended, like Coleridge, to stay in bed late and then remain up until the small hours. As his cycle of activity slipped out of step with the daylight hours he became cut off from friends and neighbours. Close friends were in any case fewer, for misfortune overtook both Charles Lloyd and Wilson. Poor Lloyd suffered a breakdown in 1813, and in 1816, after a series of crises, was taken away to an asylum near York. Wilson ran into financial difficulties in May 1813 and was forced to ask De Quincey for a loan of £200. De Quincey responded immediately although his own reserves were running dangerously low, but what had looked like a short-term embarrassment for Wilson turned out to be the prelude to disaster. In 1815 he learned that his uncle, who had the management of his fortune, had been indulging in some sort of dishonesty which had led to the loss of about £20,000 — the greater part of Wilson's capital.[97] Wilson took the blow in reasonably good spirits, but there was nothing for it but to leave Elleray and take his wife and children back to Edinburgh where they could all live in his mother's house whilst he read for the Bar.

De Quincey's own study of law, though less than half-hearted, still provided the excuse to spend a few weeks in London three times a year. He continued to keep terms at the Middle Temple until 1815 and enjoyed the social life London offered. His main contacts were Coleridge, Lamb and Crabb Robinson. Robinson found De Quincey interesting, but did not altogether like him. Meeting him in February 1814, he noted

De Quincey has a fine and very superior mind. He talks about Wordsworth with the zeal and intelligence of a well-instructed pupil, and his style, with a mixture of pedantry and high-flown sentimentality, evinces a man who thinks while he talks and who has a discriminating judgment and delicate taste.

A few days later, after an evening with De Quincey at Lamb's, his feelings were still ambivalent:

De Quincey is a dry solemn man, whose conversation does not flow readily, though he speaks well enough and like a sensible man. He is too much a disciple and admirer to have anything of his own. But he is still an amiable man, and though it is an effort to keep up a conversation with him on general subjects, he is an interesting companion.[98]

It sounds as if De Quincey had been nervous and self-conscious – perhaps through shyness – in Robinson's company. With Lamb, however, he became intimate to the point of telling him about Margaret in the early days of their acquaintance,[99] and introducing him to Richard, who was in London for a while. On one memorable occasion they met in Bond Street, where the brothers De Quincey had gone to view two 'large and splendid' paintings by Salvator Rosa. Richard was unimpressed by Rosa's lurid acreage of canvas and expressed his opinion like a true sailor. 'Damn the fellow!' he cried, 'I could do better myself', and he spat out a well-chewed plug of tobacco, which stuck to the frame of the painting. The other bystanders were horrified, but Lamb's glee was inexpressible.

Frequent coach travel between Westmorland, London and Somerset in the years from 1812 to 1817 contributed a curious element to De Quincey's fantasy-life and later to the ghastly dreams which tormented him during his periods of opium withdrawal. Travel had always held an important symbolism for him, if only because it meant an escape from the various situations in which he had grown miserable through failure to live up to his own and other people's expectations. At Oxford he has succumbed, like many students, to the cult of the stagecoach. Oxford was an important centre of coach travel and one of the sights of the town was the array of a dozen gleaming coaches and their teams which waited each morning in the High Street, ready to set off for every quarter of the kingdom. Individual drivers were well known about town and had a reputation as 'characters'. Undergraduates generally insisted on travelling 'outside' on the top of the coach, and frequently bribed the driver to let them drive for a stage or so, a dangerous practice of which the inside passengers, fortunately for their peace of mind, generally remained ignorant. De Quincey had

Thomas De Quincey, aged about two-and-a-half years

Thomas De Quincey. Oil painting by Sir John Watson Gordon, c.1845

Elizabeth Penson Quincey, De Quincey's mother

Thomas Quincey, De Quincey's father

Greenhay. Engraved from a painting, now lost, by Alexander or William Carse

Mrs Best's cottage, Everton. Watercolour by H. C. Pidgeon, 1840

Thomas De Quincey, aged sixteen

Richard De Quincey

Charles Lamb. Oil painting by William Hazlitt, 1804

Samuel Taylor Coleridge. Oil painting by Washington Allston, 1814

William Wordsworth. Chalk drawing by B. R. Haydon, 1818

Dove Cottage

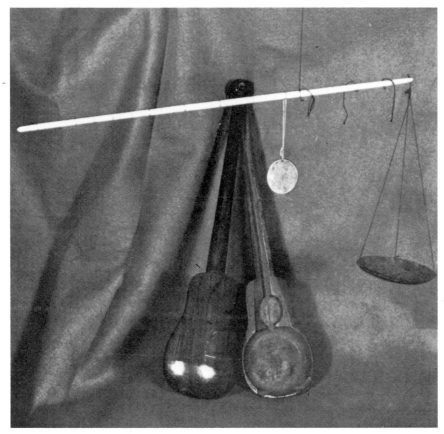

Chinese druggist's balance and case, said to be De Quincey's: his initials may be seen scratched on the case at the left

...to draw it and sometimes to run with it, though there it was not
... hill. I thought this very strange, because your carriage is hard
... when only you and Sister are in it—except when it is going
... hill; so I looked at it a long time to see how it was made; and
... I had found out.—I cannot make tell you very well, until I
... see, what it was that made it go so much easier to pull: but I
... draw here something like a picture of it:—

the boy, who is drawing it, [you see] is turning round to look at me: on...
... there is not room for me; else I ought to be drawn just before him
... asking him who made the carriage.—The children are all hid by the
... curtains: those strokes below the curtains are meant for rails

Drawing of a children's carriage in De Quincey's letter to John Wordsworth,
28 March 1809

John Wilson. Oil painting by Sir Henry Raeburn, c.1805

William Blackwood. Oil painting by Sir William Allan

Florence De Quincey. Crayon by James Archer, 1833

Thomas De Quincey. Daguerreotype, 1850

De Quincey with his daughters Emily and Margaret, and granddaughter Eva.
Pastel by James Archer, 1855

Mavis Bush Cottage, Lasswade

neither the nerve nor the physique to indulge in driving, but he was a regular outside passenger on the mail coaches, and by 1814 his standard remedy for the cold was a good dose of opium, which 'after an hour or so', he claimed, 'diffuses a warmth deeper and more permanent than could be had from any other known source'.[100] In the course of years, the box of a mail coach became, like the box of an opera house, one of his favourite settings in which to enjoy the euphoria and god-like detachment produced by opium. Memories of flirting with the coachman's granddaughter, whilst horses were changed at an inn on the Bath road, remained with him all his life, or so he claimed. Highly coloured in memory, glowing with that aura of ineffable secret meanings which opium can conjure out of the most ordinary events, conversations with 'Fanny of the Bath Road' found their way into his daydreams and later, hideously elaborated and blended with horrific sexual images, into his nightmares.[101] If 'Fanny' is not purely a figure of fantasy, he no doubt met her on his trips to Westhay in Somerset, when he would naturally take the Bath coach from London.

On the road north, in 1816 or 1817, De Quincey's drugged consciousness encountered an experience even more obsessively memorable, and one which was nearly fatal. He was taking a coach from Manchester to Westmorland some time after midnight, riding as usual on the box and fortified with 'a small quantity of laudanum'.[102] The coachman was known to him and they fell into conversation. The coachman, it turned out, was involved in a court case at Lancaster, and, driving the night mails in the intervals of attending court, had not slept properly for seventy-two hours. During the first eleven-mile stage he kept falling asleep as he drove. De Quincey felt uneasy about this, but he hoped for the best until, twenty-four miles north of Manchester, the coachman fell fast asleep in his seat as the coach continued to thunder northward at full speed. The horses knew the route; the driver had the reins firmly gripped in his hand, and had crossed one leg over that hand so that they could not slip. The guard at the rear of the coach was silent – probably also asleep. De Quincey found himself the sole waking person in charge of the mail. This predicament intrigued rather than frightened him at first and he sat comfortably enough reflecting dreamily on the silence of the night, the emptiness of the roads, the fact that it was August and his birthday would soon be coming, and whatever else the drifting currents of thought liberated by opium happened to bring him. Then he heard a sound from the road ahead. Another vehicle was approaching, and – he suddenly realized –

the mail coach was on the wrong side of the road. Reverie changed to nightmare: he tried to wake the driver, but could not rouse him. The guard was asleep at the back of a roof piled with mail bags: there was no way of getting to him. De Quincey tried to wrest the reins from the driver's hand but could not get them free. The horses swept at full tilt round a corner of the road and there appeared 'an avenue straight as an arrow, six hundred yards in length', lined with trees, at the far end of which dawn light and the coach's lamps revealed a small, fragile gig in which were seated a young couple. They were full in the path of the coach and were not even looking at the road. Struggling to think clearly and act decisively in defiance of his habitual nervous hesitancy and a recent dose of opium, De Quincey found himself paralysed as the vehicles advanced towards head-on collision. Finally he pulled himself together and yelled. The man in the gig did not hear. He yelled again and the man looked up. The scene unfolded before De Quincey's dazed eyes as if in slow motion. The man in the gig looked at the coach. Then he stood up. Dragging back the reins, he pulled his horse around, and drove it forward just in time to move the main part of the gig out of the coach's path. Then the coach was on them. It struck the gig a glancing blow which 'resounded terrifically', but when De Quincey looked back, fearing the worst, the couple in the gig were unhurt, although the sight of the woman's terror-stricken face and gestures as the coach receded made a deep impression on him, and returned to haunt him in dreams for years afterwards.[103]

Somehow the coach reached Preston without further mishap, and De Quincey was rather surprised at the tranquillity with which he was able to order breakfast at the inn as if nothing had happened. We have only De Quincey's account of the event, which may, of course, be pure fantasy. If it is true, there may still be some special pleading involved. De Quincey's narrative shows almost excessive zeal in proving that he could not possibly have taken a more active part in averting the accident. Did he really, one wonders, try so hard to take the reins from the coachman? Would he have known how to use them if he had succeeded? If the episode came to haunt his dreams it may have been less from sympathy with the terror of the girl in the gig than from a hidden anxiety that he might have done something brave and dramatic had he not been immobilized by fear. Perhaps he secretly worried that once again he had been guilty of lying down before the lion.

In 1814 De Quincey's travels took a new direction, when his brother Richard bought a house at Wetheral, a village on the River Eden not far from Carlisle in Cumberland. At about the same time Wilson persuaded him to visit Edinburgh, and since Wetheral was not far from the Edinburgh road he probably stayed with Richard on his way. Local tradition at Wetheral as late as 1920 not only recalled De Quincey's visits, but maintained that he had written a novel there containing scenes set on the River Eden: a matter to which we shall return. Richard sold the house in May 1816, so De Quincey probably stayed there in the summer of 1814 and the autumn of 1815, on his way to and from Edinburgh.[104]

John Wilson was able to introduce him to most of the men who were soon to become luminaries of the Edinburgh literary scene. They included J.G. Lockhart, the future biographer of Scott; William Hamilton, the philosopher; James Hogg, the 'Ettrick Shepherd', poet and novelist; and many other men of letters, people now almost forgotten but notable in their own day for wit and talent. De Quincey made an immediate impact: Wilson had given him a good build-up before his arrival, but no one was disappointed. People were impressed equally by his learning and by his oddness. He had an aura about him which suggested that he ought to be famous for something, and indeed he may already have been trying his hand at literature, for the journalist R.P. Gillies records that at this time 'De Quincey, though he had spent long years in assiduous study, and by his friends was regarded as a powerful author, had not, so far as I know, published a single line . . . His various literary compositions, written in his exemplary hand . . . on little scraps of paper, must have reached to a great extent, but in his own estimation they were by no means "ready for the press".'[105] And in 1813, faced with having to read a philosophical essay to the Speculative Society of Edinburgh and having neither 'time, inclination, nor ability' to write one himself, John Wilson had written to ask De Quincey frankly if he would send something suitable, as if expecting him to have an essay at hand.[106] Perhaps De Quincey was already training himself to write, but refraining from facing the public in print until he was absolutely satisfied with the results.

Edinburgh gave him the company and stimulation he had begun to lack at Grasmere. He was more at ease with Wilson's friends than he had been in London with Crabb Robinson, and no one objected to his manner or conversation. Where Robinson had seen pedantry, Gillies saw wide learning and what Robinson had felt as sentimentality was accepted in Edinburgh as evidence of a delicate sensibility. He was, however, undeniably strange. Gillies noted his preference for recondite topics of conversation, and his appearance of 'moving in a separate world'. Lockhart gives a fascinating glimpse of him in a letter:

> I dined the other day at [Hamilton's] house in company with two violent Lakers — Wilson for one, and a friend of his, a most strange creature, for the other. His name is De Quincey; he was of Worcester. After passing on half of an examination which has never, according to the common report, been equalled, he took the terror of the schools, and fled for it to the Lakes. There he has formed the closest intimacy with Wordsworth and all his worthies. After dinner he set down two snuff-boxes on the table; one, I soon observed, contained opium-pills — of these he swallowed one every now and then, while we drank our half-bottle apiece. Wilson and he were both as enthusiastic concerning the 'Excursion' as you could wish.[107]

De Quincey's personality and his curious history so impressed Lockhart that in 1819 he introduced elements of both into 'Mr Wastle' in *Peter's Letters to his Kinsfolk*, a humourous portrait of Edinburgh society.

For all his reputation as a 'violent Laker', De Quincey was now in touch with a literary circle which was outside Wordsworth's orbit. With Hogg and Wilson especially he was in the company of men who could admire Wordsworths' poetry without unconditionally worshipping the man. Towards the end of 1814 Hogg and Wilson paid a visit to the Lakes, and one evening they dined with De Quincey, Lloyd and other friends at the Wordsworths' new residence, Rydal Mount. It was a memorable night, for the sky was lit up by 'a resplendent arch across the zenith, from one horizon to the other, of something like the aurora borealis, but much brighter', in Hogg's words. The company went out on the terrace to admire the display and when Dorothy expressed some anxiety about what the extraordinary sight might portend, Hogg reassured her, jokingly suggesting that it was 'a triumphal arch, raised in honour of the meeting of the poets!' According to Hogg, 'Wordsworth, who had De Quincey's arm, gave a grunt, and turned on his heels, and leading the little opium-chewer aside, he addressed him in these disdainful and venomous words: "Poets? Poets? — What does the fellow mean? Where are they?" '[108] It was an ill-humoured remark, though certainly Wilson's *Isle of Palms*, Hogg's *Poetic Mirror* and Lloyd's sonnets scarcely challenged comparison with the *Lyrical Ballads*. Hogg admits that he did not actually hear the remark, though that turning-away must have been eloquent enough; De Quincey reported it to him later. The striking thing is that Wordsworth made the comment in private to De Quincey, expecting his agreement. It did not occur to him that De Quincey's allegiance might have changed, affection for these minor poets rendering the comment hurtful for him too. Not that De Quincey had any illusions about the merits of his friends' poetry: his supreme admiration for Wordsworth's poems remained untouched. But men like Hogg and Wilson treated him with consideration. They raised his confidence, and his gratitude to them was sufficient to lead him to betray Wordsworth's trust when a conflict of loyalties arose.

Indeed, the crisis of his relationship with Wordsworth was near, and it seems to have been precipitated by the poet's disapproval of the affair with Peggy Simpson. De Quincey continued to visit her whenever he was in Grasmere during 1815 and at first Wordsworth's concern must have been merely a protective impulse to save De Quincey from a foolish entanglement, for he continued to entrust the young man with important business, sending him to London in February to supervise the printing of a new edition of his poems.[109] Wordsworth had not forgotten the birth agonies of his ill-fated pamphlet, but he recalled them only to reassure Stuart, who it was hoped might find room in his paper for a series of 'Letters' by De Quincey answering Wordsworth's hostile critics at the *Edinburgh Review*. De Quincey, Wordsworth writes, 'is a friend of mine whom you will recollect, with no very pleasant feelings, perhaps as having caused you some trouble while my Tract occasioned by the Convention of Cintra was printing . . . I hope this letter will serve to remove any little prejudice which you may have against him . . . You need not doubt that the Letters will be a credit to any Publication, for Mr. D. Q. is a *remarkably* able man.'[110] But the 'Letters' never appeared, and Mr D. Q.'s stock fell further at Rydal Mount. 'As usual Peter is very entertaining, now that he is fresh,' Dorothy wrote coolly (using his household nickname, 'Peter Quince') when he returned in March, adding, 'The proof of his letters to the Courier is actually in the hands of the Editor.'[111] But his derelictions could not be covered up for ever and in time the truth came out. 'Notwithstanding his learning and his talents,' she sighed in April, '[he] can do nothing. He is eaten up with the spirit of procrastination.'[112]

At some point in 1815 Wordsworth began actively to intervene in De Quincey's affair with Margaret. No doubt he tried to be tactful at first and merely dampen his enthusiasm for the girl. De Quincey talked warmly of her 'angelic sweetness' – a phrase which irritated the Wordsworths [113] – and disapproval was shown. De Quincey soon decided that Wordsworth was a poor judge of female beauty[114] and probably had to endure a few choice words on Peggy's lack of education and social polish. Worse was to follow, for he began to notice that Wordsworth was showing an unwonted fondness for accompanying him on his late-night walks. Could it be that his clandestine visits to The Nab had been discovered? The secret had been closely kept, yet night after night he was denied his privacy and the company of his mistress. 'It drove me crazy,' De Quincey raged, recalling the episode years later. '[It was not] possible unless he had corresponded with fairies, that he should then know anything . . . He could not: it was impossible: I am sure it was.'[115] But there was no need to postulate fairy spies. In a small village walls have ears, and there must have been gossip. In September, receiving a letter from his mother, he was appalled to read:

> I have wavered often while writing this note, and at last resolve to say a word of the report which we now suppose had no truth in it. It seemed to come from high authority that you were about to marry, and nothing short of an oracular Voice could have made us listen to the tale, considering your want of means to meet the demands of a family . . . I cannot help begging of you to let me know your designs, and also to consider well before you trust the mere impulse of feeling, if, as I have but just now heard, the sober judgment of your Friends cannot approve the step.[116]

How had she found out? The answer seemed clear. That 'oracular Voice' was surely Wordsworth's. Directly or indirectly, and with some expurgations, he had told Mrs Quincey what was going on. Peggy's lack of education must have been stressed, for Mrs Quincey, to her credit, concedes that she 'can abate much of what the world demands in marriage', but points to 'congruities which are indispenable to *you*, which you may overlook in the delusion of fancy', with the results of lifelong misery. Her concern was natural: how could he be happy, married to an ignorant country girl?

Guilty and frightened, he seems to have taken as usual the easiest way to avoid immediate trouble, and denied everything. But he was beginning to slide into depression. His behaviour became reckless and he no longer tried to hide his opium addiction. In late November Sara Hutchinson mentioned that she and the Wordsworths had seen a good deal of him and Wilson. Wilson 'was tolerably steady' but 'Quince was often tipsy and in one of his fits had lost his gold watch . . . We believe that he will marry Peggy S[impson] after all – He doses himself with Opium & drinks like a f[ish] and tries in all other things to be as great a [?] legs as Mr. Wilson.'[117] By the spring of 1816 his guilt, or distaste for the Wordsworths' attitude, had grown so that he stopped visiting Rydal Mount altogether.[118] He was now almost isolated. Opium, books and the company of Margaret – who must have had a lot to put up with – were his only resources. Everyday life itself began to take on nightmarish qualities. In early summer Charles Lloyd arrived on his doorstep, having escaped from 'The Retreat', the Quaker asylum near York where he had been confined for several months. 'The Retreat' had a reputation for kindness but Lloyd told terrible stories of the 'brutal indignity' to which his keepers had subjected him. Whether or not these tales were true they horrified De Quincey, who was still more alarmed to realize that Lloyd was being pursued and wanted a hiding-place. Superficially his demeanour was calm but at times he would talk 'ferociously' about people against whom he held grudges. Eyeing him cautiously, De Quincey decided not to betray him to the authorities and invited him to stay the night, but Lloyd insisted on setting off at once for his home at Brathay. De Quincey walked some way with him, and once they were away from Grasmere Lloyd suddenly stopped 'in great agitation' and asked if De Quincey knew who he was. 'I dare say', he continued, 'you think you know me; but you do not, and you cannot. I am the author of all evil; Sir, I am the devil.' De Quincey ventured to doubt this, but Lloyd pursued: 'I know who you are; you are nobody, a nonentity; you have no being. You will not agree with me, and you will attempt to argue with me, and thus to prove that you do exist; but it is not so, you do not exist at all . . .' At last he calmed down, insisted on being left alone and walked off into the night. Soon afterwards he was recaptured and sent to an asylum in Birmingham.[119]

As if this were not enough, at about the same time De Quincey had – or thought he had – a visit from 'the Malay' immortalized in the *Confessions*. The whole episode may have been a dream. As De Quincey records it, there was a knocking at the cottage door and Barbara Lewthwaite, the servant girl, came to report that there was 'a sort of demon' downstairs. De Quincey, who was probably still in bed, made himself presentable and sallied down to the kitchen, where he found Barbara and a stray village child gaping in awe at a Malay in

turban and loose, dingy-white trousers. De Quincey tried him out with
some classical Greek, the nearest to an Eastern tongue that he could
muster, and the man replied in an unintelligible language – presumably Malay. All he seemed to want was rest, and he lay on the floor to
sleep for an hour, after which he was ready to leave. De Quincey, who
knew that opium was used widely in Malaya, gave him a piece, which
to his alarm the man put in his mouth and swallowed at a single gulp.
The dose was large enough, says De Quincey, 'to kill some half-dozen
dragoons, together with their horses', though for an addict it was a
tolerable amount. The man went on his way up the road, and as no one
found a dead Malay in the area De Quincey concluded that he was
probably a fellow addict.[120] Was the Malay a dream? No one can say.
Perhaps he stepped out of the frontispiece of Marsden's *History of
Sumatra* (1811) which shows a dark-skinned Malay with a striped
turban and an open jacket worn over some garment with a buttoned
waistband.[121] Marsden refers to the Malays' heavy use of opium, a
point which might well have impressed De Quincey. Still, the man may
have been real. Perhaps he was a seaman, coming from a port in the
south and making for Whitehaven or Workington.

Only one thing was wanting to complete De Quincey's troubles
and in the summer of 1816 it happened, for Margaret found she was
pregnant. Marriage was now inevitable, but for several months he did
nothing. In September Crabb Robinson paid him a visit, and was
saddened by what he found. De Quincey, he noted,

> has been very much an invalid, and his appearance bespoke ill-health.
> He was a very dirty and even squalid. I had read a bad account of him
> from Wordsworth . . . It appears that he has taken to opium, and, like
> Coleridge, seriously injured his health. I understand, too, though
> Wordsworth was reserved on the subject, he has entangled himself in
> an unfortunate *acquaintance* with a woman. He seemed embarrassed
> when he saw me, and did not ask me to walk upstairs, but said he
> should have a bed for me tomorrow. He *apologised* for not having
> written on account of bad spirits, and said he was *unfit* to see com-
> pany.[122]

He invited Robinson to go walking with him another day. Robinson
was not sure if he should accept, but the Wordsworths all urged him to
do so, for De Quincey's sake – a sign of the kindness they still felt for
him. De Quincey called at Robinson's inn late that night and seemed
'in much better spirits': perhaps he was just beginning his nocturnal
'day' on a fresh dose of opium.[123] Robinson found that Wordsworth

and De Quincey were avoiding each other: on the morning of 24 September the poet escorted him to Town End and left him near De Quincey's house; on the return journey, De Quincey took him to the gate of Rydal Mount but no further. In the evening Robinson went back to Town End, and again Wordsworth came along but left him before they reached the cottage. Robinson stayed the night and next day De Quincey took him over the fells to Coniston, asking him as they went whether the Wordsworths had mentioned his affair with Margaret. Robinson dishonestly said 'No', not wishing to create further trouble, but he had heard Mary Wordsworth speak her mind on the matter, and had no doubt about the cause of the estrangement between the poet and his former disciple.[124] No one, however, mentioned Margaret's pregnancy. If the Wordsworths knew, they kept quiet about it.

The child was born in November. He was baptized on 15 November at Grasmere Church and named William Penson, after De Quincey's elder brother. Wordsworth celebrated the occasion in a letter to Lamb which positively sparkles with malicious sarcasm:

> Bye the bye, an event has lately occurred in our neighbourhood which would raise the character of its population in the estimation of that roving God Pan,* who some years ago made his appearance amongst us. You will recollect, & Mr Henry Robinson will more easily recollect, that a little friend of our's was profuse in praises of the *'more than beauty'* – *'the angelic sweetness'* – that [?] the features of a fair young cottager dwelling upon the banks of Rydal Mere. To be brief, love and opportunity have wrought so much the tender frame of this terrestrial angel, that, to the surprise of Gods, Men, and Matrons, she has lately brought forth a Man child to be known, and honoured, by the name of William; and so called after a deceased Brother of its acknowledging Father Thomas de Q——. Such, in these later times, are the fruits of philosophy ripening under the shelter of our Arcadian Mountains. A marriage is expected by some; but from the known procrastination of one of the parties, it is not looked for by others till the commencement of the millennium. In the meanwhile he has proved employment in nursing the new-born.[125]

One might have expected more sympathy from Wordsworth, who had, after all, an illegitimate daughter of his own. Caroline, the daughter of Annette Vallon, with whom Wordsworth had had a short but intense love affair at Blois in 1792 before war had separated them and allowed them to grow into strangers, was now twenty-four,

* [Hazlitt]

recently married and living in Paris. But the secret had been kept closely within the family and De Quincey knew nothing of it, so Wordsworth was safe from revenge. As for De Quincey and Margaret, they married at last on 15 February 1817 at Grasmere. The marriage was by licence, perhaps to avoid the embarrassment of having the banns called. John Simpson and the parish clerk acted as witnesses. Possibly one or more of the Wordsworths came along as a gesture of goodwill.[126] In general the news was greeted with hilarity or tight-lipped condemnation. Sara Hutchinson told a correspondent, 'I have no news from this neighbourhood that will amuse you – except that Mr. de Quincey is at length married to his rustic beauty.'[127] Dorothy was vexed, scornful and perhaps a little jealous. She told Mrs Clarkson on 2 March:

> Mr. de Quincey is married; and I fear I may add he is ruined. By degrees he withdrew himself from all society except that of the Symp-sons of the *Nab* ... At the up-rouzing of the Bats and Owls he regularly went thither – and the consequence was that Peggy Simpson, the eldest Daughter of the house presented him with a son ten weeks ago, and they were married on the day of my return to Rydal, and with their infant son are now spending their honeymoon in our cottage at Grasmere. This is in truth a melancholy story! He utter'd in raptures of the beauty, the good sense, the 'angelic sweetness' of Miss Sympson, who to all other judgments appeared to be a stupid heavy girl, and was reckoned a Dunce at Grasmere School; and I predict that all these witcheries are ere this removed, and the fireside already dull ... As for him I am very sorry for him – he is utterly changed – in appearance, and takes largely of opium.[128]

Mary Lamb was more restrained: 'I am very sorry for Mr. De Quincey – what a blunder the poor man made when he took up his dwelling among the mountains.' Charles was more outspoken.

> It is a delicate subject [he wrote to Dorothy], but is Mr. *** really married? and has he found a gargle to his mind? O how funny he did talk to me about her, in terms of such mild quiet whispering specula-tive profligacy. But did the animalcule and she crawl over the rubric together, or did they not?[129]

The consensus was that De Quincey had let his friends down badly. It might be thought with some justice that it was the other way round. In any case, the irony is that they were wrong. Against all the odds, De Quincey had made the right choice and Margaret was to make him an excellent wife.

Still, circumstances were not propitious. De Quincey was almost penniless,[130] his legal studies had never even begun and he dared not tell his mother that he now had a wife and child to support. Worse, his capacity to confront the crisis was inhibited by opium. Concentrated thought and regular work were impossible, periods of lethargy frequent. The drug's seductive power temporarily to abolish anxiety, enabling him to forget his troubles for a few hours each day, posed the danger that De Quincey and his family would drift helplessly into ruin. But the danger was averted, and it appears that some time in 1817 he made a determined attempt to reduce his dosage and succeeded in controlling the drug's impact on his life to a point where he could work and keep his affairs in some sort of order. It seems likely that the responsibilities of marriage and fatherhood spurred him to the effort.

In the *Confessions*, he speaks of 'a year of brilliant water (to speak after the manner of jewellers), set as it were, and insulated, in the gloom and cloudy melancholy of opium': a year when his dosage had been reduced to forty grains or one thousand drops a day (an eighth of the previous level) without any difficulty, when he was happy with Margaret and at peace with the world. He paints an idyllic picture of the sitting-room at Town End on a typical evening of this year: a room full of books, a warm fire, a tea table with two cups and 'an eternal tea-pot' ('for I usually drink tea from eight o'clock at night to four o'clock in the morning'). Beside him is 'a lovely young woman' – Margaret – who will pour his tea for him. Near at hand also are 'a book of German metaphysics' and a decanter holding 'a quart of ruby-coloured laudanum'. Beyond the thick curtains rages winter weather, fierce enough to heighten the domestic cosiness of the scene.[131] He places this year of happiness, by implication, in 1816 or 1817 and claims that the 'Pains of Opium' followed afterwards, the 'brilliant' year being a last glimpse of happiness before opium revealed its true and terrible nature to the hapless addict.[132] This cannot be true. In September 1816, Crabb Robinson had found him dirty, sickly and depressed. A year later, in October 1817, he was ill and anxious again.[133] We might still be tempted to place a year of happiness between these two dates, were it credible that he could have reduced his opium intake by seven-eighths without encountering the 'Pains of Opium'. In fact, his account of the mental torment produced by opium reads like a selective account of the psychological symptoms of withdrawal such as would inevitably have attended drastic attempts at reducing the dosage. Most probably, then, there was no 'year of brilliant water'. There may have been days, weeks, even months of comparative happiness at times when his opium intake remained stable, but the 'Pains of Opium' must have dominated 1817 as he strove to break his dependence and render himself capable of work such as he did indeed undertake in 1818.

The psychological scars of this, his first 'prostration before the dark idol' of opium,[134] stayed with him for many years, and provided material for the most vivid sequence of his *Confessions*. The method he seems to have adopted was the common-sense one of gradually diminishing his daily intake in the hope of eventually reaching zero. His conclusion was that 'down to a certain point it can be reduced with ease and even pleasure, but that, after that point, further reduction causes intense suffering'.[135] How far this is accurate seems dubious, and the rationalizations of the addict have to be kept in mind. No doubt something in De Quincey wanted to believe that he still needed a certain minimum quantity of his drug. But it seems plausible enough that a gradual reduction of dosage would lead first to mild and chiefly psychological symptoms, then to increasingly unpleasant physical ones that might well scare the addict into thinking his life was in danger. Perhaps he started cutting his dose in the middle of 1817. It was then, he says, that peculiar psychological experiences began to trouble him. They started with a return of bright hypnagogic imagery such as he had not seen since childhood. As he lay in bed, 'vast processions' would move before his eyes in the darkness: elaborate, sharply defined panoramas of figures passed to and fro, forming 'friezes of never-ending stories, that to my feelings were as sad and solemn as stories drawn from times before Oedipus or Priam, before Tyre, before Memphis'.[136] The images were partly voluntary: they could be visualized by an act of will, and in fearful curiosity he experimented with this, until he found that the visions had a life of their own – he had only to think of something and he would see it before him in the dark. Worse, as he fell asleep it would persist and develop, 'drawn out, by the fierce chemistry of my dreams, into insufferable splendour that fretted my heart'. Sleep became an exhausting phantasmagoria of elaborate nightmares, the restless images bringing with them dreadful anxiety and feelings of limitless despair. He 'seemed every night to descend – not metaphorically, but literally to descend – in to chasms and sunless abysses, depths below depths, from which it seemed hopeless that I should ever re-ascend'. Terrible claustrophobia was accompanied by 'suicidal despondency' such as 'cannot be expressed by words'.

Some of the dreams brought back with startling immediacy long-forgotten incidents from childhood. Perhaps these were episodes of fear or humiliation, for other dreams elaborated the near-collision of carriages on the Preston road, the alien and frightful Malay who 'ran amuk' at the sleeper and 'led [him] into a world of nocturnal troubles', and his days of famished wandering in the London streets. Everything he wanted to forget came at him in his dreams, grotesque and magnified. Intermingled with personal memories were exhausting pageants drawn from his reading of history: armies, buildings, dances, battles. Dizzying distortions of time and space sickened him. There were architectural vistas 'in proportions so vast as the bodily eye is not fitted to receive' where distances seemed 'amplified to an extent of unutterable and self-repeating infinity'. He was reminded of the vast yet claustrophobic architectural extravaganzas of Piranesi, whose engravings of *Imaginary Prisons* Coleridge had once described to him and whose ornate, oppressive *Views of Rome* he had himself seen. Sometimes he felt he had lived for seventy or a hundred years in one night; sometimes a time far beyond any human lifespan seemed to have gone by.[137] These experiences were shaped as much by De Quincey's character as by the physiological processes of withdrawal. Always a vivid dreamer and visualizer, he had a trained imagination and a 'photographic' memory. He was very prone to obsessive, repetitious thought carried to the point of mental fatigue. His life had been lived in a continual climate of anxiety palliated by ambition and private fantasy. On one level, the dreams expressed his body's growing discomfort at deprivation of its familiar drug; on another they were the characteristic offspring of an unusual mind.

He does not describe his physical symptoms in detail. He mentions heightened 'animal spirits', an increased pulse rate, even a sense of feeling 'better'. This cannot have lasted long. As the dosage fell the typical withdrawal syndrome will have set in, with shivering, sweating, vomiting and other intensely uncomfortable symptoms. Probably he allowed this to continue for just so long – a few hours, perhaps, or a day – before having to resort to opium to relieve his sufferings, for neither he nor anyone else could feel sure that he would survive continued abstinence. 'Those', he says, 'who witnessed the agonies of those attempts, and not myself, were the first to beg me to desist.'[138] This probably means Margaret, who may well have been frightened. The fact that the symptoms would pass off harmlessly after a few days and leave him free from physical dependence was not known, and so he seems to have hovered agonizingly on the edge of withdrawal through most of 1817, 1818 and 1819, repeatedly reducing the dose, suffering, raising it again and so on. As a result his intake apparently stabilized at a lower level than before, but he did not break the dependence.

In the midst of this battle with opium he somehow managed to pull himself together and make his first serious attempt at finding work. A political struggle was developing in Westmorland, and in it he saw an opportunity. In 1818 Westmorland's two Parliamentary seats were both occupied by members of the local land-owning family, the Lowthers. The Lowthers were Tories, and two brothers, Lord Lowther and Colonel Henry Lowther held the seats, regarding them almost as hereditary property and expecting the local freeholders to vote for them in elections. Now their ascendancy was threatened. In 1818 a general election was due and Henry Brougham, a Whig and a reformer, arrived in Kendal determined to unseat one of the Lowthers, breaking the family's almost feudal grip on the politics of the county. There was likely to be a stiff fight, for the Lowthers were resented by many of the smaller landowners, of whom De Quincey's father-in-law, the 'rank Jacobin' John Simpson was fairly typical. To defend their position in public opinion the Lowthers decided to found a local newspaper to put forward their views. The key to all this from De Quincey's point of view was that Wordsworth was, unofficially, the Lowthers' chief adviser on intellectual matters. If they were to start a Tory paper in Kendal, it would need an editor; and if anyone could get the job for De Quincey, Wordsworth could. At the same time, his relations with Wordsworth had been poor for the past year. He decided to make a very cautious approach.

Accordingly, in March 1818 he sent Wordsworth a slightly formal letter mentioning the bad behaviour of Brougham's supporters at Grasmere and explaining that he had written 'two papers' on Westmorland politics which he would like the Lowthers' Political Committee to consider for publication.[139] Could Wordsworth recommend these papers to the Committee? The letter made no mention of the newspaper editorship. De Quincey was being circumspect, and wanted Wordsworth to see a sample of his political writing before the question of the editorship arose. Wordsworth agreed to read one of the papers, and De Quincey, who as it now turned out had not finished writing it, buckled to and sat up working until four-thirty a.m. on 1

April. Even then it was only three-quarters done but he sent it off, telling Wordsworth that it might be 'printed or burned' as he thought fit.[140] But the paper was a success. The Committee liked it – it was a point-by-point attack on a speech made by Brougham at Kendal the week before – and decided to publish it. It appeared in mid-April as a pamphlet entitled *Close Comments upon a Straggling Speech*. It was anonymous, but an attentive reader might have guessed that the author was a disciple of Wordsworth, for he refuted Brougham's sneers at the poet and referred to Brougham as an 'anonymous Trader in Reviews' – alluding to his connection with the *Edinburgh Review,* which was noted for its harsh criticism of the 'Lake' poets.

Close Comments was witty and well written. It at once established De Quincey as an able propagandist, and a few days later Wordsworth was thinking of publishing a letter De Quincey sent him about the iniquities of Brougham and his supporters. (Another of his letters seems to have appeared in the *Carlisle Patriot* for 25 April over the patriarchal signature 'One of the Old School'.) The ground was well prepared, so on 14 April he ventured to write to Wordsworth about the editorship. 'Do you know,' he asked, 'of any reasons which should make it imprudent or unbecoming in me to apply? . . . If you do not, and there should be no other person whose interests in this case you are inclined to prefer – I feel confident that you will do me the kindness to assist me in obtaining it with your recommendation.'[141] He took care to dissociate himself, and emphatically Margaret, from his father-in-law's radicalism: 'in spite of repeated attempts from her family to win her over to their way of thinking', he says, she has 'from the very first' taken his – the Tory – view of local politics. But he admitted two practical drawbacks. First, he could only commit himself to the job for a year, as he intended thereafter to 'remove finally to London for the prosecution of my profession as a lawyer'. Second, he did not feel competent to undertake 'the mechanical and commercial management of a Paper'. But 'perhaps this department could be conducted by some clever compositor or other person about the Press'. Certainly, he said, he was confident of his ability to select news items and produce political commentary, the paper's main function. On one crucial matter he anticipated objections and hastened to defend himself:

> In one point you may still feel some doubt of my competence . . . –
> judging from your former knowledge of me; in punctuality, I mean,
> and power of steady perseverance: but in this I am altered since I last

had the happiness to associate with you; and among other grounds of remorse, I have suffered too much in conscience on account of time left unimproved or misemployed – ever to offend in that way again, even upon calls of less importance than this would be.[142]

He added that even 'a trifling emolument' such as the job might bring in would be 'very useful' to him. He did not say so, but the situation was one of urgency, for Margaret was pregnant again. (The child, a daughter to be called Margaret, was born on 5 June.) With a certain ingenuousness he tried to entice Wordsworth by mentioning that he had nearly finished that series of replies to hostile critics which he had been promising for nearly a decade! These, he implied, could appear in the paper; and he had other 'stock' ready at hand – translations from Richter and from the minor works of Kant! – as well as original essays not begun yet, but 'very soon' to be written.

It was a brave attempt, but Wordsworth's confidence was not won. He bypassed the application and the job went to a Londoner under whose editorship the first issue of the new paper, the *Westmorland Gazette*, appeared on 23 May. But De Quincey's luck turned. The editor 'disgusted' the proprietors 'in every way'[143] and after a mere seven issues he was dismissed and the post was offered to De Quincey, whose first issue appeared on 11 July 1818.[144] A meeting of the proprietors on 19 August resolved 'that Mr De Quincey be paid £9 for the first three weeks that he was engaged and one guinea for each of the last three weeks'.[145] It was a timely rescue.

For an inexperienced editor, unused to deadlines and with a drug problem, running the *Gazette* was a formidable undertaking. Wordsworth watched with anxiety, assuring the Lowthers that the new editor was 'a most able man; one of my particular friends' but admitting some doubts about him 'on the score of punctuality'.[146] But De Quincey tackled the task with as much energy as he could summon and made, all things considered, not a bad job of it. As he had foreseen, some of the work – dealing with advertisements and subscriptions, overseeing the printing – had to be done by a clerk, one John Kilner, at Kendal, as he would not go to live there himself. The clerk was paid out of his salary, leaving a mere guinea a week[147] for De Quincey, whose task was to direct the paper's policy, write political leaders and select news items as he thought fit. He also provided miscellaneous original articles. Final sub-editing was mostly done by John Kilner. When De Quincey took over, the election had just finished and the Lowthers had held their seats. But Brougham had promised to meet them at the next election and had set up a local association to keep the reforming spirit alive in Kendal, so the political brawl continued in the local press, De Quincey's *Gazette* facing the older Whig paper, the *Kendal Chronicle*. De Quincey joined the fight with enthusiasm. Perhaps as a corrective to his social timidity, he delighted in argument and invective on paper, where he could express his feelings without personal confrontation. From the start his progress as a political writer was stormy. In the second number of the paper he had published a letter signed 'Philadelphus' in which he implied that Brougham had been a spy on the Continent – a claim which provoked Brougham to legal action against the *Gazette*.[148] As editor he continued in the same vein, bringing a new note of aggressive commitment to the paper.

In general, he took the view that local politics were of interest mainly as a microcosm of national. Brougham seemed to him significant as a democrat or, in De Quincey's words, a 'mobocrat' or 'jacobin'. Brougham was unusual, even amongst Whigs, in his custom of directing his speeches to the public as a whole, including the large section of the populace which had no vote. De Quincey, fostered in the political climate of the war with revolutionary and Napoleonic France, had no hesitation in identifying this as rabble-rousing Jacobinism. His articles repeatedly stress Brougham's tendency to mob-oratory and point with concern to his contempt for the stabilizing influence of landed property. De Quincey saw the battle between Brougham and the Lowthers as the first intimation of a 'great drama which, there is reason to fear . . . will one day be enacted, in larger proportions, upon the great theatre of the empire'.[149] Often, however, the *Gazette* deserted the philosophical heights for trivial in-fighting with the rival newspaper. Sometimes De Quincey's invective was so strong that the Lowthers themselves asked Wordsworth to persuade him to tone down his language. At times, too, *Gazette* and *Chronicle* traded insults so closely that to understand either it would have been necessary to read both. De Quincey, of course, was an inviting target for personal abuse in the *Chronicle*. For the first week or two the *Chronicle* editor could not find out who had taken over the *Gazette* and had to content himself with generalities, calling his rival 'a venal scribbler' and a 'degraded character' – terms which lacked the sting of personal relevance. But before long the secret was out and the *Chronicle* could hold up De Quincey's foibles to scorn, laughing at his 'patrician pen' and desire to inflict philosophical essays on his public,[150] and ridiculing his 'midnight rambles through and around this town (as your august personage is rarely seen anywhere between sun-rise and sun-set)'.[151]

No wonder De Quincey was moved to complain that 'in general the editors of newspapers are low-bred mercenary adventurers – without manners – without previous education – and apparently without moral principle':[152] a judgment the editor of the *Chronicle* was meant to take to heart. De Quincey, of course, saw himself as a superior sort of editor. His conduct of the paper was a characteristic blend of high-minded idealism, obsessive concern for detail and lively sensation-mongering. He put an immense amount of work into it and produced 'copy' at a rate which must have astonished everyone who knew him, but still the paper tended to slip out of control because he could not work fast enough or make firm enough decisions. A month after taking over he promised a plan 'for the future conduct of this Paper' but it failed to appear. It was the first of several promised items which never materialized. How often missing or incomplete items had to be made good for the press by Kilner is hard to say, because Kilner was a useful scapegoat when De Quincey found himself blamed for some lapse. It is plausible that Kilner and not De Quincey was to blame for a rude reply to a correspondent in June 1819; it seems less plausible that Kilner should have been responsible for printing a 'metaphysising' article on the theory of taxation as leader in the 19 September 1818 issue, instead of something more readable.[153] Sara Hutchinson mentions that some 'disgusting' articles about the Lake District had appeared in the *Gazette,* but was 'glad to say that Mr de Q. did *not know* of them being put in until too late'.[154] As the articles were taken from *Blackwood's Edinburgh Magazine* and were thought to be by John Wilson, Sara's confidence was probably misplaced.

De Quincey's own view of the paper was that it should have several functions, appealing to different classes of readers. It should be a journal of current national politics, a record of local developments, and a source of general entertainment and information. On the whole this breadth of interest, unusual for a newspaper of the day, was successfully maintained. The *Gazette* gave far more news items than the *Chronicle,* and they covered the most varied topics. Besides the usual reports of crime, accident and so on, anything remarkable or exotic might find a place – the 'Arrival of the Persian Ambassador and the fair Circassian' at Dover; the discovery of a wild boy in a German forest; a *Frankenstein*-like experiment with a galvanic battery on the corpse of a murderer, which was electrically stimulated to begin breathing, its face thrown into fearful expressions 'surpassing far the wildest representations of a Fuseli or a Kean'.[155] Such items were taken directly from the London papers, which were used as a kind of free press agency, and much of De Quincey's time was spent cutting out or summarizing news stories. For a few months he treated this task with his usual excessive care, rewriting almost every article, but in December he lost patience, informing his public that the paraphrasing of news items 'is a labour of the most unpretending rank. It is however far more fatiguing, more expensive of time, and more trying to the patience, than an equal quantity of original composition', and announcing his intention of giving up 'so unprofitable a waste of time' and printing the news without retouching.[156]

As time went on, Kilner took over more and more of this work whilst De Quincey busied himself with political leaders and essays on economics and taxation. Another of his special interests was assize court news. Early in his tenure, he had promised to reprint news of the more interesting criminal trials, partly for the intellectual interest offered by the complexities of the evidence, and partly because court cases, he thought, were a good way of impressing even the meanest intelligence with a healthy respect for morality and law. In practice, this meant that he regaled his readers with detailed accounts of murder trials and sex cases. The items on murder foreshadow the macabre essay 'On Murder considered as one of the Fine Arts' which De Quincey wrote nine years later, and record some of the murder cases discussed there. The articles on cases of rape, seduction and breach of promise are written with an eye to the titillation of the reader and take advantage of the fact that the courtrooms of those days offered no privacy to the witnesses. Full testimony had to be given to a court crowded with curious spectators and with reporters who rarely failed to comment on the personal attractions of the injured party, so that the *Gazette* was able to report, for example, that the chief witness in a rape case is 'a beautiful little girl of fifteen', or that in a prosecution for seduction the injured party is 'a very pretty interesting English girl, of 19 years of age, and apparently extremely fascinating in her manners and address'.[157]

The range of the paper was further extended in the late summer of 1819, when De Quincey began to introduce philosophical essays: 'Kant and Herder' was followed by 'Kant and Dr. Herschel' and 'The Planet Mars' – no doubt to the bewilderment of the Lakeland farming population. There were also pieces on local culture and folklore: the

229

essays on 'The Danish Origin of the Lake Country Dialect' were prepared for the *Gazette,* though they appeared after De Quincey relinquished the editorship, and the Easter custom of giving 'Pace-eggs' was recorded on 24 April 1819. The issue for 25 July 1818 includes an eloquent account of Grasmere's annual 'Rush-bearing' ceremony, clearly by De Quincey:

> Forty-one children, from the neighbouring families, both rich and poor, bearing in their hands *burthens,* composed of flowers inter-mingled with embellishments of coloured paper, walked in procession round the church; and then, according to ancient custom, entering at the great door, deposited in various parts of the church their splendid offerings . . . The lively expression of health and innocent gaiety upon the faces of so many fine mountain children assembled at this solitary churchyard, all well-dressed, and each equipped with a magnificent burthen of flowers, in connexion with the solemn beauty of the vale at this hour of a summer evening, gave an affecting interest to the whole spectacle.

The *Gazette* for 30 January 1819 gives us an unexpected glimpse of De Quincey at work, the result of a newsworthy accident at Town End:

> On Thursday night . . . an accident occurred at the house of Mr. De Quincey in Grasmere, which providentially terminated without injury to any of his family. Between one and two o'clock Mr De Quincey was sitting up and writing: in a single moment a volume of smoke passed between him and his paper so suddenly as to darken it in one instant as much as if the candles had been extinguished. On looking round to the fire, nothing was at first seen; but in half a minute, a great fork of flames . . . sprung out from a crevice in one side of the grate.

To put out the fire, the mantelpiece and grate had to be taken out, and 'the timbers about the fire-place, which were very old, were discovered to be all eaten into with fire and glowing brightly to a depth of two and a half feet within the wall'. Had De Quincey not been sitting up at his work the whole house might have been burnt. The *Gazette* mentions that the room was 'strewed on that evening with newspapers'. It was Thursday night, when De Quincey had to get his 'copy' ready for the printer, so no doubt those papers were being gutted to provide the week's quota of news for the *Gazette.*[158]

Living eighteen miles from the press, De Quincey had to meet a tight schedule. When things went according to plan, he finished writing and assembling his copy late on Thursday night. Early next morning he or Margaret took it to Ambleside post office, whence it was sent on the first coach to Kendal. There it was hastily sub-edited and set in type to be printed on Friday afternoon and evening for distribution on Saturday morning.[159] If De Quincey missed the coach on Friday morning, Kilner at the printworks filled up the paper with anything he could lay hands on. No doubt he had a store of unused pieces from previous weeks to tide him over. But such emergencies were rare. Faced with a deadline no man could delay, De Quincey drove himself hard and produced his copy week after week.

The conduct of the paper was not entirely left to his judgment, for the Lowthers naturally saw the *Gazette* as an organ for the expression of their views. They were old hands at managing the press, and though they judged it better not to own the *Gazette* the shareholders were their friends and agents and they expected De Quincey to toe the line. Rather than send their directives straight to him, they used Wordsworth as go-between. His assurance that the new editor was a 'particular friend' may have been taken to mean that he could keep De Quincey in order, and he certainly gave the impression that he had joint responsibility for the *Gazette*'s policy. His goodwill towards De Quincey continued and he allowed the *Gazette* to print six of his poems, one of them previously unpublished, but his support had its price and at times his letters read as if he were editing the paper himself. When the *Chronicle* became insolent in September 1818 he conferred with De Quincey and reported to Viscount Lowther, 'we have agreed upon the mode of noticing [the articles]'; when the Lowthers were unhappy about the contents of the paper, Wordsworth gave the editor a ticking-off and reported, 'He assured me that . . . nothing more of the kind will be admitted.' And if De Quincey failed to mend his ways, Wordsworth was not afraid to nag, announcing on one occasion, 'De Quincey has no firmness. – I shall be at him again upon the subject.'[160] De Quincey did not take all this lying down. When, two years later, the subject of the *Gazette* came up in conversation, he admitted to his London friends that, 'It was set up with a view of supporting the Lowther interest. "But," said he, "I so managed it as to preserve my independence, and it happened that during the year and a half that I was the conductor of the paper, the name of Lowther was scarcely ever mentioned in the leading articles." '[161]

As he worked at the *Gazette,* illness arising from his opium dependence continued. Withdrawal symptoms conspired with his usual hypochrondria to raise hideous terrors. About September 1818 he began to have dreams of 'lakes and silvery expanses of water' which, he says, 'haunted me so much that I feared that some dropsical state or tendency of the brain might thus be making itself . . . *objective*'.[162] When he also started to suffer from headaches, his fears were strengthened – surely it was hydrocephalus! Since Elizabeth's death he had never been free from terror of her illness. He admitted his anxiety to Wordsworth. 'She indeed was only eight years old,' he conceded, 'but you know it *may* attack an adult.'[163] His work suffered, but the headaches passed in due course. The next month a dog bit him and he decided he was developing rabies. But he survived, and an item in the *Gazette* for 28 November 1818 may shed light on the matter. It tells of a whole kennel of hounds having been treated for suspected rabies by the administration of opium, after which they all made a perfect recovery. No doubt De Quincey drew the inference, and dosed himself with his favourite medicine.

Yet the 'Pains of Opium', presumably the result of attempts to renounce the drug, were at their full intensity again in 1819. In March the *Gazette* reprinted a review of the *Travels* of Humboldt and Bonpland, quoting a horrific account of a crocodile's attack on a young Indian girl, whom it seized by the arm. The girl drove the creature off by putting her fingers into its eyes, but it bit off her arm before letting go. The episode found its way into De Quincey's nightmares, the crocodile and the girl's arm becoming focal points in a farrago of disgusting and ludicrous images. He dreamed of a crocodile 'driving four-in-hand from the box of the Bath mail'; the crocodile's granddaughter was Fanny, with whom he had flirted by the roadside on his journeys to Somerset, and she entered the dream followed by a horde of monstrous creatures who arranged themselves into massive heraldic compositions topped by a single disembodied female hand. The nightmares seemed to embody some sexual meaning which terrified and repelled the dreamer: girl, crocodile and monsters symbolized for him 'the horrid inoculation upon each other of incompatible natures'. They seemed to hint obscurely at incest, at bestiality. The worst thing about the dreams was that De Quincey recognized in himself a kind of fascination with these images, and the fear grew upon him that deep in his own mind there were alien tendencies, modes of consciousness he could not acknowledge as his own. In such a case, he explained later,

> The dreamer finds housed within himself – occupying, as it were, some separate chamber of his brain – holding, perhaps, from that station a secret and detestable commerce with his own heart – some horrid alien

nature. What if it were his own nature repeated, – still, if the duality were distinctly perceptible, even that . . . might be a curse too mighty to be sustained. But how if the alien nature contradicts his own, fights with it, perplexes and confounds it?[164]

Sometimes a sense of guilt and self-loathing mingled with the physical oppression of opium deprivation to produce lurid ordeals set in an imaginary Asia. De Quincey's extensive reading in travel literature and ancient history played its part here but the central organizing element was opium and its oriental associations. Opium, as he knew, had been used in ancient Egypt; in his own day it was the product of India and a rapidly growing curse in China (a country of which he cherished a peculiarly intense loathing, for reasons he could not himself understand, remarking in the *Confessions* that if he were forced to live there he believed he would go mad). In his worst nightmares all these things came together:

Under the connecting feeling of tropical heat and vertical sunlights, I brought together all creatures, birds, beasts, reptiles, all trees and plants, usages and appearances, that are found in all tropical regions, and assembled them together in China or Hindostan. From kindred feelings, I soon brought Egypt and her gods under the same law. I was stared at, hooted at, grinned at, chattered at by monkeys, by paro-quets, by cockatoos. I ran into pagodas, and was fixed for centuries at the summit, or in secret rooms; I was the idol; I was the priest; I was worshipped; I was sacrificed. I fled from the wrath of Brama through all the forests of Asia; Vishnu hated me; Seeva lay in wait for me. I came suddenly upon Isis and Osiris: I had done a deed, they said, which the ibis and the crocodile trembled at. Thousands of years I lived and was buried in stone coffins, with mummies and sphinxes, in narrow chambers at the heart of eternal pyramids. I was kissed, with cancerous kisses, by crocodiles, and was laid, confounded with all unutterable abortions, amongst reeds and Nilotic mud.

. . . The cursed crocodile became to me the object of more horror than all the rest. I was compelled to live with him; and (as was always the case in my dreams) for centuries. Sometimes, I escaped, and found myself in Chinese houses. All the feet of the tables, sofas, &c., soon became instinct with life: the abominable head of the crocodile, and his leering eyes, looked out at me, multiplied into ten thousand repeti-tions; and I stood loathing and fascinated . . . Many times the very same dream was broken up in the same way: I heard gentle voices speaking to me (I hear everything when I am sleeping), and instantly I awoke; it was broad noon, and my children were standing, hand in hand, at my bedside, come to show me their coloured shoes, or new frocks, or to let me see them dressed for going out. No experience was so awful to me, and at the same time so pathetic, as this abrupt translation from the darkness of the infinite to the gaudy summer air of highest noon, and from the unutterable abortions of miscreated gigantic vermin to the sight of infancy and innocent *human* natures.[165]

Contending with dreams such as this and with the *Gazette* left little time for anything else. His claim that 'for nearly two years I . . . read no book but one' may well be true if it refers to the years 1818–19. The one book was Ricardo's *Principles of Political Economy and Taxation,* which Wilson, now editing *Blackwood's Edinburgh Magazine,* had sent him for review. De Quincey did not review it, but he read it, and immediately recognized that Ricardo had made a major advance in turning economics into a science. Ricardo became his guide and prophet in matters of political economy and remained so for the rest of his life. In future years, Ricardo's theories of rent and value were to provide him with material for numerous magazine articles. Now, in 1819, he was so excited that despite his low state of physical and mental health he set to work preparing a pamphlet setting out 'briefly and elegantly by algebraic symbols' some points which he thought Ricardo had overlooked and which would form a useful supplement to the *Principles.* He hatched the grandiose, Kantian title *Prolegomena to All Future Systems of Political Economy* and got as far as assembling some notes for it.[166] He claims that the pamphlet was written and advertised, and the printers at Kendal ready to start on it, when it was given up merely because of his inability to write preface and dedication. More probably the pamphlet itself was never written.[167]

Apart from the *Gazette* his duties were neglected. Letters went unanswered, bills unpaid, except when Margaret could see to them. She carried on bravely, caring for the children, comforting De Quincey in his bouts of sickness and depression, making the most of what little money there was. The guinea-a-week from the *Gazette* proved insufficient within a few months and the sixteen pounds a year which was De Quincey's share of rent from a family property did little to improve matters.[168] By the end of 1818 creditors were pressing for £150, holding out the threat of prison if he could not pay, so he wrote to his Uncle Thomas and his mother, asking for loans. He asked Thomas Penson for £500. To inspire confidence he lied about his literary output, giving such a rosy picture that Penson may have wondered why he needed the money at all. '*Blackwood's*', he claimed, 'allows me to write as much as will produce sixty guineas a year' – perhaps a reference to some tentative offer of Wilson's which he had been too busy to take up. The *Quarterly Review*, he continued, 'has allowed me to write what has yielded 120 guineas a year'. This was untrue. The *Quarterly* had sent him Schiller's works for review four months earlier, though he had not yet opened them; Wordsworth was kindly trying to get him engaged to write for the *Quarterly* on economics, though as a Whig journal it eventually refused him. But he had never written for it, nor had it paid him.[169]

His letter to Mrs Quincey was more honest about his literary prospects but prevaricated on another subject, for he wanted to break the news of his marriage without revealing the fact that his first child had been born out of wedlock. This he did by leaving the date of his marriage vague and explaining his secrecy on the grounds that the imprudence of the marriage and Margaret's humble 'station in life' might have given his mother pain. The tone of the letter is peevish and it shows De Quincey in a poor light, however much we may sympathize with the miserably vulnerable state in which he wrote it. An immensely long document – a surviving draft of *part* of it runs to 3,000 words – it contains pages of self-justification relating in wearisome detail how each part of his fortune has been spent since 1806. Protesting at the tone of some letter already received from his mother, he indulges in an absurd blend of pomposity and self-pity:

> You would scarcely have addressed me, if I had been a member of Parliament or a distinguished Barrister or a judge or Chancellor of the Exchequer, in the tone which you hold in your last letter which addresses me sometimes as a baby and sometimes as a poor crazy nervous decayed gentleman boarded out by his friends in a retired situation where he may sit brooding and moping by the fireside and not disgrace his family by a more public exhibition. If I, instead of labouring for years to mature a great scheme of philosophy and education, had pushed myself forward in the paths of common vulgar ambition . . . I am sensible that I should have experienced a very different treatment from all my female relatives.[170]

Mrs Quincey, to her credit, chose to ignore the foolish aspects of this pitiful letter. She responded warmly and promptly, promising £160 in ten days at most. As for his marriage, she hinted that it had been unwise but concluded:

> let me at once assure you we all think there can be but one reasonable view taken of the condition of life which you have described your Wife's to be, and that view is the same as yours, that it is a happy and

respectable one, and we are greatly rejoiced to find that she has dignified it by her conduct, as well as that she answers your wishes as a Companion and a Wife.[171]

She also promised a loan from Penson. So De Quincey was saved from the debtors' prison. But his main source of income, the *Gazette*, was soon to fail him. On 29 June 1819, the management committee resolved, 'That a notification be made to the Editor expressing their sentiments of the great importance of a regular communication between the Editor and the Printer of the Westmorland Gazette by want of which it appears that great inconvenience has frequently arisen from the exclusion of the latest London news.'[172] They suggested that he move to Kendal to be near the office. They also warned him to refrain from 'direct remarks on any products or observations which may appear in the Kendal Chronicle'. But he failed to take the hints, and on 5 November the proprietors 'respectfully informed' Mr De Quincey that his resignation was accepted. John Kilner was to be the new editor.

There is no indication that the proprietors objected to De Quincey's filling the *Gazette* with murder trials and essays on Kant. Under his direction it showed a profit, which it was not to do again for years,[173] and Wordsworth mentioned that it had stolen the *Whitehaven Gazette's* readership.[174] He lost his job through a combination of practical inefficiency and over-sensitivity to the attacks of the rival newspaper. From his own point of view this period with the *Gazette*, though financially unrewarding, brought many benefits. It had kept him active and mentally alert at a time when he might otherwise have sunk into despair. It had given him a harsh, intensive schooling in the skills of journalism. And it had forced him to make actual the potential literary talent he had carried within him for years. In the *Gazette* he had developed a humorous, conversational literary style, full of thought yet engagingly personal. One example will suffice. Lamenting the dangerous haste with which he had to consign his copy to the printer, the editor confessed on 16 January 1819 that

> more than once, under anxiety at the recollection of some error uncorrected or some thought left open to misconstruction, (which being sent off by Friday morning's post would be sure to face him in print on the following day) he has fervently wished that some Eastern magician would, a few hours before publication, loosen the 'Gazette' Office from that rock on which we trust it is built – raise it into the air with all it's live and dead stock – and would transport it for one week,

– not (as angry people are apt to say) into the Red Sea, but to some comfortable place on its shore, Arabia Felix for instance . . .

Rare, even in 1819, was the editor who could make his apologies with such grace and style.

8
Confessions

For De Quincey, jobless and penniless once more, the obvious course should have been to take up the magazine work he had been offered. *The Works of Schiller* in twenty-six volumes lay about the cottage, waiting to be reviewed for the *Quarterly*, and late in 1819 Wilson came to see him and urged him to write something for *Blackwood's*. Wilson had good reason for concern, as De Quincey had recently borrowed forty pounds from him[1] and was showing a tendency to rely on Wilson to get him out of financial scrapes. If he could set De Quincey to work that problem would be solved and Wilson would be able to take credit for introducing a talented new writer to *Blackwood's*. He had begun to edit *Blackwood's* in 1817 and, with the help of his literary friends, had made it a huge and scandalous success. His inaugural number had carried insulting attacks on Coleridge and Leigh Hunt, as well as a malicious satire on Edinburgh society couched in biblical language and entitled the 'Chaldee Manuscript'. Concocted by Wilson, Lockhart and Hogg, the 'Manuscript' insulted numerous prominent citizens and provoked a series of law suits, but it sold remarkably well and set the pattern for the magazine's next few years.[2] Wilson gathered around him all those Edinburgh Tory wits who delighted in libel and literary in-fighting, and before long *Blackwood's* became a byword for cruel but entertaining criticism. Its seven-part onslaught on the 'Cockney School' of poets culminated in a violent attack on Keats, who was advised that 'it is a better and a wiser thing to be a starved apothecary than a starved poet; so back to the shop, Mr. John, back to "plasters, pills and ointment boxes, etc." ', and there were other campaigns of the same sort, now forgotten.

Wilson felt that no magazine could be kept going indefinitely in this manner, however successful it might prove in the short term, so he tried to recruit De Quincey for *Blackwood's* and De Quincey promised to send something. So convincing were his promises, indeed, that early in 1820 Wilson persuaded William Blackwood, the publisher, to hold the press for 'several days' in the expectation of a manuscript from Grasmere. It never arrived, and Wilson was left to take the blame. 'I can never again mention the subject to Mr. Blackwood', he wrote to De Quincey on 22 March. 'Unless something has occurred to make it impossible for you to send yr. contribution as you so solemnly promised when we parted, no doubt you wd. have done so.' But he added, 'It becomes daily a more difficult task for Mr. Lockhart and I to write almost the whole of the work . . . Your assistance is becoming, therefore, every day more desirable, and I have only to add that payment at the rate of £10.10s. a sheet shall be monthly transmitted for your communications ... Whatever and whenever you send, it shall be inserted, and nothing can ever come wrong.'[3]

Yet De Quincey still dallied. Worse, he drew more bills on Wilson, and by March 1820 had cost him ninety pounds. Wilson protested but continued to write kindly and to treat De Quincey with respect. This tender attitude may have been dictated by pressure of circumstances. Not only did he urgently need help with *Blackwood's*, but in July 1820 he had stood for election to the Chair of Moral Philosophy at Edinburgh University and, largely for political reasons, been successful. The attraction of the post was the income it would bring, for Wilson knew nothing about philosophy and had beaten his rival, Sir William Hamilton, only because Hamilton was a Whig and the Town Council, who made the election, was strongly Tory. Hamilton was a serious scholar, and Wilson's election was an absurdity, for he had to begin lecturing in November and so had three months in which to learn his subject. He turned, naturally to De Quincey: 'I am quite at a stand respecting my lectures, but have been reading some books, some of which I even understand . . . What should I treat of in the Senses – appetites and bodily powers? What are the books? and what theory is the true one? And your objections to Locke.'[4] Other questions followed pell-mell. What should he say about Greek philosophy? What constitutes moral obligation? What should he read on the Stoics and Epicureans? He asked De Quincey to send 'some long letters' on such points, adopting 'some ingenious disguise as to your object in writing' – so that no one would guess that De Quincey was writing his lectures for him! At the same time he was still trying to extract articles:

> You proposed to send in a day or two your review of Malthus. It is now the 5th of August, and I am beginning to fear that something may have occurred to stop your composition. *Ebony*, who is the child of Hope and Fear, and who has shown a face of smiles for some days,

begins to droop excessively, and if the article does not come soon, no doubt he will commit suicide, which will be some considerable relief to me and many others of his well-wishers. Two sheets of the magazine was a promise that raised the mortal to the skies; so do not draw the devil down! . . . I tried to convince Blackwood that you never *had engaged to* write for the Magazine, and his face was worth ten pounds – for it was as pale as a sheet. – I told him, however, that now you *were* engaged, so that if the articles don't come now, he will become a sceptic even in religion, and end in total disbelief of Earth, Heaven and Hell.[5]

Even 'Ebony' (as Wilson punningly called Blackwood) was enlisted to cajole De Quincey into action. 'It is a remark warranted by reason not to mention a higher sanction,' wrote Blackwood on 26 August 'that hope deferred maketh the heart sick – I would still however hope against hope that you will yet fulfil your long bygone engagement to the Magazine . . . Whatever you choose to send – be it long or short – will always be acceptable.'[6]

But De Quincey had troubles of his own, and neither philosophy lectures nor articles were forthcoming. He was still grappling with opium addiction: the *Confessions* records the usual exhausting nightmares from 1820, and mentions the perennial stomach troubles.[7] Without the stimulus of a rigid deadline he could finish nothing, and the wonders he had performed for the *Gazette* could not be duplicated for *Blackwood's*. Possibly he was already experiencing that 'powerful disgust with any subject upon which he had occupied his powers of composition for any length of time, and an equal disgust with the results of his exertions' which he came to regard as the worst obstacle to writing under the influence of opium, and which often led him to discard half-finished essays rather than face the loathsome task of rereading and completing them. Trying to think and write under opium, he later explained, 'You feel like one of Swift's *Strulbrugs* [sic], prematurely exhausted of life; and molehills are inevitably exaggerated by the feelings into mountains.'[8]

So nothing was done, and he continued to survive on credit, without a notion of how the bills would be paid. Some indication of how he passed his time may be given by the following jotting:

It frets me to enter those rooms of my cottage in which the books stand. In one of them, to which my little boy has access, he has found out a use for some of them. Someone has given him a bow and arrow – God knows who, certainly not I, for I have not energy or ingenuity to invent a walking stick – thus equipped for action, he rears up the largest of the folios that he can lift, places them on a tottering base, and then shoots until be brings down the enemy. He often presses me to join him; and sometimes I consent, and we are both engaged together in these intellectual labours.[9]

Meanwhile, expenses mounted. Margaret had another baby, a son born some time in 1820 – the exact date is unknown.[10] He was christened Horatio, but was usually called Horace, thereby commemorating two of De Quincey's heroes Nelson and the Roman poet. In September 1820 De Quincey complicated matters further by taking Fox Ghyll, a small house under Loughrigg Fell by the River Rothay, without relinquishing the cottage at Town End. Sara Hutchinson spread the news:

> Mr. de Quinceys Books have literally turned their master and his whole family out of doors – He is *arranging* them – so being strewed about and he meditating a journey to Edinh. he thought the safest way, as 'his wife did not understand books' (as he expressed himself to Mr Wm) and they the maids *would be dusting*, was to take another house – and now they are safely lodged at Fox Ghyll which he has taken for 6 months. I predict that there they will remain unless unsettled by an earth-quake or a second accumulation of Books.[11]

De Quincey continued 'meditating' his journey for two months more and then, on 27 November, he wrote to tell Wilson that he was on his way. Illness, he said, had delayed him: for six weeks he thought himself close to death, and 'My Laudanum', he said, 'has rendered my stomach incapable of retaining any sort of food for 2 minutes.' He may have thought it politic to stress the poor state of his health, for in the same letter he tried to reassure Wilson about all those bills, gently reproaching him for 'ascribing to me so vile a temper of mind . . . as to expect or to wish of any man that he should entangle himself in difficulties in order to disentangle me'. Unhappily, he had to break the news that to pay his coachfare to Edinburgh he had drawn on Wilson for ten pounds. But, he hastened to point out, long before the money was due he would be in Edinburgh and 'able to write it out for the Magazine'.

He went on to mention the *London Magazine*. The *London's* editor, John Scott, had taken offence at *Blackwood's* vicious treatment of London writers, and the November issue of the *London* carried a twelve-page attack on *Blackwood's*, accusing the Edinburgh group of 'staining the honour of literature'. De Quincey, of course, took Wilson's side, but with reservations:

My chief subject of anxiety at the moment is that infamous attack on you in the London Mag by John Scott (I guess): – to speak conscientiously, I cannot wholly approve of everything you have done: what I should condemn if I had any right to be your judge, is the harsh (and latterly to my mind more painful than anything simply harsh – *good-naturedly contemptuous*) treatment of Keats.

This, however, is a trifle compared with the *London's* transgressions, which provoke De Quincey to an exuberant outburst of schoolboy obscenity. Will one article against Scott, he asks rhetorically, be enough?

No! Wilson, for the love of God, make an example of the Bugger. Lampoon him in songs – in prose – by night and by day – in prosperous and adverse fortune. Make him date his ruin from Nov. 1st. 1820. – Lash him into lunacy. Tax yourself, as Voltaire did, to produce a pasquinade upon him once a day. Let the children in the streets have ballads on John Scot. Tye him up, as Ajax Mastigophoros did the old buggery ram that he took for Ulysses, at private opportunities and decent intervals for fractions of his never ending Scourging. You think perhaps I am laughing. No! I am in a hurry, and I take such words as occur to me, but my abhorrence of this beast is deep – serious – and morally grounded.[12]

Scott 'oh! slave – oh! bugger!' is, he concludes, a parasite of literature.

He reached Edinburgh early in December, and wrote to tell Margaret that he was 'tolerably well – much better, at least, than when I left home . . . All my old friends here are more kind that I can express. Without any trouble on my part, they have procured me lodgings, books, and everything that I can wish, or rather ten times more. And invitations crowd upon me so fast that I hardly know how I shall get through all my writing, &c.'[13] Whether the visit had been his idea or Wilson's, behind it was the theory that his inhibition about writing could be broken if he were on the spot to be encouraged and pestered by Wilson and Blackwood. He stayed for six weeks, but left at last after producing only one article, and the episode almost suggests that without really knowing it, he was playing an elaborate game with Wilson and Blackwood, finding out how far he could provoke them before they lost their tempers and sent him packing. He had been expected in good time to write for the January number but through various misunderstandings was late. Blackwood complained and De Quincey sent a long letter of explanation on 12 December. Blackwood replied, urging him to get to work and stop wasting his time on long letters. De Quincey's response was another long letter explaining why his previous letter had been so long, and mentioning an article on opium. 'Opium', he wrote, 'has reduced me for the last six years to one general discourtesy of utter silence. But this I shall think of with not so much pain, if this same opium enables me (as I think it will) to send you an article.'[14] The next day he was working on an 'Opium Article', and promised translations from Schiller, Richter and Kant, as well as pieces on Hannah More and political economy. In the meantime he enclosed part of a translation from Schiller, a short story of no great merit entitled 'The Sport of Fortune'.[15]

Blackwood, who had almost given up hope, replied ecstatically: 'I am so happy to receive anything from you that your two pages appear like the 24 of any one else, because now that you are fairly begun I feel confident that you will do justice to yourself. It was the knowing what you *could do*, if you once *resolved to do*, which made my repeated disappointments so very mortifying to me.'[16] This was on 13 December. Five days later De Quincey had finished 'The Sport of Fortune' and reassured Blackwood that it had been delayed only because 'finding it very irksome employment, I had intermitted it for two others far more pleasant to me'; these articles, he added, were now 'in a state of forwardness'. He sent the manuscript and asked for ten guineas, the agreed price for a 'sheet' (eight printed pages) of the magazine. At the same time he promised that, 'Tomorrow . . . I will send you *my bond* . . . selling myself soul and body to the service of the Magazine for two years.'[17]

The story arrived just in time to go into the January number. By the New Year, however, further delays had soured Blackwood's temper, and on 6 January 1821 he wrote testily to complain about De Quincey's tardiness and his recurrent fuss over hypothetical deadlines. There is no need, he fumes, for incessant inquiries 'as to when an article will be in time. A good article is always in time.' As soon as he received Blackwood's note De Quincey fired off a reply, amusing enough but edged with arrogance and culminating in a remark which a moment's cool thought might have led him to suppress: ' "A good article", you say, "is always in time". Well: mine is a good one – a very good one, and therefore in time. For he, who does not laugh at the whole latter part especially from p.8 to 20 is fit for treasons &c.' He conceded that the article was late. But then, 'I move slowly whenever I am uncommonly witty. Nevertheless, if you are more particular about quantity than quality, I am perfectly ready to oblige you by changing my style.

But articles as droll as this I really cannot produce faster: dull reviews, morality &c. and even wit such as some I saw in your December No. as fast as you please.'[18]

Blackwood's reply to this sally has not survived. If he showed anger, as he probably did, it merely stimulated De Quincey to compose a breathtakingly rude letter to accompany his next manuscript:

> If Wilson and Lockhart do not put themselves forward for the Mag. I forsee that the entire weight of supporting it must rest on my shoulders: I see clearly that I must be it's Atlas. For excepting our friend Gillies's translation (*from* a cursed dull thing though), and excepting that spirited Political article at the end, – a more dreary collection of dulness and royal stupidity never did this world see gathered together than the December No. exhibits. Positively it would sink any work in the world. No, no! I see clearly that I must write it all myself . . .
>
> And this horrible dulness, which is enough to inflict apoplexy, appears to coincide with those infernal articles from London. And to these it seems we are to knock under. What a craven the fellow must be who advised such a piece of devilish cowardice: whoever he be, I hope to God he may soon meet with a halter – even if it were my dear friend Prof. Wilson.
>
> I am hard at work, being prepared to save the Mag. from the fate which its stupidity merits.[19]

These opinions on his *Magazine*, coupled with provocative remarks on the very sensitive matter of the attack in the *London Magazine* – 'those infernal articles from London' – produced the natural reaction from De Quincey's prospective employer:

> I can only excuse your letter which I rec'd today by supposing that you were hardly awake when you wrote it. When I apply to you to be the Atlas of my Magazine it will be time enough for you to undertake the burthen. And in the mean time I beg leave to say that if you cannot send me anything better than 'The English Lakes' it will be quite unnecessary for you to give yourself any farther trouble about the Magazine.[20]

De Quincey replied in similar tone:

> You are pleased to doubt whether I was awake when I wrote my note of yesterday morning: with a good deal more reason might I doubt whether the person were awake who either read my note or wrote the answer to it which I received last night. I shall not however enter into any dispute; and shall as little as possible in future . . . trouble you with any notes at all – sleeping or waking.[21]

He ended by promising more copy, but Blackwood was not to be mollified and (after what more bickering we do not know) De Quincey left Edinburgh, having ruined his chances there. By the end of January he was back at Fox Ghyll and was again drawing bills on Wilson. The Professor wrote on 17 February stating plainly that he would refuse any further bills.[22]

Meanwhile the journalistic feud De Quincey had in his small way helped to foment reached its climax. Lockhart, who felt himself chief among those insulted by Scott of the *London Magazine*, sent his friend Christie to London to see Scott and insist on a public apology, failing which a challenge was to be delivered. Taking the quarrel upon himself, Christie insulted Scott until Scott challenged him. They met by moonlight in a field at Chalk Farm on 16 February. A duel took place and Scott received a fatal bullet wound. He died on 27 February. Four months later De Quincey went to London and in September 1821 his masterpiece, *The Confessions of an English Opium-Eater*, appeared in the pages of *Blackwood's* sworn enemy, *The London Magazine*.

It was with no enthusiasm that De Quincey went to seek work in London. He hung on at Fox Ghyll with his family until June; he saw no one, and Edward Quillinan, who was to marry Wordsworth's daughter Dora, heard that 'he remained in bed . . . all day, and only took the air at night, and then was more shy than an Owl'.[23] The Wordsworths themselves seem to have been aware of him mainly as an obstacle to the re-letting of Fox Ghyll, whose landlord was willing to let it to Mary's cousin, Thomas Monkhouse, if the De Quinceys could somehow be ousted.[24] But Wordsworth himself performed one more significant favour for his truant disciple by giving him a letter of introduction to Thomas Noon Talfourd, a contributor to the *London Magazine*.

When he reached London[25] he called on Talfourd, who put him in touch with John Taylor and James Augustus Hessey, who had just bought the *London Magazine*. Scott's death had left the *London* in chaos, but they were determined to turn it into a prosperous concern and were busy assembling a group of talented contributors. They lost no time in securing De Quincey's services – 'The terms they held out to contributors were ultra-munificent',[26] or so it seemed to the poverty-stricken author – but he had no article ready for them, and the trip to

London might have turned out a fiasco of the same kind as the Edinburgh visit but for the timely intervention of a creditor. De Quincey had lodgings at 4, York Street and there he took up again the 'Opium Article' he had begun for Blackwood and started to revise and extend it. Before the work was finished, however, payment of a bill fell due. An expected remittance from Mrs Quincey failed to arrive and he learned that unless he immediately found money he was to be arrested for debt. So desperate was he, that seeking about for any expedient, however remote or distasteful, he recalled how in 1807 Coleridge had accepted his gift of £300 under the polite fiction that it was a 'loan'. Rather than face the debtors' prison, he forced himself to write to Coleridge and ask if the money could now be repaid. The humiliation he must have felt at having to retract his generous gesture in this way may easily be imagined. And after all he was shaming himself for nothing, as he must have guessed: Coleridge was himself in debt and had, he said, not a shilling in his pocket. He sent a long tale of misfortune, concluding

> Dear De Quincey! I conjure you to feel convinced that were it in my power – let what would come next week – to raise the money, you should not have received this melancholy History as an answer – Were you to see me at this moment, you would know with what anguish & sickening of soul I subscribe myself your *obliged* & grateful
> S.T. Coleridge.[27]

De Quincey had no choice but to leave his lodgings and go into hiding, struggling meanwhile to finish the 'Opium Article' so that it could be exchanged for hard cash. On 9 August, therefore, he and part of his manuscript (the rest had already gone to the printer) left York Street and found refuge in coffee houses, amid whose 'tumult', he complained, it was 'difficult to write at all: for it happened that the only coffee-rooms, where I was known enough to expect credit, were those of great Coach-Inns'.[28] He returned from his fugitive excursion on 17 August with the manuscript much advanced, to find the first five pages of his article in proof and awaiting correction.

The article, of course, was *The Confessions of an English Opium-Eater*. Writing it in the midst of such difficulties must have made him painfully aware of the parallels between his boyhood wanderings in London and his present hole-and-corner existence: 15 August had been his thirty-sixth birthday. De Quincey, who believed firmly that walking minimized the ill-effects of opium and digestive disorders, used to walk for three or four hours every evening and on that evening, he says, 'about ten o'clock . . . I turned aside from my evening walk, down Oxford Street, purposely to take a glance' at the Greek Street house he had haunted, cold and hungry, nearly nineteen years before. Returning to his place of refuge, he recorded the experience in his manuscript:

> The house is now occupied by a respectable family and, by the lights in the front drawing-room, I observed a domestic party, assembled perhaps at tea, and apparently cheerful and gay. Marvellous contrast in my eyes to the darkness – cold – silence – and desolation of that same house eighteen years ago, when its nightly occupants were one famishing scholar, and a neglected child![29]

He found the *frisson* he sought; and his desire to communicate that sensation in all its immediacy to the reader is typical of the eager, sensitive self-revelation that makes the *Confessions* so engaging. But the work went slowly. On 22 August he had almost finished the first part, though illness was keeping him in great pain, and he promised the remaining copy by nine o'clock next morning. Taylor, mindful of the approaching end of the month, grumbled:

> One gentleman has begun a long Article and we have included it in our present No. and his copy comes in so very slow that I cannot complete anything more for want of it. That Article will be found a very curious one – it is on opium-eating. What singular Men the literary World abounds with! I sometimes doubt whether my Opium Friend be in his senses.[30]

Yet the work was done, and 'Part I' of the *Confessions of an English Opium-Eater: Being an Extract from the Life of a Scholar* appeared, signed 'X.Y.Z.', in the *London Magazine*'s September issue, followed by 'Part II' in October.

Any doubts Taylor may have had about De Quincey's work were dispelled by the success of the first part, and in October the *Confessions*, which had been placed well down the list of contents the month before, took pride of place and had a fanfare in 'The Lion's Head', the editorial page which opened each issue:

> We are not often in the habit of eulogising our own work, – but we cannot neglect the opportunity . . . of calling the attention of our readers to the deep, eloquent, and masterly paper which stands first in our present Number. Such Confessions, so powerfully uttered cannot fail to do more than interest the reader.[31]

The articles created immediate excitement. Many people wrote to the publishers and there was a demand for a third part: in December the magazine announced that it would appear in the course of the next year. But no third part was written. Late in 1822 Taylor and Hessey reprinted the work in book form, and De Quincey added an appendix explaining his failure to add a third part on grounds of illness. The *Confessions* were instantly famous and have remained so ever since. Between 1821 and 1823 some fifteen reviews appeared, nearly all of them enthusiastic about the book's style and imaginative power, though a few thought the author vain or immoral and there were doubts about the truth of his story. Imitations and parodies abounded, and before long De Quincey's literary influence, unknown to him, was spreading abroad. In 1828 his work was introduced to France by Alfred de Musset in *L'anglais, mangeur d'opium,* a very free adaptation; in 1860 a better version was to be made by Baudelaire in *Les paradis artificiels*, and before that the *Confessions* were to reach Edgar Allan Poe and contribute an important element to his style and vision.

Not all the influence of the *Confessions*, however, was literary. In 1823 a young man died from an overdose of opium. It appeared that he had been experimenting with the drug, and at the inquest a doctor testified that there had lately been an alarming increase in the number of such cases, 'in consequence of a little book that has been published by a man of literature, which recites many extraordinary cases of taking opium'. The doctor claimed to have direct knowledge of four cases in which the patients, when questioned, gave De Quincey's book as their inspiration for taking a nearly fatal dose. 'Almost every young man of practice and science', he added, 'had been induced to purchase this work, it therefore is of universal ill tendency.'[32] This was the first of many claims that the book exerted an evil influence, encouraging people to experiment with dangerous drugs. Yet the tendency was not of 'universal ill'. Thomas Carlyle, thinking of trying laudanum as a remedy for overwork and insomnia, read the *Confessions* first and 'said to himself on finishing it: "Better, a thousand times better, *die* than have anything to do with such a Devil's own drug" '.[33] Taylor and Hessey had bought the work outright for forty guineas and they had secured a bargain; though De Quincey, according to Crabb Robinson, regarded the sum as very generous.[34] Yet even in the absence of debt, such an amount would keep him and his family only for a few months. Taylor and Hessey made him a present of twenty pounds when they published the book but after that he could expect no further payment, however often the *Confessions* might be reprinted.

If ever a man 'had a book in him', that man was De Quincey and that book was the *Confessions*. It was the book he had, in a sense, been born, educated and addicted to write. The strangeness of his early life, together with his literary gifts, love of anecdote and need for self-justification, made him the perfect autobiographer. Since 1818 (and probably earlier) he had kept notes of his dreams, intending to put them to literary use. In his long letter to his mother in 1818 he had accused his guardians of dishonesty, threatening to denounce them 'in my life which I have partly written and design to publish before my death'.[35] In 1821 these ideas and the notion of an 'Opium Article' had come together and crystallized. Everything about the *Confessions* was brilliant and original, beginning with the title. Echoing the *Confessions* of St Augustine and Rousseau, it hinted at both spiritual purification and scandalous revelation. There was only one English predecessor – *Confessions of a Coquet* (1785) – though there were a number of French books with similar titles (for example *Les confessions d'une courtisane devenue philosophe*, 1784) most of them, apparently, erotic in content; and De Quincey was familiar with *The Confessions of William-Henry Ireland*, the Shakespeare forger, and *The Confessions of J.L.* (James Lackington), the spiritual autobiography of a Methodist convert. So strongly did the formula catch the public imagination that titles using De Quincey's phrase 'Confessions of a . . .' have appeared in a steady stream ever since. The term 'Opium-Eater' seems also to have been his invention. He was generally, of course, an opium *drinker*, but he expected his readers to know of the Turkish 'Theriakis' who ate solid opium and featured in many Eastern tales and travel books, and called himself an English opium-eater to imply his kinship with this exotic fraternity.

The *Confessions* was autobiography of a highly selective kind. The real interest, De Quincey felt, should centre upon opium and its effect on the faculty of dreaming. The events of his life should be recounted only in so far as they might show how he became an opium addict, explain the content of his dreams, or engage the reader's sympathy. So he gave much of his life in the briefest of summaries, emphasizing only those experiences which seemed to him crucially formative: the escape from Manchester Grammar School; the miseries of vagrancy in London and his love for the lost Ann; his first experience of opium; the idyll of cottage life at Grasmere with Margaret; the visit of the frightful Malay; and then the dreams themselves. Perhaps the most significant departure from fact was that at the end of the work he claimed to have conquered his addiction. The *Confessions* end, most effectively, on a 'dying fall': the addiction is broken, yet the former addict is still 'agitated, writhing, throbbing, palpitating, shattered'; his dreams are still disturbed, and though the disturbance gradually lessens his sleep is 'still tumultuous, and, like the gates of Paradise to our first parents when looking back from afar, it is still (in the tremendous line of Milton) –

'With dreadful faces throng'd and fiery arms.'

Such passages, with their hints of apocalyptic experience breaking into the individual life, their implication that opium opened the gates to both hell and paradise, have always fascinated De Quincey's readers. His fluent, ornamental prose style, glittering with exotic imagery but controlled by a wry humour, conveys psychological states with unique vividness and reflects his ambivalent attitude to opium by making the 'Pains of Opium', for all their nightmare quality, as dangerously enticing as its 'Pleasures'.

Although the *Confessions* remain an extended essay in form, with a narrative sequence which is not always coherent, De Quincey was not without literary models and probably had a clear idea of the effects he wished to achieve. Above all he must have been affected by his knowledge of Wordsworth's unpublished autobiographical poem, known to us as *The Prelude*. The poem's emphasis on the development of personality by means of

a dark
Invisible workmanship that reconciles
Discordant elements, and makes them move
In one society,[36]

and its view of experience as leading purposefully to culmination in the consciousness of the artist was something De Quincey wished to emulate, and his selection of episodes significant in the unfolding and shaping of the individual consciousness shows how much he had learned from Wordsworth. As Wordsworth's poem portrays the growth of a poet's mind, so De Quincey's prose-poem traces the inner development of a dreamer and philosopher.

Equally important (and ironically hinted at, perhaps, in the quasi-religious term 'Confessions') was the concern with earnest self-examination and spiritual autobiography prominent in the Evangelical thought of Mrs Quincey and her friends. De Quincey had seen a particular clear statement of this principle in the essays of John Foster, a Baptist minister whose writings were popular in Evangelical circles. Foster's essay 'On a Man's Writing Memoirs of Himself' recommends autobiography as a means to self-knowledge, stresses the importance of inner experience as opposed to outward action, and offers some interesting hints on the remembrance of things past:

> In some occasional states of the mind, we can look back much more clearly, and much further, than at other times. I would advise to seize those short intervals of illumination which sometimes occur without our knowing the cause, and in which the genuine aspect of some remote event, or long-forgotten image is recovered with extreme distinctness in spontaneous glimpses of thought, such as no efforts could have commanded.[37]

He even suggests revisiting places where one has 'conversed with happiness or misery' as a means of recovering the past. De Quincey had read Foster with attention.[38]

Other considerations may have been less personal. The stress the *Confessions* lay on De Quincey's experience of the London streets is very much in tune with the *London Magazine's* policy of taking the metropolis itself as a subject in an attempt to re-assert London's cultural dominance against the aggressively 'Edinburgh' viewpoint of *Blackwood's*.[39]

The authorship of the *Confessions* was no mystery to those who knew De Quincey. Crabb Robinson, for example, read it in Glasgow and guessed at once. He thought it 'strange': 'a melancholy composition, a fragment of autobiography in emulation of Coleridge's diseased egotism'.[40] Taylor was delighted with his new contributor and made full use of him, publishing more than twenty of his articles in the *London* over the next three years. But there is no evidence that De Quincey every signed a contract with Taylor. At the end of October Crabb Robinson recorded that 'he is necessitous and will be in great distress soon, for his talents are not marketable',[41] and tried to help him to an editorial job with the *Classical Journal*. But De Quincey did not take it and in November Taylor entrusted him with the writing of an editorial for the *London* setting out the magazine's future policy. In it De Quincey promised greater variety of articles, an emphasis on classics, and educational material which was to include 'Letters on the Transcendental Philosophy' and 'Letters to a Young Man of Talents Whose Education Has Been Neglected'.[42] The editorial never appeared, no doubt because he failed to finish it in time, though the promised 'Letters to a Young Man' were eventually written for the *London* in 1823. He did bestir himself sufficiently to produce for the December issue two short translations from Richter, one of them a piece he had partly translated in 1811 which he now snatched up, completed and sent to the press, imperfect as it was. He also found time to insert a letter signed 'X.Y.Z.' replying to criticisms of the *Confessions*, asserting that he had told the truth – though not the whole truth – and promising a third part. There, for the time being, his contributions ended.

This fragmentary magazine work brought De Quincey into contact with the social circle that gathered about the *London*, and this was something he could enjoy. As before, in Edinburgh, he was admired and invited; but he now had a notable literary success to his credit and his company was valued still more highly. He saw a good deal of Charles Lamb, another *London Magazine* contributor, and the touches of mutual suspicion that had troubled their earlier relationship gave way to real friendship. Worried, ill and unhappy at being forced to stay so far from Margaret and the children, De Quincey found the Lambs delightful company. Charles, he says, 'set himself, with all the kindness of a brother, Miss Lamb with the kindness of a sister, to relieve my gloom with the closest attentions. They absolutely persecuted me with hospitalities; and, as it was by their fireside that I felt most cheered, . . . I did not neglect to avail myself of the golden hours thus benignantly interposed amongst my hours of solitude'.[43] They often pressed him 'to dine with them and stay as late as I would'. He came to delight in the outrageous puns to which Lamb's stammer gave a peculiarly comic impact, and even learned to tolerate jokes at the expense of Coleridge, opium, Oxford Street and other sacred subjects. Dining at the Lambs' or with Taylor and Hessey (who gave dinners for their contributors) he met, among others, Alan Cunningham, Thomas Hood, Richard Woodhouse the friend of Keats, and the art critic Thomas Wainewright, later notorious as 'Wainewright the poisoner', who wrote for the magazine under the pseudonym 'Janus Weathercock'. Wainewright struck De Quincey as a critic of 'sincerity and of native sensibility', albeit dandified and rather arrogant in manner. In 1826 he was to forge an order on the Bank of England and subsequently poison three people, dying a transported convict in Van Dieman's Land. De Quincey, of course, was disappointed in retrospect that in 1821 his intuition failed to tell him with what kind of man he was dining.

De Quincey himself was often ill or depressed and attended the dinners out of sheer loneliness and boredom. But Woodhouse quickly became friendly with him and found his conversation so interesting that he kept notes of it. He found the Opium-Eater 'a short, sallow-looking person, of a very peculiar cast of countenance, and apparently much of an invalid. His demeanour was very gentle, modest and unassuming.'[44] He talked much of himself – his early life, his association with Wordsworth and other writers, his opium and his illnesses – but he also impressed Woodhouse with 'the depth and *reality* . . . of his knowledge'! 'Upon almost every subject that was introduced he had . . . that minute and accurate acquaintance with the details that can be acquired only from personal investigation of a subject and reflection upon it at the same time.'[45] Whether the company discussed economics, archaeology, languages, literature, history or politics, he seemed 'informed to considerable minuteness'. He talked just as he wrote, and Woodhouse was pleased to find that 'his conversation fully came up to' what one would expect from the author of the *Confessions*. His language had 'eloquence and scope', so that he could 'overlay every little topic with rich discussion and valuable information and reflection'.[46] He was full of anecdotes about opium: of Coleridge dropping in at a doctor's house and helping himself to more than half a pint of laudanum, which he drank by the wineglassful under the horrified eyes of the doctor's wife; of the time when he, De Quincey had been absorbed in reading and absentmindedly knocking back laudanum until he 'suddenly found himself dizzy and heavy and very much inclined to sleep' and had to force himself out of his chair and find an emetic to bring up what he had swallowed before he collapsed from an overdose. His current routine, he said, was to take a hundred drops in the morning and another hundred at four o'clock in the afternoon. He regarded the dose as rather high and attributed it to stomach pains. Visiting Woodhouse one night he tried a cigar and found that it allayed the pains, which may mean that they were of psychological origin.[47]

On one occasion he spoke bitterly about Lakeland gossip, complaining that the minds of the people in that district were 'particularly gross and uncharitable'. No doubt he and Margaret had suffered the rough side of many tongues around Grasmere, though he did not mention it. Among the examples of 'horrible' local gossip he did mention were tales that 'he was himself the father of Mrs. Wordsworth's child that died . . . The Grounds for this fiction, were the plainness of the child's appearance, the comparative want of fondness, or rather indifference of most people, even Wordsworth for the little thing, and the opium eater's partiality for it, and grief at its death . . . Again there was an unnatural tale current, and which the Opium Eater had heard even in London, of Wordsworth having been intimate with his own sister' which De Quincey thought had arisen because of the poet's habit of kissing his sister on meeting and parting – as he did with all female relatives. Both stories he vigorously denied.[48]

Late in 1821, perhaps at Woodhouse's instigation, he read Keats. He was not impressed by *Endymion* (it seemed to him 'the very midsummer madness of affectation') but a few days later he read *Hyperion* and his estimate of Keats changed entirely. *Hyperion*, he thought, possessed 'the majesty, the austere beauty, and the simplicity of a Grecian temple enriched with Grecian sculpture'.[49] He was already an admirer of Shelley, and told Woodhouse that, when Wilson had sent him *The Revolt of Islam* to review for *Blackwood's* in 1818, he had not written a review but had returned it with an enthusiastic letter, whereupon 'there appeared a flaming article by Wilson in the magazine praising the book very highly'.[50] When he mentioned Wilson now it was generally with suspicion and even dislike. The *London*'s contributors had no reason to love Wilson, but De Quincey was outspoken. Wilson, he said, had written anonymous articles 'abusing and vilifying' Coleridge, at the same time writing to De Quincey pointing out the articles and urging him to reply in Coleridge's defence! Wilson's character he called 'a compound of cruelty and meanness': ambitious and domineering yet ready to 'crouch' to those in powerful positions. 'In short he has lost his principle.'[51] All this seems odd, for whatever Wilson's obvious weaknesses, he and De Quincey had never ceased to be on good terms. But an explanation is not hard to find. Early in November Wilson came to London and seemed eager to contribute to the *London*. His overtures were not successful, though he consulted De Quincey as well as Taylor and Hessey and De Quincey made a point of dining with him and keeping up friendly contact.[52] At the same time De Quincey confided his real thoughts to Woodhouse:

> Wilson (O.E. has no doubt) came up to Town principally to learn particulars of the editorship and management of, and the writers for the London Magazine: and he feels sure that in a very short time there will be an attack upon it. Wilson has made many attempts to learn incidentally particulars – by talking a good deal on the subject, and by leading industriously the conversation that way.[53]

A month later, 'O.E.' – the Opium-Eater – admitted to 'a sort of feeling or omen of anticipation, that possibly there was some being in the world who was fated to do him at some time a great and irreparable injury . . . Many circumstances seemed to make it not improbable that Wilson might be than man.' He was surely suffering from a bad conscience about deserting *Blackwood's* for its chief rival, and feared that Wilson would take revenge. He knew the kind of treatment *Blackwood's* could mete out to writers who provoked it, and was well aware that many details of his life over the past five years would provide splendid material for a scurrilous article. In due course something of the kind did happen; but not yet.

On 29 December De Quincey went back to Westmorland. Before he left he had discussed with Taylor and Hessey a new project, which would occupy him while he lived for a few months in the tranquillity of Fox Ghyll with Margaret and the children. He was to write a novel. No details are known except that he received £157.10s. in advance.[54]

Once he was out of reach of Taylor and Hessey, however, good intentions counted for little. He stayed at Fox Ghyll for nearly a year but the novel made no progress. During the winter he was plagued with rheumatism and through the spring was still 'wretchedly ill'. To complete his misery, the rent for Fox Ghyll was overdue and the landlord, Mr Blakeney, was threatening him with the law. De Quincey sent a long, frigidly polite third-person letter informing Blakeney that 'Mr. De Quincey was surprised that any gentleman should make his . . . application . . . in such terms' and putting him in his place by mentioning that five other creditors, who had had the good manners to draw upon him at his London address at one or two months' notice, had all been duly paid. The implication was that Blakeney would get his rent when he learned better manners and understood that money was to be had in London, not Westmorland.[55]

The shortage of money grew so acute that he had to make arrangements to sell his library. In the hope of averting the sacrifice, he wrote to his mother in February asking for help. She managed to obtain fifty-four pounds for him, but tried at the same time to shame him into taking a more realistic view of things. 'I see not at the bottom of your calamities any better hope than that which has ever cheated my unfortunate children,' she wrote despondently. She had little faith in 'flattering accounts' of his 'literary expectations and successes' and the 'numerous honourable testimonies which you received from Men and Journals'. One wonders what Mrs Quincey had made of the *Confessions*. Certain facts, such as William's birth out of wedlock, had been concealed by a blurring of the book's chronology, but the fact that her son had for years been secretly indulging in opium must have come as a severe shock, and she did not fail to hint that his troubles were partly self-inflicted. He had mentioned his ailments and she expressed herself 'greatly troubled', but added, 'I cannot but believe, that your stomach is miserably injured by the Opium you have swallowed.'[56] She warned him that if he sold his library it would go for much less than the £400 he expected.

Plans for the sale of his books and some of his furniture went ahead, but as spring advanced there was still no peace. Taylor and Hessey were demanding that he redeem various promises he made in London. They wanted a novel; they wanted articles; they wanted a third part of the *Confessions*. De Quincey was too ill and anxious to produce any of these, but he kept up a kind of verbal fencing by letter, dazzling them with promises. On 20 April he told Hessey that he was working on what he called 'a sort of *Ana*' – a miscellany of short, anecdotal pieces on every imaginable subject: 'Criticism – Human Life – Love – Marriage – Courtship – Political Economy – Mathematics – Morals – Coleridge – Wordsworth – Myself in childhood . . . in short the flower of all my reading, thinking and scheming for twenty odd years.'[57] This was the first hint that he might write about his friendship with the Lake Poets, and the whole plan shows how inseparable the journalistic and autobiographical impulses were for him. But having whetted Hessey's appetite, he wrote again on 29 April to say that he had an article ready but was holding it for improvements. As soon as the sales of furniture and books were safely over, the *Confessions*, Part III would be written. But he foresaw, he said, 'nothing but disappointment from it – and, what is worse, that it will reflect disgust upon the former parts'. The book could be improved only be a 'remodelling of the whole'. Otherwise it would be 'a mere spinning out' and would spoil the overall impression. 'However,' he dutifully added, secretly hoping that Hessey would relent, 'injudicious or not, the engagement is made: and must be kept: and after all one consolation is that nobody will ever ask me for a 4th. part'. As for 'The *Novel*', that 'is a far easier task: nay, 20 novels would not task me so heavily as one Opium Eater'. It would be ready 'in a very short time' – but as it was already late in the publishing season, would Hessey not prefer to have his advance repaid from the proceeds of the book- and furniture-sales? Other promised items would be written 'the moment I am free from daily anxieties of arrests, executions &c., – they will be a perfect pleasure to me'. After this encouraging start he came to the point, which was to ask if Hessey would help him borrow some more money.[58]

By June the frantic struggle with creditors had reached a temporary lull. Still nothing had been written, but De Quincey decided to make another attempt at conquering his opium addiction. In London he had been taking large quantities to help him cope with the strains of work and loneliness. Now he was taking anything up to 300 drops a day, so on 24 June he cut this to 160 and by the beginning of July was down to 80. On 8 July he suffered a lapse of will power and took 300. Thereafter he plunged to 50, and hovered around an average of 70 until late July, when for a few days he took none at all. The misery of this period was intense. He suffered from shooting pains in his limbs as well as the habitual stomach pains. Sometimes he could not sleep for several consecutive nights. His lower jaw became swollen, his mouth full of ulcers. He was seized by fits of compulsive sneezing, results of the intense nasal irritation common in opium withdrawal. A restlessness continually goaded him into movement so that he could not sit, stand, read or write comfortably for two minutes together. At times his body was bathed in sweat which flowed hour after hour so that he felt compelled to wash himself six times a day.[59] Worst of all, he felt as if his mind were out of control: 'It seems', he wrote, 'as if all the thoughts which had been frozen up for a decade of years by opium had now . . . been thawed at once, such a multitude stream in upon me from all quarters.'

In the midst of all this, proofs arrived of the new edition of the *Confessions*. Taylor and Hessey had given up hope of a third part and were anxious to get the book out as soon as possible. De Quincey managed to write a short appendix detailing his latest attempt at breaking the accursed chain which he had previously claimed to have 'untwisted, almost to its final links'. He now admitted that this boast had been premature, though somehow he still found the optimism to argue that his own case 'establishes . . . the fact that opium may be renounced'. More honestly he admitted that he 'could not even bear to read the proofs over with attention enough to notice the press errors' and ended on a note of self-disgust by offering his 'crazy body' to the medical profession for scientific investigation once he had done with it. Then he packed up proofs and manuscript and sent them off, glad to be rid of them.

The *Confessions* appeared in book form in August. How De Quincey spent the rest of the summer is not known. He later claimed to have been approached by three publishers with offers of work, all of which he turned down. And despite his struggles, he remained addicted to opium. His agonies were in vain because he could not abstain totally for long enough. Always, after a few days without the drug he would lose his resolution and take a massive dose. In September he was as sick as ever, and suffering, he said, 'the wretchedness of a lunatic' on twenty-five drops a day.[60] By mid-autumn he had made a truce with the drug. He was back on his usual dose and, feeling ready to talk about work again, began tantalizing his publishers with promises of a treatise on political economy, a subject which was something of a hobby-horse with Taylor. He revived his old plan for a *Prolegomena to all Future Systems of Political Economy*, but it followed the same course as before. Early in October he told Hessey that it was nearly complete, but could not be finished because he was too ill to write the Preface;[61] a month later he wrote again, 'in so completely altered a tone', Hessey commented, 'that I could scarcely have believed it to be the same Man', full of optimism and urging Hessey to advertise the *Prolegomena*, 'on the faith of his supplying the Press with Manuscript as fast as it may be required'. Not only this, but 'he talks of a Third Part of the Confessions again', and miscellaneous essays 'are to flow', says Hessey, 'as fast as my pen now moves'. But still nothing was done. The less De Quincey performed the more he promised, and violent fluctuations in his state of mind and health rendered him incapable of assessing what he could or could not do. He talked of returning to London, and undertook to 'feed the press from the moment of my arrival'. As for the promised novel,

> One night in high summer, when I lay tossing and sleepless for want of opium, – I amused myself with composing the imaginary *Confessions of a Murderer*; which, I think, might be made a true German bit of horror, the subject being exquisitely diabolical; and, if I do not flatter myself, some few dozens of useless old women I could frighten out of their wits and this wicked world. – Yet do not mention this, if you please, to anybody: for if I begin to write imaginary Confessions, I shall seem to many as no better than a pseudo-confessor in my own too real confessions.[62]

This exciting proposal was made in a letter of 24 October, in which he promised to be in London within a week. He then put the letter aside and posted it at last on 1 November, having squeezed hasty postscripts into every available space on the sheet. One of these explained that his library had gone for only £170; another urged Hessey to advertise in the newspapers not only the *Prolegomena* but also *Meditations on the Philosophy of Literature* – a book of some 250 pages which he intended to write immediately!

This catalogue of unwritten books can be explained easily in psychological terms. De Quincey was a great believer in making the disapproval of others a substitute for willpower. Claiming in the *Confessions* to have given up opium, he no doubt meant to make himself give it up: after all, not to do so would make him a liar. In the same way, if the papers carried announcements that 'in a few days would be published' this or that work by himself, how could he fail to produce it? His conscience and his publishers would hold him to it. In short, the way to do things was to promise them. But Hessey had the sense not to advertise anything until he saw the manuscript, and De Quincey sank back into torpor. In November Dorothy Wordsworth wrote, 'Mr. de Q. is here as usual – the house always blinded – or left with but one eye to peep out of – *he* probably in bed – We hear nothing of him.'[63]

At last poverty forced him to make another raid on the metropolis. He reached London on 12 December, intending to stay for just two months: long enough, if he wrote intensively, to produce a bulky collection of articles and perhaps one of the various small books he had been planning. He then counted on being able to return to Fox Ghyll with money in his pocket and settle down to another period of peaceful family life. This plan was partly fulfilled, and 1823 proved to be one of the most fruitful years of his literary life. Every issue of the *London Magazine* that year carried some example of his work. There were translations, essays on German literature, articles on political economy, and the 'Letters to a Young Man Whose Education Has Been Neglected'; and in September the miscellaneous pieces promised in his letters from Fox Ghyll began to appear as 'Notes from the Pocket Book of a Late Opium-Eater'.

De Quincey was now committed to journalism. He was ready to turn his finely wrought prose style to almost any subject that would interest the magazine-buying public, and when Thomas Hood, another contributor to the *London*, paid him a visit, he found De Quincey's lodgings a literary workshop in full production, and De

Quincey himself 'quite at home in the midst of a German Ocean of Literature, in a storm, flooding all the floor, the table and the chairs – billows of books, tossing, tumbling, surging open'.[64] De Quincey would stop work and talk for as long as the visitor cared to stay, 'standing with his eyes fixed on one side of the room, seeming to be less speaking than reading from a handwriting on the wall', ready the instant the door closed again to turn back to his desk and press on with the next page of copy for the *London*. Taylor and Hessey soon came to trust De Quincey's judgment to the extent to submitting manuscripts to him before accepting them.[65] Several of his own contributions, too, were of real brilliance, and among them was his most successful piece of literary criticism, the short essay 'On Knocking at the Gate in *Macbeth*', where he tried to explain the dramatic impact of Macduff's knocking after the murder of Duncan, which 'reflected back upon the murder' such a 'peculiar awfulness and . . . depth of solemnity'.

Characteristically, he had arrived at his solution by noticing an analogy between the episode and an incident mentioned in newspaper reports of a murder in 1811. The killer had murdered several members of a family and was alone in their house with the corpses when a servant girl had knocked at the street door. The situation – innocent girl on one side of the door, murderer red-handed on the other – had caught De Quincey's imagination and he was to return to it much later in one of his essays on murder. What interested him now was the predicament of the murderer and its parallel with that of Macbeth and his wife. For the duration of the crime, the criminals have acted in a closed world, 'cut off by an immeasurable gulf from the ordinary tide and succession of human affairs'. Now, in the moment after the crime is completed, the normal world again makes itself felt 'and the re-establishment of the goings-on of the world in which we live, first makes us profoundly sensible of the awful parenthesis that had suspended them'. The essay is a good instance of De Quincey's belief that criticism must draw upon the irrational and intuitive parts of the mind. 'The mere understanding', he argued, '. . . is the meanest faculty in the human mind, and the most to be distrusted.' The critic should attend to his emotional responses. With their guidance, a sensational news item may teach him secrets about literature which no amount of logical analysis could ever reveal.

During 1823 the *Confessions* in book form became a firm favourite with the general public, successfully making the transition from critical to popular success. Even reports of accidental death by opium only helped to increase public interest. To spread his fame further, John Wilson introduced 'The Opium-Eater' into his series *Noctes Ambrosianae* in the October number of *Blackwood's*. The *Noctes* purported to be the monthly record of conversation amongst a group of *Blackwood's* writers and their friends who met to dine, drink, play practical jokes and talk scandal at 'Ambrose's Tavern'. Everything about the *Noctes* was semi-fictional. The tavern really existed, and the characters, led by 'Christopher North' (John Wilson) and 'The Ettrick Shepherd' (James Hogg), were fictional portraits of real people. The 'Opium-Eater' was therefore invited, in his fictional form, to dinner, where the 'Ettrick Shepherd' tackled him in suitably flattering style:

> Hech, sirs, yon bit Opium Tract's a desperate interesting confession. It's perfectly dreadfu', yon pouring in upon you o' oriental imagery. But nae wunner. Sax thousand draps of lowdnam! It's as muckle, I fancy, as a bottle of whusky. I tired the experiment mysel, after reading the wee wud wicked work, wi' five hunner draps, and I couped ower, and continued in ae snore frae Monday night till Friday morning.[66]

After which 'North' asked, 'Pray, is it true, my dear Laudanum, that your "Confessions" have caused about fifty unintentional suicides?' Replied the 'Opium-Eater', 'I should think not. I have read of six only; and they rested on no solid foundation.' And the feeling of the meeting was that, 'It only shows the danger that dunces run into, when they imitate men of genius.'

But phantom appearances earned no fees, and while the 'Opium-Eater' entertained Wilson's readers with his quaint manners and elaborate whimsical conversation his real-life counterpart dodged creditors, sweated over pieces of hack journalism and hid in dirty lodgings. His hopes of spending a mere two months in London were quickly dashed. He could rarely work fast enough to get his copy in before the last minute, and paying for lodgings added a new drain on his income, so that he could never quite pull himself out of debt. He was continually having to borrow money, often from Taylor and Hessey themselves, which meant that when he delivered articles he sometimes received nothing, having spent the fee in advance.[67] He was forced to pawn his watch and some of Margaret's jewellery. In July he was hiding from creditors in a tavern and begging Taylor and Hessey to keep his name a secret. ' "M.M. in the Swan" or simply "The Gent in ye Swan" is enough by way of direction,' he told them, when they had to send him his proofs. Working in these conditions told on his health. On 21 March he had declared himself 'worn out with sleep-lessness and taking laudanum three days in succession'[68] and at least once had to apologize for sending a manuscript blotched with laudanum.[69]

The terrible thing about this struggle was that it had no foreseeable end, for in truth magazine writing would not support a man, unless he could supplement it with an editorial post. Contributions were paid for by length, usually at about ten guineas for sixteen printed pages. To pay the year's rent of Fox Ghyll, therefore, De Quincey would have had to produce eighty pages of the magazine. Add to this the rent of lodgings together with the cost of food, clothing, domestic service, schooling for his children and coach fares for himself, and it becomes clear that he would have had to write the entire magazine single-handed to make ends meet. The *London* could take only so much material by one author. On the other hand, editors objected to their best contributors' writing for rival magazines. There was no solution and by August he could stand no more. He wrote to Hessey in a tone of apologetic embarrassment, to make 'an explanation' which, he said, he should have made long before, namely that staying in London, which to Hessey might seem a mere matter of course, was to him a very great 'sacrifice'. By doing so he wasted money and cut himself off from his family. He had forgotten the optimism with which he had announced his determination to come to London, and now seemed to think that he had come south to do Taylor and Hessey a favour. If he stayed much longer, he wrote ominously, 'pure anxiety will again do the same work it did before in London – viz. put an end to all power of composition, and reduce me to my old condition of an Opium-Eater'. After this unconvincing attempt at moral blackmail, he gradually came to the point, with the question——

> *Why am I now in London?* For what purpose (not as easily accomp-lished at home); on what justification; – for whose interest real or imagined? Are you aware of the enormous sacrifice which I am making in *personal happiness* by staying at a distance of 300 miles from my own family? . . . Have you ever asked – *whose interests* this residence in London was meant to serve? . . . Simply to renounce all domestic comforts – to exchange a roomy house for a single chamber – a Westmoreland valley for a London alley – attendance of servants for the necessity of doing all things for myself – a regular table for no table at all – literary leisure for the labour of writing all day long – &c.&c. Simply *these* sacrifices in the estimate of the world, would rank as very heavy, and implying some powerful motive.[70]

The purpose of the letter was probably to make Hessey responsible for De Quincey's own decisions. He hated being in London, but he feared that going home might be a mistake, and needed to believe that it was all Hessey's fault. Once he had worked himself up into a belief that Hessey had treated him badly, he could leave London in a state of indignation and whatever disaster might follow could be blamed on Hessey. Accordingly, having relieved his feelings on that score, on 6 August De Quincey was back at Fox Ghyll.

9
The Wretched Business
of Hack-Author

Margaret and the children, the country air and the summer weather, must have done him good, for he went to tea with the Wordsworths and Dorothy reported, 'he is returned quite well, and looks younger than he did seven years ago'.[1] He looked so much better that she thought he must have given up opium. He now had four children: William, Margaret, Horace and a baby called Francis John who had been baptized in February and seems to have been born while De Quincey was in London.[2] No wonder he had been so eager to leave – though it seems odd that in his complaints to Hessey he never mentioned the new baby. But troubles continued as usual: the rent was overdue, and the landlord wanted to sell Fox Ghyll. Several prospective purchasers were waiting impatiently for the De Quinceys to leave or be evicted, and had no scruples about knocking at the door and demanding to be shown over the house.[3]

Meanwhile, it appears that De Quincey may have managed to apply himself once more to writing, and to produce – of all things – the long-awaited novel. For in October 1823 appeared anonymously *The Stranger's Grave: A Tale* in one volume duodecimo, published by Longman's at six shillings. *The Stranger's Grave* is a sentimental novel, set partly in Wetheral, Cumberland – where Richard De Quincey had lived – and partly in an imaginary Spanish and Pyrenean landscape. Local tradition at Wetheral, recorded in 1870 and 1920,[4] attributed the novel to De Quincey, and despite its absurd plot and poor style there are several features which strengthen the attribution. The Spanish scenes present a landscape similar in every way to the Portuguese environment described in a short story, 'The Peasant of Portugal', which, as we shall see, De Quincey certainly wrote in 1826. No doubt his researches into the Peninsular Campaign in 1809 provided the material. The novel concludes by reprinting, slightly altered, Wordsworth's 'A Slumber did my Spirit Seal' from the *Lyrical Ballads*. And the plot is replete with material from De Quincey's past. The hero, Edward Stanley, contracts a serious pulmonary complaint, from which he recovers at Clifton; he goes to Oxford to please his parents and, having no desire for university honours, leaves without a degree but deeply in debt; he is told by a quack doctor at one point in the story that he is suffering from water on the brain, the disease De Quincey most dreaded. About to elope with the heroine, Emily, he spends an anguished evening alone in the sitting-room of an inn, listening to a storm outside and knowing that he is about to make an irrevocable mistake – an episode parallel to De Quincey's account of his evening at Shrewsbury in 1802. With equal fidelity to De Quincey's experience, the heroine, secretly escaping from her parents' home by night, nearly rouses the household by dropping (most improbably) a 'small trunk' – as the groom had done on the day De Quincey fled from Manchester Grammar School.

The style of *The Stranger's Grave* is undistinguished and shows signs of haste, but it is not uncharacteristic of De Quincey in his less polished moments – in his letters, for instance, or in the translation he made in 1824 of the trivial German novel *Walladmor*. We should remember also that part at least of *The Stranger's Grave* is said to have been written at Wetheral itself. If so, this would have been in 1814 or 1815, when De Quincey was nineteen or twenty and stayed there with Richard. Perhaps in 1823, desperate for money, he dug out a manuscript discarded years before, hastily refurbished it and sold it to Longman.

But why did he not send it to Taylor and Hessey, to whom he had promised a novel? Possibly Longman offered him more than the £157.10s. offered by Taylor and Hessey. This might explain an angry letter written by De Quincey in March 1824 to Hessey,[5] who had demanded repayment of a substantial sum previously advanced. De Quincey goes out of his way in this letter to deny that he has had dealings with any other publisher, and bitterly reproaches Hessey for detaining his manuscripts in lieu of the disputed sum. Had Hessey heard of De Quincey's selling a novel to Longman? If so, De Quincey was no doubt trusting to the anonymity of *The Stranger's Grave* and denying all knowledge of it. Another possibility is that the undistinguished quality of the writing led him to submit it elsewhere, not wanting to damage his standing with Taylor and Hessey. A third explanation, however, concerns the novel's subject. *The Stranger's Grave* deals with an incestuous relationship, a love affair between a young man and his niece, who is only three years his junior. Much of its emotional interest derives from guilt and the violation of sexual prohibitions, and it may well be that De Quincey preferred not to have it known that he was the author. Taylor would probably not have touched the novel anyway, for he was sensitive to the criticism of his father, a man of strict moral views who a few years before had congratulated his son on refusing to publish Byron.

If *The Stranger's Grave* is De Quincey's work, it holds considerable biographical interest because it appears to synthesize the two central emotional experiences of his life and present a hero who is in many ways a perceptive self-portrait. We are told that Edward Stanley is endowed with 'a natural volatility of temper, which frequently led him to perpetrate, with his eyes open, deeds for which he was all the time aware that his better reason would afterwards reproach him; and a spirit of – I know not what to call it, whether perverseness or idle romance, which led him to derive an extraordinary satisfaction in the knowledge that he was surrounded by difficulties'.[6] His customary attitude to these difficulties is to hope for the best and determine 'to be guided in his behaviour by chance or circumstances'. The author, without obvious irony, calls this 'a wise resolution' and one which is 'very general with young men who find themselves in the midst of difficulties from which they can discover no direct outlet'.[7] As a key to one aspect of De Quincey's psychology, these passages could hardly be improved. Moreover, the trials of hero and heroine look in some ways as if they were modelled on those of De Quincey and Margaret. After discovering that Emily is pregnant, the couple elope together and go to Spain where they live in a small country cottage, vainly awaiting a remittance from a friend in England and forced to sell their clothes and furniture as an insolent landlord presses for rent. This may well reflect De Quincey's experience since 1817. On the other hand the novel's concern with sexual guilt may also owe something to the experiences of 1814 and 1815, when his secret liaison with Margaret had just begun: it is a natural enough preoccupation if indeed the tale had been started at that time whilst visiting Richard. As for the theme of incest, it may (though not uncommon in the sensational fiction of the period) be derived ultimately from De Quincey's attachment to his sister Elizabeth. It may be significant that the names Margaret and Elizabeth both occur in the novel but, as it were, transposed: the hero is given a sister called Margaret, whilst Elizabeth is the name of a girl who falls in love with him shortly before his death at Wetheral. De Quincey had already shown signs of a tendency to assimilate his relationship with Margaret to that of brother and sister in a passage of the *Confessions* where he compared himself under the torments of opium to the fury-haunted Orestes of Greek tragedy, and likened Margaret to Electra – the loving sister of Orestes. Edward and Emily in *The Stranger's Grave* are, of course, uncle and niece, but their ages, and the attitude of their family, encourage the reader to think of them as siblings.

The Stranger's Grave was well reviewed and must have sold briskly, for as well as the London edition of 1823 others were published at Exeter in 1828 and at Boston, Massachusetts, in 1824. It was once more reprinted in 1848, the author's name being given as 'Henry Villiers'. Nothing is known of 'Villiers'; nor is it known whether De Quincey was even aware of this last edition. It seems probable that the novel was De Quincey's work, but unless new evidence comes to light we may never be quite certain.

His essays continued to appear in the *London* through the autumn of 1823 but their reception was not always favourable. There was an embarrassing episode in October when the Opium-Eater's 'Notes' included a short essay criticizing Malthus's *Essay on Population* and Hazlitt wrote to point out that De Quincey's arguments exhibited 'rather a striking coincidence' with a published work of his own. A flustered De Quincey replied from Grasmere for the December number, admitting that he had once glanced at Hazlitt's work but denying any close similarity. Hazlitt did not press the point, but he might have done so. The two key points of De Quincey's essay were identical in substance with the first two sections of Hazlitt's pamphlet on Malthus. Direct plagiarism is unlikely: no doubt Hazlitt's ideas had been part of De Quincey's mental furniture for so long that he had forgotten where they came from. But the incident showed the dangers of trusting entirely to memory: a serious problem for an author who could not afford to buy books and often had to work in haste, far from any adequate library. It also revealed De Quincey's extreme sensitivity. No harm would have been done by a modest admission that Hazlitt had anticipated him, but his pride was stung and he could not admit the possibility. One can imagine him secretly raging at the poverty and pressure of work which prevented his doing justice to his real abilities, feeling that circumstances were cheating him of the credit he deserved. Further evidence of this attitude may be found in a series of papers on 'The Origin of the Rosicrucians and the Freemasons', which he finished and sent to Hessey at the end of August. Hessey was so impressed that he considered publishing them as a separate book.[8] He did not, but they appeared in the magazine during the first half of 1824. They purported to be a synthesis of material from a badly written and disorganized German work, transformed by De Quincey into a stylish and lucid argument. In fact all he had done was to make a hasty summary of his German source, following the order of the original argument and giving literal translations of the crucial sentences.[9] The product was interesting but lacked even the degree of originality De Quincy claimed for it. Again, it seems, he wanted credit for what he might have done rather than for what he did.

It is easy to understand the frustration and sorrow with which he turned out his copy, and how little satisfied he must have been with the results. In December, he apologized to Wordsworth for his unsociability at Fox Ghyll, giving as his excuse

> the load of labour, under which I groan . . . when I am not utterly exhausted, I am writing: and all is too little . . . Mere correction of proofs indeed, and corresponding with London on business, is almost enough to fill up my time: for, if all that I have lately written – were published at once, it is a literal fact that I should *more* than fill the London Mag. myself.[10]

The *London*, meanwhile, had problems of its own. John Taylor was heading for a nervous breakdown and his judgment was suffering. As well as coping poorly with the routine work of keeping the magazine going, he was tending, in defiance of public taste, to push the magazine in the direction of factual exposition and away from literary concerns. Papers on economics, statistics and science occupied increasing amounts of space, and as Taylor and De Quincey shared a fascination with political economy, De Quincey's essays on such subjects began to weigh down the magazine. In spring 1824, after weathering two months of illness and debt, De Quincey was working on a series of 'Dialogues of Three Templars on Political Economy' setting forth the theories of Ricardo. Taylor began to publish these in March and soon his other contributors were growing mutinous as they saw their work rejected to make room for interminable discussions of rent and value which would surely sink the magazine altogether. T.L. Beddoes summed it up: 'Taylor has lately refused a paper of Procter's & one of Reynolds & kept back Darley's . . . for the purpose of introducing that thrice-double demoniac the oeconomical Opium-eater. Exit London.'[11] De Quincey, of course, was glad to sell Taylor anything he would take. In the intervals of composing his 'Dialogues' he was hunting through mountains of old bills and papers at Town End to draw up a long legal document explaining his financial position in order to forestall 'a series of nearly a dozen arrests' for debt which would have forced him to flee the country to avoid prison.[12] He won his battle and kept the creditors at bay, but as usual the feeling was growing on him that he could only restore his fortunes properly by going to London, and after several false alarms he arrived in late June.[13]

These helpless oscillations between Westmorland and London followed a clear pattern. He would arrive in London hopeful and primed with bright ideas. He would work hard but find himself earning less than he expected. Living in London would lead him to incur new debts. He would grow homesick and lonely. It would seem to him that he could work just as well in the lost paradise of Grasmere as in cramped London lodgings, and at last he would go home. Here he would be happy and might work again, but the distance from the press would mean delays and missed deadlines. He could not contact Taylor and Hessey quickly when he needed money. Local creditors would press him for debts. He would start to feel that only in London could he make the money he needed, and he would set off again. And in counterpoint to this rhythm was the fluctuating graph of opium-taking: too much one week, too little the next; lethargy, confusion, days spent apathetically in bed; or else withdrawal symptoms, night-mares, manic irritability. Yet somehow he survived. A sense of respon-sibility to Margaret and the children sustained him, no doubt, as much as his 'extraordinary satisfaction in the knowledge that he was sur-rounded by difficulties'.

He had to endure a new kind of blow to his confidence when he reached London in June 1824. Soon after his arrival he was reading a copy of *The Times* at breakfast. 'Strolling with my eye', he recalls, 'over the vast Babylonian confusion of the enormous columns,' he noticed an advertisement for the *John Bull Magazine and Literary Recorder*, a new comic journal which promised a series of satirical articles on the 'Humbugs of the Age'. 'Humbug No. 1', it appeared, was 'The Opium-Eater'. By nine a.m. ('an hour at which few people had seen me for years') he was on his way, full of apprehension, to the publisher's shop.[14] He bought *John Bull* and stopped in the street to find the article.

There are some humbugs [he read] with which we have no patience . . . the fellows who, on the strength of some wretched infirmity, endeavour to puff themselves into notice . . .

Conceive an animal about five feet high, propped on two trap-sticks, which have the size but not the delicate proportions of rolling-pins, with a comical sort of indescribable body, and a head of most portentous magnitude, which puts one in mind of those queer big-headed caricatures that you see occasionally from whimsical pencils. As for the face, its utter grotesqueness and inanity is totally beyond the reach of the pen to describe . . .

There is something excessively disgusting in being obliged to look into any man's private life, but when we have it tossed into our faces, we must now and then do so. Now, in the 83rd and 84th pages of Quincey's book, he bursts out into an apostrophe to his wife, very fine, and very affecting:- 'Beloved M., thou wert my Electra – thou thoughtest not much to stoop to humble offices of kindness, and to servile ministrations –' and much more trash, which we have not room to quote. The truth of the business is, that this *Electra*, who did not *think much* (affected puppy) to stoop to servile offices, was his servant-maid long before he married her, and had often made his bed before she ascended it . . . As we are fond of biographical researches, we should request De Quincey to give us an extract from his parish-register, dating the birth of his first child, and also his marriage with Electra. It would be an important addition to the chronology of the county.[15]

There was much more in the same style. It was a vicious attack, and was clearly written by someone who had personal knowledge of De Quincey. In his helpless rage, De Quincey at first thought of tracing the author and challenging him to a duel. Fortunately he thought better of it; he seems, however, to have learned in due course that the author was William Maginn, a *Blackwood's* colleague of Wilson's. No doubt Wilson had unintentionally supplied Maginn with the scandal he needed in the course of comparatively innocent gossip, although he must have known that Maginn was a dedicated libeller who could never resist the temptation to use journalistic anonymity as a cover for abusing friend and enemy alike. Wilson pointedly brought the subject up in the August *Noctes Ambrosianae*, where 'Odoherty' (a character who represented Maginn) asks 'Christopher North', 'You would disapprove, no doubt, of the attack on De Quincey in the John Bull Magazine?' 'North' replies, 'Disapprove? I utterly despised it, and so, no doubt, did he.'[16] So Maginn was rebuked, but there was no way of preventing the libel from finding its way to Westmorland, where the Whig *Kendal Chronicle* gleefully reprinted it as a final stab at its old enemy.[17] Thus did *Blackwood's* (though without Wilson's sanction) indirectly punish its renegade contributor.

De Quincey found some consolation for this and his other troubles in two new friendships. One was with Matthew Davenport Hill, barrister and educationalist. De Quincey reviewed a book of Hill's for the *London* and in July Hill, pleased with the review, sought De Quincey out and invited him to dinner. The Hill family were first astonished at De Quincey's shabby clothes and strangeness, then delighted with his courtly manners, brilliant talk and air of amiable naivety. He became a regular visitor at their house in Chelsea. There he met Charles Knight, a former newspaper editor now running his own magazine, *Knight's Quarterly*. Knight befriended De Quincey and published one of his German translations. He greatly admired De Quincey's skill as a translator: his versions, said Knight, were always very free, but 'he could not go about this sort of work without improving all he touched'.[18] Knight and Hill often invited De Quincey to spend his evenings at their houses, knowing, as Knight said, that 'he was directly beset with visitations more terrible than the normal poverty of authors'. Hill reported that one morning De Quincey arrived at his house 'wet and shivering, having slept under a hayrick in the Hampstead fields' to avoid arrest.[19] His troubles became a standing joke among the *London Magazine's* contributors. At a tea party in July Hessey entertained his guests by reporting De Quincey's latest description of his bodily sufferierings. 'He should have chosen as his publishers', said Lamb, '*Pain* and *Fuss*' (Payne and Foss were a well-known firm of literary agents).[20] But his articles continued as spirited and urbane as ever. He was prone to moods of terrible despondency, of course. 'A curse seemed to settle on whatever I then undertook,' he later recalled. 'It was rare, indeed, that I could satisfy my own judgement, even tolerably, with the quality of any literary article I turned out.'[21] But this very discontent was a safeguard, and he never submitted a paper whose style fell below a certain minimum standard of his own, so that he continually gained friends, admirers and the respect, if not the cash, of editors.

Not everyone liked his work, of course. In August and September he reviewed the first English translation of Goethe's novel *Wilhelm Meister's Apprenticeship*, by the young unknown Thomas Carlyle. Despite his enthusiasm for German literature, De Quincey knew little about Goethe and his review, although amusing, was completely inadequate to its subject. It consisted partly of an attack on Goethe, whom De Quincey chose to see as vastly overrated, and partly of a scathing criticism of the novel itself, which he portrayed as the epitome of that bad taste for which Germans were, supposedly, renowned. De Quincey, who could be extraordinarily prim when he chose, was shocked by the novel's frank treatment of adultery and illegitimacy. He announced that certain passages were indecent enough for 'the most obtuse of old libertines', and ended by declaring pointedly that, 'Our practice is to turn away our eyes from whatsoever we are compelled to loathe or to disdain, and to leave all that dishonours human nature to travel on its natural road to shame and oblivion.' [22] Poor Carlyle, who was twenty-nine and had just come to London hoping to launch his literary career, was deeply upset. He called it 'a vulgar and brutish review', adding, 'I read three pages of it . . . and said: "here is a man who writes of things which he does not rightly understand; I see clean over the top of him, and his vulgar spite, and his commonplace philosophy" '[23] – which, as far as the Goethe articles were concerned, was perfectly accurate. At the same time, what may especially have rankled was that De Quincey had hit on just those points which had infuriated Carlyle himself as he struggled to translate the novel a year before. 'When I read of players and libidinous actresses and their sorry pasteboard apparatus for beautifying the "moral world," ' he had grumbled, 'I render it into grammatical English – with a feeling mild and charitable as that of a starving hyena.'[24] Perhaps De Quincey's review aroused misgivings that some of this feeling had crept into the translation and communicated itself to the reader. Carlyle found out what he could about his critic and wrote to his wife, 'The dwarf Opium-Eater . . . lives here in lodgings, with a wife and children living or starving on the scanty produce of his scribble, far off in Westmorland. He carries a laudanum bottle in his pocket; and the venom of a wasp in his heart.' But he concluded, kindly enough, 'If I could find him, it would give me a pleasure to procure him one substantial beef-steak before he dies.'[25]

By a strange turn of events, De Quincey himself was about to embark on the translation of a German novel, by a far worse author than the despised Goethe. It happened that in 1823 Sir Walter Scott, whose work was immensely popular in Germany, had published no less than three novels. As the Leipzig Book Fair of Easter 1824 approached and it became clear that Scott's new novel, *Redgauntlet*, would not be published in England for some months, an enterprising German printer saw an opening for deception and commissioned a hack author called Haering, who wrote under the pseudonym 'Willibald Alexis', to forge in German a new Waverley novel, which could be published and distributed at Leipzig as a translation of Scott's latest romance. Alexis duly concocted a piece of nonsense in three volumes entitled *Walladmor*. The plot was an improbable brew of shipwreck, smuggling, missing heirs and picturesque landscape-description, padded out with lengthy dissertations on demonology and folklore, and it was hoped that it would pass muster as one of Scott's more fantastic creations in the vein of *Guy Mannering*.

Walladmor was good enough to have its short vogue in Germany, and it aroused the curiosity of Scott, who asked for a copy, which was obtained for him by Bohn, the leading London dealer in foreign books. At this point De Quincey enters the story. Early in September he heard that a copy of the book was in London and, with true journalistic enterprise, took immediate steps to secure it. He wrote to Hessey to tell him that he was making good progress with the first of a new series of articles, '*Epistola Critica*': four items were ready, but

> for the . . . 5th or last art [icle], we must have 'Walladmor' . . . if Heaven or Earth can get it. An abstract of the novel, which I will make in 24 hours, will be of universal interests from the circumstances. – Pray send if you can to Bohn's. They have promised to lend Sir W. Scott's copy in default of any other, on condition of a speedy return. And within 36 hours of receiving it at most I will pledge my word for returning it. What I fear is that the copy should be snapped up by somebody on the spot.[26]

The book was borrowed, and De Quincey tackled it. Reading it presented practical problems because the pages had not been cut and as it was Scott's he felt he could not take the liberty of cutting them himself. But he managed to read enough of the hidden pages by peering up between the folds 'in the attitude of a man looking up a chimney' to obtain a general idea of the novel, and he produced his review in time for the October *Magazine*, where it appeared as 'Sir Walter Scott's German Novel' – an appropriate title, for 'German' carried the slang meaning of 'cheap substitute'. The article ridiculed the book but called it 'the boldest hoax of our times', and it had unexpected consequences. Rather than merely providing an hour's amusement for the *London's* readers, it created a demand for the novel and within weeks Taylor and Hessey, anxious to keep the initiative, were asking De Quincey to produce a full translation as soon as possible.

He could not afford to decline the commission, so he shut himself up in his lodgings with a copy of *Walladmor* and began work. The task proved to be harder than he had anticipated. He had undertaken to translate as fast as the printers could work, producing forty-eight pages of print each weekday and finishing the book in three weeks. On reading the novel properly, however, he found it much worse than his first cursory examination had suggested. It was, he now realized, 'almighty nonsense': 'the very devils and runners of the press would have mutinied against being parties to such atrocious absurdities'.[27] Charles Knight visited him in November and 'saw him groaning over his uncongenial labour, by which he eventually got very little'. The novel was supposed to appear in three volumes, but, De Quincey told him, 'after weeding out forests of rubbish, I believe it will make only one decent volume'.[28] To avoid disappointing his audience and to preserve his own self-respect, he decided to solve the problem by rewriting the novel as he went along, an expedient which slowed his progress to a mere eight pages a day. He not only cut out much tedious matter but gave the plot a new climax, altered the relationships of the characters and added some splendid fantastic scene-painting. One suspects that once involved in this work of metamorphosis he was much happier. At any rate he had great fun with the details of the final product, for his peculiar position as translator of a pseudo-translation appealed to his sense of humour, and he tried to make sure that no one could take the book too seriously. His title-page announced *Walladmor* as

"Freely Translated into German from the English of
Sir Walter Scott"
and now
Freely translated from the German into the English.

The German forger had had the impudence to dedicate his 'translation' to Scott, so De Quincey dedicated his English version to the German forger, in a preface where he ceremoniously apologized for his tampering with the plot. He warned Alexis that 'your three corpulent volumes have collapsed into two English ones of rather consumptive appearance', but consoled him with the thought that where style was concerned the English version was 'a silk purse' in comparison with the 'sow's ear' of the original. As for the plot, he had had no choice but to make some alterations: for instance, 'the case of a man's swimming on his back from Bristol to the Isle of Anglesea, was more than the most indulgent public would bear. They would not stand it, Sir, I was convinced . . . Your chronology was almost equally out of order: but I put *that* into the hands of an eminent watchmaker; and he assures me that he has "regulated" it.'[29] He finished by suggesting that Alexis translate the improved *Walladmor* back into German, and signed himself 'Your obedient (but not quite faithful) Translator'. The novel appeared early in 1825, and one reader at least was satisfied. 'We are very busy reading "Walladmor",' wrote Sara Hutchinson. 'It is well worth reading – as the style and descriptions are very far beyond anything in merit that you meet with in such publications – seldom indeed anywhere – for everything that De Quincey does must be clever.'[30]

Nonetheless, he was in as much trouble as usual by the end of 1824. The *London Magazine* was taken over by a new editor who was not interested in De Quincey's work, and *Knight's Quarterly Magazine* had collapsed. As usual he was being pursued by creditors, and there exists a letter dated 26 October 1824 – from the middle of the *Walladmor* period – where he claims to be just back from Boulogne, 'Whither I had been compelled to go for the purpose of meeting an English friend on business.'[31] There is no other record of this excursion and, as he is writing to apologize for the non-payment of rent, he may be inventing an excuse. On the other hand, Boulogne was a common refuge for English debtors. Perhaps De Quincey really was 'compelled to go' there, not to meet an 'English friend' but to escape arrest. The only possible solution was to write to his mother. The flurry in which he had lived for the past few years had resulted in an almost complete loss of communication between mother and son, and though life at Westhay had been far from peaceful, De Quincey had had no emotional energy to spare for things which might otherwise have moved him deeply. His sister Mary had married a young clergyman, but after little more than year she had died in childbed in 1820. Henry, the youngest brother, had turned out as unmanageable as all the other Quincey boys. After drifting for some years and developing a tendency to 'get into scrapes about money', as Jane put it, he had married and set himself up in an expensive house at Clifton where he and his wife lived in fine style, expecting Thomas Penson, the Indian uncle, to settle a fortune on them when he retired and thus pay their debts. Possibly Henry saw himself as the virtuous son of the family and relied upon Penson to disinherit the prodigals Thomas and Richard. If so, he miscalculated: Penson heard of his conduct and determined to disinherit *him*. In the event, Henry did not live to suffer the consequences. At an early age, he succumbed, as his father had done, to consumption – the exact date of his death is not known – and Penson, really the kindest of men, gave a home and financial support to his widow.[32] As for Richard, he had not been heard of since 1819, when he was said to be in America.[33] The details of his later travels have been lost. All we know is that at some time during the 1820s he was on a ship which called at Port-au-Prince, Haiti. A party of sailors decided to go on a hunting expedition in forest country and 'Pink' went with them. Somehow he got separated from the group and disappeared. No trace of him was ever found and his fate remains a mystery. De Quincey records that 'many years' after 'Pink' was last heard of, he came across some papers belonging to his lost brother and found among them, to his surprise, the drafts of several 'wild lyrical verses' composed by 'Pink' at the age of eleven or twelve. They seemed 'of a nature to have proceeded . . . from some mystical quietist' and resembled the work of George Herbert. 'Pink' had never confessed to writing poetry.[34]

In January 1825, of course, there was as yet no great anxiety over 'Pink', who was expected to reappear in his own good time. Jane still lived with her mother at Westhay in reasonable comfort, but even there financial problems were not unknown, for Kelsall had gone bankrupt 'in consequence', Jane reported, 'of extensive speculations in which you would have fancied honest John was the last person to have thought of engaging'.[35] Some of Mrs Quincey's money had been invested in his business, though fortunately most of it had been removed before the crash. Replying to Thomas's letter, Mrs Quincey had so far lost track of her son's affairs that she had to ask, 'Do you live at Fox Ghyll? How many Children have you?' She thanked him for *Walladmor*, but could not resist adding, 'I cannot expect that your literary productions either as a Translator or Author will rise in moral tone to my point, for I suppose you must please your Readers, and unfortunately little is required.'[36] But in response to his appeal for money she proposed to make him an allowance of £100 a year. This would certainly ease the pressure of debt, though it would soon go in small payments on account to the worst creditors, to buy a brief respite in which he could tackle more work.

As usual De Quincey was unwell in the early part of the year and in February 1825 a letter to John Wilson summed up pathetically the misery of his existence:

> To fence with these ailments with the one hand, and with the other to maintain the war with the wretched business of hack-author, with all its horrible degradations, is more than I am able to bear. At this moment I have not a place to hide in . . . sometimes I meditate I know not what . . . With a good publisher and leisure to premeditate what I write, I might yet liberate myself: after which, having paid every body, I would slink into some dark corner, educate my children, and show my face in the world no more.[37]

The latest phase in 'the wretched business of hack-author' was newspaper work. A certain Dr John Stoddart, a friend of Wordsworth, edited a London morning paper called the *New Times*, and De Quincey, perhaps on Wordsworth's recommendation, became a contributor.[38] Between January and May he contributed about fifteen articles to the *New Times*, some unsigned and some over pseudonyms which included 'Defoe' and 'Lepus' ('The Hare'). Most of his pieces appeared in a miscellaneous column of literary and humorous items called 'Variorum'. The column may have been devised as a vehicle for De Quincey, for it appears only during the first third of 1825 and, apart from verses contributed by one 'Pollio', nearly all the items, however signed, look very much like De Quincey's work.

Some of the essays show a new facet of De Quincey: an interest not only in individuals but in character-types. 'Tom Pry' and 'Readers against the Grain' are humorous pen-portraits, perhaps worked up from hasty notes taken in the course of his daily encounters with the London populace. An anecdote which may date from about this time gives us a glimpse of such a process. Looking for rooms somewhere in South London De Quincey was shown over a house by a remarkably garrulous landlady who made a point of larding her conversation with long words learned from the newspapers: promising, for example, that she 'would spontaneously adapt the several modes of domestication to the reciprocal interests' of herself and the tenant.[39] Making his escape, De Quincey noted down what he could remember of her conversation for future use.

He was not altogether at the mercy of landladies, for Hill and Knight both offered him shelter, and he spent part of the summer at Knight's house in Pall Mall. Knight had come to feel great affection for the harassed little man, and in his sympathy could see clearly how much sheer impracticality and diffidence magnified his troubles at every turn. He seemed, Knight recalled, 'helpless in every position of responsibility' and 'constantly beset by idle fears and vain imaginings . . . His sensitiveness was so extreme . . . that he hesitated to trouble a servant with any personal requests without a long prefatory apology.' One evening when Knight's family were away in the country Knight entered De Quincey's room to find him working stripped to the waist. ' "You will take cold," I exclaimed. "Where is your shirt?" "I have not a shirt, my shirts are unwashed." "But why not tell the servant to send them to the laundress?" "Ah! how could I pretend to do that in Mrs. Knight's absence?" ' On another occasion Knight returned from a trip to Windsor to find that De Quincey had taken his box and disappeared, leaving word that he had 'gone home'. Knight knew that he had been expecting a remittance from his mother which would enable him at last to rejoin his family in Westmorland, and assumed that it had come. Two or three days later, however, he heard that De Quincey was still in London. He traced him to lodgings in 'a miserable place on the Surrey side of Waterloo Bridge', and found that he had indeed received 'a large draft on a banker at twenty-one days' sight'. He had taken it to a bank and been told that the cash could not be paid until the three weeks were up, and not realizing that he could borrow money on the draft had settled down to wait until he could cash it. He had taken lodgings because he felt too embarrassed to go back to Knight's house and put the servants to further inconvenience, having told them he was leaving.[40]

There were no new literary ventures after the *New Times* essays finished, although Wilson heard a rumour that De Quincey was 'going to set up a new Periodical', a plan which Wilson stigmatized as 'silly madness'.[41] He need not have worried. All De Quincey wanted was to go home, and once he had his mother's allowance he could do so. His last weeks in London were spent in a state of anguish over the plight of Margaret and the children. His tenancy of Fox Ghyll was due to expire in October, and the landlord wanted the De Quinceys out as quickly as possible. De Quincey had agreed to give up possession to the new owner, Mrs Luff, by 7 March, but the move had not been made because, as Dorothy Wordsworth reported, in De Quincey's absence 'his Wife will not dare to touch a Book, or do any thing towards removal'. There had already been one skirmish, in December, when 'poor Mrs Luff was in such haste to have possession that she set labourers into the Garden' – apparently to force Margaret and the children to leave. 'Now was not this foolish?' reflected Dorothy complacently: 'taking possession and thus having all the risk and all the trouble of ousting the De Quinceys',[42] when the former landlord might have been left to do it at his own expense!

Still, poor Margaret and her family had now been driven out and Mrs Luff moved in. The De Quinceys had gone to live at The Nab with Margaret's parents. De Quincey, fighting for his existence in London, could not go home to comfort his wife, but expected that The Nab would at least provide a comfortable sanctuary until he came back with money in his pocket. It turned out otherwise. Whether the Simpsons were away from home, or whether they had turned against Margaret and resented her presence, she had to survive at The Nab almost in isolation. On 16 July De Quincey wrote desperately to Dorothy:

> Call, I beg and pray you, my dear Miss Wordsworth, on my poor wife – who suffers greatly from a particular case of embarrassment affecting me just now . . . in a few weeks I shall be free from all distresses of the kind which have so long weighed upon me. Meantime, she writes me the most moving and heartrending letters – not complaining, but simply giving utterance to her grief. In her very last letter she concludes by begging me 'not to take her grief amiss': and in fact she disturbs my fortitude so much, that I cannot do half what I else could. For my fear is – that being thrown entirely upon herself, with no soul (unless her eldest sister) to speak a word of comfort to her – she will suffer her grief to grow upon her, and . . . will fret herself into illness. If that should happen, I know what I must look for next: and I shall never have any peace of mind, or a happy hour, again . . . Oh! Miss Wordsworth, – I sympathised with you – how deeply and fervently – in your trials 13 years ago: – now, when I am prostrate for a moment – and the hand of a friend would enable me to rise before I am crushed, do not refuse me this service . . . What I wish is – you would give my wife the relief of talking over her distress with one whom she can feel to be sympathising with her. – To do this with less constraint, perhaps you will be so good as to go over and drink tea with her – Say whatever you can think of to raise and support her spirits: beg her not to lie down too much, as she is apt to do in states of dejection, but to walk in the fields when it is cool, and to take some *solid* food, which she is very apt to neglect. – She is amused by newspapers: perhaps you could lend her a few just for the present, until I am able to send one down.[43]

He added that he hoped to be free from his difficulties in twenty-eight days at most, but it was 17 October when Dora Wordsworth told

Edward Quillinan that 'the poor little man is returned – he reached the Nab Thursday last'.⁴⁴ Rydal society found De Quincey a wonderful theme for gossip, and Sara Hutchinson reported with glee that he 'is now here *in great force*, his Mother having given him £300 to pay his debts. He tells Miss W. that he had entirely left off opium before he came hither, but has been obliged to have recourse to it again; "as he has *no Shoes* to walk in & without exercise he is obliged to take it" – I suppose it is *easier* to send to the Druggists than to the Shoe Makers'.⁴⁵

At least De Quincey had the consolation of being with his family again. He seems to have done little work, though a remark of 'North' in the October *Noctes Ambrosianae* – 'Would that we had his promised "Romance"!' – must reflect some vague plans of turning again to fiction. Wilson was trying to stimulate him to work; not altogether from altruistic motives, for he had undertaken to produce a philosophical article for the *Quarterly Review* and wanted De Quincey to help him write it! He was also trying to hold De Quincey to an old promise to write something for *Janus*, an Annual he was editing. He held out the prospect of fifty guineas 'every 1st of December until Doomsday' if only De Quincey could produce something. This, however, was in November and time was running out. 'The publisher is in a fever, and the volume must be shipped off to London in time to be published there *some weeks before the New Year*,' he wrote. 'Without your timely assistance the double-faced old gentleman will assuredly be damped.'⁴⁶ It seems that De Quincey did manage to send something: an inappropriately heavy essay called 'Hints Concerning the Universities' looks very much like his work. The annual appeared in January 1826 carrying, as if to give notice of De Quincey's presence, an 'Advertisement' explaining that

> The publication of this Work has, from circumstances not likely to occur again, been deferred considerably beyond the time intended. In future years, the volume will be produced in the first week of November. The Editor has the satisfaction to state, that he has received every assurance of steady and efficient assistance from the distinguished characters who have contributed to the present volume.

One wonders why Wilson was so sure the delay was 'not likely to occur again'. Perhaps he had decided not to employ De Quincey next time.

The family spent the winter together at The Nab, and De Quincey stayed on through the spring and summer. It may seem strange that he generally chose either to work or to be with his family; why could he not work at home, or move his family to a city where he could find work? As we have seen, distance from the press gave rise to delays and a lessened incentive to work. His dealings with editors suggest that he liked to have his copy coaxed out of him a few pages at a time. Frequently he would see to it that part of an article was already in type while he worked at the rest, as if he needed a sense that the whole staff of magazine and printing press were hanging on his pen. In the same way, he liked to receive his payment in dribs and drabs. Perhaps this was the outcome of a yearning for attention, a response to the terrifying impersonality of the literary market place. On the other hand, it seems that he resisted pressure to move his family to London because he wanted to keep his two lives separate. As he toiled in London, he wanted to know that still, three hundred miles away, there was paradise, unsullied by haste and dirt and the press. Landlords might threaten and Margaret might be lonely but at least it represented sanctuary, an assurance that the whole world was not Grub Street.

De Quincey's summer at The Nab seems to have produced one piece of literary work, a short story of no great value entitled 'The Peasant of Portugal: An Episode of the Peninsular War'. The journalist and poetaster Alaric Watts had asked Wordsworth to secure De Quincey's services for an annual, *The Literary Souvenir or Cabinet of Poetry and Romance*. Wordsworth warned Watts 'whatever hopes [De Quincey] may hold out, do not be tempted to depend on him. He is strangely irresolute.'[47] But De Quincey defeated these gloomy expectations. 'The Peasant of Portugal' is the story of Juan Taxillo, a hero of the Portuguese resistance against Napoleon. Juan's 'beautiful and newly-made bride', Marguerita, is raped and murdered by French soldiers. Vowing vengeance, Juan retreats with a band of followers to 'the fastnesses of the mountains', whence he deals out death stealthily, creeping forth at night to kill members of the occupying force until the whole regiment is in a state of terror. At last he is betrayed by one of his own countrymen but rather than endure capture he lures his betrayer and a troop of French soldiers into a cave where he kills them and himself by detonating a large store of gunpowder. The literary value of the story is negligible but it has some interest in that it resembles, in theme and treatment, aspects of both *The Stranger's Grave* and *Klos-*

terheim, De Quincey's later novel, between which it may represent a transitional stage.

In October it became necessary to work again and he went to Edinburgh. Wilson had always known that De Quincey could produce marvellous work if one could only put him into the right mood, and had never lost hope of winning him for *Blackwood's*. Now he succeeded and De Quincey began well. The November issue carried the first instalment of his abridged translation of Lessing's *Laocoön*. It was a minor literary landmark, for the *Laocoön*, one of the liveliest and most stimulating of all Romantic essays in aesthetics, had never before been seen in English. It was announced as the first of a 'Gallery of German Prose Classics, by the English Opium-Eater', which promised well for De Quincey's future security.

Wilson offered hospitality as well as work, and De Quincey stayed at his house through the winter of 1826–7. Despite his courtesy and retiring habits – or perhaps because of them – he was not an easy guest. He spent much of his time sleeping or working in an upstairs bedroom, where he also took his meals. His stomach was so delicate that he would trust it only with peculiar diets which he devised himself with the aid of medical books. He lived mainly on coffee, milk, boiled rice and small quantities of mutton, and saw the cook daily to give his instructions in minute detail. Wilson's daughter was present at some of these sessions, and reported the following:

> 'Owing to dyspepsia afflicting my system,' explained De Quincey, 'and the possibility of any additional derangement of the stomach taking place, consequences incalculably distressing would arise, so much so indeed as to increase nervous irritation, and prevent me from attending to matters of overwhelming importance, if you do not remember to cut the mutton in a diagonal rather than a longitudinal form.' [48]

When the audience was over the cook's comment was, 'Mr. De Quinshy would mak' a gran' preacher, though I'm thinking a hantle o' the folk wouldna ken what he was driving at . . . A' this claver aboot a bit mutton nae bigger than a prin!' Occasionally even the tolerant Wilson lost his patience. 'Hang you!' he exclaimed one evening, 'Can't you take your whisky toddy like a Christian man, and leave your damned opium slops to infidel Turks, Persians and Chinamen?' [49] And he kept his usual strange hours, staying in bed through the morning and becoming liveliest at night. Often he dozed in the afternoon as well and the Wilson children might enter his room to find him asleep on the hearthrug. In order to 'show him off' Wilson arranged late supper parties which went on until three or four in the morning. De Quincey's talk was at its best after midnight; earlier in the evening he was often quiet and dull.[50] He was not entirely a nocturnal creature, however, and Wilson's rowdy company stirred up energies which had slept for a long time. He and Wilson, an unlikely pair of naturalists, undertook expeditions to the seashore and countryside near Edinburgh to test various fanciful theories about nature. In particular, De Quincey recalls, they decided to find out if there was any truth in the tradition that every tenth wave is bigger, and went to stand on the beach at Portobello to count waves. They could see no difference. Perhaps Wilson was just tricking De Quincey into taking some fresh air.[51]

Alone again at The Nab, Margaret was missing her husband as sorely as ever. Dorothy Wordsworth paid a visit to the Nab on 15 November and wrote, at Margaret's instigation, to press De Quincey gently towards a change of policy:

> I called at your cottage yesterday, having first seen your son William at the head of the school-boys; as it might seem a leader of their noontide games, and Horace among the tribe – both as healthy-looking as the best, and William very much grown – Margaret was in the kitchen preparing to follow her Brothers to school, and I was pleased to see her also looking stout and well, and much grown. Mrs. de Quincey was seated by the fire above stairs with her Baby on her knee – She rose and received me cheerfully, as a person in perfect health, and does indeed seem to have had an extraordinary recovery . . . The Babe looks as if it would thrive and is what we call a nice Child – neither big nor little. –
>
> Mrs. de Quincey seemed on the whole in very good spirits; but, with something of sadness in her manner, she told me you were not likely very soon to be at home. She then said that you had at present some literary employment at Edinburgh; and had, besides, had an offer . . . of a permanent engagement, the nature of which she did not know; but that you hesitated about accepting it, as it might necessitate you to settle in Edinburgh. To this I replied, 'Why not settle there for the time at least that this engagement lasts. Lodgings are cheap at Edinburgh, and provisions and coals not dear. I then added that it was my firm opinion that you could never regularly keep up to your engagements at a distance from the press; and, said I, 'pray tell him so when you write.' She replied, 'Do write yourself.' Now I could not refuse to give her pleasure by so doing . . .
>
> I do not presume to take the liberty of advising the acceptance of this engagement, or of that – only I would venture to request you well to consider the many impediments to literary employments to be regularly carried on in limited time, at a distance from the press, in a small house, and in perfect solitude.[52]

The baby she mentions must be the De Quincey's fifth child, Paul Frederick, who was baptized in April 1827 and named after De Quincey's favourite German author, Jean Paul Friedrich Richter.

The 'permanent engagement' De Quincey had been offered may have been a position on the *Edinburgh Saturday Post*, for which he began to write in the following summer. Or it may refer to the *Argo*, a periodical of modern literature in translation which was being planned by R.P. Gillies, De Quincey's Edinburgh friend, who had fallen on hard times and was hoping that the *Argo* would repair his fortunes. De Quincey must have been considered for an editorial post, for in January 1827 he was writing to a prospective contributor on Gillies's behalf, soliciting reviews or translations.[53] But his connection with the *Argo* ended there – fortunately, perhaps, for when it appeared (under the more sober title of *The Foreign Quarterly Review*) it was as much of a failure as all Gillies's other projects.

De Quincey's work for *Blackwood's*, on the other hand, reached new heights of brilliance. The February number carried 'The Last Days of Immanuel Kant', a poker-faced account of the great philosopher's fussy domestic habits which De Quincey rendered very funny by a careful selection of incongruous detail. And this minor success was eclipsed by 'On Murder Considered as one of the Fine Arts' in the same issue, De Quincey's first and finest essay in black comedy and, after the *Confessions*, the most famous of all his works. It purported to be the text of a lecture read at a meeting of the Society of Connoisseurs in Murder. After sketching the history of murder from Cain's killing of Abel up to the eighteenth century the essay went on to subject a number of recent murders to aesthetic criticism, carrying to an absurd but logical conclusion the notion of the 'sublime' expounded by Burke and his followers, who had argued that works of art could attain power and grandeur by evoking sensations of terror in their audience. Someone (not Wilson, it seems) was nervous about the essay's reception and prefaced it with a note, reassuring the reader that, 'We cannot suppose the lecturer to be in earnest, any more than Erasmus in his Praise of Folly, or Dean Swift in his Proposal for Eating Children.' De Quincey was annoyed, feeling that this apology threatened the carefully judged tone of his paper.[54] But its impact was not destroyed and the paper consolidated De Quincey's reputation for brilliance of a rather peculiar kind, a writer whose successes were quite unlike those of anyone else.

He was back at Rydal for the spring and early summer, and then in

July returned to Edinburgh, where he had been offered work on the *Edinburgh Saturday Post*.[55] The *Post* was an old-fashioned Tory newspaper which, as a radical critic said, 'stickles for church and state, the ascendancy of the aristocracy, and every one of the exploded or faded abuses in politics and political economy'.[56] It was published on Saturday evenings to be read on Sunday mornings, a common way of evading the Sabbatarian prejudice against Sunday newspapers. Precisely what De Quincey's position on the paper was, we do not know, but it must have been important, for he contributed at least one substantial article every week, compiled general news items and helped to determine the paper's political line.[57]

His contributions to the *Post* appeared between 28 July 1827 and 12 July 1828. Most were political essays not much different from the leaders he had written for the *Westmorland Gazette*, but there were also literary pieces, usually detailed criticisms of the latest issue of *Blackwood's* or the *Edinburgh Review*. The political essays were always closely linked to some item of news – the death of Canning, a Commons debate on Slavery, or the resignation of Huskisson from the Duke of Wellington's cabinet – but these transient matters were always related to what De Quincey saw as the fundamental, permanent issues of politics. This approach enabled him to make do with rather little in the way of facts – no more, indeed, than could be gleaned from the reading of any daily newspaper – and to spin most of his contributions out of his own reflections and familiar views. The results are interesting and at times eloquent, but the views have a static and inflexible quality that makes them somewhat unsatisfying. Essentially, De Quincey's politics were a kind of prejudice, based on two fundamental assumptions which rendered inevitable a certain lack of dynamism. The first was that there were two 'great original *principles* in politics', namely 'Jacobin and anti-jacobin; principles as old as the human heart'.[58] Accepting this classification as absolute and timeless, he saw every contemporary development as the interplay of these two changeless opposites. There could thus be nothing really new in politics (though his terminology reveals a view of politics which had crystallized during the Napoleonic wars, the dominant political factor in England during his childhood and adolescence). Parliamentary reformers, Whigs, radical artisans, Irish Catholic leaders, campaigners against slavery or the corn-laws were all lumped together as 'Jacobins' and they and their ideas rejected on principle without much serious consideration.

The second guiding maxim was that, 'The Whig and the Tory . . . are reciprocally necessary, each to the philosophical existence of the other.' [59] De Quincey argued that the constitutional settlement of 1688 had left Britain with a neat two-party equilibrium where a party of change balanced a party of conservation. This system worked almost automatically as a regulator to ensure that government combined necessary change with stable continuity. It was proper for reformers to demand change, and it was equally proper for conservatives to oppose it; only such a tension could ensure that the outcome would be a workable policy. It would be a mistake to dignify this notion with the fashionable word 'dialectical', for really it is no more than the old idea of compromise. As a political theory its peculiar characteristic is that it undermines the validity of any particular commitment. If Whig and Tory are equally necessary, how is one to chose between them? The decision must be as arbitrary as choosing black or white in a chess game. In the event, as De Quincey implies, temperament makes the choice for us. The bias of our natures runs one way or the other. One suspects, therefore, that De Quincey, the Tory commentator of the *Post*, was not always expressing deeply felt commitments. Often he was just taking the side assigned to him in the political shadow-boxing, opposing for the sake of opposing. This led to some strange arguments. For example, he wrote three essays for the *Post* on demands for the abolition of slavery in the West Indies, and chose to see the question almost entirely in terms of property. The slave-owners, he argued, had invested money in their slaves and they possessed working estates which could not economically be farmed without slave labour. To abolish slavery would thus constitute an attack on the property of the West India Proprietors. The sanctity of property was a principle so basic that it could not safely be overridden. Slavery should therefore continue. The happiness and rights of the slaves themselves were hardly mentioned.

The fact is that he was often required to write on subjects of which he knew little, and concocted his arguments as best he could on the basis of the *Post*'s generally conservative line. Perhaps when he was not in the heat of composing belligerent newspaper articles he lapsed into a philosophical detachment where politics were concerned. His articles expounding political economy suggest as much, for he loved Ricardo's economics as a pure, detached science, deduced like geometry from first principles and as little affected by the untidiness of the real world. Other Tory newspapers might refer to 'that most incomprehensible, and preposterous of all things – a Tory political economist',[60] but De Quincey went his own way as if utterly unaware that Ricardo had been a Whig and that in general only Whigs and Radicals accepted his economic theories.

After three months in Edinburgh, De Quincey decided to bring his two eldest children to join him. This may have been meant as a first step towards moving the whole family; or perhaps Margaret had simply become unable to cope, for there were five children now and a sixth was on the way. De Quincey went south to meet William, who was now eleven, and nine-year-old Margaret, at Carlisle on 3 October.[61] They were to live mostly in Edinburgh from now on, Margaret spending most of the first year staying with friends, perhaps the Wilsons, and William living with his father, who was anxious about his education and wanted to teach him himself. William was an intelligent boy, fond of reading and a quick learner, though whether De Quincey's instruction kept pace with his abilities is another question: Jane Carlyle reported that 'a boy of the English Opium Eater told me once he would begin Greek presently; but his father wished him to learn it through the medium of Latin and he was not entered in Latin yet because his father wished to teach him from a grammar of his own which he had not yet begun to write'.[62] But probably this refers to one of the younger boys; William would have learnt his Latin at Grasmere.

Carlyle and De Quincey met for the first time in late November. Since De Quincey's scathing review of *Wilhelm Meister* each had regarded the other with suspicion and although they had several friends in common – including Wilson, who had amused Carlyle with his impersonations of De Quincey – they had never come face to face. At last they met, 'half accidentally', one evening at the house of J.T. Gordon, Wilson's son-in-law. 'He grew pale as ashes at my entrance,' Carlyle told his brother, 'but we soon recovered him again, and kept him in flowing talk to a late hour.' Carlyle invited him to his house at Comley Bank, Edinburgh, and he came with his two children, staying until midnight.

> He is one of the smallest men you ever in your life beheld [wrote Carlyle]; but with a most gentle and sensible face, only that the teeth are destroyed by opium, and the little bit of an underlip projects like a shelf. He speaks with a slow sad and soft voice, in the politest manner I have almost ever witnessed; . . . Poor little fellow! It might soften a very hard heart to see him so courteous, yet so weak and poor; retiring

home with his two children to a miserable lodging-house and writing all day for the King of Donkies, the Proprietor of the Saturday Post. I lent him Jean Paul's *Autobiography* which I got lately from Hamburg, and advised him to translate it for Blackwood, so that he might raise a few pounds and 'fence off' the Genius of Hunger yet a little while.[63]

De Quincey was showing signs of stress from half-a-dozen years of anxiety, hack-writing and opium addiction. At the age of forty-two the former wonder-child was already prematurely aged: still impressive but now quaint, an object of condescension, all the more pitiable because he clung so steadfastly to his dignity and tried to behave as if he had never fallen on hard times. Carlyle soon forgot the hostile reviews of *Meister*: it had not hindered his career and he was now a successful critic and essayist with a secure place in Edinburgh society. De Quincey, sometimes with, sometimes without his children, began to visit the Carlyles regularly. He was with them on 30 December,[64] and then or a little later he fell ill; Mrs Carlyle nursed him with a kindness he never forgot. Like her husband she regarded him with great affection and was similarly amused. 'What would one give,' she once exclaimed, 'to have him in a box, and take him out to talk!'[65]

How much of De Quincey's poor health was attributable simply to opium is difficult to say. On 11 March 1828 Carlyle called on him 'about two o'clock, and found him invisible in bed. His landlady, a dirty very wicked-looking woman, said if he rose at all it was usually about five o'clock!' The next day he found him 'in the *low* stage of opium-regimen, and looking rather care-stricken'. In April Carlyle heard that he had been 'in a manner living upon opium' and was 'very low',[66] and in the autumn Matthew Davenport Hill, on business in Edinburgh, called on him and heard that he had 'for the tenth time renounced opium, which he said he had not tasted for one hundred and eighty days',[67] a story which suggests that De Quincey liked to keep up the pathetic pretence of having cured his addiction when he felt there was a chance he might be believed. A kind of shame made it hard for him to admit that he was still addicted.

He returned to Rydal with William and Margaret for the summer, and when he migrated to Edinburgh again in the autumn he took his wife with him as well as the two oldest children. The younger ones, Francis, Paul Fred, and the baby Florence (born late in 1827) stayed at The Nab with their grandparents. The De Quinceys must have missed their younger children but in general the arrangement probably minimized emotional stress, for according to Dora Wordsworth De

Quincey had been coming back to Rydal 'every month, and then every week' in the early part of 1828,[68] perhaps because without him Margaret became depressed and ill.

Besides regular work for the *Post* De Quincey had been busy trying to develop his connection with *Blackwood's*. He hoped to capitalize on the success of his 'Murder' essay by submitting two sequels,[69] but neither was published, and the rejection must have been a heavy blow, for he never wrote with ease and could not afford to waste his time on unsaleable articles. He had better luck with 'The Toilette of the Hebrew Lady', an essay on the clothing, jewelry and cosmetics of the women of biblical Palestine. Trying, as usual, to claim credit for more scholarship than he had time to exercise, he presented it to the public (and to Blackwood) as a digest of huge tome by a German archaeologist. But really the essay was a translation, slightly abridged, of a single chapter of its original.[70] It appeared in *Blackwood's* in March and was his only contribution that year apart from an essay on 'Rhetoric' in the December number. His last essay for the *Post* appeared in July, and if he found any other work, no traces of it have survived. Money must have been in very short supply during the winter of 1828–9.

December brought a kind letter from the Carlyles, now living at Craigenputtock in Dumfriesshire:

> a few lines . . . to signify that two well-wishers of yours are still alive in these remote moors, and often thinking of you with the old friendly feelings . . . Come, therefore, come and see us; for we often long after you: nay I can promise too that we are almost a unique sight in the British Empire; such a quantity of German Periodicals, and mystic speculation, embosomed in plain Scottish *Peat-moor*, being nowhere else that I know of to be met with.[71]

Carlyle even suggested that they start a 'Bog School' of writers amid the 'grim hills . . . tarns and brooks' of the district, to compete with the 'Lake School'! By this time, however, De Quincey had no leisure for visiting, having involved himself in a complex scheme which promised to make him, after a fashion, a landowner at Rydal.

10
Sanctuary

For several years financial trouble had been brewing at The Nab. Until 1825 the small farm had been owned by Margaret's grandfather, William Park. Park was a stubborn, independent character who refused to truckle to the large landowners of the district, but part of the land he farmed was not his own, and for the last fourteen years of his life he had failed to pay his rent to the Rydal manor. For most of this time the steward of the estate had let him go his own way, perhaps as a calculated policy to let him fall far into arrears so that he might ultimately be evicted and his land absorbed into the Rydal estate. One of the more irritating features of Park's position was that he did not own the timber rights even to the land which was in other respects his own. This meant that he was not entitled to fell timber at his own pleasure, and towards the end of his life he was not only being pressed for arrears of rent but was sued for unauthorized tree-felling. He clung to his position tenaciously and refused to admit defeat but the law was clearly against him. Shortly before his death in 1825 he was forced to pay his arrears, which he did at the cost of mortgaging The Nab, and at his death Margaret's father inherited not only the mortgaged farm but a lawsuit which was moving inexorably towards defeat. When the case ended in victory for the Rydal Manor in 1827 the Simpsons had to face legal costs and fines.[1] In this crisis they appealed to De Quincey for help, for the farm had been in the hands of Margaret's family for generations and represented not only a valuable property but a geographical focus and symbol of 'home' for Margaret and her brothers and sisters. If it were sold the whole family would become rootless. Perhaps not grasping the fact that their son-in-law was himself living in poverty, the Simpsons hoped that De Quincey might save The Nab. And, almost incredibly, he tried to do so.

It is hard to understand how anyone could have placed the slightest confidence in the plan he worked out. One can only assume that desire to save the farm blinded all concerned to the realities of the situation, except for those outside the family, who knew too little to realize what was going on. The basic problem was that Simpson needed some £900 to pay off various debts, including the mortgage. De Quincey offered to raise another mortgage on the property, which Simpson valued at £3,000, and to buy The Nab from him. The mortgage would raise £1,400, of which Simpson was to receive the £900 he urgently needed, whilst De Quincey would take £500. Each would be responsible for the interest on his portion. De Quincey would ultimately pay off the £1,400 principal of the mortgage, and in addition, when Margaret's parents died, he would pay John Simpson's heirs £1,100. In effect, this meant that he would be buying The Nab for £2,500. Simpson wanted to leave £500 to his favourite grandchild, William De Quincey, and so De Quincey undertook also to give William, at Simpson's death, the sum of £500. In total, therefore, De Quincey would over the years pay out £3,000, the estimated value of The Nab, and become the owner. For the immediate future, however, he was committed only to pay the interest on £500, and to give Simpson 3½ per cent interest on the £1,100 he would ultimately pay Simpson's heirs. In the meantime, he would have £500 in his pocket.[2] If one could accept that in a few years' time, De Quincey would be in a position to pay out thousands of pounds as they were needed, this complicated scheme made a sort of sense. If, on the other hand, one had a realistic idea of his earning power, the whole plan was lunacy.

Surprisingly enough, someone (a Mr Pendlebury) was found willing to advance money on The Nab, and the mortgage was raised. There was controversy over the valuation, as the Rydal steward, perhaps hoping to speed the departure of the troublesome Simpsons, wrote to the valuers disparaging the estate. But eventually De Quincey had everything sorted out, and came down from Edinburgh to Rydal to take possession of 'his' estate on 1 May 1829. The De Quinceys were soon installed at The Nab, where by July there were no less than sixteen people: John Simpson, his wife and his wife's half-witted brother, William Park; De Quincey and his wife, probably some of her sisters, the six De Quincey children (ranging in age from thirteen years to nineteen months) and several servants.[3]

At the cost of storing up serious trouble for the future, De Quincey had won himself and his parents-in-law a brief respite from worry, and looked forward to enjoying several months of tranquil Lakeland life in the old house at the edge of Rydal Water. The landscape was as fine as ever, and the Simpsons in their innocence no doubt regarded him with admiration and gratitude for his financial manoeuvring. Horace attended the village school whilst De Quincey tutored William and Margaret at home,[4] and Mrs Quincey's allowance, together with the produce of the small farm, was enough to keep hunger at bay. There were, of course, the usual health problems. As soon as he reached The Nab De Quincey went down with a fever, and on 19 July wrote to apologize for failing to receive Wordsworth and his son, John, when they had called a few weeks before. He had been ill, he said,

> the last eighteen days of June, and during all that time I was able to take only a little lemonade or ginger beer. Hence, or from the malady itself, I was left so weak as to be scarcely able for a fortnight to crawl from room to room; and have not yet felt myself strong enough, though otherwise perfectly well and in good spirits, to go more than a few yards into the field behind the house.[5]

The Wordsworths still took an interest in his doings, and William at least read his magazine articles with approval: in January he had written to Crabb Robinson of the essay on 'Rhetoric', commenting, 'Whatever [De Quincey] writes is worth reading – there are in it some things from my Conversation – which the writer does not seem aware of.' [6] He seemed mildly flattered by this idea, which may be correct, as De Quincey later attributed some of his own critical theories to Wordsworth.[7] Whether he succeeded in visiting De Quincey at The Nab is not known. Certainly other friends were welcome there. On 23 July De Quincey wrote exuberantly to Charles Knight, urging him to bring his family to enjoy this earthly paradise, this 'rich farm-house, flowing with milk and honey', which 'by good management and better luck' he had been purchasing. Like many people who are used to being permanently in debt, De Quincey regarded himself as something of a financial wizard, and he saw the current escapade as rather a brilliant *coup*. He wrote to Knight, ' "Purchasing," you say, "what the devil?" Don't swear, my dear friend; you know there is such a thing as buying a thing and yet not paying for it, or, at least, paying only the annual interest. Well, that is what *I* do, can do and will do.' He was not bothering to consider how the mortgage could be repaid. In return for the hospitality he had received in London he offered Knight

> a glorious El Dorado of milk and butter and cream cheeses . . . mountain lamb equal to Welsh; char famous to the antipodes; trout and pike from the very lake within twenty-five feet of our door; bread, such as you have never presumed to dream of, made of our own wheat . . . new potatoes of celestial earthiness and raciness, which with us

last to October; and finally, milk, milk, milk – cream, cream, cream (hear it, thou benighted Londoner!), in which you must and shall bathe.[8]

Knight never accepted this tempting invitation but another London friend, Hill, went to The Nab with his family in October.[9] Unfortunately he left no record of his visit.

Life at The Nab was, of course, far from conducive to literary work. De Quincey enjoyed himself but the house was noisy and crowded and family cares kept him busy, for in November, soon after Hill's departure, Margaret gave birth to another son, Julius, who was baptized at Rydal on 14 November.[10] De Quincey's only publications during 1829 were pieces he had written before leaving Edinburgh: a political article for the March *Blackwood's* and a three-part 'Sketch of Professor Wilson' for the *Edinburgh Literary Gazette*. Wilson, never subject to excessive modesty, was flattered but not altogether satisfied by the first instalment. He wrote to De Quincey with suggestions for the subsequent parts. 'Base brutes', he complained, 'have libelled my personal character.' Could De Quincey set matters straight by a few words on the morality of his private life? And if there were any flashes of 'the sublime' in his poem 'The City of the Plague', could De Quincey mention them? Also, 'I wish you would praise me as a lecturer on Moral Philsophy. That would do me good; and say that I am thoroughly logical and argumentative – for it is true; not a rhetorician, as fools aver.' [11] But De Quincey neglected these helpful hints and Wilson had to be content with lavish praise of his adventurous temperament and sporting prowess. A promised sequel on his literary accomplishments never appeared, which may have been fortunate. De Quincey had attended lectures by Wilson and well knew their shortcomings: not merely the sheer ignorance which had led him often to beg De Quincey's aid, but the mannerisms which amused the students and made Wilson a wonderful subject for caricature – his way of running a finger down the side of his nose at the end of every paragraph, for example, and his habit of keeping his dogs under the lectern, absentmindedly treading on them as he talked and eliciting yelps of pain.

It is possible, however, that De Quincey was working on another project, for on 14 January 1830, he wrote to Wilson:

293

You remember our innumerable contracts about the novel. At length I am nearly in a condition to claim it, – that is, if you still think yourself bound by our old treaties. And the object of my present letter is to ascertain *that*. My MS. will be finished in less than a month at furthest, and it will bear the following title: 'New Canterbury Tales' . . . 'by the author of the Confessions of an Eng. Op. Eater'. It is so prepared as to make a volume of 400 pages . . . Now for this can you give me 100 guineas? and in some shape immediately negociable? Formerly you used to say that – on the same day on which I delivered the MS. – you would lay down the blunt. But say how far this holds in the present year 1830.[12]

The 'innumerable contracts about the novel' must go back to 1825, when *Noctes Ambrosianae* mentioned 'his promised "Romance"', but this is the first indication we have of the form the Romance was to take. However, no novel of this or any similar title was published by Blackwood or anyone else. If the novel ever existed, it has disappeared. It is mentioned in detailed, businesslike terms in letters by De Quincey, Wilson and Blackwood, and then suddenly nothing more is heard of it. It is possible, of course, that it was never written. The man who could instruct Taylor and Hessey to advertise two books before he had started one was quite capable of promising four hundred pages in a month without having written a word. He once told Taylor and Hessey, 'I am often obliged to compose the whole almost in my mind before I can write a line',[13] so perhaps he deduced from this the corollary that a book thoroughly composed in the mind was as good as a book on paper. Still, the negotiations seem remarkably specific. Having offered four hundred pages for a hundred guineas, he wrote again on 3 March promising to send the manuscript shortly and asking if Blackwood might consider raising his payment should the book run to more than one volume. He also asked that the book should appear anonymously. This, he explained, was not because the work was of poor quality but because he felt it prudent 'in a first attempt – first I mean in this department of literature – to provide the means of retreat by coming forward in a masque'.[14] (If indeed *The Stranger's Grave* is De Quincey's work, then the *Tales* would obviously not be a 'first attempt'; but the very fact that Blackwood knew nothing of the earlier novel perhaps proved the value of anonymity.) Blackwood agreed to pay two hundred guineas for the copyright of the book 'should it extend to two volumes of 400 pages', and added, with obvious reluctance, 'I do not insist upon your *nom de guerre* being put up[on] the title page merely trusting to the authorship becoming known in the way you mention, and that you do not disavow it.' He hoped, he said, that De Quincey would write again for the Magazine 'as soon as you have the Tales off your hands'.[15]

In April the novel was still expected and Wilson went near to betraying De Quincey's secret in that month's *Noctes*, in which the 'Opium-Eater' informs the 'Ettrick Shepherd', 'I am at present, my dear friend, . . . in treaty with Mr. Blackwood for a novel –' at which the 'Shepherd' expresses the hope that the fiction will be in 'ae volume' to prevent longwindedness. But there the matter rested and no more was heard of it – unless De Quincey's novel *Klosterheim*, which appeared in 1832, was built up from one of the proposed 'Tales'. In this connection it is odd that De Quincey speaks of anonymity as 'coming forward in a masque', for the full title of his next novel was to be *Klosterheim, or, The Masque*. Is this coincidence, or was a plot involving a 'masque' already in his mind?

The early part of 1830 was spent in a flurry of different projects. Not only were the *Tales* being planned, but on 31 January De Quincey wrote to Hill to ask, 'Is the chair of Moral Philosophy still open at the London University? And if so, by what avenues to be approached?'[16] It must have occurred to him that if Wilson could occupy a Chair in Philosophy, there was no reason why he himself should not do so. But he never applied for it. In March, as well as negotiating with Blackwood over the novel, he was announcing 'several papers in a state of forwardness for "Maga", which I am inclined to think will suit you'. ('Maga' was the *Magazine* which the contributors had nicknamed from Blackwood's way of talking proudly in his broad Scots of 'my *Mah*gazine'.) Subjects he had in mind included 'the Flight of the Kalmuck Tartars from Russia to the frontier of China', Giordano Bruno, Orators, the History of Logic, and the usual miscellanies or 'Ana'. 'On the whole,' he promised, 'you may rely upon me during the next summer as a really active contributor.'[17] He was also in touch with Lockhart, who offered a commission to write a book on the Lakes, which De Quincey declined, reluctantly, on the grounds that, 'I am ashamed to say that I want much of the commonest knowledge called for in so miscellaneous a subject. I am not an Ornithologist, nor an Ichthyologist (unless a dissertation on *Potted Char* would avail me, for *that* I could obtain).'[18] The landscape, he said, had been well treated by Wordsworth, whose *Guide* was still in print, and other aspects would be dealt with by Wilson, who was said to be writing a book on the Lakes. Wilson never produced his book, but there may not be much cause for regret in his rejection of the plan. His real strength lay in his depiction of the human landscape, and the guidebook format would probably have inhibited his use of his great store of anecdote and observation on Lakeland life. (Such material was later used in the essays which have been collected as *Recollections of the Lakes and the Lake Poets* to form one of the most entertaining of Lakeland books.) He also rejected Lockhart's proposal of a book on Oxford because he thought it would be impossible to write it without access to a large library. Instead, he suggested that the 'Family Library', of which Lockhart was an editor, might be interested in an abridged version of the Byzantine historians, as a companion to the abridged Gibbon they already published. 'Another plan of mine', he added, 'is – A *History of the Crusades*. I conceive that we have no decent one.' He did not explain how these projects were to be done without the library so essential to a work on Oxford.

But he had other, more realistic ideas in mind, and in June migrated again to Edinburgh where he stayed with Wilson and wrote busily. The move must have been prompted by poverty: no doubt there was already difficulty in paying interest on the debts he had contracted to take over The Nab. He worked hard, and Wilson gave him the right domestic conditions for high productivity, although the long-suffering cook did slip up once and, De Quincey complained, by 'an accidental blunder . . . inflicted upon me a colic which lasted the whole of [one] night', thereby delaying an article for Blackwood.[19] In the course of June he finished a paper on 'Kant in His Miscellaneous Essays', started several articles which were never finished and began a biographical paper about Bentley, the belligerent eighteenth-century classical scholar. As usual he sent in his copy piecemeal, asking for payment in dribs and drabs,[20] but Blackwood tolerated the inconvenience and De Quincey met his deadlines. The 'Kant' essay appeared in August and 'Bentley' in September and October. So reliable did De Quincey now seem that Blackwood allowed him to undertake a series of regular political essays, Tory commentaries on the month's events, which appeared in September, October, November, December and February.

As always, of course, he had to make the best of thin material. The articles on Bentley show one of the solutions he adopted. They professed to be a review of a biography of Bentley by one J.H. Monk. Reviewers in those days were not expected to stay close to the books they criticized and the articles seemed to be a short life of Bentley compiled from various sources by De Quincey himself. Bentley was a fine subject: a brilliant but hot-tempered and sometimes highly eccentric scholar, whose career was full of entertaining incidents. De Quincey told his story in a lively manner, packing in plenty of information amongst the anecdotes but repeatedly disparaging Monk, whose book he seemingly set to rights on all kinds of points. Yet recent scholarship has shown that De Quincey's account is altogether dependent on Monk's, apart from a section which is a précis of a single book by Bentley – no doubt the only one De Quincey could get hold of in time. The material for the essays had been stolen by handfuls from the book under review, whilst De Quincey tried to conceal the theft by disparaging his source.[21]

Mitigating circumstances, of course, are not hard to find. With De Quincey's medical and financial problems it is a continual wonder that he was able to write anything of value, let alone attain the note of leisurely good-humour and easy mastery of his material that characterizes most of his literary journalism. The real attraction of an essay by De Quincey lay in its style, and the style was an intensely personal one which could not comfortably be used for the straightforward summarizing of other people's work. The material had always to seem as if De Quincey had made it thoroughly his own. When he was unable to do so, he could produce his characteristic work only by putting forward someone else's material as if it were his. We should not underestimate the pressure on De Quincey to produce high-quality work in his own distinctive style. It was the only saleable skill he possessed, and he and his family lived so close to actual destitution that the rejection of an article could precipitate disaster.

Even in the latter part of 1830, with De Quincey installed at Wilson's house and doing regular work for Blackwood, there was no respite from worry. For some reason Margaret had had to leave The Nab with the children and was staying in lodgings near Penrith. Tired and lonely, she became depressed, as she often did when De Quincey stayed away for too long. The frictions incident to a life in lodgings added to her unhappiness until she felt she could stand no more. The result was announced by De Quincey in a letter to Blackwood written at five o'clock in the morning on 20 November.

> My dear Sir,
>   I am conscious that I do not stand in a very favourable position for any request of any kind – as the writer of an article still unfinished

... But ... I shall explain my situation briefly before I go for a few hours to bed. – Some days ago ... I received a letter from my wife threatening suicide in the case of my not being able speedily to release her from her present situation. It is shocking to mention such a thing, but almost necessary in my circumstances; and of course I do it in confidence. –Now, if you inquire what is distressing in her situation, I answer not much beyond what is purely imaginary. The main grievance I suppose to be this: the person, at whose house she and her children have lodgings, – a woman, and apparently coarse-minded and vulgar, has children of her own. Disputes, such as naturally arise between children, have occasionally, I suppose, arisen ... and the woman, having no other means of expressing her spite, and no doubt suspecting that her arrear cannot be paid on demand (though in fact not much is due to her), has grown insolent ... unfortunately there happens to be no other house in that neighbourhood where lodgings can be obtained; yet the neighbourhood cannot be left until *all* bills are paid.[22]

As a result, he explained, he had had to write Margaret every day for the past three days 'long and elaborate letters – arguing (or suggesting remedies upon) each particular grievance which she stated, and endeavouring to tranquillize her mind'. The previous evening he had received an ultimatum: 'she assures me peremptorily that, if I do not hold out some immediate prospect of relief in my promised letter of tomorrow night, her present application shall be the last letter she'll ever write'. There was good reason to take this threat seriously, because 'in something of the same condition of spirits at a very early period of her life she really did make an attempt of the kind she now threatens'.

Blackwood came to the rescue with money, and the crisis passed. But Margaret's desperate threats had one result which may have been in her mind all along, for they put an end to De Quincey's practice of leaving his family on some precarious perch in the Lake District while he disappeared for months at a time to work in the city. On 4 December he wrote to Blackwood thanking him for the 'very liberal' payment he had made on the rather substandard copy sent with his last anxious letter, promising never again to be late with an article (!) and announcing that Margaret and the children would be 'on the road to Edinburgh' by 19 or 20 December.[23] He had finally learned that neither he nor his wife could survive emotionally without the support of the other. From now on they never again lived apart.

The city which now became the De Quinceys' home was a remarkable place both socially and architecturally. It housed a brilliant library, educational and juridical élite as well as an extensive criminal under-world and a notable collection of eccentrics: three groups which were not altogether distinct. The city landscape is vividly described in a letter written by Coleridge to Southey in 1803:

> What a wonderful city Edinburgh is! – What alteration of Height & Depth! – a city looked at in the polish'd back of a Brobdignag Spoon, held lengthways – so enormously *stretched-up* are the Houses! . . . I climbed last night to the Crags just below Arthur's Seat, itself a rude triangle-shaped bare Cliff, & looked down on the whole City & Firth, the Sun then setting behind the magnificent rock, crested by the Castle – the Firth was full of Ships, & I counted 54 heads of mountains, of which at last [sic] 44 were cones or pyramids – the smokes rising up from ten thousand houses, each smoke from some one family.[24]

The Old Town, a maze of steep, winding streets clustered around the Castle on its jutting outcrop of volcanic rock, had been supplemented since the mid-eighteenth century by the elegant New Town, whose ordered streets and crescents covered the less precipitous land to the north. De Quincey and his family moved many times through houses, lodgings and hiding-places in both the Old and New Towns and full details of their movements cannot be recovered. Characteristically, De Quincey himself was sometimes the honoured guest of the leading citizens, sometimes a fugitive in the most squalid corners.

As soon as Margaret and the children arrived in December 1830, he took a house at 7 Great King Street, one of the elegant, recently built streets of the New Town. Writing to Lockhart in the summer he showed some embarrassment. 'You will observe', he wrote, 'that I date from a house of that class which implies a state of expenditure somewhat above the necessities of a needy man of letters', and he admitted that he was finding the rent too high.[25] The reason for choosing the house was supposedly that he had decided to take lodgers and needed a large house. So, at least, De Quincey later said; but no lodgers came and it is hard to imagine that De Quincey tried very hard to get them.[26] Apart from anything else, Margaret's poor health would have been a deterrent. Besides recurrent depressions she had suffered from several fairly serious illnesses over the past few years, including a bad attack of jaundice in March 1830, and after her arrival in Edinburgh she was often unwell. At such times the care of the children became De Quincey's responsibility, and a taxing one, even with the help of a servant, for he had to work on his magazine contributions as well as looking after Margaret and running the household. When things became difficult, his eldest daughter often went to stay at the house of Captain Thomas Hamilton, brother of Sir William the philosopher. De Quincey himself was often asked to dine with the Hamiltons when he came to fetch her. 'Your daughter's being here will be an inducement to you to offer us a dinner visit whenever you are so inclined,' writes Hamilton on one occasion, and on another he urges, 'Never mind her dress. Annette will supply her with anything she wants',[27] which implies that the De Quinceys' poverty often left Margaret without a dress fit to wear for visiting.

For the younger children the move to Edinburgh brought much happiness, for they loved their father and found his company a great comfort. Florence was later able to recall with some clarity how she saw him about this time.

> My own first awakening to the fact that I had a father grew out of the restless nights of a delicate childhood, when my small ill-regulated uproar was sure to bring the kind, careful arms which rescued the urchin from a weariful bed and the wisdom of nursery-discipline, and brought it to the bright warm room, and the dignity and delight of 'sitting up with papa'.[28]

De Quincey would let her drink coffee with plenty of sugar, show her pictures in books and tell her stories. She would resolve to 'stay up *all night* with papa' – but would soon fall asleep as he worked on at his desk.

Now and for several years to come Blackwood was De Quincey's only regular source of earned income. This meant that the publisher had to endure numerous small wrangles with De Quincey, who almost never sent a complete article at one time and was continually asking for small sums of money in exchange for work incomplete or only promised. There was plenty of work available but this did not prevent continual slight friction between author and publisher. At the end of 1830 De Quincey was hard at work on the first of four papers on the late Dr Samuel Parr, a clergyman well known for his Whig pamphlets, elegant Latin verses, and inflated estimate of his own conversational gifts, which had led him to pose as a second Dr Johnson.

De Quincey had once met Parr and taken a hearty dislike to him, so the subject was well suited for one of his opinionated anecdotal character sketches. On 16 December he promised to 'paper Dr. Parr' shortly in an article which, he said, would be 'burnished with unusual care'.[29] The first part was ready for the January number and subsequent parts appeared in February, May and June 1831. But two other articles submitted in January were rejected and when Blackwood accepted a third he promised De Quincey that although his rate of payment was ten guineas a sheet (sixteen printed pages), if a manuscript arrived early, then 'with excellent articles as yours always are' he would pay extra. If this was a ploy to encourage De Quincey to meet his deadlines in future it failed, for soon he was writing to apologize for the lateness of the new instalment of 'Parr' which, he said, he had not been able to finish, 'so continued were my suffering[s] from diarrhoea – arising out of too large a use of opium for the last 5 weeks'. He promised that it would not happen again because 'I have recovered my old system of opium &c., my old health since Saturday; and I am going to do this:- for the next 9 or 10 weeks I am going to write articles without stopping'.[30] The product of this worthy resolution was, besides the conclusion to the 'Parr' essay, a political piece for the August number 'On the Approaching Revolution in Great Britain' and a sequel, 'Reform as Affecting the Habits of Private Life'. The 'Revolution' of the first title was the proposed reform of Parliament, which would end the control of Parliamentary representation by the rural landowning class, and in the second essay De Quincey indulged in gloomy predictions of its consequences. Social life, he warned, would become 'plebeian' in tone; education would be debased; poetry and philosophy would be allowed to die as traditional values were discarded; morality would collapse and a general indulgence of 'licentious thoughts and practices' become the rule; the colonies would be lost through the incompetence of a 'mob Parliament'. The apocalyptic tone of all this apparently did not commend the essay to Blackwood, and these interesting predictions remained unpublished.[31]

On 11 May 1831 De Quincey's financial problems entered a new phase when, for the first time, legal action was taken against him by an Edinburgh creditor. A bookseller named John Carfrae entered a 'Protest' against him (the first step in the Scottish legal process for the recovery of debt) for £37. 16s. 6d.[32] Somehow Carfrae was paid or pacified, but by August De Quincey was in serious financial trouble. As usual he was living mainly on credit. His only steady income was fifty pounds a quarter sent jointly by his mother and his uncle, and less than twenty pounds a year from the family property in Manchester. His earnings fluctuated, but between 15 May and 18 October 1832 he made about fifty-five pounds by writing for Blackwood.[33] On this income a household of up to twelve had to be supported, including seven children. And there was really no way to improve the position. To live comfortably and clear his debts, he estimated that he would need to write eighty pages of Blackwood's each month, which would mean that over half of the magazine would be devoted to his work — clearly an impossible notion.[34] Creditors were continually on the attack: on 1 February he had had to ask John Wilson's brother, who was a banker, for a thirty pound loan; in July the water company was threatening to cut off the supply to his house unless he paid their bill. He had been forced to give up the house in Great King Street and move to a smaller one, 1 Forres Street, in May. The move may have had as much to do with evading creditors as with reducing expense, for on 23 July he sent some copy to Blackwood explaining that it had been delayed by creditors and family illness, and begging Blackwood earnestly to keep his address absolutely secret. His anxiety was justified, for on 14 August he had to leave home at five o'clock in the morning to escape arrest. Someone had discovered his hiding-place, and he was afraid that Blackwood had somehow let the information slip.[35]

Things grew steadily worse. On 20 September a creditor's suit reached its conclusion and De Quincey underwent a humiliation peculiar to Scottish law and was 'put to the horn'.[36] This curious ritual arose from the fact that imprisonment for debt was technically not sanctioned by Scottish law. Attitudes to debtors being no more friendly in Scotland than elsewhere, a procedure had evolved whereby a debtor could be imprisoned under the legal fiction that he was guilty of a different offence. The creditor would apply to a court which had power to issue a letter commanding the debtor in the name of the monarch to pay his debt. If he still 'refused' to pay he was held to be disobeying a royal command, and an officer of the court would go to the market-place at Edinburgh and, with three blasts of a horn, publicly proclaim him a rebel. He could then be imprisoned. De Quincey, having been 'put to the horn' on 20 September for a debt of ten pounds, managed to pay five, but he still failed to satisfy his creditor and on 2 October he was arrested and imprisoned in the Canongate Tolbooth, Edinburgh's grim, turretted, sixteenth-century gaolhouse.[37] He left no record of his feelings, but his misery must have been intense. There was, however, a way out, and De Quincey, with his usual wiliness, managed to take it. A prisoner who had been 'horned' for debt could be released if medical examination showed that he was ill and that his life would be endangered by continued captivity. In such a case a 'sick bill' was issued allowing him to leave the prison, although he must stay within the city and return when his health improved. De Quincey, who was an expert on the oddities of his own constitution and had not enjoyed normal health for years, soon convinced a physician that he was ill enough to be set free, and left the Tolbooth on the same day. He returned on 14 October but was discharged at once either because the debt had been paid or because the creditor had ceased to press for his imprisonment.[38] Another creditor had him arrested in late October,[39] but some arrangement was reached and De Quincey did not see the inside of a prison again. Nonetheless, disasters of this kind soon became a regular thing and between 1832 and 1840 he was put to the horn no less than nine times.[40]

In the midst of these troubles he somehow kept on writing and in March 1832 presented Blackwood with a novel: *Klosterheim: or, The Masque*. De Quincey's attitude to *Klosterheim* seems to have thoroughly business-like and unsentimental. An undated letter to Blackwood promising the manuscript assures him that despite delays due to illness, 'My anxiety to complete the Novel (as a pecuniary speculation), you may rely on it, is far greater than yours – because if it were to succeed it will deliver me from an abyss of evil into which few have ever descended. The moment I have any ease you may therefore be assured that I will lose no time.'[41] Subsequently, in more vigorous mood, he writes, 'I wish to know whether you would wish to have Klosterheim lengthened. To my great surprise, it makes only 299pp. But, if you wish it, I can throw in a chapter of 8-10 or 12 pp., which would carry it so far beyond 300pp. if you think that of importance.'[42] This workmanlike mood persisted – fortunately, for when the manuscript reached Blackwood a chapter was missing. De Quincey had somehow lost it in the process of revision. The missing chapter never turned up but without complaint he sat down and wrote it again.[43] The novel appeared in May, in one volume duodecimo, and the title-page identified it as by 'The English Opium-Eater'.

The story, which is set in seventeenth-century Germany, is a more effective treatment of the theme of the secret avenger which De Quincey had first used in 'The Peasant of Portugal'. A Gothic fantasy in the style of Mrs Radcliffe, whose novels he had so much enjoyed in his youth, *Klosterheim* is nonetheless distinguished by the power of its descriptive passages, several of which have a quality of distorted intensity reminiscent of certain stories by Poe. Its descriptions of dreams and torchlight processions of strangely clad figures, evidently inspired by De Quincey's own nightmares and hypnagogic visions, are highly effective. As narrative, on the other hand, it is less successful. Lacking the fictional imagination, De Quincey tended, when he wrote a story, to flesh out some basically simple plot with detail borrowed from his own past. In *Klosterheim* these borrowings are almost absurdly specific. The wicked Landgrave, for example, imposes on the students of Klosterheim, whose loyalty he doubts, a series of 'tyrannical regulations' which give 'the more offence that they seemed wholly capricious and insulting'. Chief among these are that 'students were confined to their college bounds, excepted at stated intervals; and were subject to a military muster, or calling over of names, every evening'[44] – just the features which had so disgusted De Quincey with Manchester Grammar School! Even in his most fantastic tales he could not really free himself from the autobiographical compulsion. A copy of the novel went to Coleridge, who on 26 May returned thanks for 'my old friend De Quincey's "Klosterheim" . . . I have read nothing since the "Quentin Durward" which would compare in interest with "Klosterheim": in purity of style . . . it reaches an excellence to which Sir W. Scott . . . appears never to have aspired'.[45]

As well as the novel there were the usual articles for *Blackwood's*: book reviews, an essay on Charlemagne and the first two instalments of a series on 'The Caesars', stylish and imaginative essays on the more lurid phases of Roman history, whose wit and urbanity is astonishing when one realizes that they were written in the midst of De Quincey's worst financial and legal difficulties. Appearing in October and November, they may well have been produced when lawsuits were in progress or when he was out of prison on his 'sick bill', and a covering note sent with part of the manuscript complains of harassment by creditors.[46] In the hope of finding additional work, De Quincey decided to approach other Edinburgh publications. He wrote to James Fraser of *Fraser's Magazine*[47] and to William Tait, editor of *Tait's Magazine*. He explained to Tait that 'writing for the purpose of clearing off a specific debt, I am under the necessity of asking for money as soon as the MS of each separate sheet is delivered in a state perfectly fit for the press'.[48] Perhaps Blackwood was becoming reluctant to pay for bits of copy as they arrived. But the risk of approaching

Tait was that it might damage his position with Blackwood. *Tait's* was a cheap magazine and an organ of Radicalism: Cobden, Bright and John Stuart Mill all contributed. There was an obvious danger that William Blackwood would take offence if his troublesome contributor began writing for a Radical competitor. But somehow De Quincey managed this delicate affair and an essay on Kant appeared in *Tait's* in November 1833, whilst 'The Caesars' continued to run in *Blackwood's*.

All the same, tension did start to build up. William Blackwood was now seriously ill and his sons Robert and John were taking on much of the routine work. They had less regard for De Quincey and no patience with his quirks. They laid down a 'strict rule' that no work should be paid for in advance, and treated him at times with surprising carelessness. In February 1833, for example, we find Robert Blackwood explaining that, 'Most unfortunately one of my children has I fear destroyed by mistake pages 12, 13, 14 & 15 and injured page 18 [of a manuscript], but I hope that this will not cause you much inconvenience'[49] – which shows how little he knew De Quincey. The reply was more or less what we should expect. Admitting that he was accustomed to calamity, De Quincey nonetheless wished Blackwood to understand that the accident *was* a calamity. 'Nobody, I am sure, was intentionally to blame: but the fact is not the less – that in my languishing condition from a low fever of 23 days' standing, it has cost me 1½ day[s] to repair the loss.' He tried to make Blackwood see the seriousness of his position: 'For the last 15 or 16 days, having a family of 12 persons absolutely dependent upon me, I have kept up with the demands upon me for mere daily necessities of warmth – light – food &c. by daily sales of books at the rate of about 30x. for 1s. – In that proportion have been my sacrifices; and I have now literally no more to sacrifice that could be saleable.'[50] Having sold his books, he had to borrow, and in the course of work on his 'Caesars' series described himself as 'writing like a fiend to secure the *élite* of the notes in the Augustan Hist[ory] – which book I have twice been obliged to return to the adv[ocates'] lib[rary] with slight hope of getting it again'.[51]

Apart from three instalments of 'The Caesars', the spring of 1833 produced only a single book review. Not much of De Quincey's time or attention can have been available for writing, for his financial troubles were reaching a crescendo. It is easy to forget, as perhaps De

Quincey himself forgot, that during the whole period at Fox Ghyll, The Nab and Edinburgh he had remained the tenant of the cottage at Town End, Grasmere. For ten years the house had been merely a storage-place for books and lumber but still De Quincey had been paying (or, more recently, owing) rent to the landlord, Thomas Benson. In the spring of 1833, with payments in arrears by two full years, Benson wrote to demand that De Quincey vacate the cottage by 12 April. De Quincey replied that a combination of ague, erysipelas and 'nervous illness' had prevented his attending to business over the winter, and, with his usual fantastic optimism, offered either to clear his debt by paying double rent for the next two years or to buy the cottage outright for £130.[52] Why he was so keen to hold on to the house he does not explain. Was it emotional attachment, or merely a dread of the labour involved in moving the mountains of books and papers with which it was stuffed? In any case Benson was not to be appeased, and had a notice to quit served on De Quincey, who, thoroughly provoked, dug his heels in and consulted two lawyers before sending, on 10 May, a long letter arguing that he could not legally be forced to quit the cottage before Candlemas 1834. He warned Benson that he would fight eviction every step of the way, and Benson must have been suitably intimidated, for De Quincey kept the cottage until 1835.

But the situation in Edinburgh grew worse and worse. On 10 February Carlyle told his brother, 'De Quincey is . . . said to be in jail; at all events, invisible.'[53] More accurately, in March, he told James Fraser, 'he is here in Edinr; but none of his Friends can see him by calling, he has hardly shewn face for the last two years; and is at present wholly occupied getting out what we in Scotland call a *Cessio Bonorum*; that is to say, a surrendering of all earthly property *to avoid going to Jail!*'[54] De Quincey applied for his *Cessio Bonorum* on 25 February. This process, literally a 'yielding-up of goods', was available in Scotland to a debtor who had served one month in prison (in De Quincey's case his period of release on a 'sick bill' technically fulfilled that condition) and it guaranteed immunity from imprisonment for debts previously contracted on condition that the debtor gave all his assets to his creditors. A bill had to be prepared listing everyone to whom he owed money (if the list were incomplete the *Cessio* would not be valid) and all his assets, which were made over to the creditors, with the exception of whatever the debtor could show to be necessary for his mere survival and that of his dependants. De Quincey's *Cessio* listed his assets as amounting to £762. 9s. 0d. and his debts as £617. 16s. 0d. The 'assets', however, mostly consisted of irrecoverable debts, headed by £315 owed by 'Samuel Taylor Coleridge, Poet, Hampstead, being cash lent in November 1807' – an item which cannot have comforted the creditors very much. The list of creditors, on the other hand, was imposing. There were fifty-one names in all, in London, Lancashire, Cumberland, Westmorland and Edinburgh, of occupations various enough to equip a respectable village: lodging keepers and booksellers in plenty, together with coalman, druggist, shoemaker, grocer, dancing-master, dressmaker, writing master, poulterer, confectioner, butcher, carpenter, wine merchant, glazier and stationer.[55]

Inevitably, new debts were contracted. In May he and Margaret were 'put to the horn' by their former landlady for the unpaid rent of 1 Forres Street: they had taken it for eighty pounds a year and lived there for fifteen months, paying only fifteen pounds![56] They avoided arrest and, miraculously, found another house immediately, so that on 25 May, two days after the 'horning', they were able to move. During the summer and autumn there were more narrow escapes from arrest and Carlyle heard from a friend that De Quincey was 'living on game which has spoiled on the poulterer's hand'; having made a bargain to that effect with him, and even run up a score of £15!'[57]

The new house was Caroline Cottage at Duddingston, in the country on the edge of Edinburgh. It belonged to Lady Nairne, who was letting it during her absence in Ireland. Her agent was presumably incompetent, or he would never have let it to a couple who had been 'put to the horn' two days before, but it suited the De Quinceys well. They now had eight children, a daughter, Emily, having been born on 27 February,[58] and in the summer Margaret's sister Ann came to stay.[59] The country air must have been pleasant after the crowds and smoke of Edinburgh, but perhaps equally important was that the cottage was only a minute or two's run from the precincts of Holyrood, where debtors could take sanctuary. But there was no respite from misfortune, for early in September, the youngest boy, Julius, died, aged three. Poor De Quincey was not even able to mourn in peace: a creditor, he told Blackwood, 'having somehow ascertained from some person busy about my little boy's funeral that I was at home',[60] sent an officer, and he was forced to run from the cottage to avoid arrest. He stayed hidden for some time, communicating with his publisher by notes carried by Horace, who was now thirteen and could be trusted to get to and from his father without being followed.

As if all these catastrophes were not enough, it was also in September 1833 that De Quincey's policy of 'buying, and yet not paying for', so daringly applied at Rydal, produced its natural consequences. From the start, the mortage on The Nab had led to trouble. Inevitably neither De Quincey nor his father-in-law had been able to keep up their payments. In January 1832 Pendlebury, who held the mortgage, had threatened to sell and De Quincey, already hard-pressed in Edinburgh, had been driven to the extraordinary step of going south to see his mother to try and persuade her to help him pay off the arrears. Meanwhile, Margaret promised Pendlebury firmly that her husband would pay the arrears by Easter. 'From the love we all bear to the place,' she urged, 'there need be no doubt that we will all of us make any sacrifice rather than endanger its loss . . . Nor shall any delay ever occur again.'[61] The long-suffering Mrs Quincey actually did supply £185, enough to bring the payments up to April 1832, but the money was a loan and she was to recover it by temporarily halving her son's allowance, a measure which made his position in Edinburgh still more precarious. He managed at about the same time to extract a loan of £110 from his sister Jane;[62] but this was quickly swallowed up by his most pressing Edinburgh debts.

Once Mrs Quincey had paid the arrears and De Quincey had pledged himself to pay Simpson's share of the interest in future as well as his own, matters reverted to their old state and not a penny was paid. As the months went by other members of the Simpson family became involved, and at last De Quincey's blacksmith brother-in-law, William Simpson, sent an accusing letter which drove De Quincey to defend himself by writing at once to old John Simpson:

Dear Sir,

We lately received a Letter from Ann, and this day we received one from Mr. William Simpson, so extraordinary that none of us can understand them. – Mr. W.S., after abusing me as a swindler, says that you are nearly dying of hunger and starvation; and that but for him you would have been brought to the last extremity. He requires me to send 40 or 50 pounds, or more, by return of post: and, in case I do not, he says that he will send off you and your whole family to me. – He also says that he has paid £100 to Mr. Pendlebury; and that in order to repay himself he is going to sell up your stock and crops on the 1st of October: and that he will also sell my property and books. Now let me ask – What sort of help is this, to pay £100 when it was not wanted, and in return to sell up all your moveable property – and, besides all this . . . to turn you out of your house and land. Good God! Are you really consenting to terms of this sort?[63]

Some sort of 'sale' had, apparently, taken place, but The Nab was not yet lost and De Quincey had managed to interest Pendlebury in a scheme which amounted to no more than a series of promises to repay arrears of interest and part of the principle. He urged Simpson to stay on at The Nab, to let nothing be sold and not to suffer himself 'to be sent off like a parcel directed to me'. It is clear from his letter that he could not understand William Simpson's point of view because he could not grasp that anyone might think it important to keep out of debt. While his brother-in-law was concerned only to render the family solvent again, De Quincey found it self-evident that the appropriate strategy was to hold on, tenaciously defending the position with promises as fantastic as the case required. Why anyone should hand over good money when an I.O.U. would do instead passed his comprehension. But Pendlebury, unlike Hamlet's chameleon, would not 'eat the air, promise-cramm'd', and at the end of September The Nab was up for sale at the Salutation Inn, Ambleside. It was bought by the Lefleming family and became part of the Rydal Manor.[64] Reluctantly Simpson left The Nab and travelled to Edinburgh to join the De Quinceys. His wife had died not long before but her brother, the half-witted William Park, came with him to the crowded Caroline Cottage. What became of Park is not known. Of Simpson, one glimpse is preserved in the words of Florence De Quincey, who recalled sitting up with her grandfather

> trying to lighten the sleepless nights of his old age, when a chance word would loose his reserve, and this silent man would find it most easy to express himself by words from the Bible, Milton, Shakespeare, Pope's 'Homer', and sometimes a whole 'Spectator', humorous or grave, as the exciting subject might have been, and all in the homely, kindly Westmorland dialect, which in no way spoiled the recitation to our ears.[65]

When Simpson arrived at Caroline Cottage the rent was already in arrears, but soon De Quincey sold two articles to *Tait's*: one on Kant appeared in November and a character-sketch of Hannah More in December. The latter was an amusingly malicious, gossipy account, and one suspects that the intellectual shallowness, snobbery and unctuous moralizing he imputed to Miss More were qualities he had observed in his mother's Evangelical set generally, so that the essay gave him a chance to take his revenge. He must have been awaiting his chance, for at the end of a letter to Blackwood in February he had squeezed in a rather ghoulish postscript: 'Hannah More, I have seen, is dying. I can furnish a sketch of her daily habits and conversation.' Blackwood must have rejected the idea and the essay went to Tait, instead, who also published in January a paper on 'Animal Magnet- ism'. Despite this work for Tait, however, the usual pressures built up and at last De Quincey was forced to an expedient he had so far avoided. The downward trajectory of his Edinburgh life was com- pleted in November when he was 'put to the horn' for a third time, and, to escape the inevitable arrest, fled from Caroline Cottage to take refuge among the other outcasts and unfortunates in the debtors' sanctuary at Holyrood.

The Sanctuary of Holyrood consisted of the Palace of Holyrood- house and the land to its south now known as Holyrood Park, a circle some two miles across, with the Palace at its north-west edge and Duddingston Loch at the south-east. Half of the Loch was inside the sanctuary, though whether a debtor who went out fishing could escape arrest by rowing in the proper part of the water is not recorded. Certainly matters could be as delicate as that on land, and at the east end of the Canongate near Holyroodhouse a white line was painted on the pavement. On one side of it, a debtor was safe. On the other, he could be seized and thrown into prison. Holyrood had once been an abbey, and in the Middle Ages had been a sanctuary for criminals of many sorts. The right of sanctuary for most crimes had long been abolished but for debtors the privilege continued even though the 'Abbey' was given over to secular uses. For those such as De Quincey who had undergone a *Cessio Bonorum* and subsequently been 'put to the horn' for further debts, it offered a tolerable alternative to prison. To avail himself of the privilege of sanctuary, a debtor had to register with the Bailie – the officer who governed Holyrood – and pay a fee of two guineas, after which he could enjoy in peace the open space within the precincts, which included Arthur's Seat and a couple of tiny lochs, and various small taverns and shops crowded into the crumbling old buildings. Some were there for days or weeks, others for many years. They came from all walks of life, and at one time in the early nineteenth century they included three baronets. Some never expected to leave; others were more optimistic, and it was said that there was always a good market for lottery tickets among the 'Abbey lairds', as they were jocularly called. J.G. Lockhart described the 'Abbey' and its denizens as they were in De Quincey's day:

> All around the Palace itself, and its most melancholy garden, there are
> a variety of little miserable patchwork dwellings, inhabited by a
> considerable population of gentry, who prefer a residence here to one
> in a jail . . . However, they emerge into the town of a Sunday; and I am
> told some of them contrive to cut a very fashionable figure in the
> streets, while the catch-poles, in obedience to the commandment, 'rest
> from working'.[66]

The 'catch-poles' or court officers could not arrest debtors on the
sabbath, so on Saturday night a crowd of debtors would wait at the
Canongate for the stroke of twelve, when they could sally forth and
visit friends or family, transact business or simply enjoy a change of
scene until twenty-four hours later, when officers would be lurking to
catch any fugitive unlucky enough to be on the wrong side of the white
line as the last stroke of midnight sounded.[67] On one occasion De
Quincey himself failed to get back before midnight: he was not
arrested but had to hide in the town until the following Sunday, when
he was able to emerge and return to safety. Even within the sanctuary
debts were liable to be contracted, and as in the outside world, the
creditor could sue. The Bailie's court handled the matter and could
imprison the debtor! De Quincey was sued in the Bailie's court in April
and June 1834 but seems to have escaped the ultimate perdition of
imprisonment *within* the sanctuary.[68] Outside, his affairs proceeded
much as usual, and he was 'put to the horn' for the fourth time on 10
April.[69]

The De Quinceys continued to live at Duddingston whilst the head
of the family slipped in and out of Holyrood. Having entered in
November, he emerged early in the spring of 1834, but soon had to
dive back, probably because of the 'horning' in April. He rented rooms
at various lodging houses in the 'Abbey'. He might be at 'Brotherstone's Lodgings' or at a Miss Miller's, or a Miss Craig's. Experience
was not teaching him to be practical: he paid Miss Craig eight shillings
a week and could have had her room for less, but, he said, 'knowing
her to be a woman of excellent heart who had met with serious
misfortunes, – I did not wish to drive any hard bargain with her'. Later
the same unworldly generosity led him to act as guarantor for Miss
Craig's own arrears of rent and involve himself in her debts as well as
his own.[70] Generally only De Quincey himself was liable to imprisonment for debt, though occasionally Margaret too was involved. At
least once, however, a creditor resorted to kidnapping. In an undated

letter to one of his editors (perhaps Tait) De Quincey explains, 'I have had a little child detained from me by violence at Portobello. Which I mention because it has interrupted my writing, having involved me in applications to the Sheriff &c. for 4 days – and in other measures.'[71] No further details are known.

During his first period in the 'Abbey' De Quincey was still fighting the threat of having his belongings turned out of the cottage at Grasmere. On 1 February he wrote to the landlord promising that either he or William would go to Ambleside to discuss the date of his removal. He was careful to give his address as 'Mr. Brotherstone's Lodgings . . . near Holyrood House',[72] explaining that 'Mr Brotherstone will forward the letter', a tale devised to conceal the fact that he was in the debtors' sanctuary. William was conducting his business for him and on 11 February De Quincey was promising that either he or William would soon be at Ambleside to agree on the date of removal. (In fact he held on for another year, and seems to have given up the cottage in July 1835.)[73] And even as he negotiated over the cottage, he was wrangling over the rent at Duddingston. In March he owed Lady Nairne's agents nearly forty pounds, which he regarded as 'a trifle', and the agents, he said, had been trying to throw him out with 'a system of menaces . . . perfectly uncalled for'. They wanted the cottage cleared before his agreed tenancy expired, on 25 May, as her ladyship had decided to return early from Ireland.[74] Exactly when the De Quinceys left the cottage, and where they went next, are not known.

Amid these conditions it was as necessary as ever that work should go ahead. In an essay on Goldsmith, fifteen years later, De Quincey was to lament, with the note of bitter personal experience, the plight of the author 'who has helpless dependants . . . upon himself', who knows 'that instant ruin attends his failure' and must 'win his inspiration for poetry or romance from the prelusive cries of infants clamouring for their daily bread'.[75] Yet in such conditions of grim necessity he now began to produce work that was of more consistent and enduring quality than that of any previous phase of his career. Part of the credit for this must go to William Tait, an editor who gave him great freedom in his choice of subjects and encouraged the autobiographical strain in his work. For some reason De Quincey grumbled more about Tait than any of his other editors, but he wrote more for him than for anyone but Blackwood, and it was for Tait that he produced his extraordinary sequence of twenty-five autobiographical papers which appeared at irregular intervals between February 1834 and February 1841. Other editors had generally compelled him to take some specific external topic as the pretext for his papers, and hence had left untapped the springs of memory and introspection towards which his work generally veered. Tait's stroke of genius was to allow De Quincey to write about his own past, about things that were of interest merely because he remembered them. This might have been a recipe for disaster, and at times he did become involved in a long-winded ramblings on peripheral subjects – historical outlines of the Irish rebellion of 1798, for example, or diatribes on the cost of coals and candles at Oxford. But more often he succeeded in bringing the past to life, by no means idealizing it and yet communicating memories intensified by a sense of loss and a quest for meaning. The memoirs began as 'Sketches of Life and Manners from the Autobiography of an English Opium-Eater', a title which underwent inconsequent minor variations over the years. Without trespassing on territory covered by the *Confessions*, they traced De Quincey's life before and shortly after the episodes related there. Childhood at Greenhay and education at Oxford, the holiday in Ireland with Westport, the exploits of his brothers William and Richard, literary life in London and the Lake District were all recalled and examined with humour, lively self-awareness and, naturally, some improvement in the telling.

This autobiographical venture may have been a psychological necessity. In 1834 De Quincey was forty-nine years old. Slow and, in some ways, reluctant though he had been to gain maturity, he could no longer avoid seeing that his youth was gone. His childhood friends had disappeared, his brothers and sisters were mostly dead. His mother was a distant, reproachful shadow. He had scarcely seen his second home, the Lake District, for five years, and with the cottage at Grasmere about to pass from his tenancy his last foothold there would soon be gone. His health was ruined; his great works on philosophy and mathematics would never be written; he had a wife and seven children whom he could barely support. He had no leisure for scholarship, no prospect before him but hack-authorship. He would never give up opium. Clearly, if he were not to despair utterly, some reassessment, some struggle for understanding must be made. De Quincey's intelligence and his curious optimism came into their own, and starting from an instinctive conviction that his past life contained a meaning, that in some way everything had been purposeful and worthwhile, he ques-

313

tioned his memories in search of the key. An observant reader might have noticed that from the beginning the sketches emphasized experiences of loss and alienation. Episodes of idyllic beauty would be interrupted or distanced by encounters with guilt, fear or bereavement, producing an effect of counterpoint. The implication towards which the 'Sketches' tended was that the mind grows and deepens through suffering – a conclusion which, like that of the *Ancient Mariner*, seems trite when baldly stated but acquires considerable power from the literary work which forms its context. De Quincey refrained from stating this principle explicitly until 1845, when it was elaborated in *Suspiria de Profundis*, but he must have had something of the sort in mind much earlier, when he made it a 'constant' observation that when one of his small children had been suffering real pain from some minor ailment, 'always on the following day, when a long long sleep had chased away the darkness . . . from the little creature's brain, a sensible expansion had taken place in the intellectual faculties of attention, observation and animation'.[76] The same, he thought, was true on a larger scale throughout life.

Five of the 'Autobiographical Sketches' had appeared when, on 25 July 1834, Coleridge died. For De Quincey this was an event of immediate practical importance for he knew quite well that his reminiscences of Coleridge were a rich vein which he could mine as soon as S.T.C. himself was safely past objecting. As in the case of Hannah More, he may have been ready even before his subject's death, for in the September issue of *Tait's* appeared the first instalment of a four-part series, 'Samuel Taylor Coleridge', which ran until January 1835. The first paper began with an explosion. De Quincey told the story of his visit to Thomas Poole in 1807, and attributed to Poole (probably falsely, as we have seen) the statement that Coleridge was a conversational plagiarist, given to trumpeting other men's bright ideas as his own. He went on to state that Coleridge's 'Hymn to Chamouni is an expansion of a short poem in stanzas, upon the same subject, by Frederica Brun, a female poet of Germany'; that his 'France' quoted Milton's *Samson Agonistes* and yet Coleridge denied the debt; that the *Ancient Mariner* took its 'original hint' from the shooting of an albatross in Shelvocke's *Voyage Around the World*, which Coleridge likewise denied; and – most startling – that the twelfth chapter of the *Biographia Literaria* contained several pages of 'barefaced plagiarism' from Schelling emphatically claimed by Coleridge as his own work. De Quincey presented these items as evidence mainly of eccentricity and did ample justice to the abilities of Coleridge who, he said, 'spun daily and at all hours, for mere amusement of his own activities, and from the loom of his own magical brain, theories more gorgeous by far, and supported by a pomp and luxury of images, such as Schelling – no, nor any German that ever breathed, not John Paul – could have emulated in his dreams'.[77]

Nonetheless, the revelations were meant to shock, and in the four papers De Quincey gave the public a great deal of exciting gossip. 'Coleridge's marriage,' he explained, 'had not been a very happy one.' Indeed, 'Coleridge . . . assured me that his marriage was not his own deliberate act; but was in a manner forced upon his sense of honour, by the scrupulous Southey, who insisted that he had gone too far in his attentions to Miss F[ricker], for any honourable retreat.'[78] Mrs Coleridge's jealousy of 'a young lady . . . intellectually very much superior to her' – Dorothy Wordsworth – was described in some detail, as was Coleridge's addiction to opium, which, wrote De Quincey reprovingly, 'he first began . . . not as a relief from any bodily pains or nervous irritations – for his constitution was strong and excellent – but as a source of luxurious sensations'.[79] He also laughed at Coleridge's incompetence in conducting *The Friend* – insisting on dwelling so far from the printer, handling subscriptions and mailing lists so badly.

At the same time he drew a remarkably lifelike portrait of Coleridge. His conversation, his appearance, the sense of his 'presence' were all vividly conveyed. De Quincey's admiration was as obvious as his desire to debunk. The articles were read avidly; Coleridge's friends and family were furious. Dora Wordsworth told Quillinan, 'poor Hartley says he will "give it him" & I do hope he will . . . Aunt Sara [Hutchinson] burns with indignation against the little Monster – whom she never liked over well.'[80] Carlyle reported a conversation with Southey in London. 'Do you know De Quincey?' he asked casually.

'Yes, sir,' said Southey, with extraordinary animosity, 'and if you have opportunity, I'll thank you to tell him he is one of the greatest scoundrels living!' I laughed lightly, said I had myself little acquaintance with the man, and would not wish to recommend myself by that message. Southey's face, as I looked at it, was become of slate colour, the eyes glancing, the attitude rigid, the figure altogether a picture of Rhadamanthine rage, – that is, rage conscious to itself of being just . . . 'I have told Hartley Coleridge,' said he, 'that he ought to take a strong

315

cudgel, proceed to Edinburgh, and give De Quincey, publicly in the streets there, a sound beating – as a calumniator, cowardly spy, traitor, base betrayer of the hospitable social hearth, for one thing!'[81]

Coleridge's daughter Sara was less severe and wrote, more in sorrow than in anger,

> We have been much hurt with our former friend, Mr. De Quincey . . . for publishing so many personal details respecting my parents in *Tait's Magazine* . . . He has characterized my father's genius and peculiar mode of discourse with great eloquence and discrimination . . . I cannot believe that he had any enmity to my father, indeed he often speaks of his kindness of heart; but 'the dismal degradation of pecuniary embarrassments', as he himself expresses it, has induced him to supply the depraved craving of the public for personality.[82]

The Coleridge family tried to take revenge by urging Cottle to omit from his *Early Recollections* any reference to De Quincey's £300 gift to Coleridge – a pressure which Cottle, to his credit, resisted. Carlyle, a disinterested onlooker, thought the articles had been written 'with no wish to be untrue . . . or hurt anybody, though not without his own bits of splenetic conviction',[83] which may be a fair summing-up.

Still, one cannot help feeling that the view of Coleridge offered in the articles was formed under pressure of some personal animus. The accusations of plagiarism would not have surprised a close observer of De Quincey's career, for a warning note had been sounded a decade earlier by Wilson in *Blackwood's*. On the occasion of the 'Opium-Eater's' first appearance in *Noctes Ambrosianae*, in 1823, conversation had turned to the question of whether or not Coleridge was to edit the *Quarterly Review*. The 'Opium-Eater' expressed his opinion forcibly:

> Mr. Coleridge is the last man in Europe to conduct a periodical work. His genius none will dispute; but I have traced him through German literature, poetry, and philosophy, and he is, sir, not only a plagiary, but, sir, a thief, a *bone fide* most unconscientious thief. I mean no disrespect to a man of surpassing talents. Strip him of his stolen goods, and you will find good clothes of his own below. Yet, except as a poet, he is not original; and if he ever become Editor of the Quarterly (which I repeat is impossible), then will I examine his pretensions, and show him up as imposter . . . Coleridge has stolen from a whole host of his fellow-creatures, most of them poorer than himself; and I pledge myself I am bound over to appear against him. If he stands mute, I will press him to death, under three hundred and fifty pound weight of German metaphysics.[84]

This interesting passage went without comment in 1823. Perhaps it failed to stand out amongst the high jinks of the *Noctes*. But there can be little doubt that it was based on opinions expressed by De Quincey in Wilson's hearing. The conversations in the *Noctes* were fictitious, but they were always suited to the characters who uttered them, and Wilson would never have dared to put into the 'Opium Eater's' mouth such startling revelations had there been no basis for them in reality. Moreover, the close correspondence between the opinions expressed in the *Noctes* and those in the Coleridge articles vouches for their having the same source. There is even a verbal similarity: 'I have traced him through German literature, poetry and philosophy' becomes 'having read for thirty years in the same track as Coleridge, – that track in which few of any age will ever follow us, such as German metaphysicians, Latin schoolmen, thaumaturgic Platonists, religious Mystics'.

These passages bring out also how strongly akin to Coleridge De Quincey felt himself to be. These 'two transcendentalists who are also two [opium-eater]s',[85] both of them inefficient editors, explorers of obscure literature, dreamers, procrastinators and, at times, plagiarists, belonged to a special breed, and De Quincey knew it. The tone of the *Tait's* essays is not hostile; rather it is the tone of one who is too close to his subject. How far De Quincey consciously saw Coleridge as an *alter ego* is not clear, but he certainly had strong views on how one should deal with a double.

> Any of us [he wrote in 1847] would be jealous of his own duplicate; and, if I had a *doppel-ganger* who went about personating me, copying me, philosopher as I am, I might (if the Court of Chancery would not grant an injunction against him) be so far carried away as to attempt the crime of murder upon his carcase; and no great matter as regards HIM. But it would be a sad thing for *me* to find myself hanged; and for what, I beseech you? For murdering a sham, that was either nobody at all, or oneself repeated once too often.[86]

Perhaps his attitude to Coleridge partook of this. Were the Coleridge articles a case of 'murdering a sham'? Or, at least, of making sure that the double was properly dead?

De Quincey was to justify himself mainly by insisting that he had never really been Coleridge's friend, and so had betrayed no trust. 'I was *not* the friend of Coleridge,' he wrote in 1840; 'not in any sense; nor at any time; owed him no services of friendship; nor was under any one obligation towards him but that of veracity in my facts and justice in my deductions.'[87] Not, one feels, a very convincing argument. More to the point, perhaps, is his comment on Johnson, whose *Lives of the Poets* he greatly admired. Johnson, De Quincey said (no doubt with his own case in mind), was fortunate that most of his subjects had left no descendants; otherwise 'he would have . . . passed down to posterity as a dealer in wholesale scandal, who cared nothing for the wounded feelings of relatives. It is a trifle after that to add that he would frequently have been cudgelled.'[88] Like Johnson, he was concerned to give lifelike pictures; and certainly his essays on Wordsworth and Coleridge are among the few critical-biographical sketches that can stand comparison with Johnson's *Lives*.

11

Utterly Aground

In the latter part of 1834, just as his journalistic prospects were looking particularly bright, De Quincey was shaken by a domestic tragedy. His eldest son, William, now nearly eighteen, had fallen ill in August, complaining of deafness and severe headaches. The symptoms grew gradually worse and by October he was almost totally deaf. Swellings developed around the eyes, and early in November he became blind. The doctors were unable to diagnose or treat the illness, which remained a mystery to them, but it can now be identified as chloroma or chloroleukaemia, a rare cancerous condition of the blood affecting particularly the bones of the head and face. There was, of course, not the remotest chance of a cure. De Quincey and Margaret sat up with William night after night tending him as best they could but unable to do anything to ease his sufferings. As usual there was pressure on De Quincey to work, and he did his best. A pathetic letter written in early November, probably to Tait, describes his feelings. 'My dear Sir,' he writes, 'Listen for a moment – and then judge what it was possible to have done.' He explains that William has been seriously ill for five weeks and now seems to be dying.

> Gradually over each eye a film of darkness has been spreading, until at length some days since . . . this poor boy is totally blind. He had begun with being totally deaf. And to the consummation of my despair I understand that – should he ever recover – both these affections may remain with him for life. Good God! what a destiny of horror! Scarcely 18 years of age, just entering the portals as it were of life, and already cut off from all intercourse with his fellow-creatures, and immured in endless darkness! He himself, poor boy!, anticipates this fate – a fate far worse in the eyes of us all than death – and for which I see no alleviation.
>
> These things have so harrowed up my heart with grief and agitation that even to write a note was for some days impossible to me. Doubtless you are right: the Art[icle] requires a very different conclusion: and I have repeatedly laboured to write one . . .[1]

319

William's condition steadily deteriorated and he died on 25 November.[2] It was a terrible blow to De Quincey, who had felt William to be 'the crown and glory of my life . . . Upon him, I had exhausted all that care and hourly companionship could do for the culture of an intellect, in all stages of his life, somewhat premature'[3] – for William had been highly intelligent and a great lover of books, taking very much after his father. De Quincey suspected that he had died of 'hydrocephalus', which he himself had dreaded for so long.

In July 1835 De Quincey reluctantly arranged for the removal of his books and papers from Town End. The only other incident of any importance during the year was the death of Thomas Penson. De Quincey, ever optimistic, had been hoping that his uncle's death would bring him a substantial legacy, but Penson had arranged things in such a way that almost nothing came immediately to him, except for an annuity of £100 – a sum which Penson had already been giving him for several years. The remainder of the estate seems to have gone, for her lifetime, to Mrs Quincey. De Quincey's disappointment added to the exasperation with which he regarded his mother.

> Not only [he grumbled a few years later] has she absorbed 2/3rds. of my father's fortune, but has intercepted the whole of a second, and almost the whole of a 3rd. (my uncle's). All these it is true come eventually . . . to myself. But according to all appearances I shall drop out of the series of generations, as scarcely if at all surviving my mother; and my claims will first revive effectually in my children. Now, if all men had mothers living to ages so excesssive and mothers by strange coincidence of accident absorbing one estate after another, who would escape embarrassment?[4]

Perhaps it was feelings like these that had lent such gusto to his account of Nero's farcically incompetent attempts at murdering *his* mother in the essays on 'The Caesars'. De Quincey did get immediately a trunkfull of his uncle's household goods and clothing, but Mrs Quincey could not send it off without the usual words of suspicion and reproof: 'I should be rejoicing to think of its comfort to you all, but . . . I cannot help recollecting that when, in a time past, you were contriving one of your migrations, you spoke of selling your Goods and Chattels as an agreeable expedient!' She feared that he would be tempted to sell the goods in the trunk to which, she said, she had added some of her own. This was not all.

I must now enter on some very painful subjects: 1st. I have heard and noticed before . . . that you are still an Opium-Eater, and this dreadful Drug, as it is its nature to ruin the unhappy recipient, thus acts on you, destroying alike the will and the power to discharge all bounden duties, to the full extent which the more common forms of intoxication effect! Well, with all you wrote *so well* before me, of poor Coleridge's dying opium misery, I am lost in the saddest wonder . . . That you write, in a disreputable Magazine, on subjects and in a spirit afflicting, as I hear, to your real friends, I suppose may be accounted for in this way, that to the last moment of opium delirium, you will not write where you might with honour and no compromise of your professed principles; money being spent, and no choice left, you take up with Mr. Tait.[5]

Then she began a diatribe on the subject of the children's education. She had noticed 'no less than seven false spellings of very common words' in a letter from little Margaret. 'I did not make this discovery without grief,' she goes on. The children, she fears, will grow up ignorant and 'fall into profligacy'. This was unfair: even the lists of De Quincey's debts show that he employed teachers of all kinds for the children, and he certainly tried to teach them what he could himself; though it is true that the youngest, Emily, later complained of having missed a proper education.[6] Coming so soon after William's death these aspersions seem particularly tactless. At the same time, however, she offered to pay for a school or governess to put things right. Whether or not De Quincey accepted is not known.

On other points Mrs Quincey's fears were justified. De Quincey did sell Penson's plate, and he sold his annuity for cash (£950) to the Caledonian Insurance Company: a furtive transaction, as it had to be done without his mother's finding out.[7] Nor would she have been happy to know how often the children had to act as secret messengers, threading the backstreets of old Edinburgh to evade pursuers, delivering manuscripts or fetching money. A bookseller in Prince's Street recalled how 'Mr. De Quincey's young, fair-haired English laddies' used to be sent to him to ask for loans,[8] and James Bertram, an employee of Tait's, tells us that

De Quincey's packets of 'copy' often reached Tait's in a most extraordinary fashion. Sometimes a young woman would enter the shop in the morning, whilst I was busy sweeping or dusting, and throwing down a roll of paper, with an exclamation of 'There!' would rush off as abruptly as she had entered. On examing the roll, I would find it addressed in the neatest of handwriting to 'William Tait, Esquire'.[9]

The children bore their tribulations bravely but sometimes found these missions harrowing. 'My Father' Florence later recalled, 'always liked best to have his girls about him,' so

> On me fell the main burden and I know the north and southbacks of the Canongate, George the Fourth Bridge, the cross causeway &c as hideous dreams, my heart rushing into my mouth with the natural terrors of footsteps approaching and rushing down again into my shoes when left to quiet and the ghosts. When he turned up it was all right, and I am sure I never told him what I suffered, children are but dumb dogs about some things.[10]

But there was often no alternative. De Quincey was back in the 'Abbey' in May 1836,[11] and once there he could not emerge except on Sundays. Someone had to deliver his copy. If the children were not available he had to make do with any messenger he could find. 'On more than one occasion,' says Bertram, 'a night policeman arrived early in the afternoon with a . . . packet, for which he demanded and received a shilling; a coin destined to be divided into three parts, the packet having passed through as many pairs of hands.' Another day, 'a hackney-coachman had been requisitioned as messenger, he was driving a party to visit Holyrood Palace, and whilst the company were engaged in viewing the old abbey "a little gentleman, as polite as a prince, although he wasn't dressed like one, gave me this to bring here, and he said I would get a shilling for my trouble". So said the cabman.'[12] From May 1836 the whole family lived mainly in Holyrood. Margaret (senior) had fallen ill early in the year, and as she did not regain her health De Quincey became increasingly dependent upon his children for practical help of every kind.

One consolation was that the 'Autobiographical Sketches' continued to be successful. Bertram tells us that

> The publisher of *Tait* entertained a high opinion of De Quincey's abilities as a contributor, and on the occasion of his visits to the warehouse, treated him with a certain degree of deference. For the numbers of *Tait* containing his sketches there was usually a brisk demand. At one time, when a large quantity of old numbers of the magazine was disposed of to . . . the waste-paper merchants, twenty-five sets of those containing Mr. De Quincey's articles were reserved to supply further demand.[13]

As a Radical magazine, *Tait's* could not normally print De Quincey's political work. One experiment was made but it was not a success. In December 1835 and January 1836 Tait published 'A Tory's

Account of Toryism, Whiggism and Radicalism', arguing that such a survey was of general interest to all parties and would silence the Tories' complaints that the Radical press misrepresented them. But he could not refrain from covering himself by adding sarcastic footnotes to De Quincey's Tory text. When De Quincey saw the finished product he was so angry that he immediately wrote a second essay, 'Political Parties of Modern England', to answer Tait's gibes, but Tait saw vistas of endless controversy opening before him, and refused to publish it. De Quincey's anomalous position as a Tory writer for *Tait's* continued to cause trouble. Early in 1837 the 'Autobiographical Sketches' dealt with his boyhood holidays at Everton and described with good-humoured contempt the circle of minor writers and Whig politicians he had met there – Roscoe, Shepherd, Clarke, Currie and others. De Quincey portrayed them as poetasters and dilettanti amusingly burdened with delusions of grandeur, ending his account with an elegiac passage in which he drew back from his subject and allowed these little men to become emblematic figures, types of frail mortality: 'Mr. Roscoe is dead, and has found time since then to be half forgotten; Dr. Currie, the physician, has been found "unable to heal himself"; Mr. Shepherd of Gateacre is a name and a shadow; Mr. Clarke is a shadow without a name; the tailor, who set the table in a roar, is dust and ashes; and three men at the most remain . . . [from] those convivial meetings . . .'[14]

But he had miscalculated, for the Rev. William Shepherd was still very much alive. A seasoned controversialist, he fired off an angry reply, suggesting that the 'Opium-Eater's' account was vitiated by his having been 'at one period of his life the slave of a deleterious drug, which shakes the nerves, and, inflaming the brain, impairs the memory'.[15] Tait published the letter in May 1837. In Liverpool, where Roscoe and his friends were still warmly remembered, great offence was taken. The newspapers published sarcastic critiques of the essay and relatives of De Quincey's victims raged.

> Tait's conduct is shameful [wrote Robert Roscoe] . . . in allowing a malignant Tory to insult and abuse honest Reformers in his pretended liberal Mag[azine] . . . 'Mr. De Q' – he says – 'only expressed his real *opinions*'! & his real *feelings* too, no doubt – It is nothing to me whether he thinks my father a poor poet, and a bad Biographer –. . . what excites our indignation is to see a wretch like *that*, undisguisedly exulting that men so much better than himself are *dead* and that the reputation which they had gained, is (as he believes) fast declining – This is sheer malignity.

And he relieved his feelings in a sonnet 'On reading the remarks of the Opm. Eater on several excellent characters deccd'.[16]

For three years De Quincey had published nothing in *Blackwood's*, probably because William Blackwood had died in 1834 and his sons John and Robert were less sympathetic to his ways of working. 'I know my Uncle John never forgave him some of his performances,' wrote a third-generation Blackwood, 'and turned his portrait out of the Saloon and would never allow it to be hung up, and then gave it to the Scottish National Gallery or told the artist to do so.'[17] On the other hand, De Quincey was not satisfied with *Tait's* standards of printing. An angry note is recorded in which 'Mr. De Quincey presents his compliments' and complains 'that some unknown person at the Press is constantly doing him the most serious injuries. He has a list of some 15 to 25 cases, where capricious . . . changes have been made *after* the press arrangements . . . had been closed.'[18] For some such reason his attitude to *Blackwood's* softened a little and he allowed them to publish in July 'The Revolt of the Tartars', a remarkable essay in oriental fantasy purporting to be based on historical sources but largely the product of De Quincey's imagination.

It marked the beginning of a cautious return to regular work for *Blackwood's*, which might have eased the financial position had not his addiction to trouble led him to involve himself with the difficulties of Major Miller, a friend he had made in the sanctuary at Holyrood. Having guaranteed bills of Miller's, he was faced with demands for several small sums on Miller's behalf in the spring and summer of 1837.[19] He tried to raise money by going back to the Caledonian Insurance Company to negotiate a loan against his reversionary interest in his uncle's property.[20] These affairs were further complicated by the fact that his attorney, one J.J. Smith, held some of Miller's bills and reimbursed himself by quietly taking £100 of De Quincey's money: he subsequently absconded to America and it was never recovered.[21] When Miller himself died in August, his creditors came swarming about De Quincey, who at some point in the year was again arrested for debt, but had a lucky escape. Adam Black, publisher of the *Encyclopedia Britannica*, 'found the little man one day in the hands of the sheriff's officers conveying him to Calton gaol. He stopped the melancholy procession and finding the debt for which De Quincey was seized to be under thirty pounds, he became responsible for it on condition of De Quincey's furnishing the articles on Shakespeare and Pope.'[22] The articles appeared in the seventh edition, to which he also contributed those on Goethe and Schiller. All of them are woefully inadequate, partly because as usual he had to write without books. The 'Pope' seems to have been compiled from rough notes for an unwritten review of Roscoe's 1824 *Life of Pope*; it contains two cryptic references to 'Mr. Roscoe' – presumably traces De Quincey overlooked when adapting the item for Black.[23] The 'Goethe' is based entirely on Goethe's autobiography *Dichtung und Wahrheit*, which ends with Goethe's twenty-sixth year, a problem De Quincey surmounted by asserting that the remaining fifty-seven years of Goethe's life were 'so quiet and uniform' that nothing need be said about them.[24] The 'Shakespeare' concentrated on biographical problems and, astonishingly, rejected the opportunity of discussing the plays.

The shortcomings of these papers may also be due to the fact that during the second half of 1837 De Quincey was distracted by grief, for on 7 August, after a long illness, his wife died of typhus fever. Margaret's death shook him even more deeply than William's two and a half year before. For a long time she had been a source of the emotional stability and comfort he so badly needed. Her unhappiness when they had been apart had only confirmed how much they depended on each other. He had often been unable to give her the security or understanding she wanted and her life had been a hard one, but she had remained devoted to him at all times and he apparently never ceased to see her as the girl with whom he had fallen in love long ago at Rydal. The effect of her death, coming so soon after that of William, was deep and lasting. In Florence's words,

> Looking back to that time, when I was a mere child, I yet seem to see that his mind was unhinged by these sorrows, and the overwhelming thought of being left with a family of such differing ages and needs, and with no female relatives at hand to help him, as even his eldest daughter was then so young that she must have seemed to him, as she did to others, most needing a mother's care.[25]

The psychic reverberations of this loss were considerable. Margaret became assimilated to those other emblems of lost feminine purity and affection, Ann, Elizabeth and Kate. More than ever De Quincey turned his thoughts inward and to the past, where amid his own follies and failures such innocent love seemed to embody some power of redemption. He later claimed that many years ago – as early, indeed, as five years before he met Margaret – he had had premonitory dreams in which he had seen her at the window of a cottage 'embowered with roses and clustering clematis'. Always as he approached she would signal to him, with a look of horror, to go away, warning him not to come near the place. He felt, as he dreamed, that not 'one life – so pitiful a thing – was what moved her care' but rather 'it was, or seemed, as if this poor wreck of a life happened to be that one which determined the fate of some thousand others'. Not 'one poor fifty years' was at stake, but 'nothing less than a century of centuries'.[26] It is hard to believe that these dreams actually preceded his meeting with Margaret: De Quincey was prone to 'remember' omens and premonitions long after the event. But such dreams may well have occurred after Margaret's death, founded on a recognition that the pursuit of his boyhood vision had led him to the place where his life would become blighted by opium. In retrospect it seemed as if it should not have happened, yet neither the beauty of the place nor Margaret's goodness had been enough to save him.

An indication of how frail he was in health at the time when he had to bear these troubles is given by a curious diary jotting made on 5 March, shortly before Margaret's last illness. He records that his dinner that day consisted of 'rice broth' and then 'minced collups' with 'a little potatoes' and 'abt. 2 oz of rice' – his usual meagre, bland diet. He had no breakfast, for 'over a cup of coffee brought to me in bed about ½ past 10 or 11, I fell asleep after taking two or three teaspoonfuls'. He has given up taking supper before going to bed, a precaution which he calls a 'great discovery' and regards as the secret of his present good health. He has also given up the 'multitude of pills' he formerly took (for the constipation caused by morphine), 'trusting to the power of nature under a previous impulse every fifth or sixth day'. He takes a seven-mile walk each day for exercise and often drinks four or five glasses of spirits, which he fears is rather too much. He feels at his best, he says, in the evening after dinner – the night being, it seems, the time when most of his work is done.[27] It is rather startling to realize that these notes were written on a day when he was feeling unusually well. He had come to accept ill-health as his normal condition.

In the autumn of 1837 he was twice 'put to the horn', but as debts were also building up inside Holyrood he had to leave sanctuary and take his chance in the city. The children stayed in his lodgings at Holyrood while he took rooms in the house of a Mrs Wilson at 42, Lothian Street.[28] As usual these troubles did not prevent him from writing and by the end of the year he had produced for *Blackwood's* the most effective piece of fiction he ever wrote, a story called 'The Household Wreck'. In the course of writing it he was chased from his lodgings by creditors three times and was, he lamented, able to see his children only once a week, 'that is on Sunday at 5 p.m. to dinner'.[29]

'The Household Wreck' derived its power from De Quincey's feelings at the loss of Margaret. A distinctly Kafka-esque piece set in a large city in an unidentified country, it tells of the destruction of an ideally happy and innocent family. The narrator, clearly a De Quinceyan self-portrait, has a young wife, Agnes, who seems to be modelled on Margaret. One day she fails to return from a shopping expedition and the narrator learns to his astonishment that she is under arrest, but cannot at first discover what charge has been made against her. He goes to the police office and has to force his way through a dense crowd to reach officials who are too busy to answer his questions but at last refer him to 'a vast folio volume' in which all charges are recorded, and where he discovers that Agnes has been accused of shoplifting – a crime of which he knows her to be incapable. She is confined in a huge prison whose keepers are notoriously corrupt yet will not take bribes to let the anguished husband see her. As the trial approaches he grows ill, haunting the enormous outer courts of the prison in company with crowds of vagabonds who seem to live there permanently, and at last he falls into feverish delirium. When he regains his senses he learns that the trial is already over. Agnes has been found guilty and sentenced to ten years' hard labour. The remainder of the tale is less interesting. Agnes is rescued but dies soon afterwards, and the cause of the catastrophe is revealed: she had been falsely accused by a shopkeeper whose sexual advances she had rejected. The villain is eventually torn to pieces by an angry mob. The story as a whole, however, is curiously effective because for once De Quincey made positive use of the lack of realism in his plots and settings, and embodied in the story personal anxieties which made the distortions of viewpoint appropriate. In particular one suspects that 'The Household Wreck' is connected with De Quincey's feeling of guilt at leaving Margaret so much alone. The narrator stresses at length his protectiveness towards his wife, yet the story seems to embody fantasies of the worst that might happen to an unprotected young woman.

327

The story appeared in *Blackwood's* in January 1838. Another original story, 'The Avenger', was published in August, and the autobiographical papers continued in *Tait's*. But creditors pressed as hard as ever, and there were several suits in progress against him. He was 'horned' again in April[30] and on 25 April wrote to Tait, 'Three times, in three separate lodgings, I had been traced by the emissaries of my creditors; and always through the carelessness of my children, who suffered themselves to be followed unconsciously.'[31] Eventually he found safety at the home of the three daughters of his late impecunious friend Major Miller. He stayed with them for a month – 'the very happiest month that I have known for a long, long time' – until an old charwoman from Holyrood, to whom he had given money when she was ill and unable to work, followed Paul Frederick to the house. Soon afterwards she was heard boasting of having discovered De Quincey's whereabouts, and he had to leave his comfortable hiding place before word reached his creditors.

Circumstances would neither permit him to stop writing nor give him the peace to do it to his own satisfaction. 'There being absolutely no credit in the Abbey,' he told Wilson, 'on my children's acct. I was compelled to write continued sheets of the Autob[iography] merely to obtain the amount of their daily expenditure'. And Tait was paying part of his earnings directly to the creditors.[32] Of this year's work he told Talfourd bitterly,

> if . . . you ever look into my Autob sketches in Tait, bear in mind that I disown them. They were not written, as will be thought, in monthly successions and with intervals sufficient: but all at once . . . in a coffee room of a mail coach inn; with a sheriff's officer lurking near; in hurry too extreme to allow of reading them over even *once*; – and with no after revision.[33]

On 6 June, sending 'The Avenger' to the Blackwoods, he explained that he could only meet the daughter who took his messages 'out of doors' for fear of her being followed, and that he had 'lost 2 days in seachg. for a place to write in'. He asked for one pound at once – 'I am utterly aground', he wrote, 'without even paper or pens . . . And keep out of prison I must. Doing that I shall in 6 weeks be afloat for ever. If I fail, and once get into a prison, I am booked for utter perplexity for a year and more.'[34] The Blackwood brothers must have been softening as had their father before them, for another note acknowledges five pounds paid by them towards one of his debts.[35] At the end of June he was so harassed that he agreed to let someone at Blackwood's cut and revise one of his papers, and as if this were not proof enough of sincerity, he enclosed a demand from one of his creditors to convince the Blackwoods that his plight was genuine.[36]

The constant stream of notes, often on tiny scraps of paper two inches square or less covered with microscopic handwriting, may have raised suspicions with both Tait and the Blackwoods that De Quincey's problems were partly imaginary or over-dramatized. This impression was shared by Florence, who remembered how the children saw his condition:

> It was an accepted fact among us that he was able when saturated with opium to persuade himself and delighted to persuade himself (the excitement of terror was a real delight to him) that he was dogged by dark and mysterious foes, at the same time this persuasion gave a sanction to his conscience for getting away from the crowded discomfort of a home without any competent head . . . where . . . he could by no possibility have done any work had he remained.[37]

This seems plausible, but it cannot be altogether accurate because court records in Edinburgh establish that De Quincey was constantly being pursued. There even survives a claim for expenses from a man hired to watch his house and follow him through the streets in the hope of enabling an arrest to be made.[38] A previous biographer[39] has concluded that De Quincey must have concealed the seriousness of his problems from his children, which may well be the correct solution. But if the debts were real, they were also often unnecessary. One need only consider the dealings over The Nab, or his frequent practice of renting several sets of lodgings simultaneously. Added to these were habits of business calculated to produce utter chaos. He would neither take nor give receipts, and he would never pay a debt at once if the money were available, preferring to pay part of it and let the remainder wait. Bertram recalls that he 'was exceedingly careless in money matters, and preferred to be paid by occasional small instalments. Once, when a cheque for a very moderate sum was sent to him, a messenger brought it back to Mr. Tait with the intimation that at the moment "so large an amount was not required by him, two pounds being all he wanted".'[40] This continual waste of time and money would have wrought havoc with an income far more substantial than De Quincey's.

The end of 1838 saw him as deeply in trouble as ever. On 21 December he wrote to Wilson proposing an article on 'The English

Language'. He was diffident because *Blackwood's* had taken nothing from him since August, having rejected an essay in September, but he had lost the last credit he had possessed, with a grocer, and the family had been living on one meal a day. 'Even then,' he told Wilson, 'my youngest daughter, 5 years old, besieged the ears of all about her with clamors for something to eat from morning till night.' Now, 'no article of dress, nor household utensil belonging to me, no plate received under my uncle's will, but has long disappeared (you may be sure) at the pawnbroker's'. And there was no prospect of earning more from Tait: 'I *have* written more than he can print in two years,' he says. If he could go to the University Library, he could 'make articles in abundance' if only *Blackwood's* would print them; but he is 'without any coat as well many other parts of dress – so that to go out even covered up by a borrowed cloak is now become impossible'.[41]

Fortunately Wilson accepted the proposed article and De Quincey gradually regained his position as a regular contributor to *Maga*. The fact that he did not then give up *Tait's* occasioned a certain degree of suspicion, but his defence was unanswerable: 'I should prefer writing for your journal. But my debts, though nearly at an end, still oblige me to write 2 sheets a month. Here is my reason for writing elsewhere.'[42] And in search of further outlets, he wrote to Robert Chambers, publisher of *Chambers's Journal*, offering his services:

> I should he happy to furnish a series of essays on Life, Manners, Literature and other subjects. And as I know experimentally that the discovery and shaping of subjects is in itself a laborious thing, I should be happy to make that a part of my undertaking . . . I am at present . . . condemned to fight off creditors with one hand, whilst with the other I furnish support to nine persons daily. Still, I am obliged to count all literary labours within my reach.[43]

Chambers did not want articles, but the letter won De Quincey more friends and he took to visiting Chambers and his family at their house in Doune Terrace. He used to go there on Sunday evenings, and became such a regular visitor that a spare pair of wellington boots was kept there for him in case he had to flee his lodgings without time to change his footwear.[44]

Like Tait, the Blackwoods came to an arrangement with one of De Quincey's creditors, and were soon paying a proportion of his earnings directly to the Albion Cloth Company, to whom a debt had long been outstanding,[45] but at least they continued to accept and pay for his work, which was the essential thing. The most successful *Black-wood's* venture of this period was a 'Supplementary Paper on Murder, Considered as One of the Fine Arts' which appeared in the November 1839 *Maga*. It included an account of a celebration dinner of the Society of Connoisseurs in Murder and added to the Society's catalogue of admirable crime the exploits of Burke and Hare, the Indian Thugs and the Sicarii, a band of murderers who appealed to De Quincey's imagination because of their technique of murdering their victims in the midst of crowds in Jerusalem at festival time – a practice which combined three of his interests (secret violence, the urban crowd and Eastern customs) most satisfactorily. The Roman army had eventually rooted out the Sicarii from their desert stronghold, creating a tableau which moved the Murder Club's after-dinner speaker – and De Quincey – to raptures: ' "Heavens, gentlemen, what a sublime picture! The Roman legions – the wilderness – Jerusalem in the distance – an army of murderers in the foreground!" '[46]

The best of his work, however, was still appearing in *Tait's*. The mass of autobiographical writing produced during 1838 had included a group of papers loosely connected with his residence in the Lake District, the first three of which were on Wordsworth. They appeared in January, February and April 1839, and together they constitute the most thorough and lifelike portrait of Wordsworth by one who knew him. They give a sketchy biography of the poet, framed by an account of De Quincey's first meeting with him and enriched with quotation (not always accurate) from the poems. There is some critical discussion of the poetry, fragmentary but nonetheless very perceptive, but the articles succeed above all in giving a sense of Wordsworth in his environment. De Quincey, knowing the poet's family as well as the landscape and customs of the Lake District, is able to bring us close to Wordsworth because he was himself close to him. The autobiographical talent, the ability to convey the flavour of a period in his own life, is used to illuminate the other man so that we see him with all the vigour of personal perception.

Incidentally, the articles also gave the public its first taste of the poem that was to become known as *The Prelude*. De Quincey quoted nearly thirty lines with remarkable accuracy, chiefly from Book V, claiming to quote from a memory 'not refreshed by sight of the poem for more than twenty years'. He has generally been credited, partly on this evidence, with extraordinary mnemonic powers, and undoubtedly his memory was very good. For things read he had a 'photographic' faculty of recall, which in middle age sometimes enabled him, for example, to see clearly before him as he lay in bed at night entire pages of the Greek texts he had studied at Oxford. In the case of *The Prelude*, however, there is room for doubt. In 1848 after an evening's conversation with De Quincey Emerson noted in his journal that De Quincey claimed to have 'lost 5 manuscript books of Wordsworth's Excursion (continued)', which he later amended to 'lost *five* manuscript books of Wordsworth's unpublished Poem'.[47] This seems to mean that De Quincey had at some time possessed a manuscript copy of *The Prelude*. Was he merely telling a tall story to impress Emerson? Or did he, in 1839, want to conceal the fact that he had had a text of the poem, perhaps a copy made without Wordsworth's permission? There is no knowing.

It was not to be expected that De Quincey would be able to handle his subject without offending Wordsworth and his family. As one reader put it, 'You know his articles on Coleridge. Wordsworth's turn has come now.'[48] De Quincey was well aware of the risks he ran in giving any picture, however bland, of the domestic life of a respected contemporary. Standards of privacy were strict, and to publish any information learned from private sources rendered one liable to accusations of breach of confidence. The public was not supposed to have its curiosity about an author gratified during his lifetime. Moreover, the growing tendency to regard poets as arbiters of morality made them especially sensitive to anything which might hint at personal shortcomings. These exacting standards would have prevented De Quincey from giving an honest and believable picture of Wordsworth, so he disregarded them. He had his defence ready:

> How invaluable should we all feel any record to be, which should raise the curtain upon Shakspeare's daily life – his habits, personal and social, his intellectual tastes, and his opinions on contemporary men, books, events or national prospects! I cannot, therefore, think it necessary to apologize for the most circumstantial notices past or to come of Wordsworth's person and habits of life.[49]

– an argument convincing to posterity but less satisfying to the poet's family and friends, who found De Quincey extending his licence to the whole Wordsworth household. Bad enough to have him telling the public that 'Wordsworth was, upon the whole, not a well-made man';

that he had a crooked walk; that his manners were not always perfect; that his dress was at times 'slovenly'; that he did not read much. But it was almost worse when he described Dorothy's occasional nervous stammer, or mentioned that Mary Wordsworth 'was generally pronounced very plain' and had 'a considerable obliquity of vision'. 'The fellow cannot even let Mrs. Wordsworth's squint alone!' raged Hartley Coleridge as he and Charles MacFarlane walked on the shores of Grasmere. 'I should not be very unwilling to pitch the Opium-Eater into this lake!'[50] Crabb Robinson, no great admirer of De Quincey, tried to reassure Wordsworth. 'A considerable part,' he insisted, 'published thirty years hence would be read with pride and satisfaction by your grandchildren – I dare say the unhappy writer means to be honest.'[51] But Wordsworth would not be appeased. His judgment was jotted down a few years later, its grand simplicity unvexed by any desire to consult the evidence: 'I have never read a word of his infamous production nor ever shall ... A man who can set such an example, I hold to be a pest of society, and one of the most worthless of mankind.'[52]

Yet the 'unhappy writer' did mean to be honest. In a passage whose frankness must have astonished the readers of 1839 (and which he cut from the essay when it was reprinted in 1854), he made a painful effort to define his position, sensing that his account of Wordsworth was somehow unbalanced.

One thing it is highly necessary that I should explain ... as in some measure necessary to protect myself from ... the suspicion of having, at times, yielded to a private prejudice, so far as to colour my account of Wordsworth with a spirit of pique or illiberality. I shall acknowledge then, on my own part – and I feel that I might even make the same acknowledgement on the part of Professor Wilson, ... that to neither of us, though, at all periods of our lives, treating him with the deep respect which is his due, ... yet to neither of us has Wordsworth made those returns of friendship and kindness which most firmly I maintain that we were entitled to have challenged. More by far in sorrow than in anger ... I acknowledge myself to have been long alienated from Wordsworth; sometimes even I feel a rising emotion of hostility – nay, something, I fear, too nearly akin to vindictive hatred. Strange revolution of the human heart![53]

And what was the cause of this revolution? De Quincey does not state it but asks us to 'imagine a case such as this which follows':

–The case of a man who, for many years, has connected himself closely with the domestic griefs and joys of another, over and above his primary service of giving to him the strength and encouragement of a profound literary sympathy, at a time of universal scowling from the world; suppose this man to fall into a situation in which, from want of natural connexions and from his state of insulation in life, it might be most important to his feelings that some support should be lent to him by a family having a known place and acceptation, and what may be called a root in the country . . . To look for this, might be a most humble demand on the part of one who had justified his devotion in the way supposed. To miss it might – But enough. I murmur not; complaint is weak at all times; and the hour is passed irrevocably, and by many a year, in which an act of friendship so natural, and costing so little, (in both senses so priceless) could have been availing.[54]

In other words, when he and Margaret had been in difficulties and surrounded by scandal, when their first child had been born and in the early days of their marriage, Wordsworth had turned away. Instead of comfort and support he had given cool disapproval. And now Margaret was dead: 'The ear is deaf that should have been solaced by the sound of welcome. Call, but you will not be heard; shout aloud, but your 'ave!' and 'all hail!' will now tell only as an echo of departed days, proclaiming the hollowness of human hopes.'[55]

It was Margaret's death that lent bitterness to the essays. But by the time they were approaching publication his feelings had cooled down a little and he tried to undo some of the damage. It is possible that Tait obstructed him, well knowing that the more indiscreet the essays were the better they would sell; at any rate, De Quincey several times complained to Tait that he was not being given time to bring the papers into line with his second thoughts. On 17 January he told Blackwood that Tait had inserted the words 'in this present year of our Lord 1839' into his text to conceal the fact that it had been written eight months before, and on 20 February he told Tait, 'The publication of this paper about Wordsworth and Miss Wordsworth will do me very great injury besides giving very great pain', demanding the opportunity to revise the text and threatening public complaint if Tait refused. The third article, published in April, shows signs of hasty cutting: one paragraph ends by introducing the subject of Wordsworth's occasional 'ill-humour and peevishness' which are said to have been displayed on 'two occasions' – at which point the topic is abruptly dropped.[56] Even so the essay retained the statement that William and Dorothy were both said to have been 'in childhood, irritable or even ill-tempered'. And a discussion of Wordsworth's supposed incapacity for passionate love introduces, by contrast, a rhapsody on De Quincey's feelings for his lost Margaret:

> When the gate moved upon its golden hinges that opened to me the paradise of her society – when her young, melodious laughter sounded in my too agitated ear – did I think of any claims that I could have? Too happy if I might be permitted to lay all things at her feet . . . Sometimes, after days of intellectual toil, when half the whole world is dreaming – I wrap my head in the bed clothes, which hide even the faintest murmur yet lingering from the fretful day . . . and then through blinding tears I see again that golden gate; again I stand waiting at the entrance; until dreams come that carry me once more to the Paradise beyond.[57]

As if to redress the balance, he wrote under the date 16 May 1838 a 'Letter to Mr. Tait concerning the Poetry of Wordsworth', intended for the magazine, setting out preliminaries for a critical survey of Wordsworth's work, and proposing that an extensive, cheaply printed selection of the poems be produced for the mass reading public, restoring the original texts as they were before the poet 'half ruined some dozens of his finest passages by "cobbling" them as it is called; that is, altering them when no longer under the free-flowing movement of the original inspiration'.[58] But the 'Letter' was not published: perhaps Tait thought his public had had enough of Wordsworth for the time being. Its rejection must have added to De Quincey's discontent with Tait's methods.

Yet he could not afford to leave Tait, and continued to supply him with autobiographical papers. He had begun the year 1838 in Holyrood, where he worked with books brought to him from the libraries by John Hill Burton, a former student of Wilson's who was now an advocate with literary interests and could thus help De Quincey in a dual capacity. During the following months De Quincey moved about, often staying with friends, sometimes so poor that he could not afford to buy paper. In October he made the grave mistake of visiting a Mr McIndoe of 113 Princes Street to whom he owed some seventy pounds. McIndoe and his family treated him kindly at first: it is said that Mrs McIndoe offered to mend some torn clothes he was wearing and it grew so late that he accepted the offer of a bed, after which he prolonged his stay and became a lodger.[59] But once he had moved his belongings to McIndoe's house it became apparent that he had been lured into a trap. McIndoe had his debtor on the premises, and proceeded to hold De Quincey's books and papers to ransom. De Quincey regarded his great haystack of papers with intense anxiety, for it contained most of his legal and financial documents and many years' accumulation of notes, out of which, when pressed, he could thriftily work up articles on all kinds of subjects. Summaries of books read, notes on dreams, lists of bright ideas, partly written essays and other valuable raw materials as well as many personal letters were there and the threat of their sale or destruction was a powerful weapon against him.

His plight became absurd as well as wretched. He began to accumulate a new debt to McIndoe for the rooms in which he lodged. When he could not pay, McIndoe reduced him from two rooms to one and then threatened eviction. De Quincey would have liked nothing better than to leave, but knew that he would not be allowed to take his papers and so was forced to hang on. He and McIndoe, living in the same house, communicated by means of furious but stilted third-person notes:

> Mr. McIndoe is astonished that Mr. De Quincey could have sent him such a note as that last received. Had he been requiring £1 for his own family it would have been easily procured. How Mr. De Quincey can suppose for a moment that he is to remain in his house to support an extravagant family while Mr. McIndoe is imputed with receiving all the money he acquires. Mr. McIndoe therefore regrets that Mr. De Quincey shall remove tonight . . .[60]

and so on. But De Quincey did not leave. Most of what he earned had to go to the children, still living together in Holyrood. He tried to ease matters a little by taking out life insurance, but failed, 'No Insurance Off[ice] consenting to insure my life under 13 per cent. on the argument that I had used Op[ium] to excess, and (tho' most favourably reported on by all their medical officers) might do so again'[61] – which was rather to understate the case, De Quincey being entirely dependent on his regular supply. So McIndoe continued his campaign, threatening to confiscate De Quincey's papers, 'the accumulation of two years' solitude and meditation', whilst De Quincey hid in his room and wrote articles barefoot and wrapped in a counterpane for protection against the cold, having, he told Blackwood, 'in a moment of pinching difficulty pawned every article of my dress which would produce a shilling', so that now he had 'no stockings, no shoes, no neckhandkerchief, coat, waistcoat or hat'.[62]

McIndoe maintained the siege, with brief truces, throughout 1839 and 1840. He had ways of discovering when De Quincey was due to receive money from his mother or publishers and would pounce at the appropriate moment. Seeing his money snatched away like this drove De Quincey almost to despair. On 30 November 1840, when he had just gone to bed at eight in the morning 'after a hard night's labour in writing', McIndoe awoke him to demand five pounds. De Quincey had at least that much due from Blackwood, but sent a note asking Blackwood to send him only two pounds and to enclose a letter explaining firmly that he could not possibly send more. Blackwood did as he was told and sent a note tough enough to discourage McIndoe, but De Quincey himself took fright. Blackwood's note seemed too convincing: did he, perhaps, really mean it? More notes went to and fro before he was reassured. Robert Blackwood must have lost patience with all this nonsense, for on 4 December De Quincey was defending himself in a tone of innocent perplexity: 'I know not exactly what you mean by *"mixing you up in my affairs"*: as I am not aware of ever having done anything of the kind.'[63]

In the background the usual sounds of pursuit arose. De Quincey had been 'horned' again on 22 January 1840, and suits for debt were in progress. He was reasonably safe with McIndoe, who had reasons of his own for wanting to keep him out of gaol and fit for work, but he suffered anguish on account of another 'vast body' of his papers which Miss Miller of Holyrood was detaining against a debt of £175.4s.2d. representing not only unpaid rent but also the cost of milk and vegetables, small loans and the use of her credit at shops. The children had incurred part of this debt as they had occupied her lodgings for the past four years, and on 12 August they were forced to leave.[64] Luckily they had already found a house in more congenial surroundings, a cottage near the village of Lasswade seven miles outside Edinburgh, and 'Mavis Bush Cottage', as it was called, became the first landmark in a process whereby they took charge of De Quincey's affairs. Margaret, the eldest, was now twenty-two. She had spent the past four years taking care of her younger brothers and sisters. Now the youngest, Emily, was seven. Horace, twenty, was to go into the army: De Quincey was negotiating (with Mrs Quincey's help) to buy him a commission, and Francis was beginning a business career at Manchester in the employment of Strettel Kelsall, John Kelsall's son. Margaret was able to turn some of her attention to her father's plight. By taking charge of his mother's allowance and carefully husbanding the sums he sent from his literary earnings she managed to feed and clothe herself and Paul Fred, Florence and Emily, and make the cottage a comfortable refuge for her father, should he ever be free to use it. Above all she avoided contracting further debts, so that from 1840 onwards the legal harassment of the family gradually ceased.

Cornered by McIndoe at Princes Street, De Quincey could not yet go to Lasswade, but at least he was able to work. He may even have found his besieged condition conducive to writing, for despite frequent illness he produced much. He suffered from spells of insomnia and in February, after a three weeks' illness, lamented that his manuscripts had become 'so injured by acid medicines, port wine, and ink thrown upon them – that I am obliged to patch them, piece them, and in some instances rewrite them'. In the summer his eyes were troublesome. 'For two days and a half I have not been able to see a word,' he complained in July: 'large spots of colour obscure everything' – a condition he attributed, implausibly, to a fault in the gas lighting in his room. Portraits of De Quincey in his later years show a slight but distinct divergence of the eyes; perhaps other visual defects were also developing. Certainly he mentioned sometimes that he could read with only one eye at a time.[65] But with his usual astonishing stamina he worked on, as often as his sight would let him. On 26 February he told Blackwood that he had literally two quires (48 sheets) of rough draft for a paper on 'The Essenes' and had five other articles nearly finished. They probably included papers on Plato's *Republic*, on Aristotle's *Poetics* in relation to modern fiction, on English style, and on the war with China – subjects chosen, he said, 'because they require few books, which for me at present (who have no means of consulting any) is a main point'.[66]

The Chinese war – the 'First Opium War', as it is now called – had broken out in 1839 when the Chinese government had tried to suppress the British importation of opium from India. De Quincey left the right and wrongs of opium consumption out of the discussion and took a vehemently anti-Chinese line based on the view that the Chinese were primitive barbarians. Contact with the civilizing West – and Britain in particular – constituted their only hope of improvement, and (the Chinese being treacherous by nature) such contact must be made on the West's own terms, under the protection of military power, the only sanction the Chinese understood. The basis of this view was prejudice: De Quincey had always detested the very idea of China and was not disposed to examine the case impartially especially as the war's opponents in Britain were vehement in their denunciation of opium as a pernicious drug. Articles on political topics or the China question appeared in *Blackwood's* throughout the summer of 1840, often in the same numbers of the magazine as other pieces by De Quincey. Simultaneously the autobiographical papers continued in *Tait's*, as usual causing some embarrassment *vis à vis* Blackwood. De Quincey claimed repeatedly that he was not now writing for Tait, and that Tait was still publishing material written in an intensive period of work two years before. He told Robert Blackwood that he had been quarrelling with Tait and had disowned the papers, refusing the correct the proof or make revisions.[67] Perhaps he simply wanted to conceal the fact that he was serving two masters, but none of his work appeared in *Tait's* between 1841 and 1845, which suggests that their relationship had indeed deteriorated.

His work was now attracting a great deal of public interest, and he received an increasing volume of mail from his admirers. In April arrived a long poem, 'Sir Henry Tunstall', by a young man called Branwell Brontë. Perhaps De Quincey bestirred himself and answered Branwell's letter, for the Brontës are said to have written to him many times[68] – and in 1847 Charlotte, as 'Currer Bell', sent him a copy of the Brontë sisters' *Poems*.[69] Branwell had discovered the *Confessions* some years before, and in 1839 had turned to opium as a partial substitute for alcohol, perhaps on the Opium-Eater's assurance that it was a prophylactic against consumption and did not 'intoxicate'.[70] He and his sisters sent their work to De Quincey as to one who combined the characters of passionate autobiographer and sensitive critic.

Part III
Misery is the Talisman

12
Resurrection

In March 1841, De Quincey somehow gave McIndoe the slip and got himself and his load of papers and books, including eight sixteenth-century volumes of Giordano Bruno's works, out of the house and on the train to Glasgow, where he knew he could find asylum with John Pringle Nichol, Professor of Astronomy at the university. He had met Nichol first at an Edinburgh dinner party. After dinner, according to Nichol's son, 'he and Professor Nichol stood together in a corner, engaged in talk, when in a slow, measured tone, De Quincey said to his new acquaintance, "Dr. Nichol, can you lend me two-pence?" '[1] Nichol took this in good part, and ended by inviting De Quincey to stay. This invitation he now took up, arriving 'without money, baggage or a change of linen'.[2] Nichol welcomed him and he spent several trouble-free days, although he had to keep his whereabouts a secret and Blackwood was instructed to put letters for him into envelopes addressed to Nichol. 'Do not place my name at all on the *outside* cover,' he insisted. These were wise precautions. He had put Mrs Miller off the scent by telling her he would be back in a month, but before a month had passed McIndoe was suing him, as was one John Craig, clothier.

Nichol's home was no ordinary one, for he lived in the Glasgow Observatory on Garnet Hill. It was being equipped as the finest scientific observatory of its day and De Quincey, who disliked Glasgow itself, was delighted with his new refuge. A few years later he recorded his impressions of it, seeing it as a focus of those balanced but opposite forces whose presence in a landscape or an idea always excited him so much:

> What makes the Glasgow Observatory so peculiarly interesting is its position, connected with and overlooking so vast a city ... How tarnished with eternal canopies of smoke, and of sorrow, how dark with agitations of many orders, is the mighty town below! How serene, how quiet, how lifted above the confusion, and the roar, and the strifes of earth, is the solemn observatory that crowns the heights

342

overhead! And duly, at night, just when the toil of overwrought Glasgow is mercifully relaxing, then comes the summons to the labouring astronomer!³

He listened with interest to Nichol's talk of astronomy and some of their conversations provided material for his later prose fantasies on cosmological themes. (There must have been something in Nichol's approach to astronomy that caught the attention of writers: eight years later he lectured in New York and earned himself a mention in Poe's *Eureka*.) But on 16 March a large consignment of astronomical equipment arrived and De Quincey had to leave to make room for it. He went to stay with Lushington, the Professor of Greek, but fell ill soon after his arrival. How long he had known Lushington is not clear but they developed an intimate friendship. Two undated notes survive from De Quincey to Lushington. In one he expects a visit from the Professor and apologizes that his room is 'such a scene of wreck and confusion, that I am seriously ashamed to have it seen'. In the other, he plans a visit to Lushington, and declares himself 'satisfied from your manner that I may rely on your Sisters' pardoning anything too neglected or *outre* in my costume'.⁴ Clearly he felt he could trust Lushington.

For some days he was ill with what he called 'a violent affection, inflammatory and connected with strong delirium'. But he recovered, and was well enough to enjoy a visit from his son Horace, who was about to enter the Twenty-sixth (Cameronian) Regiment on a commission bought for him by his grandmother. De Quincey had somehow found more than £200 towards the cost of fitting him out, ensuring that Horace's start in life should not be hampered by his own state of perpetual bankruptcy.⁵ Horace went to join his regiment soon afterwards and in December he was ordered to China. De Quincey stayed with Lushington until 12 April, when he went to lodgings in the High Street, and then in June to 39, Renfield Street, where he lodged with the family of a Mr Youille or Yuille, who worked at the university. He was still in poor health. 'Were it not for my extreme temperance,' he reflected sententiously, 'I should long since have been dead'.⁶ But he was managing to write. In March he sent Blackwood an article on the German historian Niebuhr, and in April a paper called 'Russia in the Summer and Winter of 1812', another of his curious works of pseudo-scholarship. It purported to be a synthesis of scattered passages from the memoirs of Arndt, a German poet and historian of the Napoleonic era. In reality it was a free translation of one section of

Arndt's book, whose sparse narrative De Quincey had richly embroidered until the original was almost lost to sight. The end-product was Arndt's narrative as it should have been rather than as it was, as if De Quincey had found the book a disappointment and, unwilling to inflict a similar disappointment on his readers, had made good the deficiency from imagination.[7] In June he was compiling 'Homer and the Homeridae', an essay concocted (despite the usual academic camouflage) from various elementary works borrowed from the University Library, and spun out to great length to extract the maximum payment from Blackwood. He also produced his usual essays of political commentary for the March, September and November issues of *Maga*. A fairly disciplined manner of work had been forced on him by the Blackwoods, who since January had flatly refused to pay for unfinished articles.[8] The manuscripts and the Blackwoods' replies seem to have been carried mainly by the fourteen-year-old Paul Fred,[9] who must have made regular trips between Edinburgh and Glasgow on the newly built railway.

Despite De Quincey's move to Glasgow, his family at Lasswade still had to endure harassment on account of his debts. Margaret in particular endured great anxiety, and in June she suffered two haemorrhages and consumption was diagnosed. De Quincey, not unnaturally, became obsessed by the notion that she would die and that it would be his fault: 'This child will die, I foresee, under the misery of her situation [he wrote]. For she has no firmness to face it; – is entirely guiltless of wrong: and I, unless I can do something effectual and sudden, shall feel myself in part the cause.'[10] The idea that Margaret had 'no firmness', however, was quite untrue, a symptom of De Quincey's growing tendency to sentimentalize over the supposed weakness of the female sex. Margaret, with her usual resilience, recovered from her illness and continued, at the age of twenty-three, to run a house and look after her younger brother and sisters. Her father was in a more precarious position. He, unlike his children, could go to prison for his debts, and he began to accumulate new ones as he lodged with the Yuilles. In September he told the Blackwoods that he had 'planned and partly executed' a book[11] – probably on economics – but had been forced to abandon it and return to magazine articles, which brought quick money. In November he was in such straits that he submitted an article with this note:

My dear Sir,
    I am in the situation of a man holding on by his hands to the

burning deck of a ship. With difficulty indeed I can keep my position even for 24 hours.

Do me therefore the kindness, when you have decided, to report.

Yours ever,

T. De Q.

This is the end[12]

Fortunately Blackwood liked the enclosure and sent ten pounds at once. Within a few days, however, De Quincey was attacked by erysipelas in his legs and feet and stepped up his opium intake to help him endure the pain.[13] This in turn brought other unpleasant symptoms and reduced his ability to work. Nonetheless, he kept at it and wrote several more essays on classical themes, chosen, perhaps, because the necessary books could be borrowed from Lushington. They appeared in *Blackwood's* during 1842, interspersed with political pieces: 'Sir Robert Peel's Policy' in April, articles on the agitation against the Corn Laws in August and September and a three-part exposition of economics, 'Ricardo Made Easy', in September, October and December. De Quincey was fervent in his support of the Corn Laws, which maintained the prices of imported grain at a high level, partly because of Ricardo's argument that a high price for corn benefited the country landowner at the expense of the manufacturer, and partly because of his general prejudice against popular reforms, on which an interesting light is shed by a letter he wrote to Blackwood on 16 September 1842. He was writing, he said, an essay on the working class in relation to revolutionary movements. It would be based upon many years' discreet observation of working-class attitudes:

> I *watched* in chance conversations; and in conversations that were *not* chance conversations I trained them and doctored them for the express manifestation of the true secret dispositions among the working poor. To a man I look upon the working poor, Scottish or English, as latent Jacobins – *biding their* time.[14]

If indeed these dire suspicions were ever embodied in an article, it has not survived.

As usual he was concerned about the quality of his work. He always hated having to work fast, and explained to Robert Blackwood:

> Whenever I have not time to let the thoughts organise their own arrangement, gradually to settle by interchanges and transpositions into the proper situations, – then the relations between sentence and sentence, thought and thought, are often harsh and abrupt: the differ-

ent ideas are not so placed owing to hurry as to lead fluently and naturally – each into the other; and that condition of the thoughts is precisely what makes the total result appear bad in composition.[15]

This in turn was related to his view that the fundamental problem in prose style was the management of the transitions between sentences. This factor alone, he held, made the difference between elegant and slovenly prose. His ideal, stated in the 1840 essay on 'Style', was a 'graceful succession of sentences, long intermingled with short, each modifying the other, and arising musically by links of spontaneous connexion'.[16] When, as so often happened, illness distracted him so that (as he put it) 'I frequently lost the whole thread of my ideas during the progress of a *longish* art[icle]', he suffered aesthetic as well as physical anguish.

At their worst, De Quincey's troubles always seem to have partaken of the ridiculous. Throughout 1842 his gravest problem was not debt or even erysipelas, but constipation, a well-known effect of morphine. For years his digestive system had been a battleground between laudanum and various purgatives, but for some reason the problem now became especially serious, as numerous plaintive notes to Robert Blackwood testify. Perhaps shortage of money was partly to blame. On 19 March he told Blackwood that his 'long habit of tampering with the digestive organs by extravagant delays in taking medicine (which to me costs 6d. in each separate case from the inefficacy of ordinary medicines as against laudanum) has for many weeks menaced me with evil. Inflammation of the bowels, apoplexy I believe, &c, sometimes occur.' On 1 June he wrote again, mentioning that he still had erysipelas (or 'purpurea', as the doctor had now re-diagnosed it) and that the inner deadlock was now lasting for ten days at a time. Only Seidlitz Powders, he explained, would shift it, and it took three doses. Would Blackwood send him immediately a quire of Scottish writing paper and twenty-one packets of Powders? Then, he said with satisfaction, 'I should be set up in business'.[17] There were, however, precautions to be observed. Blackwood must be sure to conceal the Powders inside the writing paper, as he usually bought them from his landlord, who interpreted continued purchase of Powders as a sign that De Quincey was still solvent. If the landlord found out that Blackwood was sending them he would conclude that his lodger was penniless and might turn him out! Blackwood must have done as he was asked, for De Quincey's problem was soon replaced by its opposite, which brought difficulties of a new kind, best reported in his own words: 'In the whole system of houses, to which this house is attached, there exists but one *Templum Cloacinae*. Now imagine the fiend driving a man thither thro' 8 and 10 hours successively. Such a man becomes himself a public nuisance, and is in some danger of being removed by assassination.'[18] So he left his lodgings in October to find a house more generously provided with sanitary arrangements.

At the end of the year De Quincey received the news that Horace had died of a fever on 27 August at a place called Chich Choo, apparently near Canton in China. He had reached the rank of Lieutenant. No reliable record of De Quincey's reaction has survived. (John Wilson later claimed that he had helped arrange the funeral, and that the bereaved father had shown little grief, saying only that he had warned Horace all along not to go to China. This account may possibly be true, but Wilson told it among several malicious stories against De Quincey, some of them certainly false.)[19] Horace had left debts amounting to seventy-five pounds. It was thought at first that there might be some prize money due to him, but this turned out not to be the case as he had arrived too late to take part in the siege of Canton. De Quincey could not meet the debt immediately and wrote to the War Office explaining the situation and offering to pay by instalment all that was due. Someone at the War Office (having no idea of his correspondent's fame) made an internal memorandum: 'His letter is rather a Curiosity, but it is obviously written by a Man of taste and talent. The arrangemt. which he proposes is highly creditable to him.' So Horace's effects were sold and the proceeds sent to his father, who gradually settled his son's small debts and felt more than ever confirmed in his bitter hatred of China and all things Chinese.[20]

By the spring of 1843 it was becoming clear to De Quincey and his children that he could no longer manage on his own in Glasgow and that the most sensible thing would be for him to join the family at Lasswade. He was able to work – he was writing the book on political economy which he had been planning for some twenty-five years – but his ailment showed no signs of improvement. As well as the 'purpurea' he now had gout, and 'even the touch of a muslin handkerchief' on his feet caused him pain.[21] In May Francis came to stay for a few days and found him in a state of helpless chaos, hardly able to move about his room, surrounded by mounds of papers which he was incapable of sorting out. Francis helped him extract some of the riches buried there and on 16 May De Quincey could send off an article, telling Blackwood that 'without his aid, from my dire immobility, I never could have separated the papers fm. the masses of others with which by long lying about they had confounded'.²² No doubt Francis also helped him assemble the scattered pieces of the little book on political economy which, amazingly, he had managed to complete. After Francis had left, the last part was posted unstamped. De Quincey apologized for the fact that it would cost Blackwood three shillings, but explained that he simply had no money for a stamp.

On 22 May Yuille, seeing that De Quincey would never catch up with the rent he owed, gave him notice to quit. He left in June and joined his children in their cottage at Lasswade. He found it a great comfort to have his family near at hand. Not only were they able to look after him and help him with the practical matters he was too ill or distracted to handle, but their presence gave him a sense of emotional security. His study was on the ground floor of the two-storey cottage, and the sitting-room where Margaret, Florence and Emily spent most of their time was overhead. He could hear their voices and often the music of their piano without breaking the solitude to which he had become accustomed. The one thing to mar his satisfaction was that he had had to leave his beloved papers behind with Yuille as hostage for unpaid bills.

The cottage itself stands today almost unchanged in its peaceful surroundings on the steep road that winds through wooded country between the villages of Polton and Lasswade. A small, square, grey-stone building with eight rooms, it must have been comparatively new when the De Quinceys moved in, and seems to have been built around 1820. There cannot have been much room to spare, for as well as De Quincey and his three daughters it housed Paul Fred, Francis, who began in 1845 to study medicine at Edinburgh University, walking the seven miles there and back for his lectures each day, and old John Simpson, who in January was lingering on, dying (according to De Quincey) from 'ossification of the entire intestines – heart, stomach, lungs &c.', and could not move without 'two young men' – his two grandsons, no doubt – to lift him. The only drawback in the situation of Mavis Bush Cottage was its tenuous links of communication with the nearest post office at Lasswade, a couple of miles away. De Quincey feared for his manuscripts and proofs, as mail reached the cottage by a motley selection of messengers including at times the postmistress's servant girl and a six-year-old-boy.²³ But nothing seems to have gone astray and De Quincey kept Blackwood supplied with copy. By July he was hard at work again, writing a second paper on the British aristocracy, and was ready to commit himself to other projects, but was hampered by 'the ancient difficult[y] of devising subjects'. He asked Blackwood if he had any books for review. Strauss's *Leben Jesu* might make a good subject, he mused: it was said to be making 'a commotion' on the Continent. His whole being was now so subdued to journalism that, given a subject and sufficient time, he could produce the required quantity of words with near-mechanical reliability. The days when he could not get started on an essay were long past. Some of his letters supply curious illustrations of this facility. In a letter to Hill written as early as 1830 he had wandered far from the matter in question and pulled himself up, after several hundred words, with, 'Pardon me this digression, I had forgotten for the moment that I was writing a letter. To return to the subject –.'[24] In a letter of 1842 to Francis, who had been reading the *Letters of Junius*, he produced a complete critical essay on the *Letters*, as if oblivious of the fact that he was writing to his own son. The tone of the letter as a whole is amusing and affectionate but the 'Junius' paragraphs could be set up in type unchanged as a *Blackwood's* article. It seems that part of his mind had become a finely adjusted instrument which, once set going, would turn out page after page of eloquent De Quinceyan prose until it ran down.

The 'ancient problem' of a subject was finally solved for him, however, by a chain of events that began with a severe attack of depression accompanied by physical illness:

> Why I know not [he wrote to Lushington], but for some cause during the summer months the weight of insufferable misery and mere abhorrence of life increased; but also it fluctuated. A conviction fell upon me that immense exercise might restore me. But you will imagine my horror when, with that conviction, I found, precisely in my earliest efforts, my feet gave way, and the misery in all its strength came back. Every prospect I had of being laid up as a cripple for life. Much and deeply I pondered on this, and I gathered myself up as if for a final effort. For if that fate were established, farewell I felt for me to all hope of restoration. Eternally the words sounded in my ears: 'Suffered and was buried'.[25]

A doctor had told him that the purpurea might affect the circulation of blood in his legs and lead to mortification. Yet experience had convinced him that he could alleviate his periodic bouts of opium misery only by strenuous walking. He resolved on a policy of 'kill or cure'.

349

Pacing out the tiny triangular cottage garden as soon as he was able to walk again, he found that one circuit of its perimeter measured forty-four yards, 'so that forty rounds were exactly required for one mile'. He began to exercise there daily, doggedly walking round and round the garden, keeping count of his circuits by placing pebbles on the rungs in the back of a chair to form a primitive abacus.[26] Before long he was averaging eleven or twelve miles a day so that, as he said proudly, 'I had within ninety days walked a thousand miles.'

At the same time he decided that a fundamental cause of his afflictions was that he was 'irregular as to laudanum' and 'this also', he says, 'I reformed'. As usual when he discusses his struggles with opium, his account is confused: shifting as to dates, blurred in matters of detail. Perhaps the reform was merely a stabilization of his dose. It seems likely, however, that this was accompanied by some reduction. Certainly he was soon to make a determined effort at drastically cutting his opium intake. Whatever the 'reform' may have been, it led at first to no improvement in his mental condition. 'For six months no results; one dreary uniformity of report – absolute desolation; misery so perfect that too surely I perceived, and no longer disguised from myself, the impossibility of continuing to live under so profound a blight. I now kept my journal as one who in a desert island is come to his last day's provisions.'[27] He began to fear that he was going mad; indeed, he felt he was mad already. 'I had known all along . . . that I was not in my perfect mind. Lunacy causes misery . . . But also misery, and above all physical misery, working by means of intellectual remembrances and persecution of thoughts, no doubt sometimes inversely causes lunacy. To that issue I felt all things tended.' He began to think of suicide: 'enormous irritability' and 'the consciousness of increasing weakness', he says, 'added to my desolation of heart. I felt that no man could continue to struggle.' He thought of Coleridge, and remembered how he had often heard him speak, in periods of depression, 'of the dying away from him of all hope'. For the first time he felt he understood what Coleridge had meant. Increasingly he compared his experience to the other man's and the comparison led him to a very strange revelation – strange because to us it will seem no revelation at all. Through his own 'ruin', he says,

> I looked into and read the latter states of Coleridge. His chaos I comprehended by the darkness of my own, and both were the work of laudanum. It is as if ivory carvings and elaborate fretwork and fair enamelling should be found with worms and ashes amongst coffins

and the wrecks of some forgotten life or some abolished nature. In parts and fractions eternal creations are carried on, but the nexus is wanting, and life and the central principle ... are wanting.[28]

Recognizing in himself the states he had seen in Coleridge forced him to one conclusion. 'Laying all things together, I returned obstinately to the belief that laudanum was at the root of all this unimaginable hell.' If this really struck him as a new insight, it argues a staggering degree of self-deception. Yet that it was so seems to be confirmed by a note written, probably, on Christmas night, 1844:

> This night, Wednesday, December 25, about 7 p.m., has first solemnly revealed to me that I am and have long been under a curse, all the greater for being physically and by effort endurable, and for hiding itself, *i.e.*, playing in and out from all offices of life at every turn of every moment. O, dreadful! by degrees infinitely worse than leprosy – than – But oh, what signifies the rhetoric of a case so sad! Conquer it I must by exercise unheard of, or it will conquer me.[29]

Another jotting, phrased apparently for inclusion in some future publication, seems to pursue the parallel with Coleridge:

> Not fear nor terror, but inexpressible misery, is the last portion of the opium-eater. At certain stages it is not so. We know of a man called X – who has often jumped out of bed – bounced like a column of quicksilver – at midnight, fallen on his knees and cried out, while the perspiration ran down his wasted face, and his voice waked all the house, 'O Jesus Christ, be merciful to me a sinner!' – so unimaginable had been the horror which sleep opened to his eyes ... But, generally, in its later stages, it is not horror, it is not fear: all these are swallowed up in misery.[30]

Whether X- represents Coleridge or De Quincey himself, the note (apart from the grotesque image of the quicksilver) paraphrases 'The Pains of Sleep':

> But yesternight I prayed aloud
> In anguish and in agony,
> Upstarting from the fiendish crowd
> Of shapes and thoughts that tortured me ...

Once he had confronted the fact that laudanum was the root cause of his troubles, the question naturally occurred, ' "Why then not, if only by way of experiment, leave it off?" Alas! that had become impossible. Then I descended to a hundred drops. Effects so dreadful and utterly unconjectured by medical men succeeded that I was glad to get back under shelter. Not the less I persisted; silently, surely descended the ladder,' and on Friday 23 February 1844, 'I might say for the first time, in scriptural words, "And the man was sitting clothed and in his right mind." ' Madness and misery were gone. 'Illimitable seemed the powers restored to me.' This state of well-being lasted a mere two days, but, says De Quincey, 'I drew hope from the omen,' and 'now, having tried the key, and found it the true key, even though a blast of wind has blown the door to again, no jot of spirits has gone away from me: I shall arise as one risen from the dead.'[31] He continued the struggle now hopefully, the more so as he had discerned through his torments something which held 'an interest for all the world – that I am certain of this, viz., that misery is the talisman by which man communicates with the world outside of our fleshy world'.[32]

The wealth of religious allusion in this account makes it clear that for De Quincey his fight against opium had a spiritual significance. It was a journey through Hell, or at least Purgatory. His plight at the beginning of the ordeal is one of death and entombment: 'Suffered and was buried' echoes the reference to Christ's trial, crucifixion and burial in the Apostles' Creed. The soul confronts not only bodily death but the mental Hell of madness: 'clothed and in his right mind' is a phrase from the description in St Mark's Gospel of the healing by Jesus of the man possessed by an unclean spirit, haunting the tombs in the country of the Gadarenes. At last, through endurance and perhaps prayer he sees the 'door' of the tomb open and moves confidently towards his resurrection, bearing in one hand the 'key' to that door and in the other a 'talisman', forged from his suffering, which will enable him to communicate with 'the world outside of our fleshy world'. The fruits of this season in Hell were a reduction of his opium intake to between four and six grains a day, a level he rarely exceeded for the remainder of his life; an improvement in his general health; and a new spate of creativity which itself helps us to understand the psychological experience he had undergone. Since 1838 his work had become less personal and less interesting. Politics, economics and classical scholarship had formed the bulk of it and the impetus of the autobiographical essays had run down. Now, in July and August of 1844,[33] in the midst of his renewed battle against addiction, he suddenly began writing what was to become *'Suspiria de Profundis*: being a Sequel to the Confessions of an English Opium-Eater'. This new work was to be a series of interrelated prose poems, exploring the worlds of dream and reverie, tracing the deliberate metamorphoses whereby experiences of the outer life became transformed into the matter of dream, interwoven by association, emotion and premonition into complex motifs or 'involutes' which embodied the hidden patterns of life and the soul.

Dream and autobiography were, of course, De Quincey's lifelong preoccupations, and had provided most of the material for the *Confessions*. Intimations that the mind could be fully developed only through suffering had made themselves felt in the autobiographical pieces written for Tait. Reveries and dreams tinged with a numinous quality had been a frequent experience, probably due in about equal proportions to opium and an introspective, imaginative temperament. The *Suspiria* drew together all these concerns. There can be little doubt that it was begun under pressure of the sudden upsurge of dreaming produced by a partial withdrawal from opium. That he was still in the habit of noting down his more striking dreams is rendered probable by his statement, made in 1847, that he was skilful at writing notes in the dark when he could not find his matches.[34] His periods of intense dreaming seem generally to have been symptoms of opium withdrawal and at these times his mind had a strong tendency to relive past experience, especially unhappy episodes from childhood and youth. Naturally enough, therefore, he was led to the view that the human mind, although *in* time, is not altogether *of* it. Like Proust he felt that the mind was not bound by the apparently linear flow of time, and that given the right conditions it could recapture the personal past in all its fullness. When De Quincey spoke of 'rising from the dead' in 1843, he was not exaggerating. For the third time, at the age of fifty-eight, the artist had arisen and displaced the hack-journalist to go once more in quest of the inner meaning of his life.

More mundane concerns were not entirely neglected. In February he finished a preface for his book on economics and in March it appeared, published by Blackwood. It was far from being the 'Prolegomena to All Future Systems of Political Economy' which he had conceived so long ago, but on a humbler level – as a basic outline of economics – *The Logic of Political Economy* was a useful book, and John Stuart Mill gave it a perceptive review in the *Westminster*. As an exponent of Ricardo's ideas, he thought, De Quincey 'is very successful, and would be more so if he had not a strange delight in drawing illustrations from subjects ten times more abtruse than what they are designed to illustrate'. He emphasized 'what pleasant reading De

Quincey can make of a dry scientific discussion . . . His writings treat of a hundred things besides their ostensible subjects' and are 'enriched with many acute remarks . . . on any subject, important or trifling, from the qualities of turbot to the laws of nature'.[35]

Francis had to write to Blackwood for a copy. His father had promised him one, he said, 'but tho' he thinks the greatest reliance ought to be placed in his promises, I am so stupid as to think that if I wait until he allows me to read it, the book will remain a mystery'.[36] De Quincey was still locked in mortal combat with opium and might be excused a little procrastination. On 5 May he told Blackwood, 'By a long and determined weaning from Laud. I have drawn myself down for 6 last weeks from purgatory into the shades of a deeper abyss. – Hence as to other things I am driven to the last gasp.' He sent part of an article and asked for immediate payment. The rest was sent next day. 'It is written with unusual care,' he asserted, 'and, from my dreadful condition as to laudm. in the 6 months' martyrdom I have been weathering, – has cost me unusual time.'[37] A letter to the minor author Mary Russell Mitford, who had become a friend of the family, gives a vivid glimpse of the psychological state with which he had to contend. Apoligizing for not having answered several of Miss Mitford's letters, he explains that he has actually written parts of several replies, but that their fate is not known to Margaret, who generally handles his correspondence for him.

> No purpose could be answered by my vainly endeavouring to make intelligible for my daughters what I cannot make intelligible for myself – the indecipherable horror that night and day broods over my nervous system. One effect of this is to cause, at uncertain intervals, such whirlwinds of impatience as precipitate me violently, whether I will or no, into acts that would seem insanities, but are not such in fact, as my understanding is under no delusion. Whatever I may be inviting becomes suddenly overspread with a dark frenzy of horror. I am using words, perhaps, that are tautologic; but it is because no language can give expression to the sudden storm of frightful revelations opening upon me from an eternity not coming, but past and irrevocable. Whatever I may have been writing is suddenly wrapt, as it were, in one sheet of consuming fire – the very paper is poisoned to my eyes. I cannot endure to look at it, and I sweep it away into vast piles of unfinished letters, or inchoate essays begun and interrupted under circumstances the same in kind, though differing unaccountably in degree. I live quite alone in my study, so no-one witnesses these paroxysms . . . At the worst the children put it down amongst my foibles, for which I am sure they find filial excuses.[38]

He compared this 'horror' to the depression he had suffered in 1812 (the time of Kate Wordsworth's death) but was unwilling or unable to define it further.

Essays on politics and foreign affairs formed the bulk of his published output in 1844. He was working on *Suspiria* but none of it yet saw the light. In August he was awaiting a review copy of Gillman's unfinished *Life of Coleridge*[39] and the result, 'Coleridge and Opium Eating', appeared in *Blackwood's* in January 1845.

De Quincey tried to evaluate the effect of opium on Coleridge's life and work, concluding that although opium 'creates spasms of irregular exertion' it 'defeats the *steady* habit of exertion' and had 'killed Coleridge as a poet . . . but proportionately it roused and stung by misery his metaphysical instincts into more spasmodic life'.[40] Opium had made Coleridge a philosopher. At the end of the essay De Quincey attempted to define more precisely than before the importance of opium to the visionary temperament. Certain people, he argued, were 'preconformed' to the power of opium, and 'to that . . . class whose nervous sensibilities vibrate to their profoundest depths under the first touch of the angelic poison, even as a lover's ear thrills on hearing unexpectedly the voice of her whom he loves, opium is the Amreeta cup of beatitude . . . It is in the faculty of mental vision, it is in the increased power of dealing with the shadowy and the dark, that the characteristic virtue of opium lies.'[41] And he hinted that the subject would be explored further in a 'sequel or finale' to the *Confessions*.

In the March 1845 number of *Blackwood's* there duly appeared the first instalment of *Suspiria de Profundis*, the new work which De Quincey hoped would prove the crown of his literary career. He had poured his heart into it and it had cost him, he told Lushington, 'seven months of severe labour'. He regarded *Suspiria* as 'a new *Opium Confessions*' and contemplating the proof of the first part, entitled 'The Affliction of Childhood', judged it 'very greatly superior' to the original *Confessions*. 'These final "Confessions" ', he thought, 'are the *ne plus ultra*, as regards the feeling and the power to express it, which I can ever hope to attain.'[42] Other friends who had read the manuscript, including Wilson, agreed. The four 'parts' were to appear in five instalments in March, April, May, June and July. They would then, he said, 'be gathered into a volume without any delay, and introduced by a letter to my three daughters'.

Why this straightforward and potentially lucrative plan was not carried out remains obscure, but the probable reason is that De Quincey was counting on a larger slice of the magazine than Blackwood was willing to give him, so that *Suspiria* appeared much more slowly than intended, and became a cause of bad feeling between author and publisher until it was temporarily abandoned. 'Part I' of the work appeared in three pieces, in March, April and June; some of 'Part II' appeared in July; and thereafter nothing of De Quincey's went into the magazine until 1849, when 'The English Mail-Coach', a long essay closely related to *Suspiria*, appeared in October and December.

Suspiria de Profundis contained the essence distilled from many years of introspection and psychological speculation. The process whereby experience might become transformed into dream was vividly displayed in the first part, which told of Elizabeth's death and its traumatic effect upon his own emotional life and presented two sets of 'dream-echoes' from these events, one dating from 1804, the other from 1845. The implication was that the gift of 'dreaming magnificently' had been conferred by childhood sorrow. A second factor was solitude, and De Quincey asserted that, 'No man ever will unfold the capacities of his own intellect who does not at least checker his life with solitude.' The increasing difficulty of attaining solitude in the modern world seemed to him an ominous sign, for

> The machinery for dreaming planted in the human brain was not planted for nothing. That faculty, in alliance with the mystery of darkness, is the one great tube through which man communicates with the shadowy. And the dreaming organ, in connexion with the heart, the eye, and the ear, composes the magnificent apparatus which forces the infinite into the chambers of a human brain, and throws dark reflections from eternities below all life upon the mirrors of that mysterious *camera obscura* – the sleeping mind.[43]

Amongst the 'dark reflections' De Quincey called up from his own dreams were the four women whom he named 'Levana and Our Ladies of Sorrow'. He claimed to have dreamed of them repeatedly during his years at Oxford and now he was able to identify them, albeit cryptically. Despite the obvious Catholic affinities of the title he gave them, he associated the Ladies with the three Fates, three Furies and three Graces. One was Our Lady of Tears, who presided over bereavement and mourning. The second, Our Lady of Sighs, he connected with the pariah, the outcast, the houseless vagrant. Both of these Ladies clearly represented aspects of his own experience. The third is far more difficult to interpret. She is Our Lady of Darkness, and De Quincey tells us,

> Her kingdom is not large, or else no flesh should live; but within that kingdom all power is hers . . . She is the defier of God. She also is the mother of lunacies, and the suggestress of suicides . . . she can approach only those in whom a profound nature has been upheaved by central convulsions; in whom the heart trembles and the brain rocks under conspiracies of tempest from without and tempest from within.[44]

It seems impossible to discover precisely what this third Lady meant to him. Clearly she had some profound personal significance and it seems likely that she embodied experiences connected with opium such as that 'storm of frightful revelations opening upon me from . . . eternity' of which he had tried to tell Miss Mitford. Certainly no passage in De Quincey's writings indicates more clearly his sense of belonging to a secret order of outcast initiates, chosen by powers outside the confines of normal human experience. Translating, he says, 'out of the signs which (except in Dreams) no man reads', he attributes to Our Lady of Tears a speech in which she presents him to her sisters and explains, as clearly as it can be explained, their role in his life. She herself has tempted him (through the death of Elizabeth) to fall in love with death, to 'worship the worm, and pray to the wormy grave'; the Lady of Sighs is to 'season him' in loneliness for the terrible third sister, who is commanded to

> Banish the frailties of hope; wither the relenting of love; scorch the fountains of tears; curse him as only *thou* canst curse. So shall he be accomplished in the furnace; so shall he see the things that ought *not* to be seen, sights that are abominable, and secrets that are unutterable. So shall he read elder truths, sad truths, grand truths, fearful truths. So shall be rise again *before* he dies. And so shall our commission be accomplished which from God we had – to plague his heart until we had unfolded the capacities of his spirit.[45]

From the beginning *Suspiria*'s publication was accompanied by violent argument. The better to conduct the controversy, and to be on hand for the proof correction of his important new work, De Quincey had moved to Edinburgh, lodging at 71, Clerk Street.[46] On 27 March, as the second instalment was going to press, he was protesting fiercely at the amputation of its concluding section, 'Levana and Our Ladies of Sorrow'. 'This opium article', he protested, was 'perilously dependent' upon a relaxation of the normal upper limit of sixteen pages. The rule was often waived for other papers: why not for this? 'There are many passages which will lose all – not only effect – but even *meaning*, if torn away from the context.'[47] But John Blackwood (his brother had recently died and he was running the firm alone) stuck to his rule, unwilling to risk having his magazine dominated for months by De Quincey's 'impassioned prose' and perhaps afraid that the public would find the new distillation too rich and strange for its taste. At the end of March De Quincey had an attack of pleurisy, but rest, a mustard-plaster and the air at Leith revived him[48] and on 22 April he was fighting fit again, castigating Blackwood for postponing the third instalment until June: 'Now to the *Suspiria*. I feel it will be a knock-down blow if they are interrupted. The disgust of readers from a balking, when expectation has at all been encouraged by the promises thrown out of coming effects of shocks, is profound.'[49] But Blackwood insisted, De Quincey swallowed his irritation and by 19 May he was revising the June instalment to bring it as close as possible to perfection:

> From 6 a.m. on Sat., – also fm. 6 a.m. on yesterday, – also fm. 6 a.m. this day, I have done no one thing but correct. I have declined all going out for this purpose. But of all the tasks I ever had in my life, it is – from the aerial and shadowy nat[ure] of the composition – the most over-whelming.[50]

Blackwood, as usual, was more interested in the problem of space and wanted to cut out a lengthy footnote, so there was more argument. In July one or both of the parties tired of the tug-of-war and for a while no more *Suspiria* appeared, though a reconciliation had been approached by November, when De Quincey promised Blackwood the rest of the series, 'making in all from 72 to 80 pp. of the Magazine'.[51] What became of this material is not known.

The break with Blackwood coincided roughly with a hasty departure by De Quincey from his lodgings, which he vacated without leaving an address.[52] This was probably connected with debt. He had not been 'horned' for five years now and Margaret had sorted out most of his financial tangles but there were still bills outstanding. On 30 April he had paid an unexpected visit, late at night, to some friends who knew him well enough to suspect an ulterior motive. Leaving the drawing-room to investigate, his hostess had found two bailiffs waiting in the hall.[53] He could not afford to be long without work so, as usual when he had fallen out with Blackwood, he went to Tait, who welcomed the prodigal with open arms. Beginning in September, something of De Quincey's appeared in *Tait's Magazine* every month until the following summer. He probably wrote more than Tait would print: Bertram claims that ten or a dozen papers were never used, for De Quincey was sometimes 'seized with extraordinary fits of industry' when contributions came in at the rate of two a week and had to be kept back for fear of over-exposure.[54]

In September Tait published 'On Wordsworth's Poetry', one of his finest critical essays, an attempt at defining the characteristic strengths of Wordsworth's achievement: his choice of subjects exhibiting conflict of mood and motive, the sharpness of his observation of nature, 'the extent of his sympathy with what is *really* permanent in human feelings'. Wordsworth was now Queen Victoria's Poet Laureate; Dorothy, suffering from advanced arteriosclerosis, was a helpless invalid living in mental twilight. The time of their intimacy with De Quincey at Grasmere now seemed very distant, and a generalized warning – 'Put not your trust in the intellectual princes of your age; form no connections too close with any who live only in the atmosphere of admiration and praise' – is the only reverberation in the essay of his disappointment at the failure of the relationship from which he had expected so much. But his confidence in Wordsworth's poetic gift was as full as ever. From first to last De Quincey had never wavered in seeing Wordsworth as the major poet of his day, one to be named in the same breath as Euripides or Milton.

Of his other contributions to *Tait's* the most interesting was a fanciful piece called 'The System of the Heavens as Revealed by Lord Rosse's Telescopes', which appeared in September 1846. It was the fruit of his visits to Professor Nichol, who had discussed astronomy with him and allowed him to inspect the night sky through the telescope which had forced him out of his room at the Observatory. Nichol had been a leading proponent of the 'Nebular Hypothesis' which argued that the nebulae were vast clouds of vapour slowly coalescing to make stars. In 1845 the Earl of Rosse, with the aid of telescopes more powerful than any previously used, had examined some nebulae and reported that they were not clouds of vapour but large groups of stars, apparently cloudy because of their vast distance from the earth. The discovery was much debated at the Nichols' dinner table. On the basis of these conversations, and an illustration of the Nebula in Orion from a book by Nichol, De Quincey worked up a bizarre prose poem in which he interpreted the nebula as the head of a vast demon, full of 'brutalities unspeakable', whose revelation by the telescope he compared to 'the reversing of some heavenly doom', or the opening of the Seals in the Book of Revelation. In time, further reports from Rosse contradicted the earlier findings, producing more accurate maps of the nebula and taking away the 'factual' basis for the essay. De Quincey was untroubled. His attitude to his scientific material is revealed by his reaction to Nichol's misgivings when the paper was to be republished in 1854. Nichol warned him that, 'Your resolution of the Nebula into something very different from Matter was hardly so effective as might have been . . . The Nebula, as now known, is wholly different from what it seemed then. Its form is not the same – thanks to the great telescopes, which have revealed so much more of it, and its composition is not now a mystery.'[55] De Quincey could not see the point of this objection. 'Dr Nichol perplexes me,' he confessed. 'That a new stage of progress has altered the appearances, as doubtless further stages will alter them, concerns me nothing . . . Nichol apparently misunderstood the case as though it required a *real* phenomenon for its basis'[56] – an emphatic formulation of the distinction between poetry and science.

He continued to work at recovering his health. His legs and feet were better, and he was careful to walk a minimum of six miles a day, of which one and a half were covered before breakfast. He must have made an odd figure: when not trudging around the garden at Lasswade he walked watch in hand to estimate the distance covered.[57] He was rising early, and after years of sleeping until noon suddenly found that he was waking too early. From nine o'clock, his hour of waking had retreated gradually to eight, then to seven, and at last to three, which gave him only three and a half hours' sleep.[58] But he seemed none the worse for it.

On 8 January 1846, his mother died. She was over ninety years old and for a long time had been living a retired life, forgetful, almost stone-deaf and sheltered by her daughter Jane from anything that might cause her excitement. De Quincey had not seen her for some fifteen years, and although we know nothing about his reaction to her death, we may guess that he was not very deeply affected. She had long ceased to play a major role in his emotional life. She left her home and personal property to Jane, who had not married, and the income from her capital, about £200 a year, to Thomas, who thus, at the age of sixty, at last reaped the benefit of his father's fortune. It was not much, but it represented an increase of £100 over the allowance he had been receiving and helped to make his life a little more secure. But to say that either the money, or his new home at Lasswade, brought an increase in physical comfort would be to misjudge De Quincey. Comfort and stable domesticity had been withheld from him for so long that he had no real preference for them, and he left Lasswade cheerfully in December 1846, when *Tait's Magazine* was bought by the proprietors of the *North British Daily Mail* and moved to Glasgow. Colin Rae-Brown, business manager of the *Mail*, negotiated with De Quincey about the move, which seems to have been proposed mainly so that he could write for both the *Magazine* and the *Mail*. De Quincey stipulated that he would go to Glasgow only for six months, and insisted that Rae-Brown find him cheap rooms in an area close to the offices but not heavily polluted by smoke from the factories, which he said had affected his lungs the last time he had lived there.

Rae-Brown found him lodgings with a Mrs Tosh in Rotten Row, where he settled down to work. His ways had not changed: he still sent his copy in fragments and, says Rae-Brown, 'frequently kept half-set articles standing and printers idle'. George Troup, the new editor of *Tait's*, had his own way of handling De Quincey. When he could not get him to the office to look over his proof, Troup would send word that 'he was revising the proof, and *would do his best with the Greek quotations*' which usually brought De Quincey round fast enough. Sometimes other measures were needed.[59] Once, when the errand-boy had come back for a second time to report that 'the old gentleman had no' got oot of his bedroom yet' Rae-Brown went to investigate and

> found, on entering De Quincey's room, that he was either uncommonly sound asleep or in a state of stupor. He lay stretched out on the hearth-rug before the parlour fire-grate (his bedroom entering off that apartment), clad in an old dressing-gown, with no stockings on his feet, and merely a pair of thin, loose slippers over his toes. 'I am sure the puir body's deid!' the landlady exclaimed, as I bent down to ascertain if he was really alive.[60]

He was, and Rae-Brown found the end of his article, tied up in red tape and addressed to the 'Editor of Tait's Magazine', nearby. He took it and left De Quincey to his dreams. Now that he was out of Margaret's reach De Quincey's clothes soon deteriorated to their accustomed state, and when he paid an unexpected visit to W.B. Robertson, a clergyman with whom he had made friends at the McIndoes', Robertson's landlady took him for a tramp and sent him on his way, not even allowing him to stay to write a note for his friend, who was absent on business.[61] The critic George Gilfillan called on him and reported that he lived in 'a mean room, such as students were wont to live in for five or six shillings a week',[62] but that he seemed happy enough there. By that time he may have been back at the Yuilles', for when Mrs Tosh's grandson caught scarlet fever he decided to move out and revealed, to Rae-Brown's astonishment, that he had been 'paying the rent of apartments in Renfield Street for a number of years. Many valuable books and papers', he added, 'should still be there.'[63] So, after a short sojourn in an hotel, he returned to his old lodgings and his treasure trove of half-forgotten papers.

From a business associate, Rae-Brown became a friend and enjoyed taking care of his eccentric contributor. Like so many others he was charmed by De Quincey's rich flow of curiously learned conversation and his air of vulnerability. His manner, thought Rae-Brown, was 'almost that of a retiring yet high-bred child', and his lack of practicality gave the same impression. About a month after the move to Glasgow he asked Rae-Brown for a few pounds 'in advance'. Rae-Brown reminded him that there were twenty pounds to his credit, and that he had insisted on taking no more than five pounds when they discussed the matter two days before. De Quincey was dismayed.

> 'You really must excuse me – but where can the money be?' So saying, he nervously thrust his right hand into his trousers pocket and fished out a sadly-crumpled envelope – the same into which I had placed five one-pound notes only a few days before. 'I beg ten thousand pardons. I believe I am becoming the most stupid of men.'[64]

He wrote for the *Mail* until the autumn of 1847, and contributed to every issue of *Tait's* throughout the year.

In the midst of all this he found time to help Francis, who as part of his medical course at Edinburgh University had to submit a dissertation and had chosen for his subject the new and controversial science of anaesthetics. De Quincey contributed an eloquent appendix, written with as much care as any of his magazine articles, 'On the Religious Objections to the Use of Chloroform', arguing that there could be no valid Christian objection to anaesthetics. (Francis was now the only one of his sons at Lasswade, since Paul Fred had joined the army late in 1845 and was in India, where he had seen action in the Sikh War.)

In April he returned to Lasswade to see the girls, who were about to set off for Bath to visit their Aunt Jane, whom they had never met.

The trip was financed by some of the Penson money which had come to the De Quinceys after Mrs Quincey's death, and it seems to have been the first holiday they ever had. De Quincey fussed and fretted over his girls just as his mother had fussed and fretted over him and Henry nearly fifty years before. 'On some railways', he lamented, '(and my poor girls never were on *any*), the doors of the carriages are not always securely fastened; and in the dark, or in the dusk, an accident might more easily happen than in full daylight. . . .'[65] But they travelled without mishap, and besides Jane and other relatives they met Walter Savage Landor, the poet and essayist, a keen admirer of their father's work.[66]

De Quincey himself, back in Glasgow, fell ill in September with a fever caught, he thought, from the crowds of homeless Irish immigrants camping out near the Clyde bridges, with whom he had been in the habit of chatting as he walked through the city. The fever was mild but he had little resistance to it, probably because he was not eating properly, and it was accompanied by severe stomach pains: he complained picturesquely of 'a feeling like a bar rigid as a poker in the stomach, sometimes a more tormenting one as though the stomach were filled with cotton, sometimes (though more rarely) of an indescribable corrosive acid'.[67] The fever, however, withdrew after a few weeks, and by 13 October he was cheerfully writing again and dosing himself with, of all things, hemlock. In November he deposited the last of his manuscripts at the offices of *Tait's* and returned to his daughters at Lasswade.

13
A Match Against Time

De Quincey was now sixty-two years old, and with advancing age he increasingly allowed his daughters to take charge of him. Sometimes he left Lasswade to stay in Edinburgh, but wherever he was the basic practical responsibilities devolved upon Margaret, Florence and Emily, who treated their 'poor papa' with indulgent tolerance. His health fluctuated: sometimes he was unable to stir from the house, but at other times he would walk to Edinburgh and back, a fourteen-mile round trip. His general routine was to work at night and sleep through the morning, rising at noon. In the afternoon he would go walking, often staying out until dusk. Then he would eat a very small dinner with the girls and retire to the study to write.[1] Florence described his habits as 'simple, almost to asceticism'. Often his main meal would consist only of bread with soup and coffee; but then he had been used to a meagre diet for a long time. 'I have in the course of my misfortunes fasted for thirty years,' he boasted, with some exaggeration. 'A dreadful fate, if it had been to come. But, being past, it is lawful to regard it with satisfaction, as having, like all fasting and mortification, sharpened to an excruciating degree my intellectual faculties.'[2]

The room where he worked was perpetually 'snowed up' with papers. His daughters were once unwise enough to move an old tin bath there for temporary storage. It was soon full to the brim with papers and he would never allow it to be moved. Amid all this paper his casual way with matches and candles made him rather a danger, and indeed he started several small fires. 'Five or six' prose pieces describing dreams, intended as the 'crowning grace' of a new edition of the *Confessions*, were, he says, 'burned in a sudden conflagration which arose from a spark of a candle falling unobserved amongst a very large pile of papers'. He put the fire out with the aid of 'one sole person, somewhat agitated but retaining her presence of mind', who helped him stifle it with 'a large Spanish cloak'.[3] One evening when the maid came to tell his daughters that the study was on fire they were unable to get in: he had locked the door so that no one could bring water and spoil his papers. This time he put the fire out himself, smothering it with a rug. Another source of excitement was his habit of holding a candle in his hand as he read. 'Those nights were exceptions', recalled Florence, 'on which he didn't set something on fire, the commonest incident being for some one to look up from work or book to say casually, "Papa, your hair is on fire," of which a calm "Is it, my love?" and a hand rubbing out the blaze was all the notice taken.'[4]

It is hard to avoid a suspicion that in old age De Quincey half-consciously adopted the role of a child. It had been with reluctance that he had first undertaken adult responsibilities, and now that his children were grown up he retreated to become once more the baby of the family. It is noticeable that almost everyone who recorded impressions of him in his last years was struck by his childlike appearance. The effect was heightened by the fact that his clothes always looked shabby and too big for him. It was not that he lacked good clothes: 'on the contrary,' said Florence, 'he somehow always managed to get new clothes too large in spite of the best efforts of his children, and to wear them as if they were old'.[5] J.H. Burton, in a passage of affectionate caricature, describes De Quincey paying a late-night visit to his house. At first sight, says Burton, he looks like a 'street boy':

> His costume, in fact, is a boy's duffle great-coat, very threadbare, with a hole in it, and buttoned tight to the chin, where it meets the fragments of a parti-coloured belcher handkerchief; on his feet are list-shoes covered with snow, for it is a stormy winter night; and the trousers – some one suggests that they are inner linen garments blackened with writing-ink, but that [he] would never have been at the trouble so to disguise them. What can be the theory of such a costume? The simplest thing in the world – it consisted of the fragments of apparel nearest at hand.[6]

Dressing and undressing were in any case liable to be interrupted if an idea struck him, 'and he would stop with his coat just taken off or not put on, without stockings at all, or with one off and one on, and becoming lost in what grew out of this thought, he would work for hours'. If a visitor arrived he would present himself as he was rather than cause delay, donning the forgotten garment as he greeted the guest.[7]

Such behaviour was regarded indulgently by most people and had its advantages for it conferred a sort of licensed irresponsibility. For example, 'My father', wrote Emily, 'was a terribly unguarded man in conversation . . . It never struck him that there were itching ears ready to scatter broadcast some slighting remark about a well-known person . . . A perfectly innocent and just remark, but which was sure to cause anger if repeated.'[8] And, on one occasion, the role of helpless child earned him a notable comic victory. A certain Captain Hamley had published a novel and thought himself rather a celebrity. Arriving in Edinburgh, he told a friend that he 'thought of riding out to see old De Quincey'. The friend warned him that 'Old De Quincey' saw few visitors these days. 'Oh,' said Hamley, 'but he'll see *me*.' In due course the sound of horses was heard outside the cottage and Emily, to her dismay, looked out to see Hamley advancing, together with Mr and Mrs John Blackwood, 'two young ladies' and a groom. She ran to see if she could persuade her father to meet the visitors. She found him in the dining-room, 'such a figure of fun,' she says, 'as I shall never forget'. An avalanche of soot had fallen down the chimney completely covering him, and he sat by the fire with his coat off and 'two mournful eyes look[ing] out of a completely black face'. The groom and the ladies had a good view of him through the dining-room window. Emily told the visitors that her father was unwell, and they departed – Hamley, she thought, in rather a huff.[9]

In such cases one may speculate as to whether De Quincey's innocence was as absolute as it appeared. It was essential for him to guard his privacy with care, as his occasional ventures into public amply showed. When James Hogg, who became his publisher in 1850, took him to a concert, De Quincey moved forward in the box to get a better view and found a row of opera-glasses trained on him from the press box. He retreated at once and took care to stay out of sight.[10] But to people whose company he really enjoyed he was most hospitable. They might stay as late as they liked, and when they left he would escort them on a shortcut through the woods with a big bull's-eye lantern in his hand and on his head a huge 'wideawake' hat which, says Burton, made his tiny figure look 'like the stalk of some great fungus'.[11] He was still an impressive conversationalist. David Masson, who many years later was to edit the standard edition of De Quincey's works, met him once at a friend's house in the Old Town. Masson was 'struck with the peculiar beauty of [De Quincey's] head and forehead, rising disproportionately high over his small wrinkly visage and gentle deep-set eyes', and of his talk remembered

chiefly two incidents. The birthday of some one present having been mentioned, De Quincey immediately said, 'O, that is the anniversary of the battle of So-and-So'; and he seemed ready to catch as many birthdays as might be thrown him on the spot, and almanack them all round in a similar manner from his memory. The other incident was his use of a phrase very beautiful in itself, and which seemed characteristic of his manner of thinking. Describing some visionary scene or other, he spoke of it as consisting of 'discs of light and interspaces of gloom'; and I noticed that, with all the fine distinctness of the phrase, both optical and musical, it came from him with no sort of consciousness of its being out of the way in talk, and with no reference whatever to its being appreciated or not by those around him.[12]

For some years De Quincey's reputation had been steadily growing in America, where British periodicals were eagerly read and looked upon as models of literary excellence. Suspecting that their own literature lacked polish, the more discriminating American readers placed a particularly high value upon style, and now that *Suspiria de Profundis* had crossed the Atlantic there were few American writers of any calibre who did not regard De Quincey as a master. The first to pay tribute in person seems to have been Emerson, who had listed De Quincey as one of the people he most wanted to meet on his visit to Britain and who did so on 13 February 1848, at the house of Mrs Catherine Crowe, an Edinburgh society hostess. Emerson was very nervous. Basing his expectations on the prose of the *Confessions* and *Suspiria*, he was ready to meet 'some figure like the organ of York Minster', but when the great man entered, having made his way on foot from Lasswade, the effect was rather different. 'He had walked 10 miles in the rain,' Emerson wrote in his journal 'but was so drest that 10 miles could not spoil him. He had walked home in the rain lately from Mrs. C's dinner, he told us, because . . . of two street girls one had taken his 8 shillings out of his pocket, and the other his umbrella.'[13] The conversation, however, soon took a more literary tone. De Quincey grumbled about Tait, whose magazine, he said, had 'vulgarized' his work, and said he was now writing for the *North British Review*. He mentioned that he had lost his manuscript copy of Wordsworth's unpublished poem and, growing confidential, discussed Wordsworth's character, saying, according to Emerson, that 'Wordsworth appropriated what another said so entirely as to be angry if the originator claimed any part of it'.

Afterwards Emerson's hosts regaled him with tall stories about De Quincey's adventures with grasping landladies – a red-haired beldame called 'Mrs MacBold', for example, who had 'exercised a reign of terror over him for years' and at last tried to force him to marry her –

but these fantasies seem not to have diminished his respect for the strange little man who had suffered so much. Six days later he dined with the De Quincey family at Lasswade. Emerson was to lecture at the Queen Street Hall afterwards and De Quincey was persuaded to go along. Emerson was thrilled – 'to my lecture! De Q at lecture!' he exulted in the privacy of his journal – but it is said that De Quincey fell asleep.[14]

De Quincey's literary output in 1848 was small. He published only three items, review articles on Goldsmith, Pope and Lamb in the *North British Review*. After completing the Lamb essay late in October he made himself ill by another attempt at giving up opium. This time he tried total abstinence, and the result was 'misery'. He 'descended into utter despair, the 17th to the 22nd November being days of profoundest suffering and utter hopelessness – (rigid obstruction, throbbing without intermission, and sub-inflammation)' but on 23 November he felt much better. He persuaded himself that the 'misery' was produced by drinking alcohol during a period of opium withdrawal and abstained from that too, but after sixty-one days without laudanum he was again taking his drug in what he regarded as moderation. He had decided that life was unendurable without it, and resigned himself to remaining an opium-eater until his dying day.[15] Experience, it seems, never taught him to refrain from experimenting with drugs. In 1845 he had mentioned parenthetically in an essay that 'I, for my part, have tried everything in this world except "bang" [hashish], which I believe is obtained from hemp'. Someone hastened to remedy this deficiency and he was later able to report that he had 'received from a young friend a present of *bang*' upon which he promised to 'report hereafter'. Alas, his report never appeared.[16]

Whether it was a product of this last struggle with opium or whether it had been lying in manuscript since 1845 is not known, but in 1849 an essay closely related to *Suspiria de Profundis* appeared in *Blackwood's*. This was 'The English Mail-Coach', his most remarkable and sustained exercise in 'impassioned prose'. As with the *Suspiria*, publication obscured its structure. It came out in two instalments in October and December; the two instalments comprised three 'sections', but subheadings seemed to divide it into four parts, each with a title. The starting point of the essay was his memories of stage-coach travel in the years before the railway had taken the romance out of transport. From this material De Quincey elaborated a prose poem whose themes were developed and counterpointed in the manner of music. The four parts were almost 'movements' in the musical sense. The first, 'The Glory of Motion', acted as overture, introducing the coaches factually, heightening its material with the slightly sinister banter De Quincey produced with such skill, describing briefly the thrills and dangers of riding on the box of a mail coach, indicating the coaches' role as vital bearers of news during the Napoleonic era, and ending with an account of 'Fanny of the Bath Road' and of the way Fanny, mail coaches, summer roses, a grotesque one-eyed coachman and many other associated images, bizarre and homely, had left their elaborate traces in his dreams and nightmares over the course of forty years.

The second movement, 'Going Down with Victory', is a magnificent first-person account of riding out from London on the coach bearing the first news of great but costly victory of Talavera. Its picture of a journey through an England united in anxiety and enthusiasm at a moment of national crisis is very powerful, so it comes as a surprise to realize that De Quincey had been staying at Westhay when the news of Talavera reached England early in August 1809 and had not visited London for several weeks.[17] Certain details of Talavera are essential to De Quincey's narrative; he cannot be confusing it with any other battle, so we must conclude that 'Going Down with Victory' is a brilliant piece of fantasy. The same may possibly be true of the third movement, 'The Vision of Sudden Death', which describes that terrifying near-collision long ago on the Preston road when the driver at De Quincey's side fell asleep with the reins in his hands. I have chosen to accept the account as substantially true; but it is as well to remember that De Quincey's first allegiance was to poetic, not factual truth. The fourth movement's title makes the musical analogy explicit. 'Dream-Fugue, Founded on the Preceding Theme of Sudden Death' opens with the direction 'Tumultuosissimamente' and pursues the imagery of the previous movements through the elaborate configurations of dream and nightmare, ending with an apocalyptic moment in which innocence, in the form of a being who is at once child and woman, is offered as ransom for the crimes and conflicts of humanity. How much of this is really taken from De Quincey's sleeping or waking dreams and how much is conscious literary elaboration is impossible to say. Parts of it certainly have the suggestive power and the inconsequence of dream. Most of De Quincey's favourite archetypal images are present, and the child-woman of the conclusion is a figure whose recurrent part in his own life he consciously emphasized, for she is Elizabeth, Ann, Margaret and the other girls or women whose love represented to him a redeeming element amidst the sufferings of life. 'The English Mail-Coach' is written in prose which to most present-day readers must seem intolerably 'purple'. But the ornate and the emotional were things De Quincey did well. He handled them with panache and confidence, generating a sense of extravagance entirely appropriate to the semi-hallucinated states of mind he wished to convey. There can be no doubt that the essay represents the perfection of his more elaborate manner.

One spring day in 1850 James Hogg, editor of an undistinguished weekly called *Hogg's Instructor*, was informed that a gentleman wished to see him. Emerging into the outer office he found awaiting him a small man in an Inverness cape. 'He produced from one pocket', recalled Hogg, '. . . a small roll of manuscript, and from the other a little brush with a handle. Opening the roll and carefully brushing each sheet as he handed it to me, he added that he proposed to contribute to *The Instructor*.'[18] As well as the manuscript he had a note from the head of the firm, James Hogg senior, instructing the younger Hogg to take the article, a piece entitled 'The Sphinx's Riddle', and pay cash for it. The visitor was, of course, De Quincey, and from now on James Hogg junior became responsible for his relations with the firm. It was a taxing business but he managed it well. He became De Quincey's friend and both benefited. Hogg elicited thirty-three short articles for his magazine and became the publisher of the first British collected edition of De Quincey's works. 'He was also', wrote Hogg later, 'my great Adviser while I edited the New Series of the "Instructor" and "Titan". . . DeQ. was like a father to me.'[19] In return Hogg helped him organize his work and business affairs, and persuaded his father to act as unofficial banker and accountant, paying various creditors at De Quincey's request and even making an arrangement with the Commercial Bank of Scotland so that De Quincey's 'little drafts by letter' would be met with money from the firm's account.[20]

Why he had chosen to go to Hogg, whose magazine was mainly filled with reprinted poetry and inferior fiction, is a mystery. Perhaps he was tired of *Blackwood's* high-handedness and the bustle and politics of *Tait's*, feeling that a small, non-political paper would allow him more freedom. Whatever the cause, all but one of his articles from now on appeared in the *Instructor* or its monthly continuation after

1856 as the *Titan*. Few of those in the *Instructor* were longer than five
pages and they dealt with all kinds of subjects. Those published in
1850 are a fair sample. Besides 'Conversation' and the 'Sphinx' there
were papers on 'Logic', 'Professor Wilson', 'French and English Manners' and 'Presence of Mind'. In 1851 there was an autobiographical
'Sketch from Childhood' in five instalments, recording memories of
his father and his brother William, but generally there was no unity
amongst the essays. Most of them were of the kind that had appeared
many years before in the *London Magazine* as 'Notes from the
Pocket-Book of a late Opium-Eater'.

Soon after he began writing for Hogg the idea of a 'collected
edition' came up for discussion.[21] De Quincey had suggested to
Blackwood in 1844 that a volume might be made out of his historical
essays but Blackwood, cautious as ever, had turned the idea down. By
1850 the initiative had been taken by an American publishing company, Ticknor and Fields of Boston. They were a reputable firm and
had every intention of treating De Quincey fairly, but although they
had written several times proposing an edition he 'simply . . . could
never muster the energy to answer the letters', as Florence explained.[22]
At last Ticknor and Fields gave up and decided to go ahead without his
permission. Their first volume, containing the *Confessions* and *Suspiria de Profundis*, appeared in 1851, inaugurating a twenty-two
volume edition.

De Quincey himself had at first shuddered at the idea of trying to
collect his countless scattered articles. When George Gilfillan urged
that it be done, his reply was vehement: 'Sir, the thing is absolutely,
insuperably, and for ever impossible. Not the archangel Gabriel, nor
his multipotent adversary, durst attempt any such thing!'[23] No doubt
he said much the same when Hogg again raised the matter. But once
Ticknor and Fields had begun the task he grew interested. After much
prodding from his daughters he wrote to the publishers' agent in
August 1851, sending a list of his periodical articles 'for many years
past' with permission to reprint in the United States, with such revision
and selection 'as may hereafter appear expedient or as my leisure and
. . . health may permit'.[24] This was an empty promise, for he still had a
'disgust' of returning to his old articles: the list he sent was compiled
by Margaret, and he did no revision for Ticknor and Fields, leaving
them to dig out and reprint whatever they could find in old files of the
London, *Blackwood's* and *Tait's*. They were happy to do so, and the
edition prospered. In 1852 Fields, on a visit to Britain, came to

Lasswade with a cheque for fifty pounds, De Quincey's share of the profits, which he tactfully handed over to the daughters.[25] De Quincey was pleasantly surprised: the fact that he was now an eminent author with a world-wide reputation never seems fully to have penetrated his consciousness, and he still thought of his earnings as a matter of a few pounds to tide him over. He had been embroiled in the trade of hack-authorship for so long that he had lost the habit of taking long views about his work. For practical purposes his world was still the space between Lasswade and Hogg's office in Edinburgh, his unit of time the interval between deadlines.

Before Fields left De Quincey rashly promised him a preface for the next volume. Months later he had still not done it and Margaret apologized for him. 'His besetting sin is procrastination,' she explained, 'and nothing but dire necessity can ever drive him to do any thing.'[26] It occurred to her that he might write Fields a letter which could be printed as a preface, but even this proved difficult. She and Florence nagged him for weeks and when he did write something he insisted on keeping it to make a fair copy and it was never seen again. But eventually a suitable letter was written and sent. Characteristically, it was full of gratitude for 'the services which you have already rendered me: viz, . . . in having brought together so widely scattered a collection – a difficulty which in my own hands by too painful an experience I had found from nervous depression to be absolutely insurmountable'.[27]

In the spring of 1851 De Quincey finished his connection with *Tait's Magazine*. Thereafter all his work went to Hogg. His mind was as lively as ever, and besides short literary and autobiographical pieces, in 1852 he produced two essays on the California gold rush, which interested him as a drama of equal psychological and economic importance. It amused him to argue that if the rumours of incalculably rich gold deposits turned out to be true, the result would be merely to depress the price of gold until few mines would repay the expense of working. He was still making new friends. In January 1852 John Ritchie Findlay, editor of *The Scotsman*, was introduced to him by Burton and thereafter Findlay and Burton dined regularly at Lasswade. Findlay recorded his impressions, noting De Quincey's boyish look: at first glance his face seemed quite smooth, but a closer view revealed that the skin was criss-crossed with a million tiny wrinkles. His clothing was as untidy as usual, but a new acquisition was a large white flannel jacket 'like a cricketer's coat' which he wore when working. He was much concerned about the safety of various *caches* of papers he had distributed about Edinburgh during his years of poverty, and talked of the need to contact Wilson, one of whose friends had helped him by moving into store a load of books and manuscripts. He had now forgotten both the location of the papers and the name of the friend, and hoped Wilson might remember.

De Quincey's generosity and concern for others were clearly apparent, though sometimes rather haphazardly applied. One evening, Findlay recalled, some children were heard singing at the cottage door. They were 'guisers' (carol-singers) and were duly given some money. De Quincey seemed to misunderstand the incident, imagining that the children were waifs, driven by poverty to sing from door to door. He looked shocked, and as the children departed he said gravely, 'All that I have ever had enjoyment of in life, the charms of friendship, the smiles of women, and the joys of wine, seem to rise up to reproach me for my happiness when I see such misery, and think there is so much of it in the world.'[28] To his guests he behaved with extreme modesty. He was as good a listener as he was a talker, never interrupted, and would diligently sustain his half of the most tedious conversation rather than risk giving offence. He confessed that he always avoided public transport for this reason: he might be engaged in conversation by a bore, and politeness would allow him no escape.[29]

The year 1853 was notable for two important events. One was that Margaret married Robert Craig, the son of a neighbour at Lasswade. She was thirty-five years old – the long responsibility of caring for her brothers and sisters had taken most of her youth, though there is no sign that she ever resented the fact. She went with her husband to live in Ireland at Pegsborough and then at Lisheen in Tipperary, where they ran a farm. This left twenty-six-year-old Florence to take over the household, which she did cheerfully enough, playing (to make the obvious fictional comparison) a lively Emma to her father's Mr Woodhouse. The second cardinal event was the beginning of a British collected edition of De Quincey's works. Ticknor and Fields having assembled much of the material, Hogg had overcome De Quincey's objections and planned an edition on the grand scale which would not only add items the Americans had missed but would print revised texts. The edition was still not intended to be complete, as the title indicated: it was to be *Selections Grave and Gay, from writings published and unpublished.*

From the end of 1852 or thereabouts the collected edition became De Quincey's chief task in life. By sheer charm, patience and persistence Hogg persuaded him to overcome his revulsion from his old work and brought him to see the new edition as an opportunity for improvement. He obtained back numbers of periodicals and copies of the American edition, and the labour began. De Quincey revised and added material on the pages of the American edition, which had generous margins, and made other additions on loose leaves, producing an inky labyrinth of balloons, arrows and asterisks. For the first volumes, which contained 'Autobiographic Sketches', pieces from *Hogg's Instructor* were spliced into the dismembered Boston volume with generous manuscript additions. Volume I appeared in May 1853, and thereafter further volumes were published at a rate of up to four a year.

Copyright in the work was to be the property jointly of Hogg and the author; profits would be split in equal shares. For the first time De Quincey began to earn respectable sums of money. By August 1857 his share of profits on the first five volumes was over £290, and in 1858 he sold his interest in the edition to Hogg for £808.9s.7d. At that time three more volumes were planned, and if he failed to prepare any of these he was to repay Hogg seventy-five pounds per volume. But he did not fail, and the edition ran to four volumes more than expected, for which he seems to have received fifty pounds per volume, so that his total returns from the edition must have been about £1300. In addition he no doubt received a few hundred pounds from Ticknor and Fields.[30] Prosperity had found him at last, when he was too old to have much use for it.

The progress of the work owed as much to Hogg's persistence as to De Quincey's. It was said in Edinburgh that Hogg had taken on an impossible task and sometimes he was inclined to agree.

> I soon discovered . . . that it was almost impossible to overrate difficulties – his whole constitution and habit of mind were averse from sustained and continuous work of the kind. He was constantly being caught with new plans, and when I was desirous of pushing on the publication of the works, would entertain me with the most ingenious devices and speculations . . . I soon found out that it was of no use to show impatience – that the causes of delay were for the most part beyond his control; that he did not lack the will to make efforts, but the power, and that the power was most amenable when he was left

unharassed. A gentle reminder, an indirect suggestion, rather than an expression of one's disappointment, was the most efficient spur to his will.[31]

Hogg paid countless visits to keep him in a good humour and nudge him back to the task. He would find De Quincey in a room where there was barely space to stand between stacks of books and mounds of paper, writing at one small corner of a large table otherwise completely covered with piles of books and manuscripts. 'He was pursued', says Hogg, 'by a Chinese-like reverence for written or printed paper. Newspapers and magazines, which reached him from all parts of the world, he preserved with religious care; even his MSS which had been printed he preserved'[32] as well as all his notes, letters and the miscellaneous scraps of paper which he would greedily pick up elsewhere in the house and carry off to add to his hoard. The difficulties of working in such an environment were not trivial, as some of his notes to Hogg testify. A frequent problem was that things got lost:

> Working through most part of the night, I have not yet come to the missing copy. I am going on with the search . . . yet being walled up in so narrow an area (not larger than a post chaise as regards the free space), I work with difficulty, and the *stooping* kills me. I greatly fear that the entire day will be spent in the search.

Sometimes he managed to lose a volume of the Boston edition interleaved for his use with blank paper: 'I have been unrolling an immense heap of newspapers, &c., ever since six a.m. How so thick a vol. *can* have hidden itself, I am unable to explain.' And there was the usual risk of fire. 'I fear that the seventeen or eighteen missing pages may have been burned suddenly lighting candles,' he told Hogg one day, 'and I am more surprised at finding so many than at missing so few.'[33] Hogg busied himself with tracking down published articles and rescuing lost manuscripts. De Quincey dimly remembered having left two tea-chests of papers with a bookseller in Glasgow years before. Hogg asked a friend to contact the city's booksellers, and the chests were found. Former landladies came to Hogg with bundles of papers left behind years before by their mysterious lodger, and a waiter in the Royal Exchange Hotel produced a parcel entrusted to him by De Quincey for some reason a year before. There was at least one fraudulent claim, when a stranger demanded money for a package that turned out to be full of straw.[34]

Recovering published items was equally difficult. De Quincey had forgotten much of his own work and relied on Ticknor and Fields to tell him what he had written. 'It is astonishing', he wrote in 1857, 'how much more Boston knows of my literary acts and purposes than I do myself. Were it not indeed through Boston, hardly the sixth part of my literary undertakings, hurried or deliberate, sound, rotting, or rotten, would ever have reached posterity.' Perhaps the thought of 'Boston's' investigations occasionally made him nervous. 'I should fear at times', he joked, 'that if, on any dark December morning, say forty or fifty years ago, I might have committed a forgery (as the best of men will do occasionally) Boston could array against me all the documentary evidence of my peccadillo before I should have time to abscond.'[35] Hogg's edition did give him the opportunity to atone for some literary misdemeanours by indicating, occasionally, the source of a borrowed item; but more often he seems to have forgotten his debts. About the details of revision, however, he was conscientious and took pains to explain everything to the printers as well as to Hogg. When on a proof-sheet the printer queried his spelling of 'calligraphy' with first one and then two *l*'s, he sent a note:

> According to all analogy I should have expected the word to be written with the single 'l' the adjective καλο being so uniformly spelt with a single λ; and resting upon this consideration, I had in one of the proofs, and in one single instance, altered the word to *caligraphy*. But, feeling some doubt, I consulted three or four different lexicons, all of which doubled the λ. And I have since met the word written *callig.* in a most carefully edited MS. of Porson.[36]

No wonder the work often went slowly.

There were unexpected difficulties also over obtaining permission to reprint some of the published work. Blackwood gladly gave his consent, but approaches to Black, who published the *Encyclopaedia Britannica*, 'met with a morose and churlish refusal'.[37] This was a trivial matter, but a far worse obstacle was created by John Taylor of the old *London Magazine*, who wrote to Hogg as soon as the first volume of the *Selections* was advertised, 'claimed the absolute copyright of the *Confessions*, and peremptorily forbade the use of them in any edition of the author's works'. Hogg was appalled, and went at once to consult De Quincey, who

> at first said, thoughtfully, but somewhat dubiously, that he had not parted with the 'Confessions' in any formal manner. At the same time gravely and serenely, indeed half-humorously, he said, 'Well, if the "Confessions" really are not mine, there is an end of everything. We

cannot proceed without them!' It seemed a happy deliverance from a great deal of laborious, tormenting work which he . . . would be glad to get rid of.[38]

But Hogg was not to be thwarted so easily. He took his time and induced De Quincey to recount over and over again his reminiscences of the writing and publication of the *Confessions* until he was sure that no formal agreement had ever been made. Then, after consulting an expert in copyright law, he wrote to Taylor putting his case and threatening that if Taylor still withheld permission he would be sued for the author's share of the profits on all sales of the book since 1822! Seeing that Hogg meant business, Taylor gave in, covering his retreat by pointing out that he and De Quincey were old men now and a battle would be undignified.[39]

The *Selections* were well received, and De Quincey found the reviews an effective stimulus to his flagging energies. In September 1854 he was delighted to hear that the London *Globe* had printed large extracts from volume III: it would help to keep the work 'alive in men's remembrance', he said rather wistfully.[40] Even that implacable damner-with-faint-praise, Henry Crabb Robinson, read the volumes avidly as they appeared. 'I have just finished the volume five of the Selections,' he wrote in May 1857. 'I long for the rest of De Quincey, and yet I neither love nor respect the man; I admire only the writer.'[41] Yet De Quincey sometimes chafed a little at having to work so consistently at one project. He was besieged by bright ideas and proposed all kinds of essays for the *Instructor*, most of which Hogg tactfully refused rather than risk his being distracted from the *Selections*, though he accepted just enough to keep De Quincey happy and to let him earn occasional sums of ready cash when he needed them. As for more grandiose projects, they were gently humoured but always nudged aside, and after all De Quincey may well have been teasing Hogg when he proposed, for example, to write a History of England in twelve volumes, or an historical novel, or a volume of Arabian Tales, or a 'book on the Idea of the Infinite'.[42] It was harder than ever to know when he was serious and when he was indulging in some subtle private joke.

In June 1854 he suddenly decided to leave Lasswade and set up his main headquarters at 42, Lothian Street, Edinburgh, where he had lodged several years before. His reasons for the move were obscure. Characteristically he did not explain to his daughters, preferring, perhaps, to act before they had a chance to object. The decision may have been hastened by the fact that Margaret was expecting a baby: Florence and Emily wanted to join her at Lisheen but would have disliked leaving him alone in the cottage. Francis, a rover like all De Quincey boys, had gone to Brazil in 1851 so there was no one else to take care of him. At Lothian Street he would be safe in the charge of two friendly landladies, Mrs Wilson and her sister Miss Stark. So he walked into Edinburgh one day without a scrap of luggage and engaged rooms. Mrs Wilson produced some clothes, carefully kept, which he had left behind there some sixteen years before, and thus equipped he soon became a permanent resident.[43]

He quickly had his rooms in the same condition as the study at Lasswade. Findlay visited him there and found him ready, as always, to stop work and talk. He was seeing fewer people these days, however, for he lived in such untidiness that he preferred only privileged intimates to enter his room. Persuading him to go out was also a complicated business. 'The first difficulty was to induce him to visit you,' Findlay recalls, 'and the second to reconcile him to leaving.' His poor health contributed to reducing his mobility. In the early 1850s he could still walk to Lasswade, talking all the way, at a pace that left Hogg breathless. Now he was again troubled with 'purpurea' in his leg. He told Findlay that he thought opium made it worse, but 'without opium I can't get on with my work, which the publishers are urging me to complete. The work must be done; the opium can't be left off; therefore I cannot begin to walk, and the leg must take its chance.'[44] He took his laudanum now diluted with water, explaining to Hogg that the undiluted tincture 'caused a very annoying and even painful itching in the nostrils'. He measured his dose by eye, holding a wine glass up to light to judge the quantity and then adding water.[45] During intense periods of work he sometimes grew a long beard, for he had never learned to strop a razor effectively (this, like his inability to put a decent point on a quill pen, had caused him lifelong, trivial inconvenience).

The second, third and fourth volumes of the *Selections* were prepared for the press in 1854. Volume IV contained the essay 'On Murder' which De Quincey strikingly improved by the addition of a new 'Postscript' describing with terrifying vividness the 'Williams murders' of 1811 – the murders which had suggested the *Macbeth* essay of 1825. Apparently the story of the murders had been haunting De Quincey for over forty years and now, realizing that it was his last chance, he interrupted the routine work of revision to compose this brilliant exercise in suspense, which more than doubled the length of the 'Murder' essay as a whole. There are enough factual errors in the story to suggest that it was written from memory, but it is just possible that it had been composed at some time between 1827 and 1839, for it refers to a previous 'paper' – not 'papers' – on murder. Perhaps it was a rejected effort for *Maga* and had lain, unused, in one of De Quincey's heaps of notes for fifteen or twenty years. If so, no wonder those masses of paper meant so much to him.

On 2 April 1854 John Wilson died: De Quincey's oldest and closest friend, though mutual irritation and suspicion had sometimes clouded the relationship. De Quincey's reaction to the news is not recorded, but in September he was talking cheerfully enough of Wilson's shortcomings to suggest that he viewed the loss with equanimity.[46] Wilson's repertoire had included rather a good impersonation of De Quincey. Now, perhaps with a feeling of having the last laugh, De Quincey repaid the compliment and treated Hogg to impressions of Wilson lecturing.

He published nothing in 1855, probably because he was working on a revised version of the *Confessions*, which was to be Volume V of the *Selections*. He intended to add to this new version a full text of the 'sequel', *Suspiria de Profundis*, but this proved difficult. Unpublished parts of the *Suspiria* had become scattered in the course of a decade. Some of the manuscript had to be redeemed, at a cost of £8.10s., from the Sheriff's office, where it was being held against some debt.[47] De Quincey expected to find a section called 'The Daughter of Lebanon' there, but it was missing. It eventually turned up amongst his papers, but not before it had been partly burned in one of his fits of carelessness with a candle.[48]

Between October 1855 and May 1856 he seems to have been back at Lasswade. Florence and Emily had returned from Ireland, bringing with them Margaret and her baby, Eva. Florence was about to marry Colonel Richard Bairdsmith, a native of Lasswade now in the Indian army. After the wedding they would leave for India, and Florence wanted to see her father and sisters, perhaps for the last time, before she went away. To console herself for the separation she commissioned a pastel drawing of Emily, Margaret, Eva and her father which she would take with her to India. De Quincey's descendants still have the drawing. The girls are pretty in a conventionally Victorian manner but it is the old opium-eater who dominates the picture, leaning eagerly forward in rumpled waistcoat and jacket three sizes too big for him, his face full of an intense, almost painful vitality.

Florence had known Richard Bairdsmith since about 1843. Perhaps they would have married earlier but for her anxieties about her father.

> What does stand in the way [she had told Bairdsmith] is . . . my duty to Papa, he is so quaint and eccentric and requires so much arrangement that we have long since agreed that one of us alone is not equal to it, – especially dear little Emily . . . And we *cannot* leave him without the power of enjoying a pleasant comfortable home when he wishes it even if my love for him were not strong enough to make such a thought terrible.

She had consulted Aunt Jane at Bath, but

> *She* does not regard Papa as we do, he is quaint, and none of his relations understand him but ourselves, and because he has not done everything after the pattern of the model father in one of Hannah More's little good stories they can't quite comprehend our love for him, or our passionate desire, just *because* we have been obliged by his cranky ways sometimes to rebel, to yield him everything in which only our own feelings are concerned.[49]

In fact De Quincey was delighted when Florence became engaged. Admittedly, with his usual genius for finding ambiguities he misunderstood the letter she sent him at Lothian Street and thought, to his dismay, that she had rejected Bairdsmith's proposal; but once the confusion was cleared up all was well. There had been talk of his moving to Ireland to join Margaret, or of his going to Grasmere, of all places, 'if by any means we can trundle Papa down there', as Emily put it.[50] But he stayed at Edinburgh, mostly at Lothian Street, with occasional spells at Lasswade, where Emily dwelt. Emily never married, apparently through her own choice. 'Marriage is a bore, and a melancholy bore,' she once wrote. 'Death hardly puts a greater clencher sometimes to people's old ties.'[51] She was always one to speak her mind.

De Quincey was back in Edinburgh at the end of May 1856, and hard at work on the *Confessions*, having resolved, he says, 'to avail myself most carefully of the opening thus made for a revision of the entire work'. He felt dissatisfied with the original version because it had been 'written hastily' and published without correction. 'The main narrative', he thought, 'should have moved through a succession of secondary incidents'; lacking these, the narrative 'had been needlessly impoverished'. It needed 'integration of what had been left imperfect' and 'amplification of what . . . had been insufficiently expanded'.[52] Another consideration was a simple desire to make the *Confessions* fill a whole volume of the *Selections* rather than risk having it supplemented with other essays to make up the right bulk. For commercial reasons, Hogg insisted that all the volumes must sell for the same price, 7s.6d., and to offer the public 'a beggarly amount of 120 pp.' for their money, De Quincey agreed, would 'look very much like swindling'.[53] So from May to November he worked away, rewriting and expanding to produce a transformed *Confessions*. Progress was both helped and hindered by domestic upheavals. In August, when his rooms were given their three-monthly cleaning, a lost packet of manuscript, containing interpolations for the book, turned up; but later in the month a man came to whitewash the ceiling and prevented work for several days by setting up his ladders against the chest-of-drawers in which the *Confessions* were kept.[54]

When he had finished De Quincey was not sure if the result had been worth the effort. 'The consequences', he wrote, 'have been distressing to all concerned. The press has groaned under the chronic visitation; the compositors shudder at the sight of my hand-writing, though not objectionable on grounds of legibility; and I have much reason to fear that . . . I may have . . . suffered greatly in clearness of critical vision.' He suspected that 'sometimes . . . a heavy or too intricate arrangement of sentences may have defeated the tendency of what, under its natural presentation, would have been affecting',[55] and admitted that he had often felt too ill to cope with errors when the printing schedule allowed him only a few minutes to make a correction. To Emily he wrote, rather despondently, 'To justify the enormous labour it has cost me, most certainly it *ought* to be improved. And yet, reviewing the volume as a whole, now that I can look back from nearly the end to the beginning, greatly I doubt whether many readers will not prefer it in its original fragmentary state to its present full-blown development.'[56]

The unpublished *Suspiria* which were to fill out the work had been lost or burned, apart from 'The Daughter of Lebanon', which was placed at the end as a sort of coda. Inevitably the result was an anticlimax. The lightness of touch was lost. Originally evocative, brief and rather cryptic, an extended essay moving into autobiographic rhapsody at certain points, the *Confessions* now became something more like a conventional autobiography. The account of his childhood in the first part was expanded in De Quincey's most elaborate and digressive manner. Much of the material thus introduced is interesting enough: the worrying episode of the misdirected forty-pound bank draft, for example, was now told for the first time, and served to introduce a theme of guilt and pursuit which could be seen to recur throughout the book. Another notable addition was the account of his boyhood visit to the Whispering Gallery at St Paul's, a fine piece of 'impassioned prose' based, as we have seen, on a misconception of the Gallery's shape and characteristics. Perhaps De Quincey's notion of a long gallery which amplified sounds was derived from *Phonurgia*, a work on acoustics by the seventeenth-century German Jesuit mystic and scientist Athanasius Kircher, where galleries of the 'whispering' and 'amplifying' varieties are described in successive paragraphs. A copy of Kircher's book might easily have been in Coleridge's library or in De Quincey's own, in his earlier years in London and Grasmere. Traces of his reading easily blended with the shifting forms of memory and could give rise to powerful images, but the quest for symbols and psychological patterns muffled the overall impact of the new *Confessions*. In the 1856 version they became a leisurely exploration of an old man's memories. As such they have a curious poignancy, as if at certain points the author can scarcely believe in his own former existence as the young protagonist and lingers over a scene in the hope that the mystery of time will at last resolve itself for him; but they could not replace the original work and, as De Quincey half-expected, many readers have continued to prefer the earlier version.

The American edition was still proceeding, and he kept it under observation to the extent of insisting on certain exclusions. On 8 March Emily wrote to tell Fields that her father would be 'much obliged if you would not publish *Klosterheim*',[57] and none of his fiction, short or long, appeared in the American or British editions. Perhaps he thought it too poor to preserve.

Once the *Confessions* were off his hands he grew tired of Lothian Street and wrote to Ireland asking Emily if she could come home and keep him company at Lasswade. She returned in the spring of 1857, but by that time he had become embroiled in Volume VI, *Sketches, Critical and Biographic*, so she went south to visit relatives in Lincolnshire and meet Paul Fred, who had left the army and was coming home for a while before setting out for New Zealand. Brother and sister decided to see if they could persuade De Quincey to go to Ireland with them to visit Margaret and, surprisingly enough, he accepted the proposal. They left on 21 July and stayed for about a fortnight at Lisheen, allowing De Quincey some much-needed fresh air and a rest from literary demons.[58] Early in August, however, he was back at Lothian Street, working on Volume VII. His industry, for a man of seventy-two, was astonishing, and he was still sending Hogg short articles for the *Titan* as well as work for the *Selections*. In 1856 the *Titan* had published a piece on textual criticism and another on 'Storms in English History'; in 1857 came 'The Lake District Dialect: A Letter', salvaged from material gathered for the *Westmorland Gazette* thirty-eight years before, and a series of commentaries on the crises in India and China. News of the Indian Mutiny had reached England in June. Florence and her baby were living in a dangerous area, and Richard Bairdsmith was in action against the mutineers. De Quincey was terribly anxious. There were erroneous reports that all the British at Delhi had been massacred, and the news produced strange dreams. 'Every night, oftentimes all night long,' wrote De Quincey, 'I had the same dream – a vision of children, most of them infants, but not all, the *first* rank being girls of five or six years old, who were standing in the air outside, but so as to touch the window; and I heard, or perhaps fancied that I heard, always the same dreadful word, *Delhi*.' The dreams were accompanied by sleepwalking: 'Every night, to my great alarm, I woke up to find myself at the window, which is sixteen feet from the nearest side of the bed.'[59] But the terror passed and the Bairdsmiths survived unharmed. De Quincey relieved his feelings by three papers for the *Titan*: 'Notices of Indian Affairs' in September and October 1857, and 'Suggestions Upon the Secret of the Mutiny' in January 1858.

Volume VII of the *Selections* was out by the end of 1857. He had asked Hogg's opinion on the merits of various titles for the volume, proposing 'Studies on Records Secret or Forgotten' or 'Studies on Secret Records – Ancient and Modern' and asking, 'Can you improve this a little?' – an indication of how closely he now worked with Hogg. They settled eventually on *Studies on Secret Records, Personal and Historic*. Throughout 1858 he continued to work doggedly, as if aware that he was racing against time. He would grumble, of course, about the unremitting labour even as he used it as an excuse for staying at home: 'The truth is,' he told a friend, 'that Vol. VII, but still more Vol. VIII – has placed a barrier between myself and all recreation for

many successive months . . . And even at present out of 3 insurmountable hindrances to my going abroad to-morrow, one is connected with
this accursed volume.'[60]

But despite his perennial optimism about the future, he had to
admit that his health was failing. His eyes were very weak and he
sometimes had to stop reading for days at a time. He had periods of
insomnia which opium could no longer cure. His purpurea persisted
and he had some other ailment which, he told Lushington, might
require an operation. He spoke of himself as 'crippled' and complained that 'change of position' was 'difficult and sometimes painful'
for him. Even managing pen and paper was hard, and he ended a note
to Lushington sadly: 'My note has fallen into the ashes; and you see
the result on the left hand side of that word *ashes*. All is dust and
ashes.'[61] At other times the letters give the usual impression of busy
chaos:

> My dear Sir [he wrote to Hogg on October 20],
>
>   Did you say, or is it a dream, that I could have till the 22nd.
>   Up to Sat. the *Proofs* occupied me, since then the *search after the
>   Mud[ies'] Books*. I send 4 more. All being on the floor covered 2 ft.
>   deep with papers – it killed me to stoop. Consequently I now on
>   Tuesd. noon – I have not written one line.
>   I. Say if you please how much time.
>   II. Allow me to draw on you for two pounds.[62]

By the end of the year, as work on Volume X began, he was energeti-
cally proposing improvements and additions to the 'Pope' essay and
debating matters of Pope's biography in a letter which also admitted:

> I write, move, do all things under a most distressing bodily affection,
> one which is properly a surgical case; intermittingly it gives me much
> pain, but (which is more relevant to the purpose before me) much
> nervous impatience. The shortest letter is an oppression to me; and for
> the last four months I have felt myself compelled to retreat from all
> conversation or personal communications with visitors.[63]

When Findlay came to see him in January 1859, Miss Stark sent him
away, saying that De Quincey was out walking. In fact she was only
protecting him from disturbance, as she had often done before. De
Quincey wrote to Findlay apologizing; this 'walk' was a 'romantic
fiction' of Miss Stark's, he said, and while she was about it she might as
well have said he was 'botanising on the Himalayahs', for he was
unable to walk at all and had been in his room grappling with Volume

X.[64] In May he gave a sketch of a typical day's events. Waking a little before four a.m., he would slowly get up and dress himself until half-past seven, 'not daring to stoop or stretch out my arm'. At last he would be 'in good fighting spirits' though, he admitted, 'not much of a dandy', for breakfast – 'tea and two or even three biscuits'. Then came newspapers and letters, followed by writing from nine until twelve, when 'my trifle of dinner is served up'. After dinner came visitors or other business until some time after three, when the printer's boy would soon be arriving to collect work he had not had time to finish. 'Near 4 p.m., while thinking in perplexity on this subject, most naturally I fall asleep, having accomplished and rounded a day of thirteen hours.' But on the day this was written he was awake again by seven-fifteen p.m., and perhaps worked until late at night before sleeping once more.

A business note to Hogg confirms this picture of the dreamy tenor into which the old man's life had settled. 'Throughout the day,' he writes, 'I have been falling out of dream into dream from pain and want of sleep, so as to have *lost from my memory all the course of what I have sent to the Press.*'[65] Dreams had always been very real to him, and he recorded them with as much interest as ever. Most often now his dreams concerned children, especially his own children or grandchildren. 'My dear M.,' he wrote to Margaret in a late but undated letter, 'Will you think me superstitious? . . . how many times I am not sure, more than 3 to a certainty, 5 I should think, – dear little Eva has been seen by me in dreams drinking from the spout of a boiling tea-kettle, or (as once) of a boiling tea-pot.'[66] He felt compelled to tell her of this alarming portent. The last dream recorded in detail dates from 1855. It was a Sunday morning (Sunday morning dreams seemed to hold some special importance for De Quincey) and he dreamed that he was in a large room. A door opened, and a voice announced 'Florence and Emily'. Soon Florence entered; in white walking dress and a bonnet lined with rose-coloured silk; but there was no Emily. 'A shadow fell upon me, and a feeling of sadness, which increased continually as no Emily entered at the door, which, however, still stood open, so, you know, there was nothing to hinder her coming after all, if it was that she had only been loitering.' Florence seemed to be walking towards him but he could not catch her eye or speak to her. The part of the room to which she was walking blended into 'a garden, still, solitary, and rich to excess with flowers past all counting, and gayer than any I had ever seen'. But as she walked, 'although Florence

385

continually advanced in the sense of widening her distance from the entrance-door, nevertheless she never came nearer to me, for the chamber-floor expanded concurrently with her steps, which is an awkward thing, you know, when walking a match against time.'[67] This rather sad dream he reported to his daughters, drawing a careful diagram to illustrate the spatial relations of himself, the garden, the door and Florence.

He was taking laudanum as usual in 1859 but had to avoid it for brief periods when forced to use a 'powerful medicine' (perhaps the familiar Seidlitz powders) 'with which Laudm. is quite incompatible'.[68] Somehow, quite early in the year, Volumes XI and XII were sent to press and in May Volume XIII was almost done. During the summer it was finished and he began to do a little work on the fourteenth and last, but found himself weak and tired. As autumn approached he seemed distinctly ill and his landladies, who for some time had been caring for him almost as for a child, persuaded him to see a physician, Dr J.W. Begbie, who paid him a visit on 22 October.

> I found him in the parlour [he recalled], sitting on a sofa, but resting his head on a cushion placed on a chair before him; this posture was assumed not from pain, but by reason of feebleness. He received me with all that graciousness and winning kindness of manner and of speech for which he was remarkable, and explained the nature of his indisposition.[69]

He was feverish, and though at first, with complete rest, the fever abated, it returned persistently and he grew weaker. He slept a good deal during the day and once or twice seemed, on waking, not to know where he was or who were the people around him.

Emily had been visiting Margaret in Ireland. Hogg sent word of her father's condition and she returned at once, staying in the house to nurse him. He was lucid much of the time and seemed aware that he was close to death. At times, however, he appeared to hold conversations with invisible beings and, says Emily, confused 'real and imaginary, or apparently imaginary, things'. His feet gave him pain, and once when Emily rearranged the bed clothes around them, asking, 'Is that better, papa?' he replied 'Yes, my love, I think it is; you know, my dear girl, these are the feet that Christ washed.' He became increasingly preoccupied with religious visions and the idea of children.

> He aroused one day, and said suddenly: 'You must know, my dear, the Edinburgh cabmen are the most brutal set of fellows under the sun. I

must tell you that I and the little children were all invited to supper with Jesus Christ. So, as you see, it was a great honour. I thought I must buy new dresses for the little ones; and – would you believe it possible? – when I went out with the children, the wretches laughed at their new dresses.'[70]

He spoke of his sons as if they were his brothers, and one night told Emily, 'I thought you were Horace; for he was talking to me just now, and I suppose he has just left the room.' Sometimes his thoughts went back to childhood. 'There is one thing I deeply regret,' he told Emily, 'that I did not know my dear father better; for I am sure a better, kinder or juster man could never have existed.' On another occasion he suddenly exclaimed, 'My dear, dear Mother!'

On 4 December Emily sent word to Margaret, who arrived two days later. De Quincey was delighted to see her but confused as to her identity, and several times addressed her as 'Mama'. Once he was heard to say, 'Sister, sister'. A note for the *Suspiria* suggests that he had thought of Elizabeth as a potential intercessor: 'Sister, lend us thy help, and plead for us with God, that we may pass over without much agony.'[71] Perhaps he saw her now. If so, his prayer was granted, for on 7 December, after a lucid moment in which – courteous to the last – he unexpectedly said 'Thank you' to those at his bedside, he lost consciousness. Dr Begbie judged that he was in no pain and would die peacefully. He lingered on through the night, and died at half-past nine in the morning on 8 December.[72]

Findlay came to the house that afternoon and was shown De Quincey's body laid out on his bed, small in build and very thin, the head seeming large in comparison. 'He looked like a boy of fourteen', Emily recalled, 'and very beautiful.'[73] The exact cause of his death is not known. Begbie ascribed it 'rather to exhaustion of the system than to specific disease'.[74] There was a postmortem examination, but all we know of it is a rumour 'to the effect of De Quincey's organs having received no damage from his prolonged opium eating indeed being exceptionally sound'.[75] He was buried beside Margaret in St Cuthbert's Churchyard at the west end of Princes Street, where his grave may still be seen, marked by a pointed headstone with some restrained Gothic ornament, facing eastward at the inner angle of the L-shaped burial-ground. The obituaries varied in tone. One extreme may be represented by the London *Athenaeum*, which referred to his 'sad and almost profitless career' and 'an intellect that remained active to the last, but had never at any time been of much service to his fellow-men'.[76] The opposite view was put by *The Scotsman* on 10 December.

> With his departure [it announced] almost the very last of a brilliant band of men of letters, who illuminated the literary hemisphere of the first half of our century with starry lustre – differing each from each in glory, but all resplendent – is extinguished . . . He is the absolute creator of a species of 'impassioned prose' which he seemed born to introduce, and in which he has no prototype, no rival, no successor.

He had nearly finished revising the final volume of the *Selections*, and it appeared in 1860. Besides his manuscripts he left cash, books and bills to the value of £218.3s.0d. in Edinburgh; books at Penrith worth £16.11s.3d; and £44.10s.9d in rents and dividends on property inherited from his mother, together with the property left him in trust for his children which now became theirs. There were also his spare wellington boots at Robert Chambers's house in Doune Terrace; odd banknotes hidden here and there between the pages of his books; and, according to Florence, about six rooms on which he had been paying rent for the storage of his papers in different parts of the city.[77]

Florence had come home from India with her two daughters, but too late to see her father. Awaiting her was a letter of condolence from J.T. Fields, her father's American publisher, worth quoting because it sums up the feelings of nearly all those who had known De Quincey in his last years:

> In my whole life I have never met a man who won upon my *affectionate* interest more. He was so great a man, and yet so gentle and kind! As I walked with him to Roslin he talked with an eloquence I had not heard surpassed . . . till it seemed as if it were sinful not to take down his wonderful sentences.[78]

Epilogue:
The Secrets of a Life

De Quincey's story is a strange one, and studying it we become strongly aware of how far the external events of a life may really be determined by inner, psychological factors. As he himself wrote, 'The fleeting accidents of a man's life, and its external shows, may indeed be irrelate and incongruous; but the organizing principles which fuse into harmony, and gather about fixed predetermined centres, whatever heterogeneous elements life may have accumulated from without, will not permit the grandeur of human unity greatly to be violated.' Apparently coerced at every stage of his adult career by forces beyond his control, De Quincey in fact chose with varying degrees of consciousness all the main conditions of his life. His struggles with circumstances were essentially struggles with himself, and beneath his apparent weakness lay an exceptionally powerful sense of purpose. The dreamy procrastinator whose naivety charmed or irritated his more worldly-wise friends was also a man who could set himself the highest aims and pursue them doggedly to achievement over years or decades. From first to last he seems to have been remarkably self-involved: deeply introspective, determined to do things in his own way, he could be utterly unco-operative when others tried to force him to behave as they wished. His mass of autobiographical writings do not belie a basic secretiveness, for by presenting a persuasive self-portrait he effectively forestalled public curiosity about his life and personality, telling 'the truth, but not the whole truth' and incidentally securing himself a place as collaborator in any biography that could be written.

Certain central dynamics of his personality may be traced quite easily to his childhood experience. It seems clear, for example, that lack of maternal affection left him with a craving for love and reassurance. This tendency revealed itself in a variety of ways. It probably lay behind the intense intellectual ambition of his youth, as he struggled for achievements that would win the approval of others and perhaps even overcome his mother's tantalising refusal to bestow praise. In situations where he felt fully secure, on the other hand, it led him to revert to a child-role where he could enjoy the luxury of uncritical acceptance by those around him.

The absence and early death of his father probably added an element of instability to his character, and it seems likely that his difficulties with money were related to the fact that Thomas Quincey, a successful businessman, died at a time when he was near to becoming rich. Had he lived another ten years he might have been a wealthy man, and De Quincey seems to have carried over from childhood a sense of expectation, a feeling that he was always about to come into real prosperity. Perhaps he continued, irrationally, to believe in the fortune his father should have lived to make.

There is nothing very remarkable about all this, however, and interest in De Quincey's psychology is more likely to centre on the causes and effects of his opium-addiction. Almost every aspect of the theory of addiction is highly controversial, so our conclusions must be tentative, but it seems clear that De Quincey's addiction was not a matter of chance. Contrary to his own assertion, he must have known a certain amount about opium before he first tried it in 1804, and he found it at a time when he was very vulnerable to its temptations. Perhaps the main factor in his continued use of the drug was a reluctance to face up to unpleasant situations. Opium helped him to forget or evade painful obligations, and dulled the awareness that by doing so he was laying up trouble for the future.

The specific effects of opium on his personality are harder to identify. The drug does not change people overnight, and often its effects seem to be simply an intensification of those traits which led the addict to regular drug-use in the first place. De Quincey was secretive, introverted, poor at some kinds of decision-making and fascinated by dream and fantasy long before he took opium. All these tendencies increased, but so they might have done without the drug. It is equally hard to be certain about its effects on his writing. Several scholars have investigated the relationship between opium and the creative imagination, and the question of whether the drug stimulates or dulls the creative faculty has been extensively discussed, particularly with reference to Coleridge. Yet the outcome has been inconclusive. The difficulty of generalizing may be illustrated by the obvious point that while it is tempting to attribute the decline in Coleridge's poetic powers to opium addiction, it seems just as likely that 'The English Mail-Coach' and *Suspiria de Profundis* are direct products of De Quincey's forty years of addiction. Nor have attempts at identifying patterns of imagery peculiar to opium-addicted writers proved very convincing. Vast architectural vistas, oriental fantasies, mind-boggling expansions of time and space, descents to the depths of the sea or the bowels of the earth are the common property of Romantic literature from Horace Walpole onwards, and most of the motifs taken to be hallmarks of 'opium literature' are adumbrated in Burke's influential *Inquiry into the Origin of our Ideas of the Sublime and Beautiful* (1757). The imagery of De Quincey's finest passages stems from an addiction not to opium but to the Romantic sublime.

Although he was happy at times to exploit public curiosity about opium, careful reading of the *Confessions*, *Suspiria* and related works makes it clear that his central literary concern was not with opium but with 'dreams'. This was his usual term for the visions he recorded, and he used it broadly, blurring distinctions between waking reverie and the dreams that came in sleep. Opium was important to him as an agent of vision only indirectly, in that he believed it produced more dreams, and finer ones, than would occur otherwise. But it was merely a catalyst: solitude, suffering, wide reading and native sensibility were also necessary, he thought: 'If a man "whose talk is of oxen", should become an opium-eater, the probability is, that (if he is not too dull to dream at all) – he will dream about oxen.' On the direct impact of opium on a writer's work, his comments were unequivocal. Opium took away the central creative 'nexus' so that extended work became impossible. The writer acquired a 'disgust' for his own work and would leave it unfinished rather than face completing or revising it. These are not the views fashionable today, but he stated them forcefully more than once.

Nonetheless, De Quincey certainly found the effects of opium psychologically interesting. He became unusually aware of his own mental processes and was especially acute in observing those that involved mental imagery or visualization; indeed, it seems that he regarded them as glimpses of a hidden spiritual world. There are indications that from these elements he constructed a private mystery-religion of which only a few cryptic fragments are revealed in his writings. We know surprisingly little about his churchgoing habits, but it seems likely that he was never a regular churchgoer, and his works discuss Christianity largely as an educative, ethical or political force. His mother's Evangelicalism repelled him, and contrasts strikingly with his tendency to adopt a quasi-Catholic terminology, proclaiming himself the 'pope' of opium, for example, and paying homage

391

to 'Our Ladies of Sorrow'. Most of his private mythology, however, was destined to remain secret. We may guess that it was as much pagan as Christian, and that opium became for him (as for many addicts) a kind of sacrament, but beyond that all is mysterious.

In any case, the works which deal at length with such matters are not those which are most read today. The prose of *Suspiria de Profundis* is, by modern standards, florid and overwrought. Its magnificence is of a kind unlikely to become fashionable in the near future. De Quincey's reputation has fluctuated greatly since his death and seems now to have reached a point of stability where it is generally recognized that, though not a writer of the very first rank, he excelled in certain areas which are perennially interesting though rarely analysed. Perhaps his most remarkable gift was as a creator of literary portraits – self-portraits as well as portraits of others. The *Confessions* are among the finest of all autobiographical works, and the *Recollections of the Lakes and the Lake Poets* are more popular today than ever because they communicate living perceptions of people and places that have come to seem not less but more significant since De Quincey's day. His literary influence has been inconspicuous but remarkably pervasive, a vein of fantasy, introspection and unease tingeing the work of Poe, Stevenson, Dickens, Baudelaire, Proust, Dostoevsky, Borges and many others.

But it is as the 'Opium-Eater' that he will be remembered. For better or worse, De Quincey remains the type of the literary drug-taker, which is certainly as he desired. The remarkable thing is that opium did not conquer him as it has conquered so many others. The drug dominated his life, and yet it was the creative imagination that triumphed. Though (to use the image of his childhood dream) he lay down before the lion, he did not close his eyes or resign himself to defeat, and despite the follies, indignities and failures of his life our final impression is of a man both lovable and oddly heroic.

References

The standard edition of De Quincey's writings, *The Collected Writings of Thomas De Quincey*, ed. David Masson, 14 vols., Edinburgh (A. and C. Black), 1889-90, is abbreviated as *Works*. Full details of other published items are given in the Bibliography.

Locations of the main manuscript sources are indicated by the following abbreviations:

Berg MS   Berg Collection, New York Public Library
BL MS   British Library
Cornell MS   Cornell Wordsworth Collection, Cornell University
   Library, Ithaca, New York
Dove Cottage MS   Wordsworth Library, Dove Cottage, Grasmere
Manchester MS   De Quincey Collection, Manchester Central
   Library
NLS MS   National Library of Scotland
Pforzheimer MS   Carl H. Pforzheimer Library, New York.
Worcester College MS   Library of Worcester College, Oxford

Autograph letters are identified by author, addressee and date wherever these details are not clearly indicated in the text.

Chapter 1: Brothers and Sisters

1. *Works*, III, 316; XIII, 304; Jordan (1962), 87.
2. *Works*, I, 32-3.
3. Quincey's Will, transcript in Manchester Public Library; Quincey (1775).
4. Japp (1890a), 2.
5. *Works*, I, 17.
6. Leary (1896).
7. *Manchester and Salford Directory*, 1781, 48.
8. *Manchester Mercury*, 20 November 1780.
9. *Manchester Mercury*, 2 December 1783.
10. *Works*, I, 114; gravestone in St Anne's Churchyard, Manchester.
11. Leary (1896).
12. *Manchester Mercury*, 22 November 1796.
13. *Works*, III, 299.

14. *Works*, I, 33.
15. *Works*, I, 21.
16. Eaton (1936), 10.
17. *Works*, I, 404.
18. *Works*, I, 22-3.
19. *Works*, I, 127; VI, 130; VII, 69n; I, 39.
20. *Works*, I, 24.
21. Quincey (1775).
22. *Works*, I, 19.
23. Leary (1882).
24. *Works*, I, 56.
25. *Works*, I, 275.
26. *Works*, III, 315.
27. Japp (1891a), I, 9-10.
28. Japp (1891a), I, 10.
29. Japp (1891a), I, 11.
30. *Works*, I, 33-4.
31. *Works*, I, 37.
32. *Works*, I, 38.
33. *Works*, I, 42-3.
34. *Works*, I, 44.
35. *Works*, I, 47.
36. *Works*, I, 45.
37. Fields (1851-9), V, 25.
38. Jordan (1962), 270.
39. Quincey's Will.
40. Quincey's Will.
41. *Works*, I, 61.
42. *Works*, III, 238.
43. *Works*, III, 242.
44. *Works*, XI, 438.
45. *Works*, I, 70-1.
46. Fields (1851-9), I, 211.
47. Fields (1851-9), I, 215.
48. Burnett (1773-92), I, 235.
49. *Works*, I, 102.
50. Hall (1949).
51. *Works*, I, 110.
52. *Works*, I, 110.
53. *Works*, I, 110.
54. Hammersmith Parish Registers; transcript in Shepherd's Bush Public Library.
55. *Works*, III, 244-5.

Chapter 2: A Sentence of Exile

Title: *Works*, I, 331.
1. *Works*, VII, 203.
2. *Works*, I, 288.
3. *Works*, I, 152.
4. *Works*, I, 153.
5. *Works*, I, 153.
6. Hayter (1971), 35.
7. *Works*, I, 155.
8. Japp (1890a), 20.
9. *Works*, I, 159.
10. Japp (1890a), 21.
11. Japp (1890a), 20.
12. *Works*, I, 160.
13. Japp (1891a), I, 159.
14. Japp (1890a), 24.
15. Japp (1891a), I, 18.
16. Hayter (1971), 36.
17. *Monthly Preceptor or Juvenile Library*, I (1800), 135, 350.
18. Japp (1890a), 23-4.
19. Japp (1891a), I, 19-20.
20. *Works*, III, 302.
21. Jordan (1962), 36.
22. *Works*, III, 301-2.
23. De Quincey to Mrs. Quincey, 1818; Cornell MS.
24. Japp (1890a), 26.
25. Eaton (1927), 181-2.
26. *Works*, I, 275.
27. Japp (1891a), I, 25.
28. Japp (1890a), 38-9.
29. *Works*, I, 168.
30. *Works*, I, 183.
31. *Works*, III, 296.
32. *Works*, I, 192.
33. *Works*, I, 196.
34. Japp (1890a), 32.
35. Japp (1890a), 31.

36. *Works*, I, 205-6.
37. *Works*, I, 208.
38. Japp (1891a), I, 27.
39. Japp (1890a), 33-4.
40. *Works*, I, 325.
41. Japp (1890a), 37.
42. Japp (1890a), 37-8.
43. Japp (1891a), I, 28-9.
44. Japp (1890a), 39.
45. Japp (1891a), I, 37.
46. Eaton (1936), 49.
47. Japp (1891a), I, 38.
48. Japp (1890a), 40-41.
49. Japp (1891a), I, 30.
50. Marchand (1973), I, 159.
51. *Works*, I, 268.
52. *Works*, I, 367.
53. *Works*, I, 375.
54. *Works*, I, 341.
55. *Works*, I, 348.
56. Smith (1868), II, 224.
57. *Works*, III, 247.
58. *Works*, III, 350.
59. *Works*, III, 270.
60. Smith (1868), I, 122-3.
61. Glen (1960), 14.
62. Smith (1868), I, 124.
63. Hayter (1971), 36.
64. Glen (1960), 14.
65. Hayter (1971), 36.
66. *Works*, I, 382.
67. Graham and Phythian (1965), 28.

68. *Works*, I, 136.
69. Japp (1891a), I, 48.
70. Japp (1891a), I, 61.
71. *Works*, II, 130.
72. *Works*, I, 129.
73. Japp (1891a), I, 65-7.
74. *Works*, I, 407.
75. Japp (1891a), I, 69.
76. Japp (1891a), I, 67-8.
77. *Works*, I, 385.
78. Japp (1891b), I, 322.
79. *Works*, I, 388.
80. *Works*, I, 394.
81. *Works*, I, 395.
82. *Works*, I, 396.
83. Japp (1891a), I, 70-2.
84. Pycroft (1845), 29.
85. Japp (1891a), I, 73-4.
86. Japp (1891a), I, 75.
87. *Works*, III, 275.
88. Japp (1891a), I, 77.
89. Japp (1891a), I, 80-1.
90. Japp (1890a), 53-5.
91. Japp (1891a), I, 83-7.
92. Eaton (1936), 70-1.
93. Japp (1891a), I, 107.
94. *Works*, III, 276.
95. Japp (1891a), I, 80.
96. Hayter (1971), 37.
97. *Works*, III, 286.
98. *Works*, III, 297.
99. *Works*, III, 297.

Chapter 3: The Compassion of Strangers

1. *Works*, III, 300. Altrincham market was held on Tuesdays. This fact, together with his mother's letter in Japp (1891a) I, 88, enables us to date his escape.
2. *Works*, III, 310.
3. *Works*, III.
4. Jordan (1974), 49-52.

5. Information from the Institute of Oceanographic Sciences, Bidston Observatory.
6. *Works*, III, 312.
7. *Works*, III, 312-13.
8. *Works*, III, 319-20.
9. *Works*, III, 317.
10. *Works*, III, 315.
11. *Works*, III, 312.

12. *Works*, III, 314.
13. **Works**, VII, 196; Bingley (1814), 302.
14. *Works*, III, 326.
15. *Works*, III, 322.
16. *Works*, III, 323.
17. Bingley (1814), 153, 249.
18. *Works*, I, 398; Bingley (1814), 346.
19. Bingley (1814), 489.
20. *Works*, III, 330.
21. *Works*, III, 335-6.
22. Hughes (1900).
23. *Works*, III, 337.
24. *Works*, III, 337.
25. Japp (1891a), I, 48-50.
26. *Works*, I, 338.
27. *Works*, III, 340-1.
28. *Works*, III, 344-9; Harper (1906), II, 274-9.
29. Findlay (1877), 104.
30. *Works*, III, 364.
31. *Works*, III, 350.
32. *Works*, III, 350.
33. St Anne's Parish, Westminster, Poor Rate Books, Christmas 1802 – Lady Day 1803, in Westminster Public Library.
34. *A Circumstantial Report* (1809), 417.
35. *Works*, III, 353.
36. *Works*, III, 354-5.
37. *Works*, III, 355.
38. *Works*, III, 356.
39. *Works*, III, 376.
40. *Works*, III, 355.
41. *Works*, III, 357.
42. *Works*, III, 360.
43. *Works*, III, 361.
44. *Works*, III, 361-2.
45. Japp (1891a), I, 91.
46. *Works*, III, 363.
47. *Works*, III, 366.
48. *Works*, III, 367.
49. *Works*, III, 367.
50. *Works*, III, 368.
51. *Works*, III, 375.

Chapter 4: The Secret of Happiness

1. Eaton (1927), 141.
2. Eaton (1927), 143.
3. Eaton (1927), 153.
4. Eaton (1927), 194.
5. Eaton (1927), 183, 189.
6. Eaton (1927), 179.
7. Eaton (1927), 176.
8. Eaton (1927), 158-9.
9. Eaton (1927), 147.
10. Eaton (1927), 182.
11. Eaton (1927), 181-2.
12. Eaton (1927), 145-6.
13. Eaton (1927), 154.
14. Eaton (1927), 209.
15. Eaton (1927), 152.
16. Jordan (1962), 28.
17. Jordan (1962), 30-1.
18. Eaton (1927), 191-2.
19. Japp (1891a), I, 93.
20. Japp (1891a), I, 94-95.
21. Eaton (1927), 153-4.
22. Eaton (1927), 156-7.
23. Eaton (1927), 156.
24. Eaton (1927), 177.
25. Hilbish (1941), 182.
26. Shaver (1967), 400-1.
27. Jordan (1962), 34.
28. *Works*, I, 415-16.
29. *Works*, II, 15.
30. *Works*, II, 27.
31. Oxonian (1828).
32. *Works*, II, 29.
33. Coombs and Bax, 1930, 313-20; Oxonian (1828); Pycroft (1845), 79.
34. Hogg (1895), 98.

35. *Works*, II, 62.
36. *Works*, II, 55-7.
37. Japp (1891a), I, 224-5.
38. Japp (1891a), I, 105.
39. *Works*, II, 14.
40. *Jackson's Oxford Journal*, March 1804.
41. *Works*, I, 146.
42. Jordan (1962), 41.
43. Jordan (1962), 37.

44. Shaver (1967), 454.
45. Shaver (1967), 454.
46. Jordan (1962), 38.
47. Worcester College Battells Books.
48. *Works*, III, 365n.
49. Worcester College Battells Books.
50. *Works*, III, 365.
51. Hayter (1971), 70-2.

Chapter 5: The Road to Grasmere

1. Lomax (1973).
2. Lomax (1973).
3. Japp (1890a), 38; Currie (1805).
4. Owen (1934), 54-6; *Ninth Report* (1782-3); *East India Company* (1787).
5. *Works*, I, 412-13.
6. *Works*, III, 399-400.
7. Japp (1891a), 232-3.
8. *Works*, III, 387.
9. Goodman and Gilman (1975), 250.
10. *Works*, I, 49-50.
11. *Works*, III, 38-9.
12. *Works*, III, 43.
13. *Works*, III, 388-9.
14. *Works*, III, 389-90.
15. *Works*, III, 391.
16. *Works*, III, 393.
17. *Works*, II, 87.
18. *Works*, II, 101.
19. *Works*, III, 425.
20. *Works*, III, 425.
21. Lomax (1973), 173.
22. *Works*, III, 425-6.
23. Fryer (1909), III, 100; Chardin (1927), 245; Tavernier (1684), 242; Hasselquist (1767), 299.
24. Hayter (1971), 82.
25. Jordan (1962), 42.
26. Moorman (1969), 26.

27. *Works*, II, 231.
28. Japp (1890a), 75; Jordan (1962), 368n.36.
29. Japp (1891a), II, 273.
30. Japp (1891a), II, 112.
31. Hogg (1895), 98-9.
32. *Works*, XIII, 362-6.
33. *Works*, XIII, 364.
34. Japp (1891a), I, 111.
35. Moorman (1969), 143, 144.
36. Japp (1891a), I, 240.
37. Worcester College Battells Books.
38. BL MSS Add. 35, 344.
39. Sandford (1888), II, 182.
40. *Works*, II, 140.
41. *Works*, II, 142.
42. *Works*, II, 146.
43. Sandford (1888), II, 306.
44. *Works*, II, 96, 125.
45. *Works*, II, 148.
46. *Works*, II, 150.
47. *Works*, II, 151; Lawrence (1970), 133.
48. *Works*, II, 152.
49. *Works*, II, 157.
50. *Works*, II, 161-2.
51. *Works*, II, 162.
52. Griggs (1956-71), III, 28-9; 73; 79.
53. Eaton (1936), 116n.
54. Coburn (1957-   ), 3168;

Potter (1934), 7.
55. Japp (1980a), 91.
56. Griggs (1956-71), III, 7.
57. Japp (1890a), 97.
58. Japp (1891a), I, 128.
59. Griggs (1956-71), III, 33-4.
60. Japp (1891a), I, 132.
61. Japp (1891a), I, 133.
62. Griggs·(1956-71), III, 32.
63. Potter (1934), 7-8.
64. Coleridge (1873), I, 12.
65. *Works*, II, 233-4.
66. *Works*, II, 235.
67. *Works*, II, 242-50.
68. *Works*, II, 306.

69. Jordan (1962), 90 and n.
70. *Works*, II, 303.
71. *Works*, II, 306.
72. *Works*, II, 306.
73. *Works*, II, 238.
74. *Works*, X, 117.
75. *Works*, II, 239.
76. *Works*, II, 239.
77. Moorman (1969), 180.
78. *Works*, II, 307.
79. *Works*, II, 317, 311.
80. Moorman (1965), 101.
81. *Works*, II, 322-3.
82. *Works*, II, 349.

Chapter 6: Irksome Employments

1. Jordan (1962), 86.
2. Moorman (1969), 180.
3. Griggs (1956-71), III, 47-9; *Works*, II, 190.
4. *Works*, II, 188-9.
5. Gillman (1838), I, 251.
6. Griggs (1956-71), III, 49, 51.
7. *Works*, II, 190.
8. Moorman (1969), 198.
9. Moorman (1969), 495.
10. Jordan (1962), 87.
11. Jordan (1962), 87-8.
12. *Prelude*, III, 74-5.
13. Hogg (1895), 99.
14. Jordan (1962), 87.
15. Pycroft (1845); Tatham (1807).
16. Jordan (1962), 90.
17. Hogg (1895), 109-10.
18. Moorman (1969), 257.
19. Moorman (1969), 257.
20. Japp (1891a), I, 277.
21. Moorman (1969), 272.
22. *Works*, V, 262, 282.
23. Wells (1921), 21-2.
24. Moorman (1969), 278.
25. Japp (1891a), I, 251, 281;

Jordan (1962), 115-16, 242; Coburn (1957-   ), 3471.
26. Griggs (1956-71), III, 262.
27. Griggs (1956-71), III, 177.
28. Moorman (1969), 283.
29. Coburn (1954), 12.
30. *Works*, V, 19n.
31. Japp (1891a), I, 286.
32. Wells (1921), 27-9.
33. Griggs (1956-71), III, 206.
34. Wright (1970), 160.
35. Moorman (1969), 315.
36. *Works*, V, 362-3.
37. Griggs (1956-71), III, 177.
38. Moorman (1969), 351.
39. Jordan (1962), 123.
40. Griggs (1956-71), III, 214.
41. Jordan (1962), 102.
42. Jordan (1962), 97.
43. Moorman (1969), 292.
44. Jordan (1962), 107.
45. Jordan (1962), 116-17.
46. Jordan (1962), 119.
47. Moorman (1969), 303-4.
48. Moorman (1969), 299.
49. Eaton (1936), 159n.
50. Wordsworth (1809), 207.

51. Jordan (1962), 132-3.
52. Moorman (1969), 318.
53. Jordan (1962), 105-6.
54. Moorman (1969), 293.
55. Moorman (1969), 293-4.
56. Moorman (1969), 337.
57. Jordan (1962), 178.
58. Richards (1927).
59. Moorman (1969), 357.
60. Jordan (1962), 185.
61. Moorman (1969), 357.
62. Jordan (1962), 139.
63. Jordan (1962), 144.
64. Japp (1891a), I, 250, 287.
65. Jordan (1962), 145.
66. Moorman (1969), 321.
67. Griggs (1956-71), III, 205-6.
68. Moorman (1969), 327.
69. Moorman (1969), 329.
70. Moorman (1969), 330.
71. Moorman (1969), 336-7.
72. Moorman (1969), 340.
73. Jordan (1962), 171.
74. Jordan (1962), 174

75. Japp (1891a), I, 252.
76. Japp (1891a), I, 252.
77. Moorman (1969), 342.
78. Moorman (1969), 347-8.
79. Moorman (1969), 344.
80. Moorman (1969), 350.
81. Japp (1891a), I, 262.
82. Griggs (1956-71), III, 214.
83. Jordan (1962), 183.
84. Moorman (1969), 326, 364; Jordan (1962), 158, 184.
85. Japp (1891a), II, 2, 4.
86. Japp (1891a), I, 284-5.
87. Wright (1970), 133.
88. Jordan (1962), 244.
89. *Works*, X, 116.
90. *Edinburgh Review,* XI (1807), 214.
91. Jordan (1962), 249.
92. *Works*, I, 287-315.
93. Jordan (1962), 254.
94. Moorman (1969), 371.
95. Jordan (1962), 248.

Chapter 7: The Fruits of Philosophy

1. *Works*, I, 204.
2. *Works*, II, 367.
3. Moorman (1969), 376.
4. Jordan (1974), illustration facing p. 106.
5. Jordan (1962), 108.
6. Moorman (1969), 374, 376.
7. Moorman (1969), 376.
8. Jordan (1962), 205-6; *Works*, II, 438; Moorman (1969), I, 325.
9. Moorman (1969), 374.
10. Coburn (1954), 22.
11. Coburn (1954), 27.
12. Moorman (1969), 377.
13. Moorman (1969), 389.
14. Moorman (1969), 429.
15. *Works*, II, 268-9, 278-9, 280.

16. Sealts (1973), X, 535.
17. *Works*, II, 434-5; V, 283-6.
18. Gordon (1862), I, 140-3.
19. *Works*, X, 303; XIII, 41.
20. Griggs (1956-71), III, 59.
21. Moorman (1969), 243, 244.
22. Griggs (1956-71), I, 257.
23. Moorman (1969), 243.
24. De Quincey to Lloyd: Berg MS.
25. *Works*, II, 383, 390-2.
26. Sara Coleridge to De Quincey, 1810: Cornell MS; Moorman (1969) I, 457.
27. *Works*, II, 345.
28. Japp (1891a), II, 8, 151.
29. Coburn (1957-   ), 3587.f.44.

30. *Works*, II, 145.
31. *Works*, XI, 448; Jordan, 178.
32. Hayter (1971), 100.
33. Japp (1891a), II, 111.
34. *Works*, II, 335.
35. Japp (1891a), II, 22; Griggs (1956-71), III, 286; Moorman (1969), 427.
36. *Works*, III, 397-8.
37. Chein *et al.* (1964), 159.
38. *Works*, III, 398.
39. Japp (1891a), II, 19, 76.
40. Moorman (1969), 511.
41. *Works*, II, 262-3.
42. Coburn (1954), 28.
43. Coburn (1954), 33.
44. Japp (1891a), II, 79, 81; 21.
45. Coburn (1954), 36-7.
46. Coburn (1969), I, 337.
47. Coburn (1954), 37-8.
48. Moorman (1969), 114; Jordan (1962), 260.
49. *Works*, XIII, 129.
50. *Works*, II, 325-7.
51. *Kendal Chronicle*, 3 July 1819.
52. *Works*, XIII, 374-5.
53. Moorman (1969), 159n; Hogg (1895), 156.
54. Japp (1891a), I, 287.
55. Jordan (1962), 261-2.
56. Japp (1891a), II, 114.
57. Griggs (1956-71), III, 296.
58. *Works*, II, 209.
59. Jordan (1962), 275-6; *Works*, XIII, 13-14.
60. Moorman and Hill (1970), 23-4.
61. Morley (1938), I, 103.
62. Jordan (1962), 263.
63. Jordan (1962), 266.
64. Jordan (1962), 266-7.
65. Morley (1938), I, 104.
66. Jordan (1962), 271.
67. *Works*, II, 442.
68. *Works*, II, 443.
69. *Works*, II, 444.
70. *Works*, I, 45-6.
71. *Works*, II, 444.
72. Moorman and Hill (1970), 50; Japp (1890a), 130-1.
73. *Works*, III, 400.
74. *Works*, III, 401-2n.
75. *Works*, III, 385; Hayter (1971), 88.
76. *Works*, III, 404.
77. Burton (1958), 24-5.
78. Coburn (1954), 88.
79. Moorman and Hill (1970), 80-1.
80. *Works*, III, 200-1.
81. *Works*, III, 198.
82. *Works*, II, 389.
83. *Works*, II, 313.
84. *Works*, III, 206.
85. De Selincourt (1970), I, 123.
86. Eaton (1936), 217.
87. Jordan (1962), 306.
88. *Works*, XII, 164-6.
89. Moorman and Hill (1970), 372.
90. *Works*, II, 209.
91. *Works*, XIII, 238-9.
92. Wright (1970), 186.
93. *Works*, IV, 48.
94. Jordan (1962), 226.
95. Gordon (1862), I, 208.
96. *Works*, III, 108.
97. Swann (1934), 52.
98. Morley (1938), I, 137.
99. Lucas (1903-5), VI, 507.
100. *Works*, XIV, 275.
101. *Works*, XIII, 285-9, 289n-292n.
102. *Works*, XIII, 306.
103. *Works*, XIII, 304-318.
104. Duckers (1920).
105. Hogg (1895), 240-1.
106. Japp (1891a), II, 35-6.
107. Lang (1897), I, 97.

108. Hogg (1841), V, cvii-cviii.
109. Moorman and Hill (1970), 194.
110. Moorman and Hill (1970), 198-9.
111. Moorman and Hill (1970), 222.
112. Moorman and Hill (1970), 230.
113. Moorman and Hill (1970), 372; Wordsworth to Lamb, 21 November 1816: Dove Cottage MS; Jordan (1962), 233, n.77.
114. *Works*, III, 45.
115. Jordan (1962), 227.
116. Japp (1891a), II, 110.
117. Coburn (1954), 88.
118. Moorman and Hill (1970), 298-9.
119. Hogg (1895), 78-9; *Works*, II, 396-400; Lloyd (1975), 239.
120. Hayter (1971), 20; Works, III, 402-5.
121. Marsden (1966).
122. Morley (1938), I, 187.
123. Morley (1938), I, 193.
124. Morley (1927), I, 90; Morley (1938), I, 194-6.
125. Wordsworth to Lamb, 21 November 1816: Dove Cottage MS.
126. Jordan (1962), 278-9.
127. Coburn (1954), 106.
128. Moorman and Hill (1970), 372.
129. Lucas (1903-5), VI, 506-7.
130. De Quincey to Mrs Quincey, 1818: Cornell MS.
131. Hayter (1971), 93-6; *Works*, III, 409-10.
132. Hayter (1971), 88, 95, 96; *Works*, III, 401, 410.
133. De Quincey to Mrs Quincey, 1818: Cornell MS.
134. *Works*, XIII, 337.
135. Hayter (1971), 98.
136. *Works*, III, 434.
137. *Works*, III, 435-40.
138. Hayter (1971), 97.
139. Jordan (1962), 303-4.
140. Jordan (1962), 307.
141. Jordan (1962), 319.
142. Jordan (1962), 319.
143. Japp (1890a), 153.
144. Janzow (1968).
145. *Westmorland Gazette*, Proprietors' Minute Book.
146. Moorman and Hill (1970), 478.
147. Japp (1890a), 153.
148. Janzow (1968), 63, 105-6.
149. *Westmorland Gazette*, 11 July 1818.
150. Janzow (1968), 211-13.
151. Janzow (1968), 52-3n.
152. Janzow (1968), 200.
153. Jordan (1962), 326-7, 324.
154. Coburn (1954), 152.
155. *Westmorland Gazette*, 18 May 1819; 28 November 1818; 9 January 1819.
156. *Westmorland Gazette*, 12 December 1818.
157. *Westmorland Gazette*, 5 September 1818; 8 May 1819.
158. Janzow (1968), 25.
159. Janzow (1968), 257-8, 264.
160. Moorman and Hill (1970), 488, 507, 512.
161. Hogg (1895), 75.
162. *Works*, III, 440.
163. Jordan (1962), 324.
164. *Works*, XIII, 290n-292n.
165. *Works*, III, 441-3.
166. Notes in the Library of University of Texas at Austin.
167. *Works*, III, 432-3.

168. Japp (1890a), 154.
169. Moorman and Hill (1970), 543; Japp (1890a), 153-4.
170. De Quincey to Mrs Quincey, 1818: Cornell MS.
171. Japp (1891a), II, 123.

172. *Westmorland Gazette*, Proprietors' Minute-Book.
173. Aspinall (1949), 361.
174. Moorman and Hill (1970), 608.

Chapter 8: Confessions

1. Japp (1891a), II, 40.
2. Swann (1934), 83-91.
3. Japp (1891a), II, 42-3.
4. Japp (1891a), II, 44.
5. Japp (1891a), II, 43-5.
6. Blackwood to De Quincey, 26 August 1820: NLS MSS.
7. Hayter (1971), 112-13; *Works*, III, 447.
8. *Works*, III, 72-4.
9. Japp (1891b), I, 318.
10. Armitt (1916), 685.
11. Coburn (1954), 209.
12. NLS MS.
13. Japp (1890a), 165-6.
14. Eaton (1936), 262.
15. Byrns (1956b).
16. NLS MS.
17. NLS MS.
18. NLS MS.
19. NLS MS.
20. NLS MS.
21. NLS MS.
22. Japp (1891a) II, 46-7.
23. Jordan (1962), 295.
24. Burton (1958), 76, 82, 115.
25. Eaton (1936), 270n. Chilcott (1973).
26. *Works* III, 127-8.
27. Griggs (1956-71), V, 163-4.
28. BL MS Add. 37215.
29. Hayter (1971), 49.
30. Taylor (1925), 262.
31. *London Magazine* IV (1821), 351.

32. *Morning Herald*, 22 May 1823.
33. Wilson (1923), 250.
34. Morley (1938), I, 275.
35. Cornell MS.
36. *Prelude* (1805), I, 352-5.
37. Foster (1838), 8.
38. *Works*, XI, 337.
39. Gross (1969), 12.
40. Morley (1938), I, 267.
41. Morley (1938), I, 275.
42. Chilcott (1973).
43. *Works*, III, 78.
44. Hogg (1895), 72.
45. Hogg (1895), 74.
46. Hogg (1895), 83.
47. Hogg (1895), 87.
48. Hogg (1895), 89-90; Woodhouse Notebook, Harvard.
49. *Works*, XI, 389.
50. Hogg (1895), 90-1.
51. Eaton (1936), 282-3.
52. Eaton (1936), 283.
53. Hogg (1895), 102; BL MS.
54. Eaton (1936), 288.
55. Berg MS.
56. Japp (1891a), II, 126.
57. BL MS, Add. 37215.f.10-12.
58. Berg MS.
59. *Works*, III, 470-1.
60. Eaton (1936), 289.
61. Rollins (1948), II, 138.
62. Berg MS.
63. Hill (1978), 168.

64. Hogg (1895), 240.
65. Rollins (1948), II, 435.
66. Blackwood's, XIV (1823), 485-6, 495.
67. Eaton (1936), 294.
68. Eaton (1936), 293.
69. Dove Cottage MS.
70. Undated (August 1823); BL MS, Add.37215.

Chapter 9: The Wretched Business of Hack-Author

1. Hill (1978), 218-19.
2. Armitt (1916), 685.
3. De Quincey to John White, 25 Aug. 1823: Berg MS.
4. Collins (1870); Duckers (1920).
5. Eaton (1936), 296.
6. *The Stranger's Grave*, 98.
7. *The Stranger's Grave*, 154.
8. Rollins (1948), II, 446.
9. Goldman (1965), 76.
10. Jordan (1962), 329-30.
11. Gosse (1894), 371.
12. Eaton (1936), 300.
13. *Works*, III, 171.
14. *Works*, III, 172.
15. *John Bull*, I, 21-3.
16. *Blackwood's*, XVI (1824), 242.
17. *Works*, III, 178.
18. Knight (1864), I, 327.
19. Knight (1864), I, 327.
20. Morley (1938), I, 311.
21. *Works*, III, 171.
22. *Works*, XI, 239, 256.
23. Sanders (1970-7), III, 260.
24. Sanders (1970-7), II, 434.
25. Sanders (1970-7), III, 233-4.
26. Axon (1912).
27. *Works*, XIV, 138-43.
28. Knight (1864), I, 327.
29. *Walladmor*, I, xviii-xix.
30. Coburn (1954), 354.
31. Berg MS.
32. Japp (1891a), II, 64.
33. Japp (1891a), II, 64.
34. *Works*, I, 290.
35. Japp (1891a), II, 63.
36. Japp (1891a), II, 131.
37. Gordon (1862), II, 79.
38. Hill (1978), 494 and n.
39. *Works*, X, 151.
40. Knight (1864), I, 330.
41. Swann (1934), 232.
42. Hill (1978), 318.
43. Jordan (1962), 331-2.
44. Hill (1978), 388.
45. Coburn (1954), 310.
46. Japp (1891a), II, 49.
47. Hill (1978), 455.
48. Gordon (1862), II, 157.
49. MacFarlane (1917), 80.
50. Gordon (1862), II, 158.
51. *Works*, VII, 68-9n.
52. Hill (1978), 494.
53. Musgrove (1953), 7.
54. Byrns (1956a), 994.
55. Jordan (1962), 298.
56. Tave (1966), 9.
57. Tave (1966), 10.
58. Tave (1966), 51.
59. Tave (1966), 352.
60. Tave (1966), 119-20.
61. Tave (1966), 4.
62. Eaton (1936), 363n.
63. Sanders (1970-7), IV, 291.
64. Sanders (1970-7), IV, 300.
65. Wilson (1924), 39.
66. Sanders (1970-7), IV, 341-2.
67. Hill (1878), 85.
68. Dora Wordsworth to Edward Quillinan, 12 April 1829: Dove Cottage MS.
69. Byrns (1956a), 994.

70. Goldman (1965), 75-7.

71. Sanders (1970-7), IV, 433.

Chapter 10: Sanctuary

1. Armitt (1916), 689.
2. Eaton (1936), 320-1; Armitt (1916), 689-96.
3. Armitt (1916), 692-6; Clowes (1892), 171-3.
4. Armitt (1916), 698.
5. Cornell MS.
6. Morley (1927), I, 201.
7. *Works*, X, 48n.
8. Knight (1864), I, 341-2.
9. Eaton (1936), 313n.
10. Armitt (1916), 685.
11. Swann (1934), 197.
12. NLS MS.
13. Green (1958).
14. Oliphant (1897), I, 432.
15. 6 March 1830: NLS MS.
16. Eaton (1936), 328.
17. Oliphant (1897), I, 432-3.
18. 10 March 1830: NLS MS.
19. De Quincey to Blackwood, 16 December 1830: NLS MS.
20. De Quincey to Blackwood, 18 June 1830: NLS MS.
21. Goldman (1965), 29-33.
22. NLS MS.
23. NLS MS.
24. Griggs (1956-71), II, 988.
25. Eaton (1936), 339.
26. Forward (1939), 517.
27. Japp (1891a), II, 54-5.
28. Japp (1890a), 278.
29. De Quincey to Blackwood: NLS MS.
30. De Quincey to Blackwood, 1831: NLS MS.
31. Byrns (1956a), 992-3.
32. Eaton (1936), 340.
33. Eaton (1936), 339-40.
34. Eaton (1936), 354.
35. De Quincey to Blackwood, 11 September 1832: NLS MS.
36. Eaton (1936), 519.
37. Forward (1939).
38. Forward (1939).
39. De Quincey to Blackwood, 29 October 1832: NLS MS.
40. Eaton (1936), 519.
41. Worcester College MS.
42. De Quincey to Blackwood, '1832': NLS MS.
43. Eaton (1936), 347-8n.
44. *Klosterheim*, 112.
45. Oliphant (1897), I, 419-20.
46. De Quincey to Blackwood, '1832': NLS MS.
47. Sanders (1970-7), VI, 339.
48. De Quincey to Tait, 25 July 1832: BL MS, Add. 37021.f.62.
49. Robert Blackwood to De Quincey, February 1833: NLS MS.
50. 13 February 1833: NLS MS.
51. De Quincey to Blackwood, 6 March 1833: NLS MS.
52. McCusker (1939), 66.
53. Sanders (1970-7), VI, 322.
54. Sanders (1970-7), VI, 339-40.
55. Forward (1939), 522.
56. Eaton (1936), 344.
57. Sanders (1970-7), VI, 362.
58. Eaton (1936), 346.
59. Eaton (1936), 361.
60. September 1833: NLS MS.
61. Armitt (1916), 700.
62. Eaton (1936), 344.
63. De Quincey to John Simpson, 27 September 1833: Berg MS.
64. Armitt (1916), 704.
65. Japp (1890a), 144.
66. Lockhart (1819), I, 33.

67. Hannah (1927); Halkerston (1831).
68. Eaton (1936), 343, 345.
69. Eaton (1936), 519.
70. De Quincey to Benson, 1 February 1834: Berg MS; Eaton (1936), 378.
71. Dove Cottage MS, 59(b).
72. Berg MS.
73. 5 July 1835: Berg MS.
74. Gray (1926), 182.
75. *Works*, IV, 292.
76. Japp (1891b), I, 11.
77. *Works*, II, 146.
78. *Works*, II, 159.

79. *Works*, II, 184-5.
80. Jordan (1962), 336.
81. Froude (1881), II, 315-16.
82. Coleridge (1873), I, 109.
83. Froude (1881), II, 316-17.
84. *Blackwood's*, XIV (1823), 500.
85. *Works*, X, 21-2,
86. *Works*, XI, 460-1.
87. De Quincey to T.N. Talfourd, 5 March 1840: Pforzheimer MS. Quoted by permission of the Carl H. Pforzheimer Library.
88. Japp (1891b), 117.

Chapter 11: Utterly Aground.

1. n.d. [November 1834]: NLS MS.
2. Balfour (1835).
3. 'Letter from a Modern Author on the Useful Limits of Literature considered as a Study for Females': Dove Cottage MS.
4. Eaton (1936), 365n.
5. Eaton (1936), 366.
6. Eaton (1936), 460.
7. Eaton (1936), 367n.
8. Moore (1933), 176.
9. Bertram (1893), 62.
10. Eaton (1936), 375n.
11. Eaton (1936), 368n.
12. Bertram (1893), 62-3.
13. Bertram (1893), 62.
14. *Works*, II, 135-6.
15. *Works*, II, 136n.
16. Robert Roscoe to W.S. Roscoe, 12 March 1837: Roscoe Papers, Liverpool Record Office.
17. Tredrey (1954), 236.
18. Japp (1891a), II, 179.
19. De Quincey to J.J. Smith, 15

April and 6 June 1837, quoted in undated extract from Maggs Bros. sale catalogue in De Quincey collection, Manchester Central Library.
20. Eaton (1936), 368n.
21. Eaton (1936), 399n.
22. Eaton (1936), 378.
23. Goldman (1965), 34-7.
24. Goldman (1965), 42-3.
25. Japp (1890a), 219-20.
26. Japp (1891b), I, 20.
27. Eaton (1936), 370-1.
28. Eaton (1936), 519.
29. De Quincey to Blackwood, n.d. (1837): NLS MS.
30. Eaton (1936), 519.
31. Eaton (1936), 372.
32. De Quincey to Wilson, 25 May, 1838: NLS MS.
33. 5 March 1840: Pforzheimer MS. Quoted by permission of the Carl H. Pforzheimer Library.
34. NLS MS.
35. 25 May 1838: NLS MS.
36. De Quincey to Blackwood, 21

June 1838: NLS MS.
37. Eaton (1936), 374n.
38. NLS MS, 1670.
39. Eaton (1936), 374.
40. Bertram (1893), 72.
41. Eaton (1936), 380-1.
42. De Quincey to Blackwood, 3 January 1839: NLS MS.
43. Priestley (1908), 56-7.
44. Priestley (1908), 58.
45. Eaton (1936), 383.
46. *Works*, XIII, 64.
47. Sealts (1973), X, 220, 535.
48. Japp (1890a), 199.
49. Wright (1970), 145.
50. MacFarlane (1917), 82.
51. Jordan (1962), 347.
52. Jordan (1962), 347.
53. Wright (1970), 145-6.
54. Wright (1970), 147-8.
55. Wright (1970), 148.
56. Jordan (1962), 350.
57. Wright (1970), 187.
58. Cornell MS.
59. Eaton (1936), 384-5.
60. McIndoe to De Quincey, 2 May 1840: NLS MS.
61. De Quincey to Blackwood, 4 May 1840: NLS MS.
62. 22 May, 1840: NLS MS.
63. NLS MS.
64. Eaton (1936), 368n; De Quincey to Blackwood, 13 August 1840: NLS MS.
65. De Quincey to Blackwood, 19 February 1840: NLS MS
66. De Quincey to Blackwood, 21 July 1840: NLS MS.
67. 30 August 1840: NLS MS.
68. Japp (1891a), II, 212-26.
69. Gérin (1971), 206.
70. Gérin (1961), 159-60.

Chapter 12: Resurrection

1. Hill (1895), 99-100.
2. Mackay (1887), I, 75.
3. *Works*, VIII, 28.
4. NLS MS 10998.
5. Eaton (1936), 409.
6. De Quincey to Blackwood, 7 June 1841: NLS MS.
7. Goldman (1965), 83-4.
8. De Quincey to Blackwood, 7 January 1841: NLS MS.
9. De Quincey to Blackwood, 7 September 1841: NLS MS.
10. Eaton (1936), 408.
11. 26 September 1841: NLS MS.
12. 25 November 1841: NLS MS.
13. Eaton (1936), 398.
14. NLS MS.
15. 18 February 1842: NLS MS.
16. *Works*, X, 150.
17. NLS MSS.
18. De Quincey to Blackwood, 28 August 1842: NLS MS.
19. Cranbrook (1884), 158.
20. Fairbrother (1915).
21. Eaton (1936), 400.
22. NLS MS.
23. De Quincey to Blackwood, 27 October 1843; 8 July 1844: NLS MSS
24. Hill (1878), 495.
25. Japp (1890a), 242.
26. *Works*, XIV, 274-5.
27. Japp (1890a), 243.
28. Japp (1890a), 241-2.
29. Japp (1890a), 244-5.
30. Japp (1890a), 245.
31. Japp (1890a), 244.
32. Japp (1890a), 244.
33. Eaton (1936), 423.
34. *Works*, XI, 465.

35. Robson (1967), IV, 392-404.
36. n.d. (1844): NLS MS.
37. 5 May and 6 May 1844: NLS MS.
38. Japp (1890a), 255.
39. De Quincey to Blackwood, 15 August 1844: NLS MS.
40. *Works*, V, 206-7.
41. *Works*, V, 210-11.
42. Japp (1890), 253-4.
43. *Works*, XIII, 335.
44. *Works*, XIII, 368.
45. *Works*, XIII, 368-9.
46. Eaton (1936), 421.
47. NLS MS.
48. De Quincey to Blackwood, 9 April 1845: NLS MS; Eaton (1936), 422.
49. NLS MS.
50. NLS MS
51. 10 November 1845: NLS MS.
52. De Quincey to Blackwood, 3 July 1845: NLS MS
53. Eaton (1936), 422.
54. Bertram (1893), 64.
55. Japp (1891a), II, 187.
56. Japp (1891b), I, 277.
57. Letter dated 6 October 1847: Hornby Library, Liverpool.
58. *Works*, XIV, 274-5.
59. Japp (1890a), 274.
60. Hogg (1895), 115.
61. Eaton (1936), 393.
62. Gilfillan (1881), 32.
63. Hogg (1895), 119.
64. Hogg (1895), 113.
65. Letter dated 28 April 1847, Bodleian Library, MS Eng.Lett.e.28,Fol.95.
66. Japp (1890a), 262-3.
67. Letter dated 6 October 1847: Hornby Libary, Liverpool.

Chapter 13: A Match against Time

1. Japp (1890a), 277.
2. Japp (1891b), I, 275.
3. *Works*, III, 221.
4. Japp (1890a), 283.
5. Eaton (1936), 445.
6. Burton (1862), 33-4.
7. Eaton (1936), 445.
8. Eaton (1936), 449-50.
9. Eaton (1936), 461-2.
10. Hogg (1895), 185-6.
11. Burton (1862), 37.
12. Masson (1881), 107-8.
13. Sealts (1973), X, 536.
14. *Blackwood's* April 1894; Japp (1890a), 310.
15. Japp (1890a), 271.
16. *Works*, XIV, 282.
17. Jordan (1962), 248.
18. Hogg (1895), 170.
19. Hogg to W.E.A. Axon, 12 May 1908: Manchester MS.
20. 'Memorandum', Hogg to W.E.A. Axon: Manchester MS.
21. Japp (1890a), 315.
22. Eaton (1936), 472n.
23. Gilfillan (1857), II, 161-2.
24. Bonner (1936), 13.
25. Hogg (1895), 230.
26. Bonner (1936), 16.
27. Bonner (1936), 16-17; Eaton (1936), 472.
28. Hogg (1895), 133.
29. Hogg (1895), 236-7.
30. Eaton (1936), 477-8.
31. Japp (1890a), 315-16.
32. Japp (1890a), 318.
33. Curwen (1873), 174-6.
34. Japp (1890a), 318-19, 324.
35. *Works*, VII, 232.
36. Japp (1890a), 331.
37. Eaton (1936), 479.

38. Hogg (1895), 203-5.
39. Hogg (1895), 203-5.
40. Japp (1891a), II, 189.
41. Morley (1938), 768.
42. Eaton (1936), 482n; Japp (1891b), I, 228, 239, 273.
43. Eaton (1936), 483.
44. Hogg (1895), 147.
45. Japp (1890a), 333.
46. Hogg (1895), 151.
47. Eaton (1936), 428n.
48. *Works*, III, 221.
49. NLS MS 10984.
50. Sotheby's Catalogue, 27 October 1970, Lot 455.
51. NLS MS 10984.
52. *Works*, III, 219.
53. Japp (1890a), 387.
54. Bonner (1936), 55-6.
55. *Works*, III, 220.
56. Japp (1890a), 387.
57. Bonner (1936), 32.
58. Eaton (1936), 497-8.
59. Japp (1890a), 409.
60. Undated extract from Maggs Bros. sale catalogue in De Quincey collection, Manchester Central Library.
61. Eaton (1936), 501.
62. De Quincey to Hogg 'October 20': Manchester MS.
63. Japp (1890a), 290.
64. Eaton (1936), 501.
65. Bonner (1936), 92.
66. Berg MS.
67. Japp (1890a), 371-2.
68. Eaton (1936), 458n.
69. Japp (1890a), 443.
70. Alden (1863).
71. Japp (1891b), I, 26.
72. Japp (1890a), 442-51; Alden (1863), 368.
73. Alden (1863), 368; Hogg (1895), 163.
74. Japp (1890a), 447.
75. G. Steell to W.E.A. Axon: Manchester MS.
76. *Athenaeum* (1859), 814-15.
77. Japp (1890a), 281.
78. Japp (1891a), II, 240.

Bibliography

This bibliography lists only works to which specific reference is made in the text. Systematic De Quincey bibliographies may be found in Green, J.A., *Thomas De Quincey: A Bibliography*, Manchester, 1908 and Dendurent, H.O., *Thomas De Quincey: A Reference Guide*, Boston Mass. (Hall), 1978.

Items are listed chronologically. Where two works by a single author appear in one year, they are lettered (a) and (b).

1684   Tavernier, Jean Baptiste, *Collections of Travels through Turkey into Persia and the East-Indies*, 2 vols., London.

1767   Hasselquist, Frederick, *Voyages and Travels in the Levant*, London (C. Davies and C. Reymers).

1773-92 Burnett, J., Lord Monboddo, *Of the Origin and Progress of Language*, 6 vols., London (T. Cadell).

1775   Quincey, Thomas, *A Short Tour in the Midland Counties of England*, London (Printed for the Author).

1782-3   *Ninth Report from the Select Committee on the Administration of Justice in Bengal*, London.

1787   *East India Company: Copy of All Accounts Received of the Ships Betsey and Nonesuch &c.*, London.

1800-3   *Monthly Preceptor and Juvenile Library*, 6 vols., London.

1805   Currie, James, *Medical Observations on the Effects of Water*, London (Cadell and Davies).

1807   Tatham, E., *An Address to the Members of Convocation at Large, on the Proposed Statute on Examinations*, Oxford.

1809   *A Circumstantial Report . . . upon the Charges . . . Against his Royal Highness the Duke of York*, London (James Cundee).

           Wordsworth, William, *Concerning the Relations of Great Britain, Spain, and Portugal, to each other, and to the common enemy, at this crisis; and specially as affected by the convention of Cintra*, London (Longman).

1814   Bingley, W., *North Wales, Delineated from Two Excursions*, 2nd ed., London (Longman).

1819   Lockhart, J.G., *Peter's Letters to his Kinsfolk*, 3rd ed., Edinburgh (Blackwood).

1823   *The Stranger's Grave*, London (Longman, Hurst, Rees, Orme, Brown, and Green).

1825   *Walladmor: 'Freely translated into German from the English of Sir Walter Scott' and now freely translated from the German of G.W. Haering into English*, 2 vols., London (Taylor and Hessey).

1828   Oxonian, An, 'Three Years at Oxford', *Blackwood's Edinburgh Magazine*, XXIV, 862-9.

1831   Halkerston, Peter, *A Treatise on the History, Law, and Privileges of the Palace and Sanctuary of Holyroodhouse*, Edinburgh (Maclachlan and Stewart).

1832   *Klosterheim; or the Masque. By the English Opium-Eater*, Edinburgh (Blackwood).

1835   Balfour, J.H., 'Case of Peculiar Disease of the Skull and Dura Mater', *Edinburgh Medical and Surgical Journal*, XLIII, 319-25.

1838   Foster, John, *Essays in a Series of Letters to a Friend*, 13th ed., London (Samuel Holdsworth).

        Gillman, James, *The Life of Samuel Taylor Coleridge,* Vol. 1, London (W. Pickering).

1841   Hogg, James, *The Poetical Works of the Ettrick Shepherd*, 5 vols., Glasgow.

1845   Pycroft, James, *The Collegian's Guide; or Recollections of College Days*, London (Longman and Co.).

1851-9 Fields, J.T., ed., *De Quincey's Writings*, 20 vols., Boston, Mass. (Ticknor, Reed and Fields).

1857   Gilfillan, George, *Galleries of Literary Portraits*, 2 vols., London and Edinburgh (J. Hogg).

1859   'Thomas De Quincey' [obituary], *Athenaeum*, 814-15.

1862   Burton, J.H., *The Book Hunter*, Edinburgh (Blackwood).

        Gordon, Martha H., *Christopher North: A Memoir of John Wilson*, Edinburgh (Edmonston and Douglas).

1863   Alden, H.M., 'Thomas De Quincey', *Atlantic Monthly*, XII, 345-68.

1864   Knight, Charles, *Passages of a Working Life During Half a Century*, 3 vols., London.

1868   Smith, J.F., *The Admissions Register of the Manchester School*, 2 vols., Manchester (Chetham Society).

1870   Collins, Mortimer, 'Praed's Country', *Belgravia*, 2nd Series II, 445-52.

1873   Coleridge, Sara, *Memoir and Letters of Sara Coleridge, Edited by her Daughter*, 2 vols., London (Henry S. King and Co.).

        Curwen, Henry, *A History of Booksellers, the Old and the New*, London (Chatto and Windus).

1877   Findlay, J.R., 'Thomas De Quincey', *Encyclopaedia Brittanica*, 9th ed., Edinburgh (A. and C. Black).

1878   Hill, Rosmund and Florence Davenport, *The Recorder of*

1878	*Birmingham: A Memoir of Matthew Davenport Hill*, London (Macmillan).
1881	Froude, J.A., ed., *Reminiscences* by Thomas Carlyle, 2 vols., London (Longman).
	Gilfillan, George, *Sketches, Literary and Theological*, ed. Frank Henderson, Edinburgh (D. Douglas).
	Masson, David, *Thomas De Quincey*, London (Macmillan).
1882	Leary, F., Letter in *Manchester Guardian*, 9 March.
1884	Cranbrook, Lord, 'Christopher North', *National Review*, III, 151-60.
1887	Mackay, Charles, *Through the Long Day, or, Memorials of a Literary Life During Half a Century*, 2 vols., London (W.H. Allen and Co.).
1888	Sandford, Mrs Henry, *Thomas Poole and his Friends*, 2 vols., London (Macmillan).
1889-90	Masson, David, ed., *The Collected Writings of Thomas De Quincey*, 14 vols., Edinburgh (A. and C. Black).
1890	Japp, A.H., (a) *Thomas De Quincey: His Life and Writings. With Unpublished Correspondence*, 2nd ed., London (John Hogg).
	—— (b) ed., *Uncollected Writings of Thomas De Quincey*, 2 vols., London (Heinemann).
1891	Japp, A.H., (a) *De Quincey Memorials*, 2 vols., London (Heinemann).
	—— (b) ed., *Posthumous Works of Thomas De Quincey*, 2 vols., London (Heinemann).
1892	Clowes, Alice A., *Charles Knight: A Sketch*, London (R. Bentley and Son).
1893	Bertram, J.G., *Some Memories of Books, Authors and Events*, London (Constable).
1894	Gosse, Edmund, ed., *The Letters of Thomas Lovell Beddoes*, London (E. Matthews and J. Lane).
1895	Hogg, James, *De Quincey and his Friends: Personal Recollections, Souvenirs and Anecdotes of Thomas De Quincey, his Friends and Associates*, London (Sampson Low and Co).
1896	Leary, F., Letter to *Manchester City News*, 25 April.
1897	Lang, Andrew, *The Life and Letters of J.G. Lockhart*, 2 vols., London (J.C. Nimmo).
	Oliphant, Margaret, *Annals of a Publishing House: William Blackwood and his Sons, their Magazine and Friends*, 2 vols., Edinburgh (Blackwood).
1900	Hughes, Henry, 'De Quincey, a Chymru, a'r Methodistiaid', *Y Drysorfa*, 292-9.
1903-5	Lucas, E.V. ed., *The Works of Charles and Mary Lamb*, 7 vols., London (Methuen).
1906	Harper, C.G., *The Old Inns of Old England*, 2 vols., London (Chapman and Hall).

1908   Priestley, Lady Eliza. *The Story of a Lifetime*, London (Kegan Paul).

1909   Fryer, John, *A New Account of East India and Persia*, ed. William Crooks, London (Hakluyt Society).

1912   Axon, W.E.A., 'The Canon of De Quincey's Writings, with References to Some of his Unidentified Articles', *Transactions of the Royal Society of Literature*, XXXII, Part 1.

1915   Fairbrother, E.H., 'Lieutenant Horatio De Quincey', *Notes and Queries*, 11th Series, 273-5.

1916   Armitt, Mary L., *Rydal*, ed. Willingham F. Rawnsley, Kendal (Titus Wilson).

1917   MacFarlane, Charles, *Reminiscences of a Literary Life*, London (John Murray).

1920   Duckers, J. Scott, 'The De Quincey Family', *Times Literary Supplement*, XIX, 684.

1921   Wells, John Edwin, 'The Story of Wordsworth's "Cintra" ', *Studies in Philology*, XVIII (1921), 21-76.

1923   Wilson, David Alec, *Carlyle Till Marriage (1795-1826)*, London (Kegan Paul).

1924   Wilson, David Alec, *Carlyle to 'The French Revolution' (1826-1837)*, London (Kegan Paul).

1925   Taylor, Olive M., 'John Taylor, Author and Publisher', *London Mercury*, XII, 262.

1926   Gray, W. Forbes, 'De Quincey as Lady Nairne's Tenant', *Chambers's Journal*, 7th Series XVI, 181-4.

1927   Chardin, Sir John, *Sir John Chardin's Travels in Persia*, ed. Percy Sykes, London (Argonaut Press).

        Eaton, H.A., *A Diary of Thomas De Quincey, 1803*, London (Noel Douglas).

        Hannah, Hugh, 'The Sanctuary of Holyrood', *The Book of the Old Edinburgh Club*, XV, 55-98.

        Morley, Edith J., ed., *The Correspondence of Henry Crabb Robinson with the Wordsworth Circle, 1806-66*, 2 vols., Oxford (Clarendon Press).

        Richards, A.E., 'The Day-Book and Ledger of Wordsworth's Carpenter', *Philological Quarterly*, 75-9.

1930   Coombs, H. and Bax, A.N., eds., *The Journal of a Somerset Rector, John Skinner, 1772-1839*, London (John Murray).

1933   Moore, H. Hamilton, 'Some Unpublished Letters of Thomas De Quincey', *Review of English Studies*, IX, 176-85.

1934   Owen, David, *British Opium Policy in China and India*, New Haven (Yale Historical Publications).

        Potter, Stephen, ed., *Minnow Among Tritons: Mrs S.T. Coleridge's Letters to Thomas Poole, 1799-1834*, London (Nonesuch Press).

1934   Swann, Elsie, *Christopher North (John Wilson)*, Edinburgh
        (Oliver and Boyd).
1936   Bonner, W.H., *De Quincey At Work: As Seen in One Hundred
        and Thirty New and Newly Edited Letters*, Buffalo, New
        York (Airport Publications Inc.).
        Eaton, Horace A., *Thomas De Quincey: A Biography*, London
        (Oxford University Press).
1938   Morley, Edith J., ed., *Henry Crabb Robinson on Books and Their
        Writers*, 3 vols., London (J.M. Dent).
1939   Forward, Kenneth, 'De Quincey's *Cessio Bonorum*', *Publications
        of the Modern Language Association of America*, LIV,
        511-25.
        McC[usker], H[elen], 'De Quincey and the Landlord', *More
        Books*, XIV, 66.
1941   Hilbish, F.M.A., *Charlotte Smith, Poet and Novelist*, Philadelphia
        (Doctoral Dissertation).
1943   Sousa-Leao, J. de, 'Robert Southey', *Revista do Instituto Historico
        e Geografico Brasiliero*, CLXXVIII (1943), 33-60.
1948   Rollins, Hyder E., ed., *The Keats Circle: Letters and Papers,
        1816-1878*, 2 vols., Cambridge, Mass. (Harvard University
        Press).
1949   Aspinall, Arthur, *Politics and the Press, 1780-1850*, London
        (Home and Van Thal).
        Hall, Edward, *The Strange Affair of De Quincey's Tutor,
        1793-1803* (typescript in Manchester Public Library).
1953   Musgrove, S., 'De Quincey's Translation of *Niels Klim*', *Auckland
        University College Bulletin*.
1954   Coburn, Kathleen, ed., *The Letters of Sara Hutchinson from 1800
        to 1835*, London (Routledge and Kegan Paul).
        Tredrey, F.D., *The House of Blackwood, 1804-1954: The History
        of a Publishing Firm*, Edinburgh (Blackwood).
1956   Byrns, Richard H., (a) 'Some Unpublished Works of De Quincey',
        *Publications of the Modern Language Association of
        America*, LXXI, 990-1003.
        ——   (b) 'De Quincey's First Article in *Blackwood's Magazine*',
        Bulletin of the New York Public Library, XL, 333-7.
1956-71 Griggs, E.L., ed., *The Collected Letters of Samuel Taylor
        Coleridge*, 6 vols., Oxford (Oxford University Press).
1957-   Coburn, Kathleen, ed., *The Notebooks of Samuel Taylor
        Coleridge*, London (Routledge and Kegan Paul).
1958   Burton, M.E., ed., *The Letters of Mary Wordsworth, 1800-1855*,
        Oxford (Clarendon Press).
        Green, David Bonnell, 'A Thomas De Quincey Letter', *Notes and
        Queries*, CCIII, 392-3.
1960   Glen, Robert, *The Manchester Grammar School in the Early*

1960   *Nineteenth Century: A New Account* (typescript in Manchester Public Library).

1961   Gérin, Winifred, *Branwell Brontë*, London (Nelson).

1962   Jordan, John E., *De Quincey to Wordsworth: A Biography of a Relationship*, Berkeley and Los Angeles (University of California Press).

1964   Chein, Isidor, *et al.*, *Narcotics, Delinquency and Social Policy: The Road to H*, London (Tavistock).

1965   Goldman, Albert, *The Mine and the Mint: Sources for the Writings of Thomas De Quincey*, Carbondale, Southern Illinois (Southern Illinois University Press).

            Graham, J.A. and Phythian, B.A., *The Manchester Grammar School, 1515-1965*, Manchester (Manchester University Press).

            Moorman, Mary, *Wordsworth: The Later Years: 1803-50*, Oxford (Oxford University Press).

1966   Marsden, William, *The History of Sumatra*, New York (Oxford University Press).

            Tave, Stuart M., ed., *New Essays by De Quincey: His Contributions to the* Edinburgh Saturday Post *and the* Edinburgh Evening Post, *1827-8*, Princeton, New Jersey (Princeton University Press).

1967   Robson, J.M. ed., *The Collected Writings of John Stuart Mill*, Toronto (University of Toronto Press), Vol. IV.

            Shaver, Chester L. (revised by), *The Letters of William and Dorothy Wordsworth: The Early Years, 1787-1805*, ed. E. De Selincourt, Oxford (Clarendon Press).

1968   Janzow, F.S., *De Quincey Enters Journalism: His Contributions to the* Westmorland Gazette, *1818-1819*, Chicago (University of Chicago Doctoral Dissertation).

1969   Gross, John, *The Rise and Fall of the Man of Letters*, London (Weidenfeld and Nicholson).

            Moorman, Mary (revised by), *The Letters of William and Dorothy Wordsworth: The Middle Years, Part I, 1806-1811*, ed. E. De Selincourt, Oxford (Clarendon Press).

1970   De Selincourt, E., ed., *Journals of Dorothy Wordsworth*, 2 vols., London (Macmillan).

            Moorman, Mary and Hill, Alan G. (revised by), *The Letters of William and Dorothy Wordsworth: The Middle Years, Part II, 1812–1820*, ed. E. De Selincourt, Oxford (Clarendon Press).

            Wright, David, ed., *Recollections of the Lakes and the Lake Poets*, by Thomas De Quincey, Harmondsworth (Penguin Books).

1970-7   Sanders, C.R., ed., *The Collected Letters of Thomas and Jane*

Welsh Carlyle, 7 vols., Durham, North Carolina (Duke University Press).

1971   Gérin, Winifred, *Emily Brontë*, Oxford (Clarendon Press).

Hayter, Alethea, ed., *Confessions of an English Opium-Eater*, by Thomas De Quincey, Harmondsworth (Penguin Books).

1973   Chilcott, Tim, 'De Quincey and the *London Magazine*', *Charles Lamb Bulletin*, New Series I, 10-19.

Lomax, Elizabeth, 'The Uses and Abuses of Opiates in Nineteenth-Century England', *Bulletin of the History of Medicine*, XLVII, 167-77.

Sealts, Merton M., ed., *The Journals and Miscellaneous Notebooks of Ralph Waldo Emerson*, Vol. X, Cambridge, Mass. (Belknap Press).

1973-80   Marchand, Leslie A., ed., *Byron's Letters and Journals*, 10 vols., London (John Murray).

1974   Jordan, John E., ed., *A Flame in Sunlight: The Life and Work of Thomas De Quincey*, by Edward Sackville-West, new ed., London (Bodley Head).

1975   Goodman, L.S. and Gilman, A., eds., *The Pharmacological Basis of Therapeutics*, 5th ed., New York (Macmillan).

Lloyd, Humphrey, *The Quaker Lloyds in the Industrial Revolution*, London (Heinemann).

1978   Hill, Alan G. (revised by), *The Letters of William and Dorothy Wordsworth: The Later Years, Part I, 1821-1828*, ed. E. De Selincourt, Oxford (Clarendon Press).

Index

De Quincey's family name varied between 'Quincey' and 'De Quincey'. In this index Thomas De Quincey himself, his brother Richard, his wife and children are listed under 'De Quincey'; all other members of the family are listed under 'Quincey'. Within entries, 'Thomas De Quincey' is abbreviated as 'De Q.' The main entry for Thomas De Quincey gives an outline of his career, followed by separate entries for 'Characteristics', 'Dreams and visions', 'Finances', 'Illnesses', 'Letters', 'Opium use', 'Political and economic views', 'Projected works', 'Pseudonyms', 'Published works', 'Reading', 'Residences and lodgings' and 'Unpublished writings'. Streets and public places in Edinburgh, London, Manchester and Oxford are listed as subheadings under those cities.

Index

421